# THE MISSING

## True Disturbing Files Vol. 1

Compiled By
Marie Tayse

# DEDICATION

This book is dedicated to all the missing people in the world, and to their friends and families who continue to hold out hope that one day they will be found.

# ATTENTION:

This book contains true stories of the missing. Some of the circumstances are graphic. Reader discretion is advised.

# TABLE OF CONTENTS

# UP IN SMOKE

Each year in the United States, more than 400,000 residential fires account for approximately 3,600 deaths and 18,600 injuries. About 59% of fatal residential fires occur in homes without smoke alarms, according to an article in Parents Magazine.

When a fire occurs, you have only minutes to escape. As stated by the Purdue University Fire Department, a fire can spread by doubling its size in seconds.

According to the National Institute of Fire and Safety Training Blog, the average house fire burns at a temperature of about 1,100 degrees Fahrenheit. The cremation of a body at a mortuary is carried out at temperatures ranging from 1,400 to 1,800 degrees Fahrenheit. Some mortuaries use an afterburner to help burn the remains completely. As a result, the body is reduced to skeletal remains and bone fragments. Finally, the bone fragments are further ground into a finer sand-like consistency. On average, it takes about one to three hours to entirely cremate a body.

According to Officer.com, in the case of an arson fire or a faked car accident and fire, the body is generally badly decomposed but the skeletal structure remains intact.

The reason the above details are so important is because some believe that an average house fire can completely incinerate a body. Based on my research, however, that is highly unlikely, unless in the case of some type of explosion.

The cases in this section all have one thing in common: the person or persons disappeared immediately prior to, during, or after a fire. Feel free to draw your own conclusions as to what you think happened.

## Chloie Leverette & Gage Daniel

On September 23, 2012, in Unionville, Tennessee, the home of Leon and Molly McClaran and their two grandchildren caught fire. After the fire was extinguished, the bodies of seventy-two year old Leon McClaran Sr. and his seventy year old wife, Molly, were found inside the home. The remains of their grandchildren, nine year old Chloie Leverette and her seven year old brother Gage Daniel, were not found amid the ashes. Fire investigators with the Tennessee Bureau of Investigation (TBI) brought in cadaver dogs and used infrared cameras attached to helicopters to search for the children.

Initially investigators thought all four family members perished in the fire, but the children's remains could not be located. Chloie and Gage were reportedly last seen near the home around 6:30pm, about three hours before the fire started. The children's mother was later spoken to, but investigators determined she neither had them nor knew where they were. Chloie and Gage have not been seen or heard from since the night of the fire.

A TBI spokesperson stated eight months after the fire that they had no evidence that the children died in the fire, but they also had no leads to indicate that they did not die in the fire.

Investigators ruled the cause of the blaze undetermined, but the Bedford County Sheriff said his investigators thought it was accidental. The cause of death of Leon and Molly McClaran was also undetermined, but they both had soot in their windpipes.

Chloie and Gage's remaining living relatives continue to hold out hope they will be found alive and well.

*(Age Progressions: Gage, 9 & Chloie, 11)*

At the time of her disappearance, Chloie Leverette had brown hair, stood 4'8", and weighed 75 pounds. She is Caucasian with blue eyes. As of this writing, she is fifteen years old.

At the time of his disappearance, Gage Daniel had brown hair, stood 4', and weighed 50 pounds. He is Caucasian with brown eyes. As of this writing, he is thirteen years old.

If you have any information about this case, you are urged to call one of the following numbers:

*Tennessee Bureau of Investigation 1-800-TBI-FIND*

## Lauria Bible & Ashley Freeman

On December 30, 1999, Danny and Kathy Freeman were found shot to death just outside of Welch, Oklahoma, after firefighters extinguished a fire that had completely engulfed their home. Their daughter, sixteen year old Ashley, and her best friend, sixteen year old Lauria Bible, had been having a sleepover in the home that night, but after the fire they could not be found. The girls were last seen on December 29th, when they celebrated Ashley's sixteenth birthday.

Lauria's car was found near the charred home with her keys still in the ignition. Investigators found her purse, with money inside, among the ruins. Several weapons were also found inside the home, but Danny's arrowhead collection was gone and has never been located. Arson investigators determined that the fire had been deliberately set by an accelerant placed near the wood-burning stove.

For years, investigators worked on the premise that someone had killed the Freemans and the girls had been collateral damage, but there was no evidence to suggest the girls had died in the fire.

In 2005, convicted rapist and murderer, Jeremy Jones, confessed to the murders and claimed to have drove the girls to Kansas, where he shot them and left their bodies in a mineshaft. However, police found no evidence of their remains in the area. The suspect later recanted his confession. He has never been charged in the case, and is currently awaiting execution in Alabama in a separate rape and murder case.

In January 2018, investigators stated that they had found new information and additional leads in the eighteen year old cold case, but would not elaborate. The Oklahoma State Bureau of Investigation (OSBI) is offering a reward of up to $10,000 for credible information in this case.

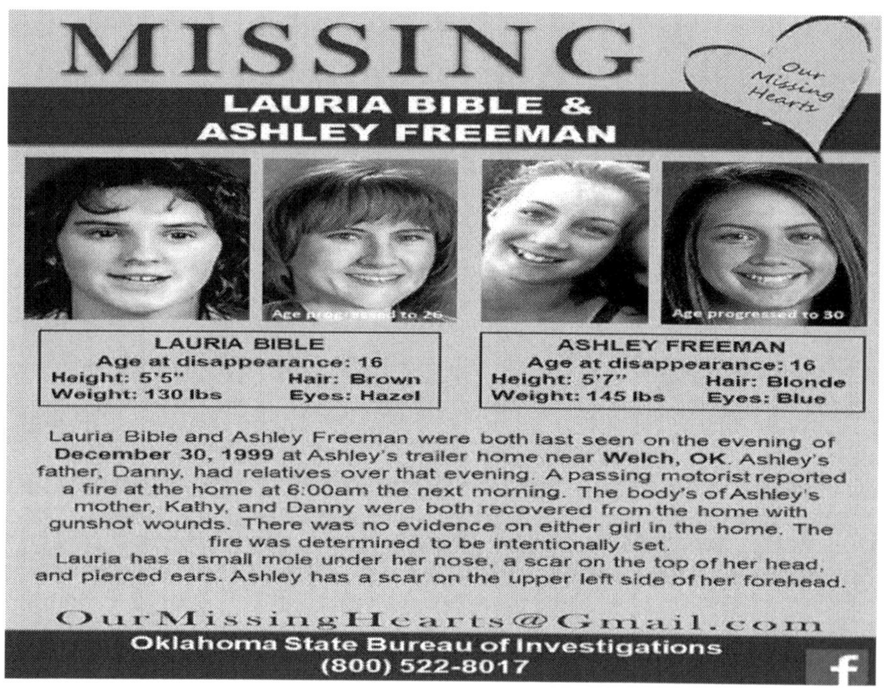


*(Age Progressions: Lauria, 26 & Ashley, 30)*

At the time of her disappearance, Lauria Bible had brown hair, stood 5’5”, and weighed 130 pounds. She is Caucasian with hazel eyes, a small mole under her nose, a scar on top of her head, and pierced ears. As of this writing, she is thirty-five years old.

At the time of her disappearance, Ashley Freeman had blonde hair, stood 5'7", and weighed 145 pounds. She is Caucasian with blue eyes and a scar on the upper left side of her forehead. As of this writing, she is thirty-five years old.

Anyone with any information about this case is urged to call the Oklahoma State Bureau of Investigation at 1-800-522-8017 or email them at tips@osbi.ok.gov.

## The Sodder Children

On the night before Christmas 1945, George and Jennie Sodder and nine of their ten children went to sleep in their home in Fayetteville, West Virginia (one son was away in the army). Around 1am, a fire broke out. George and Jennie and four of their children escaped, but the other five did not and have never been seen again.

After the fire was extinguished and the grounds searched, no human remains could be located in the rubble. The chief of police suggested that the fire had been hot enough to completely incinerate the bodies, and the coroner's office issued five death certificates, attributing the causes of death to the fire or smoke inhalation. But the Sodders began to wonder if their children were still alive. Several reports stated that George and Jennie believed the children had been kidnapped and the fire set intentionally to cover it up. Witness statements and rumors supported their beliefs.

According to investigators, faulty wiring was the cause of the blaze. But why then had the family's Christmas lights still been aglow and seen by all surviving members of the family once outside the burning house? Also, a ladder that George had always kept propped up against the house was nowhere to be found when he was in desperate need of it while trying to rescue the children he assumed where still inside the house. A telephone repairman told the Sodders that the telephone lines had been cut not burned. Plus, George had recently had an electrician rewire the house. So again, the faulty wiring conclusion just raised more questions than answers.

*(Maurice, 14, Martha, 12, Louis, 10, Jennie, 8, & Betty, 6)*

Months after the fire, the family found a shell from a military explosive device in the yard. They wondered if that could have been the source of the fire.

A medical examiner involved in the case stated that it was very unlikely that all of the remains from five children would have been completely destroyed in such a quick burning fire. An employee at a crematorium told Jennie that a body would have to burn for two hours at 2,000 degrees Fahrenheit to leave nothing but ash. The Sodder house fire was extinguished in forty-five minutes.

In 1968, a detective wrote an article about the events of that night twenty-three years prior. A few months later, the Sodders received a photograph in the mail postmarked from Kentucky with no return address. The photo was of a young man, supposedly Louis

Sodder. Most thought it was a hoax brought on by the article, but the photograph did resemble the missing child. The Sodders took it as a sign that their children were still alive, and hired a private investigator to go to Kentucky to follow leads on the photo. The private investigator vanished after traveling to Kentucky and has never been heard from again. The person in the photo and who sent it remains a mystery to this day.

*(Possible image of Louis Sodder)*

George died in 1969 and Jennie in 1989 without ever knowing what really happened to five of their children. Sylvia, the youngest of the surviving children, who was only two when her siblings disappeared, continues to believe they did not die in the fire.

As of this writing, Maurice is eighty-seven, Martha is eighty-five, Louis is eighty-three, Jennie is eight-one, and Betty is seventy-nine years old.

If you have any information regarding this case, you are urged to contact the West Virginia State Police at 304-746-2100.

**Cynthia Wilkins**

Fifty-one year old Cynthia Wilkins was last seen at her downstairs apartment on 11th Avenue in Fulton, Illinois on March 9, 2004. A fire ripped through the building at 10:30pm that night. First responders rescued a couple and their cat from an upstairs window, while all the other occupants were able to escape on their own. Cynthia's neighbors and local law enforcement authorities believed she was at home when the fire started, because her car was there. However, extensive searches through the ashes with cadaver dogs did not turn up any sign of her remains. She has never been seen again. Investigators now say it is possible she wasn't home when the fire started, but she has not surfaced anywhere else in the years since the blaze. Fire officials have not released the cause of the fire.

*(Cynthia at the time of her disappearance)*

At the time of her disappearance, Cynthia Wilkins had sandy blonde to brown hair, wore upper dentures, wore eyeglasses with bronze oval-shaped frames, stood 5'2", and weighed 160 pounds. She was last seen wearing two Black Hills gold rings on her ring finger. She is Caucasian with hazel eyes, and her nickname is Cindy. As of this writing, she is sixty-five years old.

If you have any information about this case, you are urged to call the Fulton Police Department at 815-589-3617.

## Steven Hendricks

Twenty-two year old Steven Hendricks was last seen on September 4, 1988 in Washington, Indiana. On the morning of September 5$^{th}$, his girlfriend, Rebecca Harvey was found murdered inside the couple's heavily-damaged home on Oak Grove Road. It had burned during the night. Evidence showed Rebecca had been doused with gasoline and set on fire. Steven was missing, and it was quickly determined that he too was probably the victim of foul play. However, him nor his remains have ever been found.

*(Steven at the time of his disappearance)*

At the time of his disappearance, Steven Hendricks had black hair, stood 5'7", and weighed 135 pounds. He is Caucasian with hazel eyes. As of this writing, he is fifty-two years old.

If you have any information regarding this case, you are urged to call the Daviess County Sheriff's Office at 812-254-1060.

## Brookelyn Farthing

Eighteen year old Brookelyn Farthing was last seen at a house on Dillon Court in Berea, Kentucky on June 21, 2013. Early the next morning, a fire was reported at that location. The homeowner told police that he had left Brookelyn there and gone elsewhere, and when he returned the house was on fire and she was gone. The strange parts of this story are that the house was in foreclosure and had no running water or electricity. Also, the fire originated on a couch.

At 4am on the morning she disappeared, Brookelyn sent several text messages to friends asking for a ride home and saying she was scared. At 7am, the fire department received a call from the owner of the house saying that it was on fire. The blaze was extinguished before it destroyed the whole house. The couch was badly burned, leaving a hole in the floor. Several of Brookelyn's belongings were inside the house, including her cowboy boots, but the clothes she was last seen wearing and her cell phone were gone. The fire was ruled suspicious.

Authorities searched both land and water in the days that followed, but no clues as to her whereabouts were discovered. A reward is being offered for information leading to her return or the capture and conviction of those responsible for her disappearance.

*(Brookelyn at the time of her disappearance)*

At the time of her disappearance, Brookelyn Farthing had blonde hair, stood approximately 5'1", and weighed 105 pounds. She was last seen wearing a gray Madison County FFA shirt and light blue denim shorts. She is Caucasian with brown eyes, pierced ears, and a birthmark on her left hip. Her nickname is Brooke. As of this writing, she is twenty-three years old.

## Kaidena Lozelle "Kay" Wood

Seventy-nine year old James William "Bill" Wood and his wife, seventy-two year old Kaidena Lozelle "Kay" Wood, lived in rural Norwalk, Iowa. On the night of July 30, 2011, their home was completely destroyed by a fire that is believed to have started on the front porch. Five fire departments responded to the blaze. Once the fire was out, authorities realized Bill and Kay were missing. The couple had last been seen midmorning that day at an auction house in Stuart, Iowa.

On July 13th, their red Chevrolet pickup truck was found at an apartment complex in Kansas City, Missouri. Witnesses described the man who had been seen with the truck as being in his late forties to early sixties with a slender build, short gray and white hair, and between 6'2 - 6'6" tall. That man has never been identified. That same day, fire officials found charred remains in the rubble of the Wood's home. It would take weeks to get DNA testing results back to determine if the deceased was Bill or Kay.

Authorities announced on August 1st that the fire was suspicious. While they waited for news of which of their loved ones had already been found, Bill and Kay's family and friends spent days searching the area around their home.

On August $19^{th}$, authorities announced that the remains found in the house were those of Bill Wood. Autopsy results showed he had died from multiple gunshot wounds.

Kay is not a suspect in her husband's murder, and is believed to have been taken against her will. Foul play is suspected.

*(Kay & Bill at the time of her disappearance)*

At the time of her disappearance, Kay Wood had gray hair, wore hearing aids in both ears, stood 5'2", and weighed 128 pounds. She was last seen wearing a braided wedding band with a small diamond. She is Caucasian with blue eyes, pierced ears, and a vertical scar on her abdomen. As of this writing, she is seventy-nine years old.

If you have any information regarding this case, you are urged to call one of the following numbers:

*Warren County Sheriff's Office at 515-961-1122*

*Iowa Division of Criminal Investigation 641-342-6263*

## William "Bill" Francis Rogers

Forty-six year old William Francis Rogers was last seen at his North English, Iowa home on February 25, 2001. That night his house burned down. No trace of him could be found in the rubble. It is possible he was abducted before the fire began. The cause of the fire has not been released. Few details are available in his case.

*(Bill at the time of his disappearance)*

At the time of his disappearance, William "Bill" Rogers was balding with a mustache and goatee, stood 5'8", and weighed 160 pounds. He was last seen wearing a tan jacket, a Comfort Inn t-shirt, blue jeans, and black sneakers. He is Caucasian with hazel eyes. As of this writing, he is sixty-three years old.

If you have any information regarding this case, you are urged to call the Keokuk County Sheriff's Office at 641-622-2727.

## Paul Ward Shrout

Eighty-five year old Paul Ward Shrout was last seen lying in bed at 2pm on January 4, 1999 in Sharpsburg, Kentucky. His son, who lived with him, left minutes later to go run errands. At 3:41pm, a neighbor noticed the house was on fire and called the fire department. It took seventeen hours to fully extinguish the blaze, and the house was a total loss.

No trace of Paul or his remains were located in the ruins. He has never been seen again. Authorities are not sure he was at home when the fire broke out, but he couldn't drive and no one saw him leave. He also had limited mobility.

*(Paul at the time of his disappearance)*

At the time of his disappearance, Paul Shrout had brown hair, wore eyeglasses, stood 5'9", and weighed 170 pounds. He was last seen wearing a blue flannel shirt and dark-colored pants. He is Caucasian with brown eyes and a pacemaker. He has had three prior heart attacks and two strokes. As of this writing, he is one-hundred-and-five years old.

If you have any information regarding this case, you are urged to call the Kentucky State Police at 606-784-412

**Richard Dewain Hess**

Twenty-five year old Richard Dewain Hess was last seen in Barnett, Missouri on December 5, 2010. He was visiting a cousin there. His cousin left, and while Richard was alone in the house there was an explosion causing the house to catch fire. Someone who saw the explosion went in through a window in an attempt to rescue him, but was forced back out by the smoke and flames.

Police later searched through the rubble with cadaver dogs, but found no trace of Richard's remains. He has not been heard from since. The cause of the explosion has not been released.

*(Richard at the time of his disappearance)*

At the time of his disappearance, Richard Hess had brown hair, stood 5'10", and weighed 155 pounds. He is Caucasian with brown eyes and a scar on his right knee and right elbow. His nickname is Dick. As of this writing, he is thirty-three years old.

If you have any information regarding this case, you are urged to call the Morgan County Sheriff's Department at 573-378-5481.

## Anwar Green

Nineteen year old Anwar Green and his friend, nineteen year old Rahim Qua'am Martin, planned to cash a check from a civil lawsuit in Newark, New Jersey on January 19, 2001. They were last seen on a surveillance camera at Independence Community Bank at Broad and Academy Streets. Anwar appeared to be nervous and kept glancing toward the door. Rahim cashed the check, which was for over $8,000. He had also been issued a second check for $4,000, but it was never cashed. The two left the bank and went next door to the Prudential Building on Broad Street, where Rahim had once worked as a security guard. He called his uncle from a payphone in the lobby and talked briefly, and then they left. They have never been heard from again.

Both men were close to their families and it is uncharacteristic for them to leave without warning. Neither had a driver's license at the time and relied on other people for transportation. Anwar has not used his credit card, and he left his cell phone behind.

Anwar has a juvenile record for car theft, but did not get involved in any other criminal activity after spending time in a juvenile detention center. Rahim has no criminal record.

The day after Anwar and Rahim were reported missing, a man's body was found in a burned house in Newark. He had been murdered and the house intentionally set on fire.

In August 2010, the remains were positively identified as Rahim Martin. No sign of Anwar was at the scene. Foul play is suspected.

*(Anwar at the time of his disappearance)*

At the time of his disappearance, Anwar Green had brown hair, a chipped left front tooth, stood at 5’8”, and weighed 140 pounds. He was last seen wearing a gray parka and blue jeans. He is African-American with brown eyes, and his nickname is Head. As of this writing he is 36.

If you have information regarding this case, you are urged to call the Newark Police Department at 973-733-5400.

## Michael Brendan Nash

Sixty-one year old Michael Brendan Nash resided in the Pelham Bay area of the Bronx, New York in 2000. He called his sister on April 8, 2000, and said that two men had arrived at his home uninvited earlier in the day. He said they ordered him to leave the property for unspecified reasons. Michael was last seen at approximately 2:30pm on April 10th at his home. A fire broke out in his basement that day.

Once the fire was extinguished, the rubble was searched, but no human remains were found. Michael has never been seen again. Authorities later determined the fire to have been arson. No arrests have been made, but foul play is suspected.

*(Michael at the time of his disappearance)*

At the time of his disappearance, Michael Nash had gray hair, wore eyeglasses, stood 5'10", and weighed 200 pounds. He was last seen wearing a multicolored plaid shirt, jeans, and a watch. He is Caucasian with blue eyes. As of this writing, he is seventy-nine years old.

If you have any information regarding this case, you are urged to call the New York Police Department at 646-610-6914.

## Pamela Marie Callahan

Forty-three year old Pamela Marie Callahan was last seen at her apartment in the Melrose Apartments complex on Country Club Drive in Concord, North Carolina on March 6, 2006. That day the Concord Fire Department responded to a fire at her apartment.

An investigation into the cause of the fire later determined it had been intentionally set. According to the Concord Police Department, Pamela is not suspected of having started the fire, but there is concern that the blaze may have been set to cover up a crime.

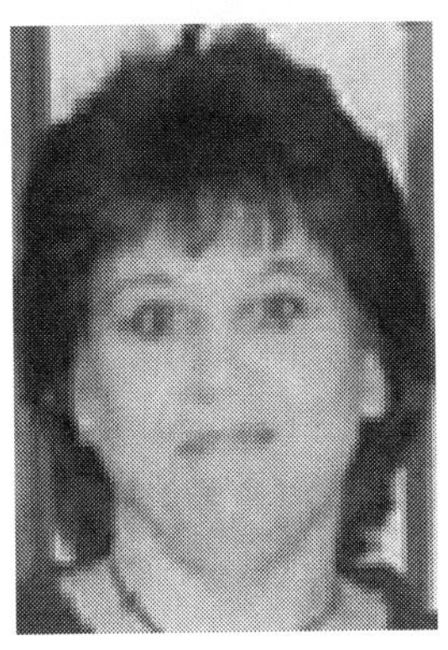

*(Pamela at the time of her disappearance)*

At the time of her disappearance, Pamela Callahan had brown hair, stood 5'6", and weighed 160 pounds. She is Caucasian with brown eyes and pierced ears. Her nickname is Pam. As of this writing, she is fifty-six years old.

If you have any information regarding this case, you are urged to call one of the following numbers:

*Concord Police Department at 704-920-5000*

*Cabarrus County Crime Stoppers 704-93-CRIME*

## Daniel McCoy Moses

Fifty-nine year old Daniel McCoy Moses last spoke to his brother on June 13, 2011. On June 16th, his home in Rich Square, North Carolina caught fire. He could not be found at the time of the fire, and his remains were not located in the ruins. He has never been heard from again. Few details are available in his case.

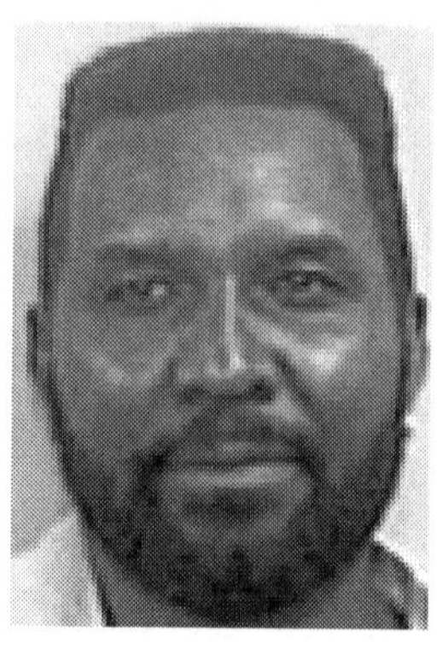

*(Daniel at the time of his disappearance)*

At the time of his disappearance, Daniel Moses had black hair, stood 6'3", and weighed between 200 - 220 pounds. He is African-American with brown eyes, a piercing in his left ear, and a known back injury. As of this writing, he is sixty-six years old.

If you have any information regarding this case, you are urged to call one of the following numbers:

*Northampton County Sheriff's Office at 252-532-2611*

*FBI VICAP at 1-800-634-4097*

## David Cook Morse

Fifty-four year old David Cook Morse was last seen in Ashville, Ohio on July 22, 2009. At approximately 6pm that day, his home on Perrill Road was found completely destroyed by fire. He lived alone with his dogs.

Authorities found the remains of two dogs, but there was no sign of David. He was in poor health at the time and couldn't walk far without assistance. His van was parked outside of his home. Five investigators were unable to determine the cause of the fire, but they suspect foul play. David has never been seen or heard from again.

*(David at the time of his disappearance)*

At the time of his disappearance, David Morse had brown hair, stood 6'2", and weighed 155 pounds. He was last seen wearing a blue long-sleeve t-shirt and brown corduroy pants. He is Caucasian with blue eyes. As of this writing, he is sixty-three years old.

If you have any information regarding this case, you are urged to call the Pickaway County Sheriff's Office at 740-477-6000.

## Joey Lynn Offutt

Thirty-three year old Joey Lynn Offutt was last seen at her home on Fugate Drive in Sykesville, Pennsylvania on July 4, 2007. In the early morning hours of July 12th, an explosion from inside her house awoke the neighbors and they called the fire department.

Once the fire was extinguished, the remains of Joey's six-week-old son were found in a bathtub. Her two older children were not in the home at the time. Joey, nor her remains, was located at the scene. She has never been heard from again.

An autopsy revealed that the baby had been deceased before the fire started. It was determined that the fire had been intentionally set using some type of accelerant.

On July 15th, Joey's red 1994 Saturn was found abandoned along Waupelani Drive in State College, Pennsylvania at the Nittany Gardens Apartments, where she used to live. There was no sign of her, and no one in the vicinity remembered seeing her recently. Authorities believe she met with foul play and is deceased, but her remains have never been located.

*(Joey at the time of her disappearance)*

At the time of her disappearance, Joey Offutt was petite with reddish brown hair, wore glasses, stood at approximately 5'3", and weighed 110 pounds. She is Caucasian with brown eyes. As of this writing, she is forty-four years old.

If you have any information regarding this case, you are urged to call one of the following numbers:

*Pennsylvania State Police at 814-371-4652*

## Kenny Dwayne Ebarb

Twenty-seven year old Kenny Dwayne Ebarb was last seen on Countryside Road in Humble, Texas on July 15, 2005. He had gone there to collect money from someone he knew. He has never been heard from again. His vehicle was found the next day abandoned and burned on Huffman Road in Huffman, Texas.

He resided in Spring, Texas at the time. He is married and has two children. Foul play is possible in his case.

(Kenny at the time of his disappearance)

At the time of his disappearance, Kenny Ebarb had brown hair, stood 5'9", and weighed 140 pounds. He was last seen wearing a white t-shirt or tank top, shorts, brown leather sandals, and silver hoop earrings. He is Caucasian with green/hazel eyes, two piercings in his left ear, one piercing in his right ear, a burn scar on his right cheek, a scar on top of his head near the scalp, and a previously fractured wrist. He has the following tattoos: Betty Boop on his upper left arm, a cross on his outer left forearm near the elbow, a cross above his left knee, the name Kathryn in Old English Script in the middle of his back, The names Brooke and Heather on the side of his right calf, a sun on the right side of his chest, his last name on the back of his neck, and the initials K.E. on his left fingers. He may spell his last name Ebard and his middle name Dewayne. As of this writing, he is forty-one years old.

If you have any information regarding this case, you are urged to call the Harris County Sheriff's Office at 713-967-5810.

## Aleman Bautista Gustavo

Forty-one year old Aleman Bautista Gustavo was last seen by his daughter at the H-E-B supermarket on Fairmont Parkway in Pasadena, Texas on August 3, 2006. He was reportedly going to pick up some cars from an unknown location at the time. He has never been heard from again. His truck and trailer were found abandoned and burned in Fort Bend County, Texas five days later. There were no clues as to his whereabouts at the scene.

*(Aleman at the time of his disappearance)*

At the time of his disappearance, Aleman Gustavo had dark brown hair, stood 5'9", and weighed 210 pounds. He was last seen wearing a red, white, and blue Tommy Hilfiger shirt, jeans, and a black and yellow baseball cap. He is Hispanic with brown eyes. As of this writing, he is sixty-three years old.

If you have any information regarding this case, you are urged to call the Pasadena Police Department at 714-475-7803.

## Ricky Jean "Jeannie" Bryant

Four year old Ricky Jean "Jeannie" Bryant was last seen in Mauston, Wisconsin on December 19, 1949. Her grandparents were watching her and two of her siblings. Sometime during the day, a fire broke out in the house. Jeannie's grandmother said she took Jeannie's brother and sister outside when the fire started, and then went back inside and called out several times for Jeannie, to no avail.

However, Jeannie's five year old brother stated that they were all standing in the yard together watching the fire when a woman drove up in an expensive-looking car and urged him to get help. She directed him to a house down the road, even though there was a residence closer by.

Most authorities believe Jeannie died in the fire, although no trace of her remains was found in the rubble. Her siblings believe she may have been hidden by other family members and is possibly still alive. It was at her siblings' request that authorities reopened the investigation into her disappearance over fifty years after she vanished.

*(Age Progression to 66)*

At the time of her disappearance, Jeannie Bryant had blonde hair, stood 3'4", and weighed 40 pounds. She is Caucasian with hazel eyes. As of this writing, she is seventy-two years old.

If you have any information regarding this case, you are urged to call the Juneau County Sheriff's Department at 608-847-5649.

## Wayne Moore

Forty-nine year old Wayne Moore was last seen at his Pasadena, Texas residence on March 14, 1992. A handgun disappeared with him that day, and the front door of his home was left open. Later, his vehicle was found abandoned and burned. Few other details are available in his case, but foul play is possible.

*(Wayne at the time of his disappearance)*

At the time of his disappearance, Wayne Moore had brown hair, stood 5'9", and weighed 140 pounds. It is unknown what he was last seen wearing, but he usually wears a gold chain with a Leo medallion. He is Caucasian with green eyes, wears a pacemaker, and has a square-shaped scar on the left side of his chest. His nickname is Buddy. As of this writing, he is seventy-six years old.

If you have any information regarding this case, you are urged to call the Pasadena Police Department at 713-477-1221.

## Amelia Martinez Smith

Fifty-one year old Amelia Martinez Smith worked for a taxi company in Irving, Texas in 2000. Her shift ended at 10pm on February 3, 2000, and she drove to her mobile home in Weatherford, Texas. Her husband was visiting his mother, and their children weren't home either. At approximately 4am the following morning, neighbors called to report Amelia's home on fire. By the time the fire department arrived, the residence was fully engulfed in flames. Investigators discovered that someone had also attempted to set fire to the interior of her car, which was parked nearby. They determined both fires were the result of arson. No sign of Amelia or her remains could be located in the ashes or the surrounding area. Foul play is suspected.

Jeffrey Maxwell is considered a possible suspect in her disappearance. In March 2011, he was charged with kidnapping and sexually assaulting a sixty-two year old woman, who also went missing after her house burned down. Thirteen days later, she was found alive in a secret compartment in his home. She had been bound, raped, and tortured. Authorities have not found any evidence that he knew Amelia, but the two cases are remarkably similar. He is also the prime suspect in the 1992 disappearance of his wife, Martha.

*(Amelia at the time of her disappearance)*

At the time of her disappearance, Amelia Smith had brown hair, wore eyeglasses, stood 5'3", and weighed 111 pounds. She is Caucasian with brown eyes and pierced ears. His nickname is Amy. As of this writing, she is seventy years old.

If you have any information regarding this case, you are urged to call the Parker County Sheriff's Office at 817-594-8845.

## Charles William "CW" Monroe Jr.

Thirty-four year old Charles William "CW" Monroe Jr. was last heard from at 9pm on May 7, 2005. Early that next morning, his residence caught fire. He lived in an apartment inside a barn on twenty acres of land at Edgewood Farm in Loudoun County, Virginia. The barn burnt to the ground. Investigators found the remains of his three dogs in the rubble, but no trace of CW was found. Fire investigators do not believe his body could have been completely consumed by the fire. The cause of the blaze has not been determined.

*(CW at the time of his disappearance)*

At the time of his disappearance, CW Monroe Jr. had brown hair, stood 6'3", and weighed 160 pounds. He was last seen wearing a long-sleeve striped shirt, blue jeans, brown or black work boots, and carrying a black digital wristwatch in his pocket. He is Caucasian with blue eyes, a scar on his right knee, and a previously fractured left foot. As of this writing, he is forty-seven years old.

If you have any information regarding this case, you are urged to call the Loudoun Sheriff's Office at 703-777-0475.

## Gloria Marlene Plunkett

Fifty-four year old Gloria Marlene Plunkett was residing in Lakewood, California in a self-storage unit she had converted into a living space in 2001. The unit was located at Anchor Self-Storage on Alondra Boulevard. She rented two and lived in one of them. Fire destroyed her living space on December 12, 2001. The rubble was sifted through, but no sign of Gloria was found.

Authorities do not believe she died in the fire. They think that the destruction of her home may have caused severe psychological trauma, and that she may be living in a psychiatric care facility or on the streets. She frequented Barstow, California and Las Vegas, Nevada at the time.

*(Gloria at the time of her disappearance)*

At the time of her disappearance, Gloria Plunkett had red hair, stood 5'6", and weighed 132 pounds. She is Caucasian with hazel eyes. As of this writing, she is seventy-one years old.

If you have any information regarding this case, you are urged to call the Los Angeles County Sheriff's Department at 323-890-5500.

## Patricia Jean Schneider

Twenty-five year old Patricia Jean Schneider completed her shift as a cocktail waitress at the Palomino Station in Indian Hills, California early on the morning of July 31, 1982. At 3:45am, she made a call from a Circle K on Limonite Avenue in Pedley, California and said her car had broken down. She has never been heard from again.

Between 5-6am, a Riverside County Sheriff's deputy found her brown and white 1974 Toyota Celica on fire in a field near the intersection of Van Buren Boulevard and Doolittle Avenue. The fire had been deliberately set, but there were no clues as to Patricia's whereabouts at the scene. Foul play is suspected.

*(Patricia at the time of her disappearance)*

At the time of her disappearance, Patricia Schneider had blonde hair, stood 5'4", and weighed 115 pounds. She was last seen wearing a cocktail waitress uniform. She is Caucasian with blue eyes. Her nickname is Patti, and she may use the last name Underhill. As of this writing, she is sixty-one years old.

If you have any information regarding this case, you are urged to call the Riverside County Sheriff's Office at 951-826-5700.

# TRAVELS GONE AWRY

When you start making preparations for your next dream vacation or just a drive through an unfamiliar part of your own state, it would be wise to do your research on how to stay safer in those locations. When we planned our Florida vacation this year, I googled tourist safety information and found several helpful tips. There are several websites and blogs out there with good information. If you can't find your vacation or destination spot on google, check out the local police department website or call and ask them for tips on keeping you and your family safe while visiting the area. The best two pieces of information I found was that it is very important that you stay aware of your surroundings and don't 'advertise' your valuables. In other words, play on your phone on Facebook in your hotel room not out in clear view of every person within eyeshot, who can tell it's obvious that you are oblivious to what is going on around you. Also, leave that $1,000 necklace at home. There is no reason to take a chance on someone swiping it from your hotel room or kidnapping you to get it.

While the kidnapping rates of several countries overseas are in the hundreds and thousands per year, most of those are locals not tourists. But that doesn't mean to go on vacation in Paris and flaunt your $800 engagement ring to anyone who will look in your direction, while posting to Instagram every ten minutes. It may sound funny, but it happens.

There are, however, instances where you do everything right and something still happens. People who have followed all the safety precautions disappear never to be seen or heard from again. You can't change the course of life, but you can make sure that you and your family are as safe as possible to the best of your ability.

According to NamUs, over 600,000 people go missing in the United States every year. It is unknown how many of that number disappear while traveling or on vacation. However, the numbers of disappearances from planes, cruise ships, and other large means of transportation are fairly well documented.

Since 2000, nearly 300 people have gone overboard or believed to have gone overboard from cruise ships and ferries, according to a professor at Memorial University of Newfoundland in Canada. He estimates that 49 people have gone missing while traveling or working onboard cruise ships.

As you can probably guess, all the cases in this section involve traveling either for vacation or other reasons. Perhaps you can give investigators that one missing clue to one of these cases, and help the missing's families either find their loved one or at least find closure.

## Willie Manuel Tobias

Sixty-one year old Willie Manuel Tobias was last seen in McComb, Mississippi on July 24, 1993. He was traveling to Baton Rouge, Louisiana to attend a family member's funeral at the time of his disappearance. He was driving a dark blue 1987 Chevrolet Silverado pickup with temporary plates. He never arrived at his destination and has never been heard from again. It is unknown if his vehicle has ever been located.

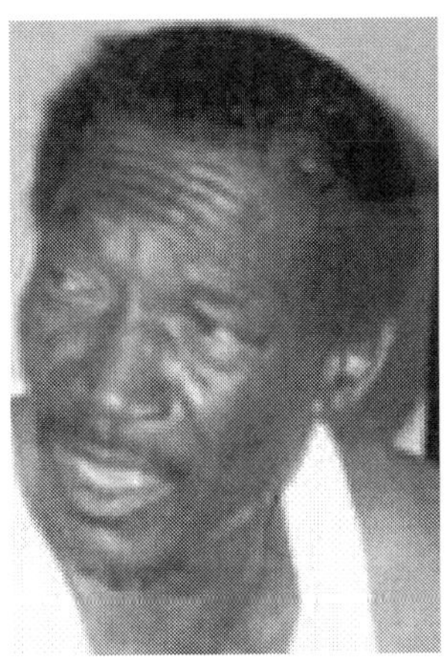

*(Willie at the time of his disappearance)*

At the time of his disappearance, Willie Tobias had black hair, stood 6'2", and weighed 160 pounds. He is African-American with brown eyes, a scar on his chest, and a surgical scar on his abdomen. He may have a mustache, beard, or goatee. As of this writing, he is eighty-six years old.

If you have any information regarding this case, you are urged to call one of the following numbers:

*Jefferson Parish, Louisiana Sheriff's Office at 504-364-5300*

## Mariah Ann Mickelwait

Thirty-one year old Mariah Ann Mickelwait was last seen in Detroit, Michigan on October 25, 2009. That day she took a Continental Airlines flight to Veracruz, Mexico, to see a man she had met online. She never returned, and has never been heard from again. None of her social media accounts have been accessed since she disappeared. Few other details are available in her case.

*(Mariah at the time of her disappearance)*

At the time of her disappearance, Mariah Mickelwait had black hair, wore contact lenses, stood between 4'11" - 5'3", and weighed between 140 - 150 pounds. She is Caucasian with green eyes, two piercings in each ear lobe and one in her nose. She has multiple tattoos, including an Egyptian symbol called an ankh on her upper left arm and a black widow spider on her left breast. His nickname is Mice. As of this writing, she is forty years old.

If you have any information regarding this case, you are urged to call the Michigan State Police at 269-948-8283.

## Randall Dean Leach

Twenty year old Randall Dean Leach left his home in November 1980 in Sheboygan, Wisconsin to hitchhike to his sister's home in Bend, Oregon. He last spoke to his mother on November 6th to wish her a happy birthday. He was last seen in the Idaho Falls, Idaho area on November 7th. His family reported him missing on February 2, 1981. He has never seen or heard from again.

*(Randall at the time of his disappearance)*

At the time of his disappearance, Randall Leach had brown hair, stood 5'8", and weighed between 140 - 160 pounds. He is Caucasian with blue eyes and a pierced ear. He had previously fractured his clavicle. As of this writing, he is fifty-eight years old.

If you have any information regarding this case, you are urged to call one of the following numbers:

*Sheboygan County Sheriff's Department at 920-459-3112*

## Garren Rudolf Beller

Thirty-eight year old Garren Rudolf Beller was visiting family and friends in Northwest Indiana from November 15 - 19, 2009. On November 19th, he was dropped off at a Chicago train station to take an Amtrak train home to Oregon. He was scheduled to be back in Ashland, Oregon on November 21st, but he never arrived. His roommate reported him missing on November 24th.

It was later learned that he bought a ticket, but did not use it. He never boarded the train. Since the day he disappeared, he has not used his credit card or cell phone. The circumstances of his disappearance are considered suspicious.

*(Garren at the time of his disappearance)*

At the time of his disappearance, Garren Beller had shoulder-length brown hair, stood 5’6”, and weighed 160 pounds. He was last seen wearing a one-quarter-carat diamond earring in his left ear. He is Caucasian with hazel eyes, a tattoo on his back, a tattoo of a scorpion on his right shoulder, and a half-inch scar on the bridge of his nose. Both of his ears and nipples are pierced. As of this writing, he is forty-seven years old.

If you have any information regarding this case, you are urged to call one of the following numbers:

*Ashland, Oregon Police Department at 541-552-2172*

*Porter County Sheriff's Department at 219-477-3136*

## Cecil O. Baker

Forty-seven year old Cecil O. Baker was last seen in Barbourville, Kentucky on May 1, 2011. He said he was going to visit his daughter in Michigan, but it is not known if he ever even left the state of Kentucky. He has never been heard from again. His lime green four-door 1994 Geo Metro with Kentucky plate number 474CDH is also missing. His family believes he may have come to harm.

*(Cecil at the time of his disappearance)*

At the time of his disappearance, Cecil Baker had sandy brown hair, wore prescription eyeglasses with black frames, stood between 5'10" - 6', and weighed between 185 - 200 pounds. He was last seen wearing a brown and white striped button-down polo shirt, tan or brown khaki pants, and a watch. He is Caucasian with hazel eyes and a tattoo of the name Tammy with a heart underneath it on the inside of his right forearm. As of this writing, he is sixty-four years old.

If you have any information regarding this case, you are urged to call the Kentucky State Police Post 10 at 606-573-3179.

## Andrew Memmelaar

Seventeen year old Andrew Memmelaar was last seen on October 25, 1975. He left Lehigh, Kansas en route to Jeffersonville, New York. He never arrived and has never been heard from again. Few details are available in his case.

*(Andrew at the time of his disappearance)*

At the time of his disappearance, Andrew Memmelaar had red hair, stood between 5'11" - 6'1", and weighed 150 pounds. He is Caucasian with blue eyes, a one-inch scar on his lower left arm, and a scar near his right armpit. His collarbone was previously broken on the right side and didn't heal properly. As of this writing, he is sixty years old.

If you have any information regarding this case, you are urged to call the Sullivan County, New York Sheriff's Office at 845-794-7100.

## Mohammed Abdulmohsen Alghannam

Twenty-five year old Mohammed Abdulmohsen Alghannam was last seen in New Orleans, Louisiana on March 28, 2015. He lived with his sister in San Antonio, Texas and was studying mechanical engineering at the University of Texas. He went missing while he and his uncle were visiting New Orleans. The two men spent three nights at the Extended Stay America hotel on Interstate 10 in Metairie, Louisiana. On March 28th, Mohammed's uncle dropped him off near Bourbon Street at 9:30pm, and then drove overnight to Arkansas. They exchanged text messages on the morning of March 29th. That was the last time anyone saw or heard from him. He was supposed to take a Greyhound bus back to San Antonio, but it is not known if he did so or not.

*(Mohammed at the time of his disappearance)*

At the time of his disappearance, Mohammed Alghannam had black hair, stood between 5'6" - 5'8", and weighed between 150 - 185 pounds. He is Asian with brown eyes. He was born in Saudi Arabia, and his nickname is Mo. As of this writing, he is twenty-eight years old.

If you have any information regarding this case, you are urged to call the San Antonio Police Department at 210-207-7660.

## Wilson Dumars Jr.

Thirty-two year old Wilson Dumars Jr. was last seen driving his white 1981 Dodge pickup truck in Natchitoches, Louisiana at 2pm on June 13, 1988. He lived in Houston, Texas at the time and had traveled to Louisiana to visit a relative for the weekend. He has never been heard from again.

*(Wilson at the time of his disappearance)*

At the time of his disappearance, Wilson Dumars Jr. had black hair styled in a shoulder-length Jheri curl style, stood 5'8", and weighed 170 pounds. He is African-American with brown eyes. As of this writing, he is sixty-three years old.

If you have any information regarding this case, you are urged to call the Natchitoches Parish Sheriff's Office at 318-357-7832.

## Robin Anne Vaudreuil

Thirty-two year old Robin Anne Vaudreuil was last seen in Worcester, Massachusetts on April 17, 1995. She spoke to her mother on the telephone and said she was going to Oswego, New York. She has never been heard from again. She has a history of hitching rides with long-haul truckers, but it is not known if she did on this occasion. Few details are available in her case.

*(Robin at the time of her disappearance)*

At the time of her disappearance, Robin Vaudreuil had brown hair, stood between 5' - 5'1", and weighed between 110 - 125 pounds. She was last seen wearing a dark-colored sweatshirt, sweatpants, and a dark-colored satin motorcycle jacket with a patch-type emblem on the back. She is Caucasian with blue eyes, a one-inch scar on her chin, and a two-inch scar on her cheekbone. She is far-sighted and requires eyeglasses, but she doesn't wear them. She wears a size five and a half shoe. At the time of this writing, she is fifty-five years old.

If you have any information regarding this case, you are urged to call the Worcester Police Department at 508-799-8651.

## John Block & Jean Gertrude Block

Fifty-seven year old John Block and his wife, fifty-eight year old Jean Gertrude Block, were last seen in Utica, Michigan on July 4, 1977. They took off from Macomb Airport at 11:10am in their green and white two-seater, single-engine Cessna airplane with the Michigan tag number N 50935. The couple planned to visit their son in Northern Michigan, and their destination was Lost Creek Sky Ranch Airport in Luzerne, Michigan. They never arrived and have never been heard from again.

John is an experienced pilot with thirty years of experience. An extensive search in North Central Michigan turned up no sign of them or their plane.

*(John & Jean at the time of their disappearances)*

At the time of his disappearance, John Block had gray hair, stood 5'6", and weighed 140 pounds. He is Caucasian with brown eyes. As of this writing, he is ninety-eight years old.

At the time of her disappearance, Jean Block had red hair, stood between 4'9" - 4'11", and weighed between 160 - 170 pounds. She is Caucasian with green eyes. As of this writing, she is ninety-nine years old.

## Georgia Ann Clock Smith

Seventy-six year old Georgia Ann Clock Smith left her son's home in Champlin, Minnesota at approximately 6:30pm on June 30, 1999. She was planning to travel 125 miles northeast to her summer lake residence in Minong, Wisconsin. She was driving her dark metallic blue two-door 1984 Mercedes Benz 1900 with Wisconsin plates TXP-401. She has never been heard from again and her vehicle has not been located.

As a result of a miscommunication problem, she was not reported missing for three days. She normally avoided interstates, and instead took smaller highways or country roads. Her family members are unsure what route she may have taken. Her children believe she may have met with foul play.

*(Georgia at the time of her disappearance)*

At the time of her disappearance, Georgia Smith had brown hair, wore eyeglasses for reading, and was in the early stages of Alzheimer's disease. Her height and weight at the time are unknown. She was last seen wearing a black shirt with purple flowers and black shoes with a zipper on top. She is Caucasian with blue eyes, pierced ears, a surgical scar from her chest to her groin, a surgical scar from the top of her left leg to her ankle, and a scar on her wrist. As of this writing, she is ninety-five years old.

If you have any information regarding this case, you are urged to call the Champlin Police Department at 612-525-6216 or 763-421-2971.

## Shelia St. Clair

Forty-eight year old Shelia St. Clair was last seen at the Cascade Apartments on west Third Street in Duluth, Minnesota on August 20, 2015. She was planning to travel to the White Earth Reservation, but never arrived there. She also wanted to go to Red Cliff, Wisconsin, but she never arrived there either, as far as anyone knows. She was reported missing on September

10th. She didn't own a vehicle at the time and may have tried to get a ride to where she was going. She is considered missing under suspicious circumstances.

*(Shelia at the time of her disappearance)*

At the time of her disappearance, Shelia St. Clair had brown hair, stood 5'4", and weighed 115 pounds. She was last seen wearing a knee-length black sleeveless dress and light-colored shoes. She is Native American with brown eyes, a tattoo of an eagle on her right arm, and pierced ears. Her right foot is damaged and she may walk with a limp. She may use the last name Jackson. As of this writing, she is fifty-one years old.

If you have any information regarding this case, you are urged to call the Duluth Police Department at 218-730-5050.

**Deborah Lois Dean**

Twenty-five year old Deborah Lois Dean was last seen on May 3, 1985. She was riding a Greyhound bus home to Tucson, Arizona from Pennsylvania, where she had been visiting a friend. It has been confirmed that she did make it to St. Louis, Missouri, where she called a family member in Tucson. She was to be picked up by a family member in Phoenix, Arizona, but she never arrived there. Her luggage went on to Los Angeles and was then sent back to her family. Her purse was found at a truck stop café outside of St. Louis on the Greyhound route. It was mailed to her address in Tucson in August 1985. She has never been heard from again.

*(Deborah at the time of her disappearance)*

At the time of her disappearance, Deborah Dean had brown hair, stood 5'2", and weighed between 125 - 130 pounds. What she was wearing is unknown, but she had her prescription contacts with a slight green tint and her prescription eyeglasses with tinted lenses on her person at the time, and neither of them has been found. She is Caucasian with green eyes, a scar on the third finger of her right hand, pierced ears, and a cartilage piercing in one of her ears. As of this writing, she is fifty-eight years old.

If you have any information regarding this case, you are urged to call one of the following numbers:

*St. Louis, Missouri Police Department at 314-444-5371*

*Tucson, Arizona Police Department at 520-837-7988*

**Bengie Lynn Tyson**

Thirty-two year old Bengie Lynn Tyson was last seen in Billings, Montana on November 26, 2009. She was traveling with her boyfriend at the time. The two were driving a blue 1999 Chevrolet Silverado pickup with Montana plates AFM487. That vehicle has never been located. The vehicle tracker was disabled on January 15, 2010 in Portland, Oregon. Bengie has never been heard from again. She lived in Phoenix, Arizona at the time and was employed as a waitress.

*(Bengie at the time of her disappearance)*

At the time of her disappearance, Bengie Tyson had light brown hair, a few freckles on her face, stood between 5'5" - 5'7", and weighed between 120 - 140 pounds. She is African-American with brown eyes, a two-inch scar on her forehead, and multiple tattoos. She may use the name Phyletta D. Mueck. As of this writing, she is forty years old.

If you have any information about this case, you are urged to call one of the following numbers:

*Billings Police Department at 406-657-8461*

*Carbon County Sheriff's Office at 406-446-1234*

## Emma Francis Tresp

Seventy-one year old Emma Francis Tresp left her daughter's home in Stillwater, Oklahoma on August 31, 1998. She was planning to drive to a religious retreat at a Benedictine monastery near Pecos, New Mexico. It is known that she bought gas at a station in Santa Rosa, New Mexico at approximately 3pm that day. Her white four-door 1997 Honda Civic was found locked and abandoned on Forestry Road 63A near Pecos, New Mexico later that day. It was lodged on a large rock in the road, which had cracked the oil pan. Authorities believe she may have walked away from the vehicle to get help. Extensive searches of the area turned up no clues as to her whereabouts. Her purse disappeared with her and has never been found.

When her children discovered she never arrived at the monastery, they all traveled to New Mexico to search for her. After not being able to locate her, they reported her missing on September 8th.

*(Emma at the time of her disappearance)*

At the time of her disappearance, Emma Tresp had graying brown hair, wore eyeglasses, had varicose veins, stood between 5'6" - 5'7", and weighed between 120 - 135 pounds. She is known to have been wearing a mother's ring. She is Caucasian with green eyes and a mole on the right side of her nose. As of this writing, she is ninety-one years old.

If you have any information regarding this case, you are urged to call the New Mexico State Police at 505-827-9076.

## Michelle Lyn Hundley Smith

Thirty-eight year old Michelle Lynn Hundley Smith was last seen leaving her residence in Eden, North Carolina at 8:30pm on December 9, 2001. She planned to go Christmas shopping in Martinsville, Virginia. She never returned home and has never been heard from again. Her green 1995 Pontiac Trans Sport van with North Carolina plates ROK-N-ON has never been found.

*(Michelle at the time of her disappearance)*

At the time of her disappearance, Michelle Smith had brown hair, stood between 5'3" - 5'5", and weighed

150 pounds. She was last seen wearing a green blouse, blue jeans, brown moccasins, a wedding ring, and a gold ring with four birthstones. She is Caucasian with hazel eyes, a scar on her upper arm, and a birthmark shaped like a baseball bat on her ankle. As of this writing, she is fifty-four years old.

If you have any information regarding this case, you are urged to call the Rockingham County Sheriff's Office at 336-634-3238.

## Nicholas Alexander-Lee McCray

Thirty-one year old Nicholas Alexander-Lee McCray left Detroit, Michigan en route to North Dakota in mid-October 2016. He said he had a construction job there. He kept in regular touch with his mother, but her last contact with him was on November 16th. He last posted to his social media account the next day. He was planning to return to Detroit for a child custody hearing involving his daughter. He never arrived at the hearing and has never been heard from again. Authorities have not been able to confirm that he was ever even in North Dakota, nor has any evidence been found to determine that he returned to Detroit.

*(Nicholas at the time of his disappearance)*

At the time of his disappearance, Nicholas McCray had black hair styled in dreadlocks, a mustache and goatee, stood between 5'10" - 6', and weighed between 150 - 160 pounds. He is African-American with brown eyes and numerous scars all over his body. His nickname is Nick. As of this writing, he thirty-three years old.

If you have any information regarding this case, you are urged to call the Bismarck Police Department at 701-223-1212.

## Courtland Lee Mumford

Sixty-five year old Courtland Lee Mumford was last seen in Portland, Oregon on July 7, 2007. He had recently purchased a bright yellow single-engine 2007 Cub Crafters Sports Cub aircraft with the tail number N222TB and was making local familiarization flights. He flew out the Aurora airport shortly after 5am on July 7th and never returned. His family reported him missing that night.

The plane had a full tank of fuel and could have flown as far as 400 miles without stopping. Neither the plane's emergency responder nor his cell phone emitted any signals after he went missing. He is a very experienced pilot. He worked for Trans World Airlines (TWA) and American Airlines for over 35 years, and was in excellent health. An extensive search turned up no sign of him or his plane.

*(Courtland at the time of his disappearance)*

At the time of his disappearance, Courtland Mumford had gray hair and was balding, stood at 6'1", and weighed 170 pounds. He was last seen wearing white striped Asics sneakers, white calf-length sport socks, a gold wedding band, and possibly a polo shirt with a flying-type logo. He is Caucasian with blue eyes, an appendectomy scar on his abdomen, and large surgical scars on both knees and both shoulders. His nickname is Court. As of this writing, he is seventy-six years old.

If you have any information regarding this case, you are urged to call the Portland Police Bureau at 503-823-0446.

## Byron Augustus Freeman

Seventy year old Byron Augustus Freeman was traveling to a class reunion in Palestine, Texas at the time of his disappearance. He was last seen on U.S. Highway 79 in Franklin, Texas on June 24, 2006, walking away from his rental car. He has never been seen again. His rental vehicle, a gray 2006 Lincoln Town Car with

Texas plates 332KWK was found along U.S. Highway 79 the next day. He lived in Los Angeles, California at the time.

*(Byron at the time of his disappearance)*

At the time of his disappearance, Byron Freeman had gray hair, wore wire-framed eyeglasses, stood between 5'8" - 5'10", and weighed between 150 - 160 pounds. He is believed to have been in the early stages of Alzheimer's disease at the time, and he may be disoriented and confused. He was last seen wearing a green jumpsuit, a watch, and possibly a ring. He is African-American with brown eyes. His nickname is Babe. As of this writing, he is eighty-two years old.

If you have any information regarding this case, you are urged to call the Anderson County Sheriff's Office at 903-729-6068.

## Jose Benjamin Hernandez

Sixty-eight year old Jose Benjamin Hernandez was last seen in Knippa, Texas on November 30, 2009. He was en route to Guanajuato, Mexico, over 700 miles away. He never arrived there and has never been heard from again. Few details are available in his case.

*(Jose at the time of his disappearance)*

At the time of his disappearance, Jose Hernandez had black hair, stood 5’5”, and weighed 150 pounds. He is Hispanic with brown eyes. As of this writing, he is seventy-seven years old.

If you have any information regarding this case, you are urged to call the Texas Department of Public Safety at 1-800-346-3243.

## Eulaila Renee LaPorte

Forty-two year old Eulaila Renee LaPorte was last seen on west Cardinal Loop F-105 in Del Valle, Texas on May 11, 1998. She was going to Matamoros, Mexico to visit her boyfriend for the day. She has never been heard from again. She was driving a 1989 blue/gray two-door Dodge Ram pickup truck with Texas plates 5MDFT with handicap tags and the VIN number 3B4GED7Y7KM939283. That vehicle has never been located.

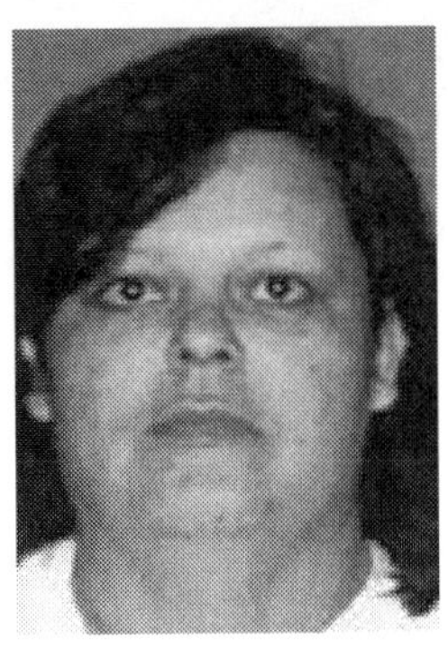

*(Eulaila at the time of her disappearance)*

At the time of her disappearance, Eulaila LaPorte had brown hair, stood 5'6", and weighed 230 pounds. She is Caucasian with brown eyes. As of this writing, she is sixty-two years old.

If you have any information regarding this case, you are urged to call the Austin Police Department at 512-974-5000.

## Timothy James McKye

Fifty year old Timothy James McKye was last seen in Beaumont, Texas on October 13, 2006. He was in the process of moving to Florida from Glendale, Arizona at the time. An apartment complex security guard in Beaumont assisted him when his U-Haul trailer got stuck in a ditch. He left it behind and didn't return for it. He has never been heard from again. His silver/blue 1999 Plymouth Voyager van with Arizona plates 161TTM, along with his female German Shepherd are also missing.

*(Timothy at the time of his disappearance)*

At the time of his disappearance, Timothy McKye had light brown hair, stood 5'9", and weighed 200 pounds. He is Caucasian with hazel eyes. His nickname is Tim. As of this writing, he is sixty-two years old.

If you have any information regarding this case, you are urged to call the Glendale Police Department at 623-930-3000.

## Charles Ray Koller Sr.

Fifty-six year old Charles Ray Koller Sr. was last seen in Bremerton, Washington on August 10, 1992. He was riding a Greyhound bus to Dallas, Texas to visit relatives, but he never arrived. He has never been heard from again.

(Charles at the time of his disappearance)

At the time of his disappearance, Charles Koller Sr. had shoulder-length gray hair with a beard and goatee, wore an upper denture, and calloused fingertips on his left hand. He was last seen wearing a cowboy hat and cowboy boots. He is Caucasian with hazel eyes. He has the following tattoos: a fish above each breast with the words sweet and sour, a sailing ship on his upper right arm, a butterfly on his right shoulder blade, a rose with the words mom and dad on his right forearm, an unknown tattoo on his left forearm, and a star on the bottom of his right thumb. As of this writing, he is eighty-two years old.

If you have any information regarding this case, you are urged to call the Bremerton Police Department at 360-478-5220.

## James Elwood Brady

Thirty-five year old James Elwood Brady was last seen boarding a Trailways bus in Logan County near Bluefield, West Virginia on September 1, 1965. He was en route to his sister's home in South Carolina, but he never arrived. He has never been heard from again.

(James at the time of his disappearance)

At the time of his disappearance, James Brady had brown hair, stood 5'7", and weighed 145 pounds. He is Caucasian with hazel eyes and a scar on his head. As of this writing, he is eighty-eight years old.

If you have any information regarding this case, you are urged to call the West Virginia State Police at 304-746-2100.

## David Vernon Lovely

Nineteen year old David Vernon Lovely was moving with his family from Massachusetts to California in August 1985. His family was traveling in a large Ryder truck, and David rode his burgundy 1978 Model 1100 Yamaha motorcycle. The motorcycle was outfitted with saddlebags and a luggage rack. It had California plates 8N3477. His family wanted to stop in Evanston, Wyoming, but David wanted to keep going. So he continued on his way.

Later, he called his aunt and said his motorcycle had broken down in Fort Bridger, Wyoming, but that a 'rough-looking' man with his own motorcycle had fixed the Yamaha at Bingo Truck Stop. David claimed to be afraid of the man. He has never been heard from again. He was carrying approximately $150 in cash at the time.

Nine days later, campers found his motorcycle in an isolated area off South Baxter Road on a dirt road west of the Sweetwater County Airport in Rock Springs, Wyoming. The keys were in it, and it was in working condition with half a tank of gas. An extensive search of the surrounding area turned up no clues as to his whereabouts.

*(David at the time of his disappearance)*

At the time of his disappearance, David Lovely had brownish-blonde hair, stood 6'4", and weighed 160 pounds. He was last seen wearing a white pullover sweatshirt or polo shirt, a red nylon windbreaker, a green Army fatigue jacket, brown cotton pants, and sneakers. He is Caucasian with blue eyes and large scars across his abdomen below his ribcage. As of this writing, he is fifty-two years old.

If you have any information regarding this case, you are urged to call one of the following numbers:

Sweetwater County, Wyoming Sheriff's Department at 307-872-6350

*Wyoming Division of Criminal Investigation at 307-777-7181*

*Huntington Beach, California Police Department at 714-536-5641*

## Randal Paul Gary

Fifty year old Randal Paul Gary was last seen on May 16, 2003. He was on vacation onboard the cruise ship Veendam. He boarded the ship in Ketchikan, Alaska, and spent most of his nights in the ship's casino.

The ship made stops in Juneau and Skagway, but he didn't disembark in either place. He was last seen at 10:30pm on the last day of the cruise. When the ship docked in Vancouver, British Columbia, he was nowhere to be found. He has never been seen again.

He left all of his personal belongings, including his passport, credit cards, insulin, driver's license, wallet, cash, and key card in his cabin. His room had only a sealed window and no balcony. He is described as a very private person but was in good spirits and not having any personal problems at the time.

*(Randall at the time of his disappearance)*

At the time of his disappearance, Randal Gary had brown hair, stood 6', and weighed 200 pounds. He is known to have a worn a Medic Alert bracelet at the time. He is Caucasian with brown eyes. He has diabetes and is insulin-dependent. As of this writing, he is sixty-five years old.

If you have any information regarding this case, you are urged to call the Vancouver Police Department at 604-717-2530.

## Robert Joseph Thompson

Fifty-six year old Robert Joseph Thompson was in the process of moving from Sarasota, Florida to Colorado in May 1993. On June 7th, his vehicle was discovered abandoned at mile marker 1289 on Alaska Highway near Northway, Alaska. Robert has never been heard from again. Few details are available in his case.

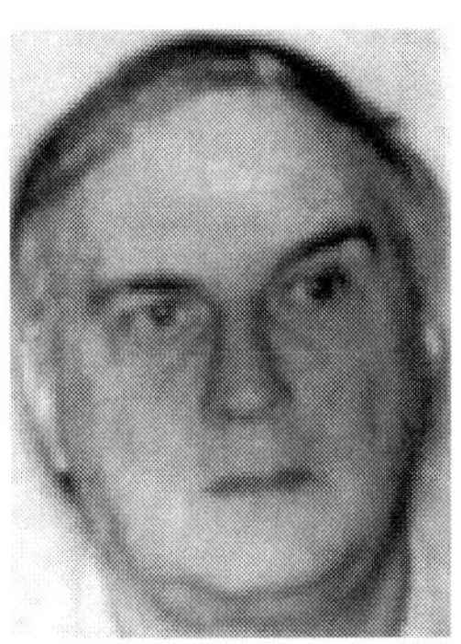

*(Robert at the time of his disappearance)*

At the time of his disappearance, Robert Thompson had gray hair and was partially balding, stood 6', and weighed 200 pounds. He is Caucasian with hazel eyes and a scar on his left cheek. As of this writing, he is eighty-one years old.

If you have any information regarding this case, you are urged to call the Alaska State Troopers at 907-269-5018 or 907-883-5111.

## DeAnna Kay Brooks

Seventy year old DeAnna Kay Brooks was last seen in Santa Cruz, California at 11am on August 23, 2012. She said she was going to a birthday party at her mother's home in San Diego, California, almost 500 miles to the south. She never arrived there and has never been seen again. She was driving a gold 2003 Chrysler PT Cruiser with damage on both sides and California plates 5EEV387. It is unknown whether or not the vehicle has been located.

*(DeAnna at the time of her disappearance)*

At the time of her disappearance, DeAnna Brooks had brown hair, stood 5'3", and weighed 218 pounds. She is Caucasian with blue eyes and pierced ears. She suffers from diabetes, and uses a walker to aid her mobility. As of this writing, she is seventy-six years old.

If you have any information regarding this case, you are urged to call the Santa Cruz Police Department at 831-420-5870.

## Jose Abel Munoz Leon

Twenty-six year old Jose Abel Munoz Leon was last seen in Santa Maria, California on July 3, 1988. He left on a Greyhound bus at 7:45am that day en route to Los Angeles, California. He was supposed to be traveling to Michoacan, Mexico, but he never arrived and has never been heard from again. Few details are available in his case.

*(Jose at the time of his disappearance)*

At the time of his disappearance, Jose Leon had brown hair, stood 5'11", and weighed 155 pounds. He was last seen wearing a blue sweatshirt, gray pants, and a white felt hat with a small brim. His is Hispanic with brown eyes. As of this writing, he is fifty-six years old.

If you have any information regarding this case, you are urged to call the Santa Maria Police Department at 805-928-3781.

## Roberta Musquiz Pagan

Thirty-five year old Roberta Musquiz Pagan went on a Carnival Cruise in January 2003 with her husband and their five year old son. The ship, called Elation, was between Mazatlan and Cabo San Lucas, Mexico when she disappeared.

She had an argument with her husband on the evening of January 26th. Afterwards, he took their son back to their cabin, and the two of them went to sleep.

When her husband awoke later, he realized she was missing.

When the ship docked at San Pedro, California on January 31st, the investigation began. Her husband was ruled out as a suspect early on. The U.S. Coast Guard was unable to assist in the search because she vanished in Mexican waters. Although there is no evidence to suggest it, her family believes foul play was involved.

*(Roberta at the time of her disappearance)*

At the time of her disappearance, Roberta Pagan had brown hair, stood 5'5", and weighed 160 pounds. She was last seen wearing a cream-colored shirt and shorts set with the words Puerto Vallarta and dolphins on the front of the shirt and black flips flops. She is Hispanic with brown eyes, a scar on her left ankle, a mole on her right cheek, and scars on her left thigh and breast. As of this writing, she is fifty-one years old.

If you have any information regarding this case, you are urged to call the Federal Bureau of Investigation (FBI) at 310-477-6565.

**Manuelita Dejos Pierce**

Thirty-nine year old Manuelita Dejos Pierce was traveling aboard the Royal Caribbean cruise ship Enchantment of the Seas in late October 2000. The ship was approximately 140 miles outside of Fort Lauderdale, Florida on October 29th. It was returning to Port Everglades, Florida after having stopped in Key West, Mexico, the Cayman Islands, and Jamaica. A crew member saw Manuelita in a hallway on the ship at approximately 1am that day. She has never been seen again.

Her possessions were found unpacked in her cabin after all the other nearly 2,000 passengers disembarked the ship. She was reported missing at that time. Local law enforcement and the Coast Guard searched both the ship and the water, to no avail.

*(Manuelita at the time of her disappearance)*

At the time of her disappearance, Manuelita Pierce had auburn hair, stood 5', and weighed 115 pounds. She was last seen wearing black dress with spaghetti straps. She is Asian with brown eyes, a triangle-shaped birthmark above her right breast, a birthmark on the left side of her back near her kidney, skin abrasions on both of her calves, tattooed eyebrows, and surgical scars from breast augmentation. Her ears and navel are pierced. Her nickname is Mandy, and she is of Filipino descent. As of this writing, she is fifty-seven years old.

If you have any information regarding this case, you are urged to call the North Miami Beach, Florida Federal Bureau of Investigation (FBI) Office at 305-944-9101.

## Sandy Seligman

Twenty-six year old Sandy Seligman traveled from his home in Vancouver, British Columbia to the Virgin Islands, the Bahamas, and Florida for vacation in the summer of 1980. He called his mother from Miami, Florida on August 15th and said he would be returning home in two days. He also told her he had purchased a Columbian emerald worth $1,500 as a gift for her. He was supposed to take an 11:15am flight to Seattle, Washington, and then travel onto Vancouver by bus. He was last seen in Miami on August 17th. He checked out of his hotel and returned his rental car to the Hertz rental car company, but he never made his flight. He has never been heard from again.

*(Sandy at the time of his disappearance)*

At the time of his disappearance, Sandy Seligman had blonde hair, stood between 5'11" - 6', and weighed 165 pounds. He is Caucasian with hazel eyes. As of this writing, he is sixty-four years old.

If you have any information regarding this case, you are urged to call the Miami-Dade Police Department at 305-471-1700.

## Francis Xavier McKenna

Seventy-two year old Francis Xavier McKenna left his Taylorsville, North Carolina home on October 10, 2011 to go to his vacation home in Sarasota, Florida. He checked into the Orange Blossom Motel in Citra, Florida on the night of October 11th and left the next morning. When he checked out, he appeared to be confused and disoriented. That was the last time anyone saw him. He never arrived in Sarasota.

On October 14th, his white 1998 Ford Econoline E150 minivan was found abandoned on Interstate 75 at the County Road 484 exit ramp in Marion County, Florida. It was in operable condition, and his belongings were still inside it. His brother reported him missing on November 9th. His credit and debit cards have not been used since he was last seen.

*(Francis at the time of his disappearance)*

At the time of his disappearance, Francis McKenna had gray hair, wore eyeglasses, stood between 6'3" - 6'4", and weighed between 190 - 200 pounds. He was last seen wearing a light-colored t-shirt, khaki cargo shorts, and sneakers. His is Caucasian with green eyes and a small tattoo on his shoulder. As of this writing, he is seventy-nine years old.

If you have any information regarding this case, you are urged to call one of the following numbers:

*Marion County, Florida Sheriff's Office at 352-732-8181*

*Alexander County, North Carolina Sheriff's Office at 828-632-4658*

## Wallace Tolar Gerrald

Eighty-five year old Wallace Tolar Gerrald was last seen in Palatka, Florida at 12pm on October 20, 2015. He traveled from Galivants Ferry, South Carolina to Palatka to get some legal documents and was supposed to return to South Carolina later that day. He never did and has never been heard from again. He was driving a white 2013 Ford F-150 pickup truck with a dented tailgate, South Carolina plates DEQ188, and the VIN number 1FTMF1CM1DFB14841. It is unknown whether or not the vehicle has been located.

*(Wallace at the time of his disappearance)*

At the time of his disappearance, Wallace Gerrald had graying brown hair, stood 5'11", and weighed 165 pounds. He was last seen wearing a plaid shirt, khaki pants, and a baseball cap. He is Caucasian with blue eyes and hardwire installed in his hip. He has had surgery on both of his hips, his knee, his prostate, and open-heart surgery. His nickname is Buster. As of this writing, he is eighty-eight years old.

If you have any information regarding this case, you are urged to call one of the following numbers:

*Putnam County Sheriff's Office at 386-329-0801*

*Palatka Police Department at 386-329-0115*

## Lloyd Raymond Gilsdorf Jr.

Thirty-one year old Lloyd Raymond Gilsdorf Jr. was last seen in Pensacola, Florida on July 29, 1984. He told his parents he had gotten a phone call from an offshore oil company offering him a job. A man from Houston, Texas had sent him a prepaid bus ticket, and someone was going to meet him in New Orleans, Louisiana and take him to the job site. He boarded a Trailways bus at the downtown bus station en route to

Louisiana, but it is unknown whether or not he arrived there. He has never been heard from again.

After three months passed with no word from him, his mother sent a registered letter to the Houston man who had paid for her son's bus ticket. The letter was returned undeliverable. She reported him missing on January 10, 1985, almost six months after he was last seen.

Foul play is suspected. His mother believed he was purposely lured to the bus station to be murdered. She passed away in 1998, but his siblings would still like to know what happened to their brother.

*(Lloyd at the time of his disappearance)*

At the time of his disappearance, Lloyd Gilsdorf Jr. had brown hair that he wore in a hippie-like style with a mustache and full beard, stood between 5'6" - 5'7", and weighed 160 pounds. He was last seen wearing a sport shirt, blue jeans, and moccasins. He is Caucasian with blue eyes, a tattoo of Snoopy on his left arm, and a tattoo of a zigzag on his right arm. As of this writing, he is sixty-five years old.

If you have any information regarding this case, you are urged to call the Escambia County Sheriff's Office at 850-436-9199.

## Rebecca Coriam

Twenty-four year old Rebecca Coriam of Chester, England, disappeared on March 22, 2011 while onboard the cruise ship Disney Wonder. She was an employee onboard the ship and been employed by Disney Cruise lines since June 2010. She was last seen just before dawn on the day she disappeared. When she did not report for work that morning, an alarm was raised. The crew searched the ship but could not find her. When she was discovered missing, the ship was off the coast of Mexico and heading to Puerto Vallarta.

Security camera footage timestamped at 5:45am shows Rebecca looking distraught and talking on the phone in the crew quarters. After the captain of the ship learned of her disappearance, he notified the U.S. Coast Guard, the Bahamas Maritime Authority, the Royal Bahamas Police Force, the FBI, and the Mexican Navy. While there were several agencies notified of her disappearance, supposedly only a few of the crew and none of the passengers were questioned. The investigation concluded there had been no foul play.

Weeks after her disappearance, a bank informed her parents there had been some activity on her account. Near the one-year anniversary of her disappearance, someone claimed to have spotted her with a dark-haired man in Venice, Italy. But after an investigation there, she was not found. In September 2011, her family learned that someone had changed her Facebook password. All of these bits of information have given her parents and her sister hope that she is still alive.

Her family insists she was not suicidal, and proof of that could be that she had bought tickets to Disneyland as a surprise, so she and her family could go when she got back from the cruise.

Her parents hired private investigators who disagreed with the original investigation's findings. They believed she did not commit suicide and that there was a possibility of foul play. Unfortunately, she is still listed as being lost at sea.

*(Rebecca at the time of her disappearance)*

No distinguishing characteristics for Rebecca Coriam could be found. As of this writing, she is thirty-one years old.

If you have any information regarding this case, you are urged to go to www.rebecca-coriam.com or email help@rebecca-coriam.com or contact your nearest FBI Field Office.

# Jorge Luis Pintado & Enrique Oscar Valles

Forty-three year old Jorge Luis Pintado and forty year old Enrique Oscar Valles were last seen in Miami, Florida on May 17, 1991. They were driving a rented vehicle to Georgia to purchase a used dump truck. They never arrived and have never been heard from again. Their rental vehicle was later found abandoned and burned in a wooden area in Huntsville, Georgia.

*(Jorge at the time of his disappearance)*

At the time of his disappearance, Jorge Pintado had brown hair, stood 5'11", and weighed 210 pounds. He was last seen wearing black pants, a black shirt with blue stripes, and possibly carrying pink rosary beads. He is Hispanic with brown eyes and a circular scar on the left side of his chest. As of this writing, he is sixty years old.

*(Enrique at the time of his disappearance)*

At the time of his disappearance, Enrique Valles had brown hair, stood 5'11", and weighed 180 pounds. He was last seen wearing a white shirt and brown pants. He is Hispanic with brown eyes. As of this writing, he is sixty-seven years old.

If you have any information regarding this case, you are urged to call the Miami-Dade Police Department at 305-471-1700.

## Annette Mizener

Thirty-seven year old Annette Mizener, from Waukesha, Wisconsin, disappeared on December 4, 2004 while onboard the Carnival Cruise ship Pride off the coast of Mexico. She was on vacation with her parents and her seventeen year old daughter. On the last night of the cruise that had originally departed from Los Angeles, California, Annette left her cabin to go play Bingo. She was supposed to meet her parents for the 10pm Bingo game but didn't. When she didn't show up, her parents became concerned and began to look for her. A witness placed her in the casino at 9:30pm. At around 10:10pm, her name was paged after members of the crew found her beaded handbag on deck. They had paged her in an attempt to return it.

Later, it was discovered that beads from the purse were located on the deck, appearing to have been ripped from the purse. A security camera in the same vicinity had been covered by a paper, and therefore didn't catch anything of interest. Supposedly, a spot of blood was also found near the beads on the deck.

The cruise line's crew conducted a room-by-room search after she was reported missing, but the ship did not stop. Once the Coast Guard was notified, the ship turned around to search the water. The FBI also investigated, but found no explanation for her disappearance. She is presumed deceased, but her body has never been located.

*(Annette at the time of her disappearance)*

No distinguishing characteristics for Annette Mizener could be found. As of this writing, she is fifty-one years old.

If you have any information regarding this case, you are urged to call the Federal Bureau of Investigation (FBI) at 1-800-225-5324.

## Glenn William Sheridan

Fifty-four year old Glenn William Sheridan, from Williamsburg, Virginia, disappeared while vacationing with his wife on board the Carnival Cruise line ship Celebration. The ship was returning from a five-day cruise to the Bahamas at the time. He was last seen by his wife at 1:30pm on November 24, 2004. His wife later reported him missing. At that time a search was conducted, but he wasn't located. When the ship docked in Jacksonville, Florida, his wife officially reported him missing. Documents show that he did not leave the ship once it docked.

A boat and a helicopter searched the Atlantic Ocean and the St. Johns River, to no avail. He has never been seen again. He is presumed deceased, but his body has never been located.

*(Glenn at the time of his disappearance)*

At the time of his disappearance, Glenn Sheridan had gray hair and was balding, stood 5'7", and weighed 170 pounds. He was last seen wearing a green or teal polo shirt and blue jeans. He is Caucasian with blue eyes. As of this writing, he is sixty-eight years old.

If you have any information regarding this case, you are urged to call the Federal Bureau of Investigation (FBI) at 1-202-278-2000.

## Rama Forman

Forty-eight year old Rama Forman disappeared on November 9, 2004 while sailing aboard the Silversea Cruise ship Silver Cloud. The ship was sailing from

North London, United Kingdom. It is believed she went missing while the ship was near Mumbai, India on the Arabian Sea. The crew discovered she was missing when they docked in Mumbai.

Upon investigating, the crew found her balcony room locked from the inside. Her handbag was there, but her jewelry was missing. There was no sign of a struggle and no evidence of foul play. The case was closed and she was presumed lost at sea, but her body has never been found.

Her sister, Roya, insists Rama was not suicidal. She continues to believe there is some other reason for her sister's disappearance.

*(Rama at the time of her disappearance)*

No distinguishing characteristics for Rama Forman could be found. As of this writing, she is sixty-two years old.

If you have any information regarding this case, you are urged to call your local law enforcement agency.

## John Halford

Sixty-three year old John Halford, of Milton Keynes, Buckinghamshire, set off for a 7-day Egyptian cruise, which had been his dream for many years. Although married with three children, he went on the cruise alone, because they could not afford to go as a family. On the evening of April 6, 2011, he packed his suitcase and left it outside his cabin door on the cruise liner Thomson Spirit. It was the last day of the trip, and the ship was due to dock at Sharm-el-Sheikh, Egypt the next morning. He texted his wife to say he would see her at the airport the next day, and then he went to dinner. At about 12:30am, he was seen drinking cocktails in an upper deck bar. Sometime after that he vanished.

Mrs. Halford learned of her husband's disappearance as she was about to leave for the airport to go pick him up. Passengers at the bar said he was not drunk shortly before he disappeared. His family said he was not depressed or suicidal. A search of the sea was carried out, but no trace of him has been found.

*(John at the time of his disappearance)*

No distinguishing characteristics for John Halford can be found. As of this writing, he is seventy years old. His family is pleading for anyone who saw him that night or knows what happened to please come forward.

If you have any information regarding this case, you are urged to call one of the following numbers:

*Thames Valley Police at 0845 8 505 505*

*Federal Bureau of Investigation (FBI) at 1-202-278-2000*

## Sister Eileen Christie

Seventy-two year old Sister Eileen Christie, a Roman Catholic nun from Brentwood, New York, disappeared in July 2016 while vacationing in Austria. Along her way, she kept in contact with her nephew via email. Her last contact with him was on July 6th, saying she had arrived safely at Haus Jodler, a hostel in the village of Hallstatt, Austria. After responding to her email and not getting a reply for three days, her nephew knew something was wrong.

According to her itinerary, she was scheduled to stay at Hallstatt for six days, and then arrive at Innsbruck, Austria on July 9th. When her nephew contacted the hostel in Hallstatt, which was her last known location, he was told she had not been seen since the first day she arrived. Her nephew then notified the police of her disappearance. Sister Eileen had vacationed in the same area the previous three summers, so the location was not new to her.

The only thing missing from her room was her swimsuit. There was no indication of foul play inside her room. Divers with Austria's Special Forces unit, EKO Cobra, began searching the lake on July 19th, after dogs picked up her scent nearby. Submersible robotic cameras were used in areas divers could not reach. A helicopter and search teams were also used in the area, but no sign of her whereabouts was found.

Her family and friends have stated it is not like her to not keep in contact with her loved ones. While most believe she drown, her family is not convinced. They continue to hold out hope of her being found.

*(Sister Eileen at the time of her disappearance)*

Sister Eileen had only recently retired from teaching at St. Anthony's High School in South Huntington, New York. She is described as being friendly and always in motion. No distinguishing characteristics could be located. As of this writing, she is seventy-eight years old.

If you have any information regarding this case, you are urged to call either the Federal Bureau of Investigation (FBI) at 1-202-278-2000 or your nearest American Embassy.

## Althea Blankenship & Jeffrey Blankenship

Twenty-three year old Althea Blankenship and her three year old son, Jeffrey, disappeared on March 27,

1973 after being dropped off at Sea-Tac International Airport in Seattle, Washington. They had made plans to travel to Greece to meet Althea's parents, who were already there on vacation. However, Althea and Jeffrey did not arrive in Greece and have never been heard from again. Foul play is suspected.

*(Althea & Jeffrey at the time of their disappearance & Jeffrey's Age Progression to 47)*

At the time of her disappearance, Althea Blankenship had brown hair, stood 5'6", and weighed between 135 - 145 pounds. She is Caucasian with blue eyes. As of this writing, she is sixty-eight years old.

At the time of his disappearance, Jeffrey Blankenship had brown hair, stood 3'4", and weighed 75 pounds. He is Caucasian with brown eyes. As of this writing, he is forty-eight years old.

If you have any information regarding this case, you are urged to call one of the following numbers:

*Washington State Patrol Missing Persons Unit at 1-800-543-5678*

*The National Center for Missing and Exploited Children at 1-800-843-5678*

## Matthew Paul Garnes

Sixteen year old Matthew Paul Garnes left his Tacoma, Washington home on December 26, 1984 to drive to Portland, Oregon. The drive should have taken just under three hours, but he never arrived. He has never been seen or heard from again. He was driving a gold 1974 Plymouth Duster with Washington plates BUX-160. It is not known whether or not the vehicle has been located.

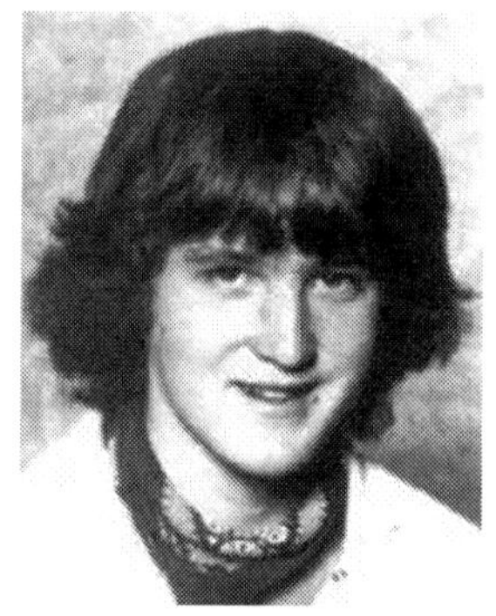

*(Matthew at the time of his disappearance)*

At the time of his disappearance, Matthew Garnes had brown hair, stood 5'7", and weighed 135 pounds. He was last seen wearing a black leather jacket, a sleeveless black Iron Maiden t-shirt, size 30 jeans, a black maroon and gray scarf, size 9.5 Nike tennis shoes, and a silver chain necklace. He was a student at Curtis High School, employed part-time at Texaco, and a member of the high school baseball team. He is Caucasian with hazel eyes and a three-inch scar on his right cheek. He had previously fractured his upper right foot and right elbow. As of this writing, he is fifty years old.

If you have any information regarding this case, you are urged to call one of the following numbers:

*Pierce County Sheriff's Office at 253-798-7530*

*The National Center for Missing and Exploited Children at 1-800-843-5678*

According to The National Center for Missing and Exploited Children (NCMEC), the most frequently reported missing child cases are runaways and family abductions. Between 2008 and 2017, there were 11,581 children abducted by a parent or family member. Of those, fifty-one percent remain active. Forty-seven of them were recovered deceased. However, 99.7% of them were located alive.

Of the nearly 25,000 runaways reported to The National Center for Missing and Exploited Children (NCMEC), one in seven were likely the victims of sex trafficking. This crime is occurring in all types of communities throughout the United States, and traffickers are making an alarming profit while victims endure countless days and nights of rape, abuse, torture, and violence. Traffickers 'recruit' victims in schools, online through social media, at shopping malls, bus stations, and even foster care and group homes. A trafficker can be anyone who profits from the selling of a child for sex to a buyer, including family members, foster parents, friends, gangs, trusted adults, or 'boyfriends'. Much of the trafficking of children has moved from street corners and truck stops to the internet.

The National Center for Missing and Exploited Children operates the CyberTipLine, the nation's centralized reporting system for suspected child sexual exploitation. In 2017 alone, they received more than 10.2 million reports. The CyberTipLine uniquely positions the NCMEC to spot patterns and trends in child sexual exploitation and the online enticement of children. Online enticement can include: enticing a child to share sexually explicit images, meeting in person for sexual purposes, engaging the child in a sexual conversation or role-playing, mutually sharing explicit images, offering an incentive such as a gift card or drugs, grooming through compliments and discussing shared interests, 'liking' their online posts, and pretending to be someone the child's own age or near their age. These types of victimizations take place across every platform: social media, messaging apps, gaming platforms, etc. If you suspect child sex trafficking, you are urged to call 1-800-THE-LOST or visit www.cybertipline.org.

Many (not all) abduction attempts involving children involve one of the following circumstances: a suspect driving a vehicle, occur when the child is traveling to or from school, occur between the hours of 2pm - 7pm, and involve girls between the ages of 10 - 14. The top five methods used during abduction attempts involving children are offering a ride, offering candy or sweets, asking questions or for directions, offering money or gifts, offering to show or needing help looking for an animal.

According to The National Center for Missing and Exploited Children (NCMEC), forty-five percent of infant abductions take place at a hospital or health care facility, while 41% involve the infant being abducted from their home. Most medical facilities now have measures in place to prevent abductions and keep newborns safe. The two most common circumstances where an infant was kidnapped from their home involved someone posing as a social worker or hospital employee or the baby being taken by someone the parent trusted.

Code Adam was created in memory of six year old Adam Walsh, who was abducted from a Florida department store and later found murdered. It is designed to help businesses, parks, government buildings, and other establishments ensure that they have safety protocols in place to respond quickly and effectively when a child is missing.

The Amber Alert Program was named in honor of nine year old Amber Hagerman, who was abducted while riding her bicycle in Arlington, Texas and later found murdered. It is a partnership between law enforcement agencies, broadcasters, transportation agencies, and the wireless industry to activate an urgent bulletin to the community to assist in the search and safe recovery of a missing child. The program is used in all fifty states, the District of Columbia, Puerto Rico, and the U.S. Virgin Islands. As of March 20, 2018, the program was responsible for 924 successful recoveries of missing children.

Federal law requires no waiting period before law enforcement can accept a missing child report. It also requires law enforcement to enter a missing child into the National Crime Information Center (NCIC) within two hours of receiving the report.

## Sherry Marler

Twelve year old Sherry Marler was last seen on June 6, 1984 as she left the First National Bank in downtown Greenville, Alabama to go to the gas station across the street. She had ridden downtown with her stepfather, who had business to attend to at the bank. She has never been seen or heard from again.

*(Age Progression to 39)*

At the time of her disappearance, Sherry Marler had brown hair, stood 5'4", and weighed 120 pounds. She was last seen wearing a red shirt, faded jeans, and tennis shoes. She is Caucasian with brown eyes and a two-inch scar on her stomach. As of this writing, she is forty-seven years old.

If you have any information regarding this case, you are urged to call one of the following numbers:

*Greenville Police Department at 334-382-3107*

*The Polly Klaas Foundation at 1-800-587-4357*

## Stella Evon

Seventeen year old Stella Evon walked out of her sister's apartment in Bethel, Alaska in the early morning hours of September 26, 1996 and disappeared. She had been out with friends the night before and had arrived home to find the door locked, and she could not get in. So she walked across the street to the Bethel Police Department. The officer tried to get her grandmother, whom she lived with, to wake up at the house across the street, to no avail. About 4:30am, the officer left Stella in her sister's care at the BNC Apartments. Within an hour of arriving there, she left. She was last seen by her sister walking down the street.

*(Age Progression to 32)*

At the time of her disappearance, Stella Evon had long curly brown hair, stood 4'11", and weighed 100 pounds. She was last seen wearing a blue hooded Georgetown sweatshirt underneath a brown leather jacket, jeans, and black shoes. She is Native American with brown eyes, and double pierced ears. As of this writing, she is thirty-nine years old.

If you have any information regarding this case, you are urged to call the Bethel Police Department at 907-543-3781.

## Jacqueline Vasquez

Four month old Jacqueline Vasquez was abducted while at a Swap Meet with her mother and two year old sister in Avondale, Arizona on May 6, 2001. Her mother set down the car seat she was in beside a port-a-john and stepped inside with the older child. When they came out, Jacqueline and the car seat were gone. Authorities suspect that whoever took her raised her as their own.

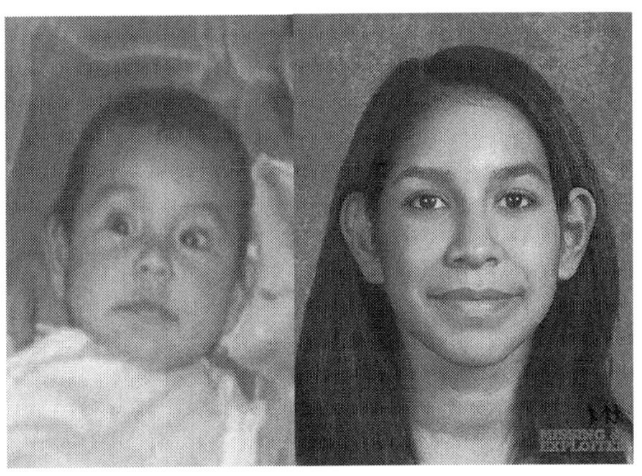

*(Age Progression to 15)*

At the time of her disappearance, Jacqueline Vasquez had black hair, was 24", and weighed 13 pounds. She was last seen in a white baby carrier car seat with a green and white striped cushion. She was wearing a white jumpsuit with snaps on the legs and a diaper. She is Hispanic with brown eyes and a heart-shaped birthmark on her upper right arm. As of this writing, she is sixteen years old.

If you have any information regarding this case, you are urged to call the Avondale Police Department at 623-333-7000.

## Mikelle Diane Biggs

Eleven year old Mikelle Diane Biggs was abducted after buying ice cream near her home in Mesa, Arizona on January 2, 1999. Her change and her bicycle were found about four houses west of her own home.

*(Mikelle at the time of her disappearance)*

Her family held a funeral for her on the five-year anniversary of her disappearance, although her remains have never been found. They hope that even if she is deceased that they will someday get some answers.

At the time of her disappearance, Mikelle Biggs had blonde permed hair, stood 4'8", and weighed 65 pounds. She was last seen wearing a solid red t-shirt, bell bottom blue jeans with embroidered seams on the side of each leg, and plain white canvas shoes. She is Caucasian with hazel eyes, two or three small moles on the left side of her neck, and pierced ears. As of this writing, she is thirty years old.

If you have any information regarding this case, you are urged to call the Mesa Police Department at 602-644-2211.

## Morgan Chauntel Nick

Six year old Morgan Chauntel Nick was abducted from a little league baseball game in Alma, Arkansas on June 9, 1995. She was last seen standing near her mother's car where she had stopped to empty the sand from her shoes after catching fireflies with friends.

*(Age Progression to 26)*

At the time of her disappearance, Morgan Nick had blonde hair, stood 4', and weighed 55 pounds. She was last seen wearing a green Girl Scouts shirt, blue denim shorts, and white tennis shoes. She is Caucasian with blue eyes and five visible caps on her molars. As of this writing, she is twenty-nine years old.

If you have any information regarding this case, you are urged to call one of the following numbers:

*Alma, Arkansas Police Department at 479-632-3930*

*The Polly Klaas Foundation at 1-800-587-4357*

## Vanessa Smith

Fifteen year old Vanessa Smith left her home in Winton, California on May 31, 1997 at 7pm to go for a walk and has never been heard from again. She was last seen walking near an orchard behind her house.

*(Age Progression to an unknown age)*

At the time of her disappearance, Vanessa Smith had a fair complexion with freckles, blonde hair, stood 5'6", and weighed 130 pounds. She was last seen wearing a light blue dress with an elastic waist and metal buttons. She is Caucasian with blue eyes, a birthmark from her shoulder to her elbow on her right arm, and a scar on her left ear. As of this writing, she is thirty-seven years old.

If you have any information regarding this case, you are urged to call one of the following numbers:

*Merced Major Crimes Unit at 209-385-7472*

*The Polly Klaas Foundation at 1-800-587-4357*

## Crystal Ann Tymich

Six year old Crystal Ann Tymich disappeared on June 30, 1994 from her neighbor's yard on Brynhurst Avenue in South Central Los Angeles, California sometime between 2pm - 5pm. There are few details available in her case.

*(Age Progression to 29)*

At the time of her disappearance, Crystal Tymich had dark blonde hair, stood 4', and weighed 60 pounds. She was last seen wearing a pink t-shirt, flowered shorts, and Little Mermaid sneakers. She is Caucasian with hazel eyes. As of this writing, she is thirty years old.

If you have any information regarding this case, you are urged to call one of the following numbers:

*Los Angeles Police Department at 877-275-5273*

*Federal Bureau of Investigation (FBI) at 1-202-278-2000*

## Melissa Ann Espinoza

Twelve year old Melissa Ann Espinoza disappeared on December 2, 1993 from White Rock Road in Rancho Cordova, California. She had had an argument with her mother at 11pm on December 1st and left the house angry. At 3am, she was seen sitting on a car hood in the parking lot of an apartment complex on White Rock Road. That was the last sighting of her.

In 1993, the area was frequented by pimps and drug dealers and was a dangerous place for anyone to be, let alone a twelve year old child.

Melissa had lived with her father and two older siblings in Sacramento, but had moved in with her mother and younger brother a month before her disappearance. She had a history of running away, but had always returned within a short time. She normally talked to her grandmother daily and would have never gone so long without contact.

Her brother said he saw some suspicious people near their apartment in the days before she went missing. He believes they may have somehow been involved. No one has been charged or named as a suspect, but foul play is suspected.

*(Age Progression to 35)*

At the time of her disappearance, Melissa Espinoza had long brown permed hair, stood 5’1”, and weighed 125 pounds. She was last seen wearing a black Chicago Bulls jacket, a black low-cut blouse, black pants, and black low-top Nike sneakers. She usually wore her hair in a ponytail and slicked back with gel at the time. She is Hispanic with brown eyes, a homemade tattoo of a heart around the letter M near her thumb on one hand, scars on both knees, and a one-inch scar on her chin. As of this writing, she is thirty-six years old.

If you have any information regarding this case, you are urged to call the Sacramento County Sheriff's Office at 916-874-5115 or 916-874-5467.

## Abby Jo Blagg

Six year old Abby Jo Blagg and her mother, Jennifer Blagg, were last seen at their home in Grand Junction, Colorado on November 12, 2001 between 3 - 3:30pm. Jennifer's remains were found in a Grand Junction landfill in June 2002. Her death was ruled a homicide. Abby has never been seen again.

Abby's father, Michael Blagg, told authorities that his daughter went to sleep in her bedroom at approximately 7pm on November 12, 2001. He said that his wife, Jennifer, received a phone call at 8pm from a neighbor regarding a possible lunch date the following day. Michael stated that he and Jennifer went to bed by 10pm, and that there was no indication of anything amiss during the overnight hours. He said he left for work at approximately 6am on November 13th. He claimed his wife and daughter were asleep when he left. He told investigators that he called home multiple times throughout the day to speak to Jennifer, but his calls went unanswered. He said that by afternoon he was concerned, but not to the point that he thought something was wrong. He told them that he returned home by 4pm and noticed that their home showed signs of a struggle. A large amount of blood was on the mattress in the master bedroom, but there were no sign of his wife or daughter. He notified the police at 4:20pm.

Investigators learned that someone had called Abby's school and told them she would be absent on November 13th. Authorities questioned friends and relatives of the Blaggs to try and determine if there was anyone who stood out as a possible suspect.

In late March 2002, investigators announced they believed Jennifer and Abby were the victims of foul play. They also stated that they believed the family's maroon and gold 2000 Ford Windstar had been used in their disappearances.

Jennifer's remains were discovered in the Mesa County landfill on June 5, 2002. There was no evidence of Abby's remains being there. Michael was charged with first-degree murder in his wife's case shortly after her body was identified. An autopsy showed she had been killed by a single gunshot wound to the left eye. Authorities believe she had been murdered while she was asleep, because the dental retainer she only wore at night was found near her body.

A witness told investigators that Jennifer had visited a law office several days prior to her disappearance, telling of being abused by her husband and saying she was afraid of him. Another witness said they saw Michael pushing a pallet jack with two large cardboard boxes on it at his work on the day he reported Jennifer and Abby missing. The witness stated Michael discarded the items on the loading dock near the trash compactor.

Authorities believe that Jennifer's murder was premediated and that Abby was killed as an afterthought. That is if he did indeed murder his daughter. Jennifer's blood was found in the house and the van, but Abby's was not found anywhere.

Michael Blagg attempted suicide in February 2002 after being questioned about his involvement in his wife's murder and his daughter's disappearance. He was tried for Jennifer's murder in the spring of 2004. On April 16, 2004, after deliberating for twelve hours, the jury found Michael Blagg guilty of murdering his wife and sentenced him to life in prison. His conviction was upheld in a 2008 appeal.

Abby remains listed as a missing child. Her father has never been charged in connection with her disappearance.

*(Age Progression to 17)*

At the time of her disappearance, Abby Blagg had blonde hair, stood 4', and weighed 44 pounds. She is Caucasian with blue eyes. As of this writing, she is twenty-three years old.

If you have any information regarding this case, you are urged to call one of the following numbers:

*Mesa County Sheriff's Office at 1-970-244-3500*

*The National Center for Missing and Exploited Children at 1-800-THE-LOST*

## Trenton Duckett

Two year old Trenton Duckett was last seen at approximately 7pm on August 27, 2006 in Leesburg, Florida. His mother said she put him to bed at around 7pm, but when she went to his room to check on him two hours later, he was gone.

His bedroom's window screen had been cut leading authorities to speculate an abductor had entered through the window and taken the little boy. But upon further investigation, they learned Trenton's mother, Melinda, and father, Joshua, were in the middle of a heated divorce and bitter custody battle when he went missing. Melinda had won a temporary restraining order in July 2006, after accusing Joshua of threatening both hers and Trenton's lives. Joshua denied the allegations and has been cooperative in the investigation into the disappearance of his son. He also passed a polygraph. Melinda failed both a polygraph and voice stress test.

On September 8th, thirteen days after her son's disappearance, Melinda took her own life. She left two notes, but neither of them disclosed any information of what had happened to Trenton. Her family cited the stress of Trenton's disappearance and the subsequent media scrutiny that followed as the reasons behind her suicide.

On September 21st, police officially named Melinda as the prime suspect in Trenton's disappearance, but they didn't necessarily believe she had harmed him. Authorities remain hopeful that he is alive, and continue to investigate his disappearance.

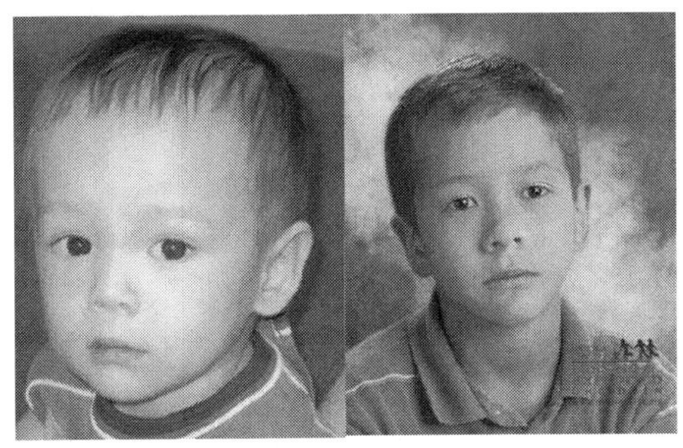

*(Age Progression to 11)*

At the time of his disappearance, Trenton Duckett had brown hair, stood 3', and weighed 35 pounds. He was last seen wearing a green and blue striped shirt, denim shorts, and a diaper. He is Biracial (Asian/Caucasian) with brown eyes and a small mark above his left eye. As of this writing, he is fourteen years old.

If you have any information regarding this case, you are urged to call one of the following numbers:

*Leesburg Police Department at 352-787-2121*

*The National Center for Missing and Exploited Children at 1-800-THE-LOST*

## Zachary Bernhardt

Eight year old Zachary Bernhardt disappeared from his Clearwater, Florida home sometime during the early morning hours of September 11, 2000. His mother told investigators that he had fallen asleep in her bed around 11pm. She said she went for a walk around the apartment complex and then a quick swim between 3am - 4am. After she returned to the apartment and took a shower, she realized Zachary was missing. She called the police at 4:45am.

There were no signs of a struggle or a break-in. Police took DNA evidence, secured the scene, and launched a large search around the apartment complex. Dogs were used but they found no trace of the child outside of the apartment.

Early on in the investigation, authorities said they thought his mother knew more than she was telling them. They also questioned her decision to go for a swim without a towel at that hour, leaving the door unlocked. She maintained her innocence, however.

On New Year's Eve 2001, another child, this time a five year old, went missing from the same apartment complex. Ten hours after the abduction, the child was found alive in a dumpster. He said a white man with stringy hair had taken him. Authorities tried to link the two cases but could not find a connection.

Zachary's mother has since relocated to Hawaii and stopped being involved in the investigation. However, other members of his family are still searching for answers.

*(Age Progression to 23)*

At the time of his disappearance, Zachary Bernhardt had blonde hair, stood 4'6", and weighed 60 pounds. He was last seen wearing only boxers. He is Caucasian with hazel eyes, a scar under his chin, a scar on the bridge of his nose between his eyes, and a scar on the right side of his top lip. As of this writing, he is twenty-seven years old.

If you have any information regarding this case, you are urged to call one of the following numbers:

*Clearwater Police Department at 727-562-4420*

*The Polly Klaas Foundation at 1-800-587-4357*

## Sabrina Paige Aisenberg

Five month old Sabrina Paige Aisenberg was abducted from her crib in her Brandon, Florida home sometime between midnight and 6:30am on November 24, 1997.There were no signs of forced entry into the home, but the garage door was open.

Her parents and their two other children moved to Maryland in 1999. Sabrina's father has been quoted as saying that their trust that his daughter's disappearance will be solved lies more with the public than with law enforcement. The statement came after nearly two years of the authorities focusing on Sabrina's parents as suspects in her disappearance. In 1999, the couple was indicted in connection with their daughter's disappearance, after the federal prosecutor claimed the couple had been recorded making incriminating statements. When the static-filled tapes were played back, however, most of the supposed statements were inaudible. Both a former FBI agent and the U.S. District Attorney listened to the tapes and agreed. The charges against Sabrina's parents were then dropped.

At the time of her disappearance, Sabrina Aisenberg had brown hair, was 30", and weighed 20 pounds. She was last seen wearing a lavender sleeper with a floral pattern. Her blue and yellow handmade blanket with yellow piping and decorated with animals went missing with her and has not been located. She is Caucasian with blue eyes. As of this writing, she is twenty-one years old.

If you have any information regarding this case, you are urged to call one of the following numbers:

## Brandon Wade & Paula Wade

Three year old Brandon Wade and his twenty-six year old mother, Paula Wade, were reported missing on October 13, 2002 from Valdosta, Georgia. Paula, who was employed at Sam's Club in Valdosta, failed to show up for work or call to say she would not be in. Being uncharacteristic of her, her coworkers became concerned and went to her apartment twice that morning. Her vehicle, a 1998 Chevrolet Blazer, was there but there was no sign of Paula or Brandon. Her coworkers reported them missing after their second trip to the apartment.

The police, along with the landlord, checked inside the apartment and again found no trace of Brandon or his mother. Paula's roommate, a nineteen year old male, allegedly has been uncooperative with the investigation and refused to take a polygraph. He has since hired a lawyer. Paula's husband, and Brandon's father, is a soldier who was stationed at the Shaw Air Force Base in Sumter, South Carolina when they disappeared. He passed a polygraph and has been ruled out as a suspect.

Paula's loved ones say she would never have taken her son and left without warning. She had received a transfer notice to Kissimmee, Florida for a new job. Her father was supposed to help her move the following week.

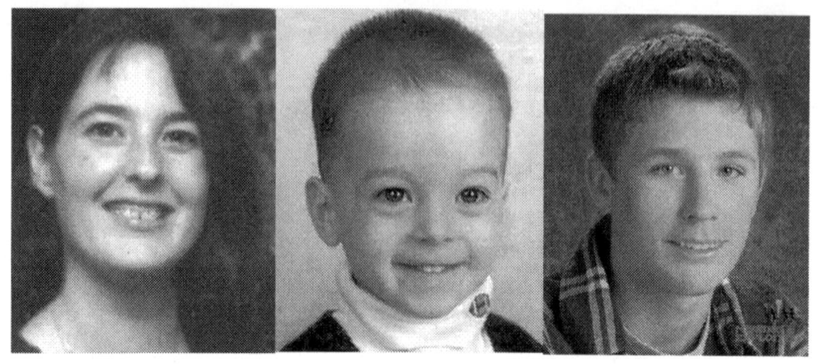

*(Paula & Brandon at the time of their disappearances & Brandon's Age Progression to 16)*

At the time of his disappearance, Brandon Wade had brown hair, stood 2'9", and weighed 33 pounds. He is Caucasian with hazel eyes. As of this writing, he is nineteen years old.

At the time of her disappearance, Paula Wade had brown hair, stood 5'7", and weighed 150 pounds. She is Caucasian with brown eyes, a birthmark on the upper part of one of her legs, and her top canine teeth protrude in front of her other top teeth. As of this writing, she is forty-two years old.

If you have any information regarding this case, you are urged to call one of the following numbers:

*Valdosta Police Department at 229-242-2606 or to remain anonymous 229-293-3091 (Valdosta PD Crime Tip Line)*

*The Polly Klaas Foundation at 1-800-587-4357*

## Ruben Felix

Two year old Ruben Felix was last seen by his stepfather on February 23, 1997 in his front yard drinking from his bottle in Shoshone, Idaho. His stepfather went inside for only a moment and when he came back, Ruben was gone.

Dogs tracked his scent to the edge of the Little Wood River, but upon searching it several times nothing related to him was found. Some sources suggest that he was taken to Mexico and sold.

*(Age Progression to 17)*

At the time of his disappearance, Ruben Felix had blonde hair, stood 2'6", and weighed 32 pounds. He was last seen wearing a red sweatshirt, blue sweat pants, and brown hiking boots. He is Biracial (Caucasian/Hispanic) with blue eyes and a scar on his right wrist. As of this writing, he is twenty-four years old.

If you have any information regarding this case, you are urged to call one of the following numbers:

*Lincoln County Sheriff's Office at 208-886-2259*

*The Polly Klaas Foundation at 1-800-587-4357*

## Trudy Leann Appleby

Eleven year old Trudy Leann Appleby was just two weeks shy of her 12th birthday when she disappeared.

Her father left home going to work at approximately 9am on August 21, 1996 in Moline, Illinois. A neighbor saw her enter a silver or gray four-door box-style vehicle in the driveway of her home between 9:30am and 10:30am. Her father reported her missing when he returned home from work and could not find her.

The driver of the vehicle is described as being Caucasian and in his twenties at the time with curly brown or black hair down to his shoulders and wearing a baseball cap.

Authorities believe that Trudy may have known the vehicle's driver. Her home was located off of the main road and was not visible from the street. Her case was initially investigated as a possible runaway, but investigators now believe Trudy was abducted.

Police are appealing to anyone who might have seen any suspicious activity in the areas of Campbell's Island, Black Bird Island, Dynamite Island, or the boat launch at Empire Park in East Moline, Illinois around the time Trudy was abducted.

*(Age Progression to 30)*

At the time of her disappearance, Trudy Appleby had long brown hair, stood 5', and weighed 85 pounds.

She was last seen wearing black bicycle shorts, white socks, and blue Nike sneakers with white laces. She is Caucasian with blue eyes. As of this writing, she is thirty-three years old.

If you have any information regarding this case, you are urged to call one of the following numbers:

*Moline Police Department at 309-797-0401*

*The Polly Klaas Foundation at 1-800-587-4357*

## King Walker & Diamond Bynum

Two year old King Walker and his aunt, twenty-one year old Diamond Bynum, were last seen on July 25, 2015 at their home on Matthews Street in Gary, Indiana. They were reported missing when Diamond's stepmother awoke from a nap and discovered they were gone.

Their family believes they left the residence together, possibly to go to a local store. But Diamond was still unfamiliar with the area and may have gotten lost. Their loved ones continue to hold out hope that they are alive somewhere.

*(Diamond & King at the time of their disappearances)*

At the time of his disappearance, King Walker had black hair styled in dreadlocks, stood 3', and weighed 34 pounds. He was last seen wearing a blue t-shirt and red pants. He is African-American with brown eyes. As of this writing, he is five years old.

At the time of her disappearance, Diamond Bynum had black hair, stood 4'8", and weighed 210 pounds. She was last seen wearing a shirt and blue jeans. She is African-American with brown eyes. She has Prader-Willi Syndrome, characterized by mild to moderate intellectual impairment, and she walks with a limp. She also has a noticeable speech impediment and may not be able to express what she wants to say. She is known to smile and laugh a lot. As of this writing, she is twenty-four years old.

If you have any information regarding this case, you are urged to call one of the following numbers:

*Indiana State Police at 1-800-843-5678*

*Gary Police Department at 219-881-1260*

*The Polly Klaas Foundation at 1-800-587-4357*

## April Wiss

Sixteen year old April Wiss was last seen leaving an apartment complex on Marion Road in Wichita, Kansas on January 11, 2000. Her friend told police she saw April heading towards Pawnee and Broadway Streets between 10pm and 10:30pm that evening. Investigators believe she had her pager, apartment keys, and wallet with her at the time.

April was scheduled to testify in a felony statutory rape case two days after she disappeared. Authorities do not know if her disappearance is connected to the trial or not. Her mother theorizes that she was abducted and possibly became a victim of human trafficking.

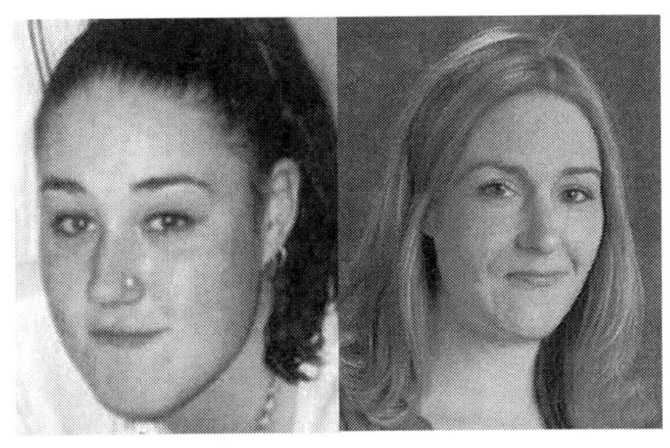

*(Age Progression to 27)*

At the time of her disappearance, April Wiss had dark brown dyed hair, stood 6', and weighed 165 pounds. She was last seen wearing a white t-shirt, a navy blue jacket with gray lining, flared-leg blue jeans, white tennis shoes, gold loop earrings, a gold cross of Jesus on a gold chain, and a silver ring. She is Caucasian with hazel eyes, a scar on her right hand, three black dots tattooed on her right hand, double pierced ears, and a nose piercing. She may wear glasses. As of this writing, she is thirty-four years old.

If you have any information regarding this case, you are urged to call one of the following numbers:

*Wichita Police Department at 316-268-4111*

*The Polly Klaas Foundation at 1-800-587-4357*

## Erica Lee Fraysure

Seventeen year old Erica Lee Fraysure disappeared on October 21, 1997. She was last seen with friends at a party in Brooksville, Kentucky at around 9pm. Her car was found the following morning in a field on an isolated road near Brooksville. Her keys were found in the field, but her purse and other belongings were still inside the car.

Erica was a resident of Germantown, Kentucky at the time. She was a senior at Bracken County High School. She had no history or running away, and authorities do not believe she left of her own accord.

*(Age Progression to 30)*

At the time of her disappearance, Erica Fraysure had long light brown hair with bangs, stood 5’6”, and weighed 115 pounds. She was last seen wearing a purple sweater with white stripes, Levi jeans, white Keds sneakers, a Winnie the Pooh watch, a gold sapphire ring, and a gold diamond heart ring. She is Caucasian with blue eyes and a strawberry birthmark on the back of her neck. As of this writing, she is thirty-seven years old.

If you have any information regarding this case, you are urged to call one of the following numbers:

*Bracken County Sheriff’s Department at 606-735-2700*

## Randy Lee Sellers

Seventeen year old Randy Lee Sellers went to the Kenton County Fair in Independence, Kentucky on August 16, 1980 where he got into a fight with another individual and was picked up by police. He was charged with disorderly conduct and public intoxication. The police stated that they drove him home, but dropped him off one mile from his residence, as a courtesy to him. He was last seen walking through the L & N Railroad underpass. He never arrived home and has never been heard from again.

Some believe he may have slipped and fallen into the Licking River, but a search on land and in water there turned up nothing. Others thought he may have been a victim of a drifter in the area, who was eventually sentenced to death for the murders of several women and children from 1975 to 1991. Donald LeRoy Evans confessed to murdering Randy, but his remains have never been found. However, his mother continues to hold out hope that her son is alive somewhere.

*(Age Progression to 49)*

At the time of his disappearance, Randy Sellers had brown hair with a beard and goatee, stood 5'9", and weighed 149 pounds. He was last seen wearing a black shirt, blue jeans, and work shoes. He is Caucasian with hazel eyes, a crooked letter R tattoo on his right forearm, a scar on his left elbow, a scar above his right eye, and a surgical scar on his right knee. He may have a crowned tooth. As of this writing, he is fifty-six years old.

If you have any information regarding this case, you are urged to call one of the following numbers:

*Kenton County Police Department at 606-356-3191*

*The Polly Klaas Foundation at 1-800-587-4357*

## Kristopher Lewis

Thirteen year old Kristopher Lewis was last seen getting off the school bus in Boston, Massachusetts on February 4, 2014. The bus dropped him off at the corner of Morton and West Selden Streets. The bus driver confirmed he was on the bus and was dropped off at the usual time. A friend said he walked with Kristopher up to within a block of his home. He has not been seen or heard from since.

*(Kristopher at the time of his disappearance)*

At the time of his disappearance, Kristopher Lewis had black hair worn in a shaved style, stood 5'11", and weighed 87 pounds. He was last seen wearing a navy blue polo shirt, a black coat, khaki pants, white Nike sneakers, and a yellow backpack. He is African-American with brown eyes and a scar on his bottom lip. As of this writing, he is seventeen years old.

If you have any information regarding this case, you are urged to call one of the following numbers:

*Boston Police Department at 617-343-4687*

*The National Center for Missing and Exploited Children at 1-800-THE-LOST*

## Andrew Amato

Four year old Andrew Amato was playing in the woods behind Ash Street Trailer Park in Webster, Massachusetts with his sister and cousin during the morning hours of September 30, 1978. Andrew fell and was crying when the other children ran for help at about 10:30am. When they returned, he was gone. Authorities believe it is possible that he walked out to Route 52 and was abducted by a passing motorist. The National Guard assisted in a ten-day search for him but no clues as to his whereabouts were found.

For a time, it was believed that a man named Nathaniel Bar-Jonah, who had been convicted of the abductions and attempted murders of two Massachusetts boys in 1977, could be involved in Andrew's disappearance. Nathaniel was convicted of child molestation in Montana in February 2002 and died in prison of a blood clot in April 2008. Investigators have been unsuccessful in tying him to Andrew's disappearance, however. Foul play is suspected.

*(Andrew at the time of his disappearance)*

At the time of his disappearance, Andrew Amato had blonde hair, stood 3'6", and weighed 38 pounds. He was last seen wearing a hooded maroon-colored zip-up jacket, dungarees, a white Mickey Mouse t-shirt, and brown suede shoes with dark brown stripes on each side of the instep. He is Caucasian with hazel eyes, a one-inch scar on the right side of his head, and a mole behind his right ear. His nickname is Andy. As of this writing, he is forty-four years old

If you have any information regarding this case, you are urged to call one of the following numbers:

*Webster Police Department at 617-943-1212*

*The Polly Klaas Foundation at 1-800-587-4357*

## Angelo "Andy" Puglisi

Ten year old Angelo "Andy" Puglisi was abducted from Higgins Memorial Pool about a hundred yards from his home in Lawrence, Massachusetts on August 21, 1976. A four year old boy claimed to have witnessed Andy's abduction, but because of the witness's age the tip was not pursued.

Andy had called home that day about 3:30pm and talked to one of his brothers. He gave no indication that anything was wrong at the time. A lifeguard at the pool reported that he saw Andy walking around the pool area at approximately 5:45pm. That was the last time he is known to have been seen. Despite an intensive search and investigation, no trace of him has ever been found, and foul play is suspected.

In 1975, an eleven year old boy was abducted and raped near the swimming pool. Wayne Chapman was convicted of the rape. Authorities suspect he may have had something to do with Andy's disappearance as well. His vehicle closely resembled the description of one that Andy's friends said was near the pool that day. However, Wayne Chapman has never been charged in connection with Andy's case.

*(Age Progression to 50)*

At the time of his disappearance, Andy Puglisi had brown hair, stood 4', and weighed 65 pounds. He was last seen wearing a bathing suit, towel, and sneakers. He is Caucasian with brown eyes, three scars along his spine, and a discoloration on his chest. As of this writing, he is fifty-two years old.

If you have any information regarding this case, you are urged to call one of the following numbers:

*Lawrence County Police Department at 978-794-5925*

*The Polly Klaas Foundation at 1-800-587-4357*

## Leigh Savoie

Ten year old Leigh Savoie went missing from the vicinity of Suffolk Downs Race Track in Revere, Massachusetts on April 7, 1974. He left home, on State Road, with his shoeshine kit at 11am that day. He shined shoes after school and in his free time to earn pocket money. He stopped at a restaurant for a sandwich and a glass of milk. He asked the owner to watch his kit for a few minutes until he returned, but he never came back to get it. He has never been seen again.

In 2009, Revere Police revisited the thirty-five year old cold case to try and bring some answers to his then seventy-four year old mother. They hoped that a new $5,000 reward and DNA testing that was not available all those years ago might generate some new leads. His parents and seven siblings continue to hold out hope of one day being reunited.

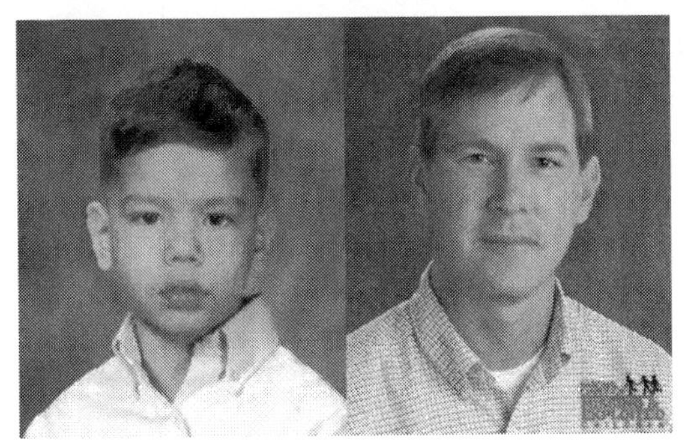

*(Age Progression to 50)*

At the time of his disappearance, Leigh Savoie had light brown hair, stood 4'4", and weighed 60 pounds. He was last seen wearing a white t-shirt with the words Try It You'll Like It, cut off blue shorts, and sneakers. He is Caucasian with brown eyes. His nickname is LeeLee. As of this writing, he is fifty-four years old.

If you have any information regarding this case, you are urged to call one of the following numbers:

*Massachusetts State Police at 508-820-2121*

*The Polly Klaas Foundation at 1-800-587-4357*

**Steven Earl "Stevie" Kraft II**

Twelve year old Steven Earl "Stevie" Kraft II was last seen playing with his two dogs on Holly Drive in Benton Harbor, Michigan on February 15, 2001 between 7pm - 8pm. He was about half a block away from his home. He has not been seen or heard from since. He could not have survived long outdoors without shelter, as temperatures in the area were below freezing and remained that way for several days.

One of his dogs returned home three days after Stevie's disappearance, and the next day the other one was found near Blue Creek, a mile and a half from home. The area was searched but no clues as to Stevie's whereabouts were found.

Stevie is described as being a quiet boy who had few friends. He had only recently returned to school from a five-day suspension after he had defended himself during an altercation. Both boys had been suspended. It is not known whether or not that incident had any connection to his disappearance.

*(Age Progression to 25)*

At the time of his disappearance, Stevie Kraft had sandy brown hair, stood between 5' - 5'2", and weighed between 90 - 100 pounds. He was last seen wearing a white and tan striped shirt, an aqua and purple Hornets jacket, tan pants, and black Lugz boots. He is Caucasian with green eyes and a small red birthmark on the left side of his rib cage. As of this writing, he is twenty-nine years old.

If you have any information regarding this case, you are urged to call one of the following numbers:

*Federal Bureau of Investigation (FBI) – St. Joseph Missouri Office at 313-965-2323*

*The Polly Klaas Foundation at 1-800-587-4357*

## LeeAnna Susan Marie Warner

Five year old LeeAnna Susan Marie Warner was last seen walking home from a friend's house in Chisholm, Minnesota on June 14, 2003. Her friend's home was a block and a half from her own home. Her mother reported her missing between 8pm and 9pm after searching the neighborhood for her. An extensive search by police officers, firefighters, volunteers, bloodhounds, and tracking experts was conducted on the entire city in the first forty-eight hours after she was reported missing. Later, more searches took place in hopes that LeeAnna had just gotten lost.

When no clues surfaced, investigators began to treat her disappearance as an abduction. They have since announced that no one has forgotten about her, and they continue to follow even the smallest lead to this day.

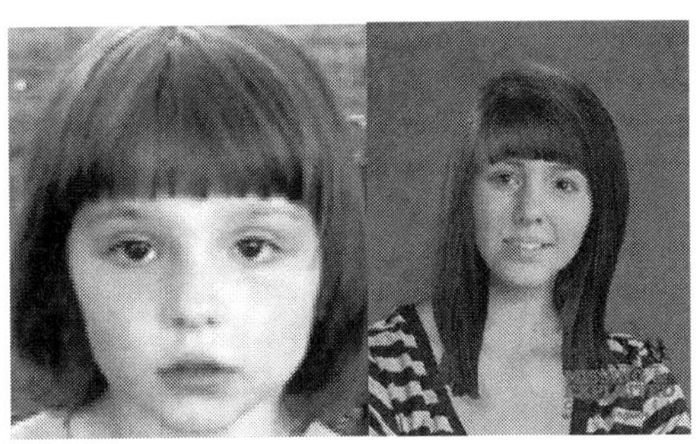

*(Age Progression to 15)*

At the time of her disappearance, LeeAnna Warner had brown shoulder-length hair, stood 3', and weighed 50 pounds. She was last seen wearing a sleeveless dark blue denim dress with an attached belt, orange Hanes panties, and no shoes or socks. She is Caucasian with brown eyes. As of this writing, she is twenty years old.

If you have any information regarding this case, you are urged to call one of the following numbers:

*Chisholm Police Department at 218-742-9825*

*The Polly Klaas Foundation at 1-800-587-4357*

## Myra Lewis

Two year old Myra Lewis disappeared from her home in Camden, Mississippi on March 1, 2014 between 10:30am and 11am. Her mother left to go to the store and told Myra and her sisters to go inside the house where their father was. Each parent thought the little girl was with the other, so she was not reported missing until about 4pm. A search of the area turned up no clues as to her whereabouts. The FBI is offering a reward of up to $20,000 for information regarding Myra's whereabouts.

*(Age Progression to 4)*

At the time of her disappearance, Myra Lewis had black hair, stood 2'10", and weighed 27 pounds. She was last seen wearing a turquoise sweater with a bear on the front, off-white or khaki pants, and pink tennis shoes. She is African-American with brown eyes. As of this writing, she is six years old.

If you have any information regarding this case, you are urged to call one of the following numbers:

*Madison County Sheriff's Office 601-987-1530*

*Federal Bureau of Investigation (FBI) at 1-202-278-2000*

*The Polly Klaas Foundation at 1-800-587-4357*

## Leigh Marine Occhi

Thirteen year old Leigh Marine Occhi was last seen at her home on Honey Locust Drive in Tupelo, Mississippi on August 27, 1992. Her mother saw her before she left for work at 7:35am. There were severe storms forecasted that day and her mother was concerned about her daughter being home alone. Her mother tried to call her at 8:30am, but got no answer. She tried to call again before returning home, but there was still no answer.

Leigh planned to go to an open house at her new school that morning. She was waiting for her grandmother to pick her up. It was the first time she had been left home alone.

When Leigh's mother arrived back home, she discovered the garage door open and another exterior door unlocked. There was no sign of Leigh and she has never been seen again. She had only been home alone for about an hour. Both her mother and her grandmother said she would never open the door for a stranger.

There were no signs of forced entry, but there were signs of a struggle. There was blood on the wall, a door frame, some carpeting, and on the bathroom countertop. Leigh's nightgown and her bra were in her bedroom and both had bloodstains. There was evidence that someone had tried to clean up the blood in the bathroom. Leigh's glasses, shoes, and some undergarments were missing.

About a month after her disappearance, someone mailed Leigh's glasses to her home in an envelope addressed to her stepfather, who no longer lived at the residence. The envelope was postmarked Booneville, Mississippi, a town about thirty miles from Tupelo. Handwriting and forensic tests yielded no results on the person who mailed the envelope, and the sender remains unidentified.

Several persons of interest were interviewed, but no one has been charged in connection to her disappearance. An award of up to $1,000 is being offered by Crime Stoppers of Northeast Mississippi for information leading to an arrest in Leigh's case. An undisclosed reward is also being offered by Leigh's mother.

*(Age Progression to 31)*

At the time of her disappearance, Leigh Occhi had blonde hair, stood 4'10", and weighed 95 pounds. She is Caucasian with hazel eyes. As of this writing, she is thirty-eight years old.

If you have any information regarding this case, you are urged to call one of the following numbers:

*Crime Stoppers of Northeast Mississippi at 1-800-773-TIPS*

*Tupelo Police Department at 662-841-6491*

## Shemika Keyanta Cosey

Sixteen year old Shemika Keyanta Cosey disappeared from her cousin's home on Napier Drive in Berkeley, Missouri between 1:30am and 8:30am on December 28, 2008. When her family awoke that morning, she was gone. Her clothes and other belongings were still in the apartment. The front door was unlocked, but there were no signs of foul play.

Authorities believe she left on her own and that she may still be in the local area. Her family, however, believes that someone abducted her. They have continued to pass out flyers and other information through the years since she went missing.

*(Age Progression to 19)*

At the time of her disappearance, Shemika Cosey had black hair, stood 5'5", and weighed between 135 - 160 pounds. She was last seen wearing a black long-sleeve shirt, a tan Old Navy jacket, and blue jeans. She is African-American with brown eyes and pierced ears. She wears glasses, and her nickname is Mika. As of this writing, she is twenty-five years old.

If you have any information regarding this case, you are urged to call one of the following numbers:

*Berkeley Police Department at 314-524-3311*

*The Polly Klaas Foundation at 1-800-587-4357*

## Karla Rodriguez

Seven year old Karla Rodriguez was last seen riding her bike at about 7pm on Bonita Avenue, just around the corner from her home, in Las Vegas, Nevada on October 20, 1999. Her mother had walked her to school that morning and then returned home to lie down before work. Her father returned home from work about 3pm and Karla wasn't home, but her bicycle was.

It wasn't unusual for her to go play without it, so her father wasn't worried. When he left to go to a meeting and then returned at 5pm, Karla still wasn't home but now her bike was gone too. After being seen by a neighbor at approximately 7pm, she has not been seen or heard from since. Because her father assumed she was staying the night with a friend, she wasn't reported missing until the following morning when she didn't show up for school.

Authorities have had few leads to go on, but they are convinced she was the victim of a stranger abduction. Her immediate family has all been cleared, and they continue to hold out hope that she is alive somewhere.

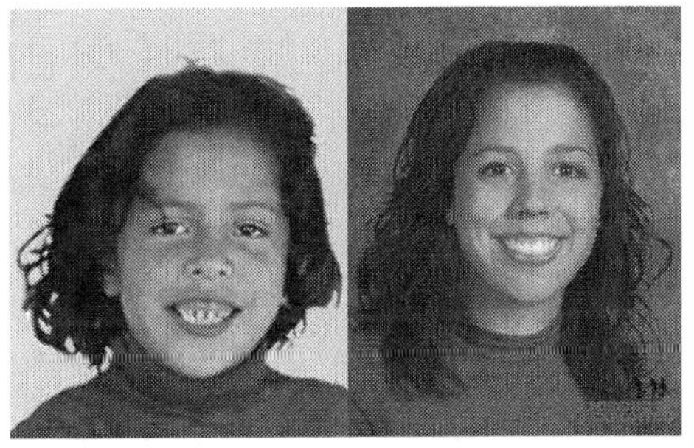

*(Age Progression to 20)*

At the time of her disappearance, Karla Rodriguez had black hair, stood 3'5", and weighed 49 pounds. Her teeth were unevenly spaced and had wide gaps between them with visible cavities. She spoke Spanish and only limited English at the time. She was last seen wearing a blue and white striped shirt, a black jacket, red pants, and her fingernails were painted green. She is Hispanic with brown eyes, moles above her right eyebrow and on her lower lip near the right corner of her mouth, and a surgical scar on her abdomen. As of this writing, she is twenty-five years old.

If you have any information regarding this case, you are urged to call one of the following numbers:

*Las Vegas Missing Persons Section at 702-828-2907*

*Las Vegas Metropolitan Police Department at 702-229-5678*

*The Polly Klaas Foundation at 1-800-587-4357*

## Tristen Alan Myers

Four year old Tristen Alan Myers disappeared from his great-aunt and uncle's home, where he lived, in Roseboro, North Carolina on October 5, 2000. His great-aunt was napping at the time. He has not been seen or heard from since.

When he disappeared, he was accompanied by the family's two dogs, a black Doberman puppy and a three-legged Chihuahua-mix. A search over the ten-acre section of wooded land near their home turned up no evidence as to Tristen's whereabouts. The Chihuahua-mix returned home on October 10$^{th}$, and the search resumed. On October 14$^{th}$, the Doberman puppy returned. Neither showed signs of being in the woods.

Eleven days prior to his disappearance, Tristen had been taken to a hospital for testing because of his severe behavior problems. But due to his inability to understand simple directions or speak more than a few words, full testing could not be performed. Three days later, he wandered away from his home. Neighbors found him half a mile away and brought him back. Three days after that, he disappeared for good.

Tristen's mother was killed in March of 2004 in a car accident. His father is unknown. His grandparents had custody of him until his grandfather accidentally ran him over with a car while drunk. Custody was then given to his great-aunt and uncle. Authorities believe he was either abducted by a stranger or fell into a body of water and drown.

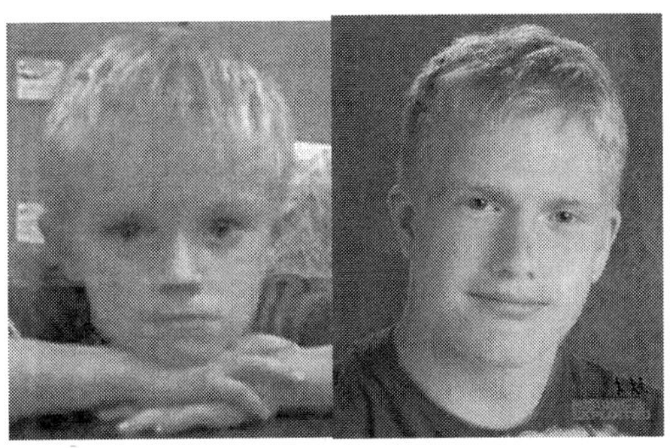

*(Age Progression to 19)*

At the time of his disappearance, Tristen Myers had blonde hair, stood 3'1", and weighed 38 pounds. He was last seen wearing a black t-shirt, blue jeans, and white Mickey Mouse sneakers. He is Caucasian with blue eyes, scars on the left side of his neck and on top of his head, and his leg was previously broken. He is described as being emotionally and physically underdeveloped, and he has a speech impediment. His nickname is Buddy. As of this writing, he is twenty-one years old.

If you have any information regarding this case, you are urged to call one of the following numbers:

*Sampson County Sheriff's Office at 910-592-4141*

*The Polly Klaas Foundation at 1-800-587-4357*

**Aaron Cody Stepp**

Three year old Aaron Cody Stepp was supposedly last seen playing in a neighbor's backyard in Columbus, Ohio at approximately 7pm on March 11, 1997. He was supposed to be living with his aunt and grandmother at the time. His aunt told authorities she thought he was being supervised by the grandmother while she went to the store. The grandmother claimed she thought Cody had gone with the aunt. However, multiple family members insisted they had not seen the child for several months prior to March 1997.

Cody disappeared, according to the missing person report, the day before his mother was released from prison after serving seventeen months on theft convictions. His mother's sister, Mickey Stepp, had had custody of Cody since December 1996.

Investigators were unable to locate evidence suggesting Cody even resided in the home. There were no toys, photographs, or clothing connected to the child in the home. Neighbors stated that they had not seen Cody for about a year prior to his disappearance. Both his aunt and grandmother denied allegations that they had handed him over to another family member. Mickey failed a polygraph, but there was no solid evidence of her involvement in his disappearance. Both his aunt and grandmother are now deceased.

Investigators suspect foul play, but they do not necessarily believe he is deceased. His mother continues to hold out hope that he will one day be reunited with her.

*(Age Progression to 22)*

According to the report filed by his aunt and grandmother, at the time of his disappearance, Cody Stepp had had blonde hair, stood 3'2", and weighed 39 pounds. He is Caucasian with blue eyes. As of this writing, he is twenty-four years old.

If you have any information regarding this case, you are urged to call one of the following numbers:

*Columbus Police Department at 614-645-4670*

*The Polly Klaas Foundation at 1-800-587-4357*

## Amber Renee Barker

Ten year old Amber Renee Barker was last seen leaving a friend's house at approximately 6pm on December 18, 1997 in Oklahoma City, Oklahoma. She was on her way home on northwest 39th Street. She never arrived and has never been seen or heard from again.

The following day, her bicycle was located one mile from her home in Denniston Park in Oklahoma City. On December 20th, her sweater, a ring, one sock, and one shoe were found along the same street where her bike had been found. A second shoe belonging to her was found a block away. Investigators stated that blood, hair, and fiber evidence was found near her possessions, and a partial DNA profile of an unidentified man was pulled from it.

*(Age Progression to 21)*

At the time of her disappearance, Amber Barker had medium brown hair that she wore pulled into a ponytail on top of her head with the rest left straight down, stood 4'11", and weighed between 65 - 70 pounds. Besides the clothing located after her disappearance, she was last seen wearing a long-sleeve beige shirt and black jeans. She is Caucasian with brown eyes and pierced ears. As of this writing, she is thirty-one years old.

If you have any information regarding this case, you are urged to call one of the following numbers:

*Oklahoma City Police Department at 405-297-1290*

*Oklahoma City Police Missing Persons Unit at 405-297-1000*

## Jamie Michelle McChurin

Sixteen year old Jamie Michelle McChurin was last seen sitting on the front porch of a friend's residence on

March 18, 1997 near the corner of F and Elmira Streets in Muskogee, Oklahoma. Her friend's mother went inside the house for a few minutes, and when she returned Jamie was gone. The woman saw a dark-colored four-door sedan turning the corner, but it is not known if the unidentified car was involved in Jamie's disappearance or not. An extensive search provided few clues as to her whereabouts.

She has no history of running away. She had a job and had just cashed her first paycheck. She had also been talking about buying a car. She left behind a one year old child, who was raised by her parents after she went missing. Authorities suspect she was taken against her will.

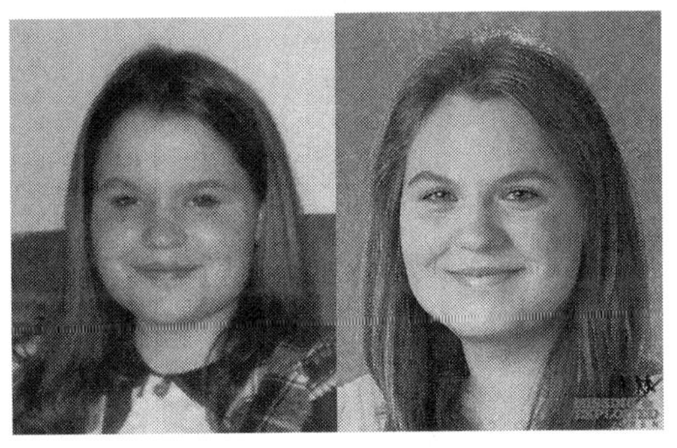

*(Age Progression to 35)*

At the time of her disappearance, Jamie McChurin had straight brown shoulder-length hair, stood at 5'11", and weighed 133 pounds. She is Caucasian with brown eyes, a small heart tattoo on her right hand, and a scar over her right eye. At the time of this writing, she is thirty-seven years old.

If you have any information regarding this case, you are urged to call one of the following numbers:

*Muskogee Police Department at 918-683-8000*

*The Polly Klaas Foundation at 1-800-587-4357*

## Tabitha Danielle Tudors

Thirteen year old Tabitha Danielle Tudors was last seen walking toward her school bus stop at 14th and Boscobel Streets in Nashville, Tennessee on April 29, 2003. She was supposed to board the bus at 8am. Witnesses saw her walking in that direction and reading some papers. She did not get on the school bus and never arrived at school. Her parents contacted the school that evening when she failed to return home. When they found out she had been absent from school that day, they reported her missing shortly before 6pm.

She has no history of running away, and she left behind all her possessions. She was a straight-A student and was active in her church choir at the time.

A young boy waiting at the bus stop said he saw Tabitha get into a red car with a 30 - 40 year old African-American man wearing a baseball cap.

On October 30, 2003, a trucker reported a possible sighting of Tabitha in Linton, Indiana. The trucker saw a man and another teenage girl, along with the one he believed to be Tabitha. A hotel clerk in Linton also reported seeing a girl resembling Tabitha, accompanied by a man and a teenage girl.

Authorities initially treated Tabitha as a runaway due to her age, but they now believe she was abducted. Her parents and two adult siblings were all investigated and none are being called suspects in her disappearance. Investigators believe she is in danger.

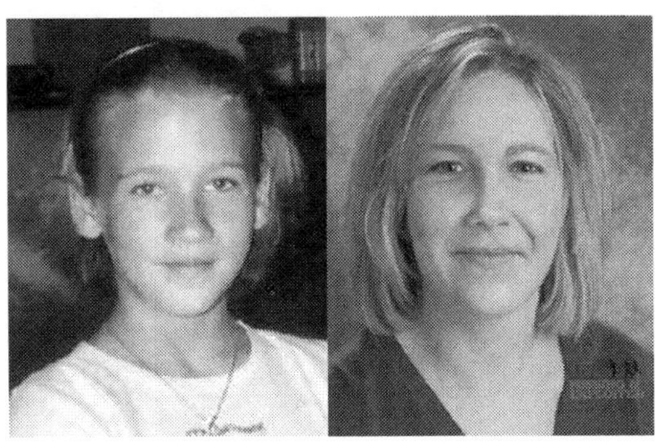

*(Age Progression to 24)*

At the time of her disappearance, Tabitha Tudors had sandy blonde hair, stood 4'9", and weighed 97 pounds. She was last seen wearing a light blue shirt, Mudd jeans, and Reebok sneakers. She is Caucasian with blue eyes, a birthmark on her stomach, a scar on her finger, and pierced ears. As of this writing, she is twenty-eight years old.

If you have any information regarding this case, you are urged to call one of the following numbers:

*Nashville Metro Police Department at 615-862-8600*

*The Polly Klaas Foundation at 1-800-587-4357*

## Alexandria Joy "Ali" Lowitzer

Sixteen year old Alexandria Joy "Ali" Lowitzer was last seen walking toward Treaschwig Road in Spring, Texas shortly before 3pm on April 26, 2010. She was en route to the Burger Barn, where she worked. Her last communication was a text message sent to a friend at 2:57pm asking them to come over later that afternoon.

When her mother arrived home from work and Ali wasn't home, she thought her daughter was working. She assumed Ali would text or call when she had a break. After not hearing from her for a few hours, her mother sent a text around 7pm to check on her. Then after a while of not getting a response, she began to get concerned and sent her another text. By 8pm that night and getting no responses to the text messages, her mother began calling and leaving messages. Shortly after 9pm, she went to the Burger Barn to pick Ali up after the end of her shift, but the restaurant was already closed. Her mother contacted family members and her daughter's friends to see if anyone had seen Ali. With no results, she then contacted law enforcement and reported her missing. However, after questioning Ali's co-workers and the boys she regularly exited the school bus with the police listed her case as a runaway. But many do not believe that was the case.

Ali regularly texted and made calls on her cell phone throughout the day, yet all communication including pings on cell towers stopped at approximately 3pm. Her phone charger, clothes, makeup, and other belongings that were important to her were all left behind in her room. In addition, her paycheck at the Burger Barn hadn't been picked up. None of the employees there claimed to have seen her.

Displeased with the reaction of local law enforcement, Ali's family contacted the Laura Recovery Center for Missing Children, who immediately began coordinating search teams and volunteers to search the area and distribute flyers. Unfortunately, no clues leading to her whereabouts were found.

A white truck was seen in the area around the time of her disappearance, and police would like to talk to the owner. If you were in the area at the time and happened to see anything unusual or otherwise, you are urged to contact police. It may seem insignificant to you, but it could make all the difference in Ali's case.

*(Age Progression to 23)*

At the time of her disappearance, Ali Lowitzer had dark red dyed hair, stood 5'2", and weighed 145 pounds. She was last seen wearing a white top, a gray zip-up hoodie, black and white checkered skinny jeans, and black sneakers. She was carrying a multicolored checkered backpack and her blue AT&T LG slide cell phone. She is Caucasian with blue eyes, pierced ears, a nose piercing, pink braces on her upper and lower teeth, and a faint chicken pox scar between her eyes. Her nicknames are Ali, Alex, and AJ. As of this writing, she is twenty-four years old.

If you have any information regarding this case, you are urged to call one of the following numbers:

*Harris County Sheriff's Office 713-221-6000*

*The Polly Klaas Foundation at 1-800-587-4357*

## Angela Jaramillo

Sixteen year old Angela Jaramillo was last seen leaving a party in Dallas, Texas on January 23, 2010 at 2am. She had left home at 11:30pm to go to the party. Later, she sent a text to her mother asking for permission to spend the night at a friend's house. Her mother consented, but Angela never arrived at her friend's house.

She has no history of running away, and she hasn't accessed her bank account since she disappeared. Although authorities originally classified her case as a runaway, they now believe foul play may have been involved. Her mother, however, does not.

Authorities found her cell phone in a local park. They also stated they located unspecified evidence that indicated Angela had been injured. There have been some sightings of her in the Dallas area, but none have been confirmed.

Even after her phone was found in the park, her mother says that she thinks Angela ran away to prove a point, but took it too far. She says she does not believe her daughter is being held against her will.

*(Age Progression to 18)*

At the time of her disappearance, Angela Jaramillo had black hair with two sections at the front dyed blonde, stood 5'8", and weighed 190 pounds. She was last seen wearing a gray Hollister sweatshirt, light-colored blue jeans, black Vans shoes, and handmade jewelry. She is Hispanic with brown eyes, a tongue and lower lip piercing, double pierced ears, and braces. As of this writing, she is twenty-four years old.

If you have any information regarding this case, you are urged to call one of the following numbers:

*Dallas Police Department at 214-671-4268*

*The Polly Klaas Foundation at 1-800-587-4357*

## Dorien Deon Thomas

Nine year old Dorien Deon Thomas of Amarillo, Texas, was last seen on October 26, 1998 riding his bike along 9th and Lipscomb Streets around 5:30pm. Neither he nor his bicycle has ever been seen again.

A search of vacant fields and buildings, knocking on doors asking questions, and handing out fliers began once he was reported missing. But no clues as to his whereabouts were found. He is described as a streetwise boy who knew his way around the neighborhood. Foul play is now suspected.

His bicycle was aqua blue with small white tires, white handle bars, and a rusty chain. The words Free Style were imprinted on one side.

*(Age Progression to 24)*

At the time of his disappearance, Dorien Thomas had black hair, stood 4', and weighed 60 pounds. He was last seen wearing a red shirt and jeans. He is Biracial (Caucasian/African-American) with brown eyes. As of this writing, he is twenty-eight years old.

If you have any information regarding this case, you are urged to call one of the following numbers:

*Amarillo Police Department at 806-378-3038*

*The Polly Klaas Foundation at 1-800-587-4357*

## Shelby Raistlin Wright

Fourteen year old Shelby Raistlin Wright was last seen at the residence of a family friend on Cemetery Road off 135$^{th}$ Avenue southeast in Machias, Washington on July 26, 2004. He was living with and caring for his great-grandmother in Snohomish, Washington at the time. His scooter was left behind at the friend's residence, but his laptop disappeared with him. He has never been seen or heard from again.

He enjoyed surfing the internet and was known to frequent chat rooms. He has no history of running away.

In April 2008, authorities announced they had reason to believe that Shelby had been murdered. They used a backhoe, ground-penetrating radar, and cadaver dogs to search the property where he was last seen, but they didn't find anything useful. The couple who lived on the property insisted that the last communication they had had with Shelby was when he said he was going back to his great-grandmother's home. The couple has since passed away. His family requests that anyone who may have seen or know anything about Shelby's whereabouts to please call police.

*(Age Progression to 20)*

At the time of his disappearance, Shelby Wright had sandy brown hair, stood between 5'4" - 5'5", weighed between 140 - 150 pounds, and wore glasses. He is Caucasian with gray eyes, a half-inch scar on his left elbow, and a left ear piercing. His nickname is Shelb. As of this writing, he is twenty-eight years old.

If you have any information regarding this case, you are urged to call one of the following numbers:

*Snohomish County Sheriff's Tip Line at 425-388-3845*

*Crime Stoppers of Puget Sound at 1-800-222-8477*

## Teekah Latres Lewis

Two year old Teekah Latres Lewis was last seen playing a race car game in the arcade section of New Frontier Lanes bowling alley on Center Street in Tacoma, Washington on January 23, 1999 between 10 and 10:30pm. She was only a few feet from her family. Her mother said she turned away for a moment and when she looked back, Teekah was gone. She has never been seen or heard from again.

An extensive search of the area was launched, but she wasn't located. A witness at the bowling alley told police that a maroon Pontiac Grand Am sped out of the parking lot that night, but they didn't know if they were involved in Teekah's disappearance or not. The vehicle was described as being either a late 1980s or early 1990s model with dark tinted windows and a large spoiler.

Two months before Teekah's disappearance, a man with brown curly hair and a beard molested a four year old in the bathroom of the same bowling alley. A few weeks after that, a Caucasian man attempted to lure a six year old boy from the bowling alley. Earlier on the day that Teekah was kidnapped, a man with curly brown hair tried to abduct two children from a park less than a mile from the bowling alley, but was chased away by their father. He fled in a blue 1995 Pontiac Grand Am. No arrests were made in those cases, and authorities have been hesitant to say that they are related to Teekah's abduction; although it is difficult to not see a connection.

*(Age Progression to 17)*

At the time of her disappearance, Teekah Lewis had black hair, stood 3', and weighed 35 pounds. She was last seen wearing a Tweety Bird t-shirt, white sweatpants, and Air Jordan sneakers. Her hair was pulled into a ponytail, and she was carrying a clear purse with a fish design that contained Starburst candies. She is Multiracial (African-American/Caucasian/Native American) with brown eyes, a large birthmark on her left buttock, red natural highlights in her hair, patches of light discoloration on her face and the left side of her buttocks, dimples on her face, and pierced ears. She has asthma and used an inhaler at the time. As of this writing, she is twenty-one years old.

If you have any information regarding this case, you are urged to call one of the following numbers:

*Tacoma Police Department at 253-798-4721*

*Federal Bureau of Investigation (FBI) at 1-202-324-3000*

*The Polly Klaas Foundation at 1-800-587-4357*

## Jeffrey Allen Klungness

Fourteen year old Jeffrey Allen Klungness disappeared on March 2, 1996 from his home on east 113th Street in Bonney Lake, Washington. His mother, Susan Klungness, was found deceased inside the home by his father when he came home from work between 4pm and 4:30pm. The door was unlocked and the television was on, but Jeffrey was gone. He has never been seen or heard from again. A trail of blood, believed to be Susan's, led from an armchair in the living room to the bedroom where she was found. His father's gold watch and about $700 cash was missing. Jeffrey's father had spoken to his son at 9:30am and all had seemed well.

A handyman employed at the home told authorities he had been the one to find Susan deceased and that he panicked and drove away in her Toyota Camry. The car was found abandoned the next day at a convenience store in Auburn, Washington. The handyman turned himself in that same day. He was arrested and charged with possession of stolen property. He spent forty-five days in jail and was released. He then declined to take a polygraph and hired a lawyer. He has never been charged in Jeffrey's disappearance or Susan's murder, however.

Police are interested in locating Jeffrey's father's watch. It is a Seiko Quartz with a gold finish and the serial number SGF 206. It is engraved with the name Ron Klungness and a message thanking him for thirty years of service with Boeing. Authorities believe the watch was taken by Susan's killer, and possibly sold afterwards. Police do not believe Jeffrey left of his own accord, and he is not considered a suspect in his mother's murder.

*(Age Progression to 35)*

At the time of his disappearance, Jeffrey Klungness had curly brown hair, stood between 5'10" - 5'11", and weighed between 155 - 160 pounds. He is dyslexic and has a speech impediment. He slouches when walking. He may go by the names Jeffrey Haynes or Stanley Ipkiss. As of this writing, he is thirty-six years old.

If you have any information regarding this case, you are urged to call one of the following numbers:

*Pierce County Sheriff's Office at 253-591-5959*

*The Polly Klaas Foundation at 1-800-587-4357*

## Bryce Herda

Six year old Bryce Herda was hiking with his family on Shi Shi Beach on the Makah Indian Reservation in Neah Bay, Washington, when he disappeared during the early evening hours of April 9, 1995. His grandfather was the chief of police at the time, so resources were deployed quickly. Coast Guard helicopters, as well as, searchers on foot combed the area. Within a week, dogs, divers, rock climbers, and members of the U.S. Air Force also joined in the search. But eventually, when no clues as to Bryce's whereabouts were found, the search was called off. He has never been seen or heard from again.

Bryce was unable to follow his family up the trail they were on, so they agreed to meet him back at the beach. It is unclear how much time passed before they returned and noticed him missing. His family believes he was abducted. Police believe he may have been washed out to sea, but his body has never been recovered.

*(Age Progression to 19)*

At the time of his disappearance, Bryce Herda had sandy brown hair, stood 4', and weighed 60 pounds. His upper front teeth were large and had a wide gap between them. He was last seen wearing a white t-shirt, green pants, white socks, and white Power Rangers sneakers with red and white lightning bolts on them. He is Native American with brown eyes, a scar at his hairline extending at an angle down the right side of his forehead, a mole or freckle on his right temple, and a light colored birthmark on the back of his upper thigh. He is left-handed. As of this writing, he is twenty-nine years old.

If you have any information regarding this case, you are urged to call one of the following numbers:

*Makah Indian Reservation Police Department at 360-645-2701*

*The Polly Klaas Foundation at 1-800-587-4357*

## DaShawn Leon McCormick

Four year old DaShawn Leon McCormick was living with his father in Anchorage, Alaska in 2013. On April 1st, the police went to the home to arrest his father on federal fraud charges. DaShawn wasn't with him, and he refused to reveal his whereabouts. However, authorities have reason to believe he may be in the Matanuska Susitna Borough area.

*(Age Progression to 9)*

At the time of his disappearance, DaShawn McCormick had blonde hair, stood 3'6", and weighed 45 pounds. He is Biracial (African-American/Caucasian) with brown eyes, a U-shaped scar in the center of his forehead, and a burn scar on his left thigh. As of this writing, he is ten years old.

If you have any information regarding this case, you are urged to call The National Center for Missing and Exploited Children at 1-800-THE-LOST.

## Matthew Wade Crocker

Four month old Matthew Wade Crocker was abducted from his home in Van Buren, Arkansas by an adult female on June 9, 1983. Authorities believe the suspect had been working at a carnival in Fort Smith, Arkansas at the time. She was using the name Kathy Johnson. She is described as a Caucasian female with a tattoo of a white unicorn on her upper left arm, the name Kathy with a ribbon above it tattooed on her upper right arm, and a green and yellow star with a burst tattooed on the left side of her chest. She had a long scar on the back of her right shoulder. Authorities believe Matthew is alive and was raised as the suspect's own son.

*(Age Progression to 32)*

At the time of his disappearance, Matthew Crocker had brown hair and a concave chest, was 29", and weighed 15 pounds. He is Caucasian with brown eyes. As of this writing, he is thirty-five years old.

If you have any information regarding this case, you are urged to call one of the following numbers:

*Van Buren Police Department at 479-474-1234*

*The National Center for Missing and Exploited Children at 1-800-THE-LOST*

## Daniel Barter

Four year old Daniel Barter was last seen playing near the banks of Peridido Bay, Alabama between 9:30am and 10am on June 18, 1959. He, his parents, a cousin, and three of his six siblings had gone camping there. His other three siblings were staying with relatives. Daniel apparently wondered away from his family while his parents were readying some fishing equipment. The family searched for him and bloodhounds were brought in to help, to no avail. He has never been seen or heard from again.

A month before Daniel's disappearance, his mother saw a mysterious vehicle parked in front of their house. She approached the car and driver, a man who quickly covered his face with a newspaper and drove away. One evening not long afterward, a neighbor saw a strange man peering into the Barter boys' bedroom, where Daniel and his brothers were asleep. The police were called and found footprints in the dirt by the window. They took photographs and made casts of the prints, but there was little more they could do.

On the morning before Daniel's disappearance, he and one of his brothers accompanied their mother to the store. She went inside and left them in the car. While she was gone, an unknown man drove his car up next to the

Barter's car and stared in at the boys without speaking to them. He then drove away. Daniel's brother told their mother about it when she returned. Those incidents led the Barters to suspect that Daniel was abducted by someone who had been stalking their family.

Investigators do not believe he wandered into the woods or fell into the water, but they have never been able to find any clues at the scene to suggest he was the victim of a kidnapping.

*(Age Progression to 58)*

At the time of his disappearance, Daniel Barter had brown hair, stood 3', and weighed 50 pounds. He was last seen wearing only gray boxer shorts. He is Caucasian with brown eyes and scars on his fingers and tongue. His nickname is Danny. As of this writing, he is sixty-three years old.

If you have any information regarding this case, you are urged to call one of the following numbers:

*Baldwin County Sheriff's Office at 251-972-8589*

*The National Center for Missing and Exploited Children at 1-800-THE-LOST*

## Tarasha Benjamin

Seventeen year old Tarasha Benjamin was last seen in Selma, Alabama on June 26, 2010. She said goodbye to her mother and left home at 10am to go to a flea market. On the way there, she stopped at a yard sale and met with a relative, who borrowed her cell phone to make a call. It is not clear whether or not Tarasha ever made it to the flea market. She never returned home and has never been heard from again. She has no history of running away. Foul play is suspected.

The car she was driving, a gray Mazda she had borrowed from a friend, was found abandoned on the Cecil Jackson Bypass. The car was located one mile from the flea market and facing the opposite direction. The two windows on the driver's side were broken out, and the driver's side door handle was broken.

*(Tarasha at the time of her disappearance)*

At the time of her disappearance, Tarasha Benjamin had black hair, wore tinted contact lenses, stood 5'2", and weighed 125 pounds. She was last seen wearing a yellow turquoise and white shirt, blue shorts, a silver necklace, and silver sandals. She is African-American with brown eyes, a tattoo of her nickname

Pooh on her upper right arm, and pierced ears. As of this writing, she is twenty-five years old.

If you have any information regarding this case, you are urged to call one of the following numbers:

*Selma Police Department at 334-874-2134*

*The National Center for Missing and Exploited Children at 1-800-THE-LOST*

## Christina Lynn Carter

Three year old Christina Lynn Carter and her mother, Janet Gail Carter, were last seen in Hueytown, Alabama on September 17, 1973. Janet and Christina's father had gotten divorced two months prior, and he was seeking custody of his daughter. It was originally believed that Janet and Christina went into hiding to prevent that from happening. However, on October 7th, Janet's nude bound body was found inside a duffle bag alongside Clingman's Dome Road in the Great Smoky Mountains National Park. She had been suffocated within only hours of being found. An extensive search of the park turned up no clues as to Christina's whereabouts. No one has ever been charged in Christina's disappearance or Janet's murder.

*(Age Progression to 43)*

At the time of her disappearance, Christina Carter had blonde hair, stood 3'2", and weighed 30 pounds. She walked pigeon-toed and wore a toddler's size 3 shoe. She is Caucasian with blue eyes. As of this writing, she is forty-seven years old.

If you have any information regarding this case, you are urged to call one of the following numbers:

*Hueytown Police Department at 205-491-3587*

*The National Center for Missing and Exploited Children at 1-800-THE-LOST*

## Fred Wright

Thirteen year old Fred Wright was last seen at his home in Tuskegee, Alabama on December 6, 1998. He disappeared during the evening hours, and was last seen by an adult male who was inside the house at the time. There was a suspect in his disappearance, but that person is now deceased. Few details are available in his case.

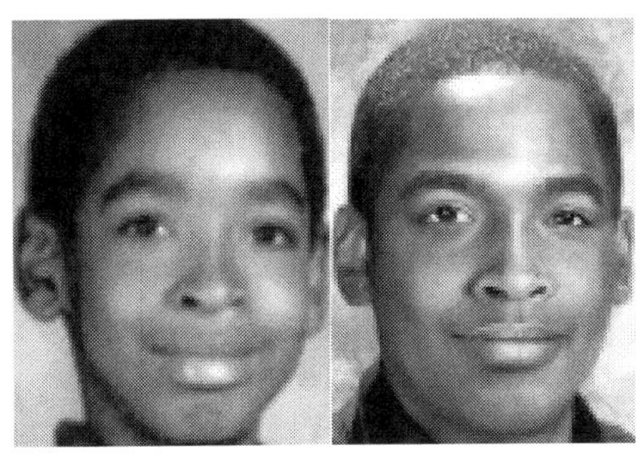

*(Age Progression to 32)*

At the time of his disappearance, Fred Wright had black hair, stood 5'9", and weighed 115 pounds. He is African-American with brown eyes and a chipped front tooth. As of this writing, he is thirty-three years old.

If you have any information regarding this case, you are urged to call one of the following numbers:

*Tuskegee Police Department at 334-727-0200*

*The National Center for Missing and Exploited Children at 1-800-THE-LOST*

## **David Michael Borer**

Eight year old David Michael Borer was last seen walking on Parks Highway, eleven miles north of his hometown in Willow, Alaska on April 26, 1989 at 5pm. It is not clear where he was going. He was reported missing at 7pm that evening. Search dogs traced his scent to where he was last seen, but the trail ended there. He has never been seen or heard from again. He is believed to have been abducted.

*(Age Progression to 36)*

At the time of his disappearance, David Borer had blonde hair, stood 4', and weighed between 55 - 65 pounds. His front teeth protruded slightly at the time. He was last seen wearing a red coat, green jeans, a green plaid shirt, and Sorel winter boots with felt inserts. He is Caucasian with blue/green eyes and scars under his right eye and above his left eye. He is left-handed. As of this writing, he is thirty-six years old.

If you have any information regarding this case, you are urged to call one of the following numbers:

*Alaska State Troopers at 907-733-2256*

*The National Center for Missing and Exploited Children at 1-800-THE-LOST*

## Amy Lee Fandel & Scott Curtis Fandel

Eight year old Amy Lee Fandel and her thirteen year old brother, Scott Curtis Fandel, were last seen during the evening hours of September 4, 1978. The siblings lived in a cabin located in a heavily wooded area of Scout Lake Road in Sterling, Alaska. Their mother and aunt dropped them off at home and then returned to a bar they had been at earlier in the day. Their next-door neighbors said that Scott and Amy came over to play with their children after being dropped off. Later on, the siblings returned home. When their mother and aunt arrived back at the cabin between 2am and 3am on September 5th, all the lights were off. A package of macaroni sat on the kitchen counter and a pot of water was boiling on the stove, but the adults still thought the children were next-door. So, they went to bed. However by afternoon, once they realized neither Amy nor Scott had attended school that day, their mother called the police and reported them missing.

Bullet casings were found outside the cabin, but it is unknown if they were related to the children's disappearances or not. For many years, Amy Fandel's father was a suspect in the case, but authorities no longer believe he was involved.

*(Amy's Age Progression to 46)*

At the time of her disappearance, Amy Fandel had blonde hair, stood 4', and weighed 52 pounds. She was last seen wearing a sweater, a red and blue vest, and striped jeans. She is Caucasian with brown eyes. As of this writing, she is forty-seven years old.

*(Scott's Age Progression to 46)*

At the time of his disappearance, Scott Fandel had brown hair, stood 4'11" and weighed 74 pounds. He was last seen wearing a striped t-shirt and jeans. He is

Caucasian with blue eyes. As of this writing, he is fifty-three years old.

If you have any information regarding this case, you are urged to call one of the following numbers:

*Alaska State Troopers at 907-262-4453*

*The National Center for Missing and Exploited Children at 1-800-THE-LOST*

## Michael Timothy Palmer

Fifteen year old Michael Timothy Palmer was last seen riding a bicycle down Pittman Road in the direction of his family's home in Wasilla, Alaska at approximately 4am on June 4, 1999. His friends had been riding with him, but he fell behind them. They waited for him at the 7-Eleven on Parks Highway, but when he did not show up shortly, they assumed he went home. He never arrived home and has never been heard from again. He has no history of running away.

His mother, who originally assumed he was at a friend's house, reported him missing at 3pm, eleven hours after he was last seen. The bicycle, which he had borrowed, was later found in the Little Susitna River, which runs parallel to Pittman Road and Silver Drive Intersection. However, tracker dogs did not track his scent to the river.

His Converse sneakers were discovered near a private runway for a homeowner's personal plane. They were wet and muddy. No other evidence related to his disappearance has ever been found.

Coincidently, Michael's older brother, thirty year old Charles Palmer, disappeared near Talkeetna, Alaska in April 2010. He had gone out on a snowmobile ride and never returned. The snowmobile was later found stuck in the snow. Charles was presumed to have died of exposure, and was declared legally dead in April 2011. Authorities do not believe the brothers' disappearances are related.

*(Age Progression to 28)*

At the time of his disappearance, Michael Palmer had brown/blonde hair shaved on the sides and longer in the middle, stood between 5'5" - 5'6", and weighed 110 pounds. He was last seen wearing a t-shirt, blue jeans, a black jacket with red stripes on the sleeves and the Marlboro logo on the lapel. His nickname is Mike, and he is left-handed. As of this writing, he is thirty-four years old.

If you have any information regarding this case, you are urged to call one of the following numbers:

*Alaska State Troopers at 907-745-2131*

*The National Center for Missing and Exploited Children at 1-800-THE-LOST*

## Victor Manuel Tolentino Cruz

Sixteen year old Victor Manuel Tolentino Cruz was last seen somewhere in southern Arizona on January 7, 2011. He was crossing the Mexican border at the time. Few details are available in his case.

*(Victor at the time of his disappearance)*

At the time of his disappearance, Victor Cruz had black hair, stood 5', and weighed 160 pounds. He was last seen wearing a black sweatshirt, a blue sweater, and blue jeans. He is Hispanic with brown eyes, and he may use Tolentino as his last name. As of this writing, he is twenty-three years old.

If you have any information regarding this case, you are urged to call one of the following numbers:

*Monterey County Sheriff's Department at 831-755-3722*

*The National Center for Missing and Exploited Children at 1-800-THE-LOST*

## Richard "Richie" Gorham & Roland Himebrook

Eleven year old Richard "Richie" Gorham and his grandfather, fifty-two year old Roland Himebrook, were last seen in Avra Valley, Arizona on July 7, 1986. They were reported missing by Roland's friend on July 12th. Roland's vehicle, a 1966 Chevrolet El Camino, was found abandoned in the Silverbell area on September 27th. There was no sign of Richie or Roland at the scene.

Richie's mother's live-in boyfriend is considered a possible suspect. Richie was living with his grandfather after allegations were made of the boyfriend being abusive to him, his mother, and his sister. Roland and the boyfriend had supposedly had several confrontations in the past.

*(Richie & Roland at the time of their disappearances)*

At the time of his disappearance, Richie Gorham had red hair, stood 4'8", and weighed 60 pounds. He is Caucasian with hazel eyes. As of this writing, he is forty-three years old.

At the time of his disappearance, Roland Himebrook had gray hair, stood 6'1", and weighed 215 pounds. He is Caucasian with blue eyes. As of this writing, he is eighty-four years old.

If you have any information regarding this case, you are urged call the Pima County Sheriff's Department at 520-351-4900.

**Karen Rosalba Grajeda**

Seven year old Karen Rosalba Grajeda was last seen playing outside her home at the Saguaro Crest Apartments on west Valencia Street in Tucson, Arizona on January 11, 1996. She was roller skating with her younger sister and some friends that evening. She was last seen when she returned to their apartment to drop off her skates before going back out to play. Her mother reported her missing when she called in both girls for dinner at 6:30pm, and Karen was nowhere to be found. None of the other children had seen her wonder off or heard any screams. She has never been seen or heard from again.

Authorities believe she was abducted, possibly by an unidentified man seen in the area around the same time she went missing. He is described as being either Hispanic or Caucasian, approximately thirty to forty-six years old in 1996, with light brown hair, green eyes, between 5'6" - 5'8" tall, and weighing about 170 pounds. He also may have had a mustache. That same man is believed to have also been responsible for the abduction, rape, and murder of another child. Investigators say that the circumstances of both cases were very similar, except that Karen's remains have not been found.

*(Age Progression to 28)*

At the time of her disappearance, Karen Grajeda had black hair, was missing several baby teeth, stood 3'5", and weighed 50 pounds. She was last seen wearing a faded purple or turquoise t-shirt with white lettering on the front, multicolored pastel floral shorts, Guess shoes, a gold chain with a pendant reading Little Angel, a ring with a red stone, and another ring engraved with the letter K. She is Hispanic with brown eyes, a pea-sized mole behind one ear, and pierced ears. She speaks both Spanish and English. As of this writing, she is twenty-nine years old.

If you have any information regarding this case, you are urged to call one of the following numbers:

*Tucson Police Department at 520-791-4444*

*The National Center for Missing and Exploited Children at 1-800-THE-LOST*

## James Hendrickson

Twelve year old James Hendrickson disappeared while walking home on the morning of June 12, 1991 in Tucson, Arizona. He was last seen near Oracle and Grant Roads. He resided on east Delano Street at the time. He has no history of running away.

A male suspect was questioned in the years following James' disappearance, but no one has ever been charged. Foul play is suspected.

*(Age Progression to 35)*

At the time of his disappearance, James Hendrickson had dark blonde hair, stood 5'5", and weighed 140 pounds. He was last seen wearing a white t-shirt with some sort of design, blue shorts, and white shoes. He is Caucasian with blue eyes and a scar on the top of his head. His nickname is Jimmy. As of this writing, he is thirty-eight years old.

If you have any information regarding this case, you are urged to call one of the following numbers:

*Tucson Police Department at 520-791-5159*

*The National Center for Missing and Exploited Children at 1-800-THE-LOST*

## Cynthia Ardina Leslie & Jackie Lynn Leslie

Fifteen year old Cynthia Ardina Leslie and her sister, thirteen year old Jackie Lynn Leslie, were last seen walking down Baseline Road near Power Road in Mesa, Arizona on July 31, 1974. They were headed to a friend's home that was located three blocks away from their own residence in the Desert Shores Mobile Home Park. They left a note for their mother saying they were going to babysit, but she learned later that they planned to attend a party. Neither girl has ever been seen or heard from again.

When authorities questioned the people who attended the party, some said they had seen Cynthia and Jackie there, while others said they had never arrived. They had no history of running away, and foul play is suspected.

*(Cynthia's Age Progression to 54)*

At the time of her disappearance, Cynthia Leslie had brown hair, wore glasses, stood 5'6", and weighed 109 pounds. She was last seen wearing a summer shirt and light blue jeans. She is Caucasian with hazel eyes, a half-inch mole on the outer side of her right armpit, and pierced ears. Her nickname is Cindy. As of this writing, she is fifty-nine years old.

*(Jackie's Age Progression to 52)*

At the time of her disappearance, Jackie Leslie had brown hair, stood 5'4", and weighed 110 pounds. She was last seen wearing a summer top, jeans, and carrying a white hairbrush. She is Caucasian with blue eyes, a mole on her right cheek bone, and pierced ears. As of this writing, she is fifty-seven years old.

If you have any information regarding this case, you are urged to call one of the following numbers:

*Maricopa County Sheriff's Office at 602-256-1087*

*The National Center for Missing and Exploited Children at 1-800-THE-LOST*

## Robert Parks

Thirteen year old Robert Parks was last seen leaving his home in Mesa, Arizona on April 11, 1974. He has never been heard from again. He has no history of running away, and he left all his belongings behind. Foul play is suspected. Few details are available in his case.

*(Age Progression to 51)*

At the time of his disappearance, Robert Parks had brown hair, stood between 5'6" - 5'7", and weighed between 120 - 130 pounds. He was last seen wearing bell-bottom pants with blue and purple cuffs. He is

Caucasian with blue eyes. His nickname is Robbie. As of this writing, he is fifty-seven years old.

If you have any information regarding this case, you are urged to call one of the following numbers:

*Mesa Police Department at 480-644-2211*

*The National Center for Missing and Exploited Children at 1-800-THE-LOST*

## Randy Doyle Parscale Jr.

Ten year old Randy Doyle Parscale Jr. was last seen hiking with his grandfather and two brothers in Peppersauce Canyon in the Santa Catalina Mountains near Oracle, Arizona on April 7, 1979. He wandered ahead of the rest of the group, and has never been seen again.

A search of the area provided only some child's footprints leading to the road and then nothing. Investigators theorized that he may have gotten into a vehicle at that spot. His case is classified as a nonfamily abduction.

*(Age Progression to 43)*

At the time of his disappearance, Randy Parscale Jr. had brown hair, stood 4'6", and weighed 70 pounds. He was last seen wearing a green jacket, blue pants, and shoes with a bullseye pattern on the soles. He is Caucasian and has blue eyes. As of this writing, he is forty-nine years old.

If you have any information regarding this case, you are urged to call one of the following numbers:

*Pinal County Sheriff's Office 520-866-5149*

*The National Center for Missing and Exploited Children at 1-800-THE-LOST*

## Danielle Therese Pitcher & Dorothy Jeanne Pitcher

Fourteen year old Danielle Therese Pitcher and her mother, forty-seven year old Dorothy Jeanne Pitcher, were last seen walking back to their home from the RV Park store on the corner of Highway 666 (now 191) and Highway 181 in Sunizona, Arizona on May 23, 1993. They had gone to get a pack of cigarettes for Dorothy's husband (Danielle's father). It was a three mile walk one way from their home to the store. The rest of Dorothy's children stayed back at home with their father.

Search dogs tracked their scents for approximately one and half miles along the route they would have taken home, but then lost it close to the road. Investigators theorize that they may have been picked up by a vehicle at that spot. Foul play is suspected.

*(Dorothy & Danielle at the time of their disappearances & Danielle's Age Progression to 34)*

At the time of her disappearance, Danielle Pitcher had blonde hair, stood 5'1", and weighed 112 pounds. She was last seen wearing a white shirt or tank top, white shorts, and black or brown heeled boots with fringe. She is Caucasian with blue eyes. As of this writing, she is thirty-nine years old.

At the time of her disappearance, Dorothy Pitcher had brown hair, wore dentures and eyeglasses, stood between 5'2" - 5'3", and weighed 145 pounds. She was last seen wearing a white short outfit with a duck design. She is Caucasian with brown eyes. As of this writing, she is seventy-two years old.

If you have any information regarding this case, you are urged to call one of the following numbers:

*Cochise County Sheriff's Office 520-432-9500*

*The National Center for Missing and Exploited Children at 1-800-THE-LOST*

## Jennifer Anne Douglas

Seventeen year old Jennifer Anne Douglas was last seen riding her brand new bike north on Monaco Parkway in Denver, Colorado on July 16, 1984. She was supposed to be at her ballet class at 4pm, but she never arrived and has never been heard from again.

An extensive search turned up no clues as to her whereabouts. She has no history of running away. Both authorities and her parents believe she was taken against her will.

Jennifer's bicycle was a boy's black Univega 12-speed model with the tag number 12083.

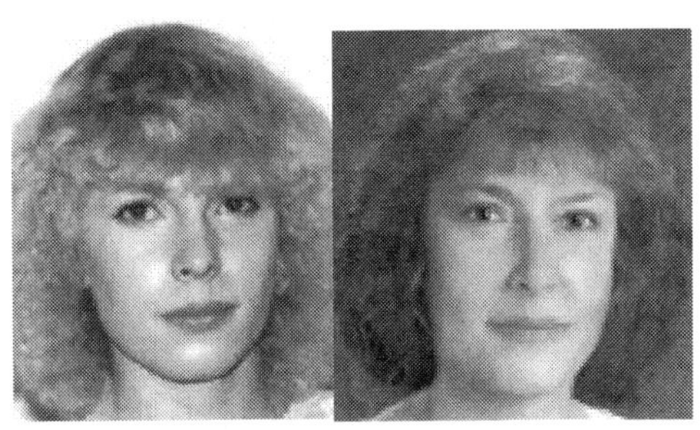

*(Age Progression to 44)*

At the time of her disappearance, Jennifer Douglas had blonde hair, wore contact lenses, stood 5', and weighed 87 pounds. She was last seen wearing a blue green top, khaki shorts, black Nike sneakers, and a blue fanny pack. She is Caucasian with blue/green eyes. His nickname is Jenny. As of this writing, she is fifty years old.

If you have any information regarding this case, you are urged to call one of the following numbers:

*Denver Police Department at 303-640-3875*

*The National Center for Missing and Exploited Children at 1-800-THE-LOST*

## Jonelle Renee Matthews

Twelve year old Jonelle Renee Matthews was last seen when she was dropped off by friends at her home on 43rd Avenue Court in Greeley, Colorado on December 20, 1984 at approximately 8:15pm. She was returning from a Christmas program at a nursing home where she had sung with her middle school choir. There was no one else home at the time, because her father and her sister were at a basketball game and her mother was out of state visiting relatives. Jonelle was last heard from when she took a message over the telephone from her father's acquaintance. She has never been seen or heard from again.

Her father and sister arrived home at around 9:30pm and found the television and lights on, but Jonelle was gone. The garage door was open, and there were footprints from inside the garage leading around to the back of the house. But there were no indications of a struggle in the snow or inside the house.

Authorities suspect that an intruder or intruders broke into the house and abducted Jonelle while she was home alone. She was adopted by the Matthews when she was a baby, but neither her biological mother nor her adoptive parents are suspects in her case.

*(Age Progression to 42)*

At the time of her disappearance, Jonelle Matthews had brown hair, had a full set of braces on her teeth, stood 5'3", and weighed 115 pounds. She was last seen wearing a light blue ski jacket, a red blouse, a dark gray sweater vest, a charcoal gray shirt, and house slippers. She is Caucasian with brown eyes, pierced ears, and a scar on her chin. As of this writing, she is forty-six years old.

If you have any information regarding this case, you are urged to call one of the following numbers:

*Greeley Police Department at 303-350-9670*

*The National Center for Missing and Exploited Children at 1-800-THE-LOST*

## Lashaya Nae Stine

Sixteen year old Lashaya Nae Stine was last seen in Aurora, Colorado in the early morning hours of July 15, 2016. She left home without permission to meet an unspecified individual and never returned. The last sighting of her was on a surveillance camera, walking near a bus stop on Peoria Street at 2:23am. She has no history of running away, and she left all of her belongings at home.

Her family believes she was abducted by sex traffickers. There have been sightings of her in Kansas City, Missouri. Witnesses have stated that a girl resembling Lashaya was being kept and forced into prostitution.

She was an honors student at George Washington High School at the time. She dreamed of becoming a nurse.

*(Lashaya at the time of her disappearance)*

At the time of her disappearance, Lashaya Stine had black hair styled in corn rows, stood 5'6", and weighed 150 pounds. She was last seen wearing a white long-sleeve shirt, black stonewashed jeans, silver metal hoop earrings, and a silver watch on her left wrist. She is African-American with brown eyes and a quarter-sized round scar on her chest. As of this writing, she is eighteen years old.

If you have any information regarding this case, you are urged to call one of the following numbers:

*Aurora Police Department at 303-627-3100*

*The National Center for Missing and Exploited Children at 1-800-THE-LOST*

## Christopher William Vigil

Nine year old Christopher William Vigil was last seen hiking with his mother and brother on Grey Rock Mountain Trail in the Poudre Canyon in Poudre Park, Colorado on April 30, 1978. He hiked out ahead of them a bit and disappeared. His mother reported him missing at 5:30pm, three hours after she had last seen him.

Two women who were also hiking that day came forward and said they had saw Christopher. They also said they had seen a man sitting on some rocks. They described the man as being dark-haired and dark-complexioned, wearing a straw cowboy hat, with a camera hanging around his neck. That man has never been identified. The women said they sat down to have lunch not far from the dark-haired man. During their meal, they heard two voices, one of which was a young boy's. They assumed it had been Christopher. They couldn't make out what was being said, but then the boy started yelling and they felt that something was wrong. They started to investigate but were afraid to do so. After a short time, the yelling stopped. When they had finished eating, they passed by where the man had been sitting, but he was gone.

An extensive search turned up no signs of him. He has never been seen or heard from again. The night of Christopher's disappearance was very cold and overnight temperatures dropped below freezing. It is very doubtful he would have survived the night without shelter.

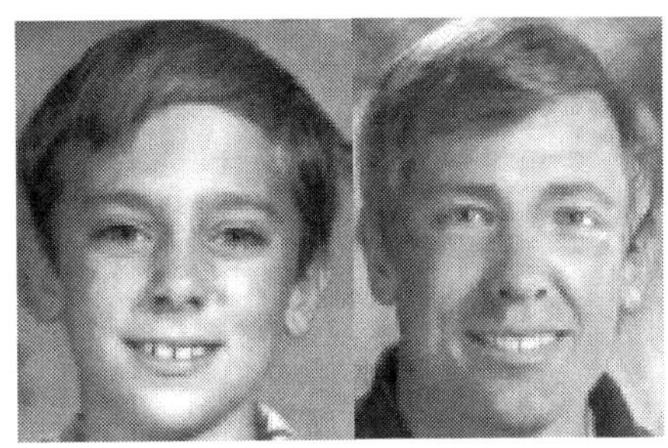

*(Age Progression to 44)*

At the time of his disappearance, Christopher Vigil had brown hair, stood 4'8", and weighed 74 pounds. He was last seen wearing a dark green knit shirt, green plaid pants, white socks, blue sneakers, and a maroon or purple denim jacket. He is Caucasian with green eyes. His nickname is Chris. As of this writing, he is forty-nine years old.

If you have any information regarding this case, you are urged to call one of the following numbers:

*Larimer County Sheriff's Office at 970-498-5100*

*The National Center for Missing and Exploited Children at 1-800-THE-LOST*

## Bianca Elaine Lebron

Ten year old Bianca Elaine Lebron was last seen getting into a vehicle she claimed was being driven by her uncle outside Elias Howe School in Bridgeport, Connecticut at 8:30am on November 7, 2001. She has never been seen or heard from again.

The vehicle was an older model two-tone brown and tan van with tinted windows. Witnesses said the exterior was in poor condition and it appeared to have been sanded down in several areas. The driver was described as a Hispanic male, approximately twenty to thirty years of age, standing between 5'8" - 5'11" with an average build. He had curly hair styled in a short afro with long side burns and a beard, brown eyes, a prominent nose, and scratches on his cheeks. He was wearing a long-sleeve blue pullover shirt with GAP imprinted on the front and along the right sleeve, Fubu jeans with an image of Fat Albert on the right rear pocket, and scuffed Timberland boots. The man made no attempt to conceal his face from witnesses.

Bianca's classmates believed her when she said he was her uncle and didn't interfere with her getting into his van. Her family told authorities, however, that she does not have an uncle, nor does anyone in their family own a van similar to the one she left in. School officials received widespread criticism for their handling of Bianca's disappearance. Her teacher counted her absent, and did not know she was missing until into the following day. Stronger security measures and new attendance policies were put into place afterwards.

Her mother and stepfather initially thought she had gone over to a friend's house after school and had forgotten to call them, but by 8:30pm they realized something was wrong and reported her missing. Neither Bianca's mother, stepfather, nor biological father are suspects in her disappearance. No other suspects or persons of interest have been identified.

*(Age Progression to 23)*

At the time of her disappearance, Bianca Lebron had brown hair, stood 4'11", and weighed 115 pounds. She was last seen wearing a green beige and brown camouflage shirt, beige pants, black boots, and a dark blue denim jacket. She is Hispanic with hazel eyes and a birthmark on her forehead. As of this writing, she is twenty-six years old.

If you have any information regarding this case, you are urged to call one of the following numbers:

*Bridgeport Police Department at 203-576-7671*

*The National Center for Missing and Exploited Children at 1-800-THE-LOST*

## Marisela Pino

Eleven year old Marisela Pino was last seen in the vicinity of Nash's Pizza & Groceries on Cherry Street in Waterbury, Connecticut on March 20, 1993. She has never been seen or heard from again. Few details are available in her case.

*(Age Progression to 33)*

At the time of her disappearance, Marisela Pino had brown hair, stood 4'5", and weighed 85 pounds. She was last seen wearing a black and gray jacket, a green and white shirt, a green denim skirt, white socks, and blue shoes. She is Hispanic with brown eyes. She may use the last name Vasquez. As of this writing, she is thirty-six years old.

If you have any information regarding this case, you are urged to call one of the following numbers:

*Waterbury Police Department at 203-574-6941*

*The National Center for Missing and Exploited Children at 1-800-THE-LOST*

## Diana Belinda Alvarez

Nine year old Diana Belinda Alvarez was last seen in her home on Unique Circle in Fort Myers, Florida on May 29, 2016. At 2am, she was asleep, wrapped in a green floral print blanket. Sometime after that, she disappeared and has not been heard from again.

Jorge Guerrero, who had lived in the home up until two weeks prior, was quickly identified as a person of interest in Diana's disappearance. Her parents had asked him to leave, because they were concerned about the way Diana was behaving around him and about the remarks he had made about her.

On June 3rd, Jorge was detained as an illegal immigrant, and police found pornographic photos of Diana on his cell phone. He admitted to using crystal meth while living with Diana's family and touching her inappropriately, but he denied having had sexual intercourse with her. He claimed to have had no contact with her since moving out. He was charged in connection with child pornography in an unrelated case.

In August 2017, Jorge was sentenced to forty years in prison. Diana's mother visited him in prison in an attempt to get answers as to her daughter's whereabouts. According to her mother, Jorge told her that Diana was not dead, but he would not give her a straight answer as to where she is. Her family believes she is either dead or being held in a sex trafficking ring.

*(Diana at the time of her disappearance)*

At the time of her disappearance, Diana Alvarez had black hair, stood 4'4", and weighed 95 pounds. She was last seen wearing a short-sleeve shirt, blue shorts, and shoes. She was possibly carrying a green floral print blanket. She is Hispanic with brown eyes and two scars on her leg. As of this writing, she is eleven years old.

If you have any information regarding this case, you are urged to call one of the following numbers:

*Lee County Sheriff's Office at 239-477-1000*

*The National Center for Missing and Exploited Children at 1-800-THE-LOST*

## Jeremy Lee Dages & Bonnie Lee Dages

Four month old Jeremy Lee Dages and his mother, eighteen year old Bonnie Lee Dages, disappeared while en route to a shopping center located at the intersection of Lumsden Road and Lithia Pinecrest Road in Brandon, Florida at approximately 9pm on April 28, 1993. They were going to do some shopping and meet an unknown individual. Neither of them have ever been seen or heard from again.

Their silver 1986 Dodge Caravan was found abandoned in the parking lot later that night. It was locked and Bonnie's purse, which contained $75 cash, was inside. Jeremy's diaper bag was also there, but his car seat was gone. Foul play is suspected.

Bonnie's mother had them both declared legally dead in 1999, but their remains have never been located.

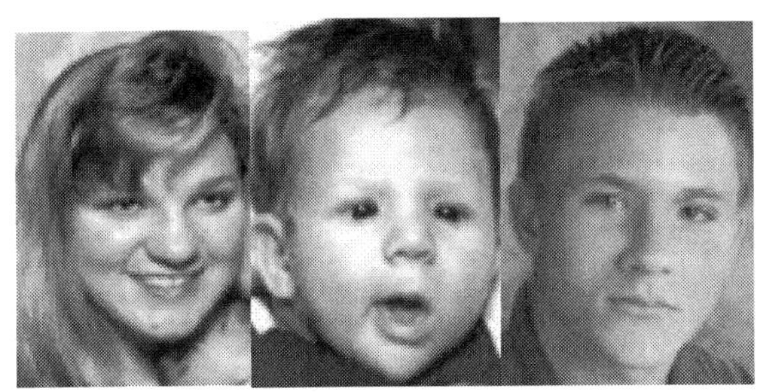

*(Bonnie & Jeremy at the time of their disappearances & Jeremy's Age Progression to 20)*

At the time of his disappearance, Jeremy Dages had brown hair, was 20", and weighed 15 pounds. He is Caucasian with blue eyes. As of this writing, he is twenty-five years old.

At the time of her disappearance, Bonnie Dages had blonde hair, stood 5'6", and weighed between 145 - 150 pounds. She was last seen wearing a blue t-shirt, pink denim shorts, and white leather thong sandals. She is Caucasian with blue eyes, a surgical scar on her abdomen, a scar on the shin of her left leg, and pierced ears. As of this writing, she is forty-three years old.

If you have any information regarding this case, you are urged to call one of the following numbers:

*Hillsborough County Sheriff's Office at 813-247-8660*

*The National Center for Missing and Exploited Children at 1-800-THE-LOST*

## Adji Desir

Six year old Adji Desir was last seen at approximately 5:15pm on January 10, 2009 on Grace Street in Immokalee, Florida when he went outside at his grandmother's house to play with some other children. About half an hour later, his grandmother realized he was missing and called police.

An extensive search of the area turned up no clues as to his whereabouts, and he has not been seen or heard from since. None of his family members are considered suspects. Authorities believe he either wandered away or was abducted.

Adji is mentally disabled. He functions at the level of a two year old and is almost completely nonverbal. He understands Haitian Creole, but cannot speak it. He knows his name, but cannot speak it either. He can speak a few words in English, and can nod and shake his head to indicate yes and no. Due to his disability, he may be unable to ask for help.

*(Age Progression to 10)*

At the time of his disappearance, Adji Desir had black hair, stood 3', and weighed 45 pounds. He was last seen wearing a blue t-shirt with thin yellow stripes, blue shorts with pink flamingos down the sides, and two-tone blue sneakers. He is African-American and of Haitian descent with brown eyes. His nickname is JiJi. As of this writing, he is fifteen years old.

If you have any information regarding this case, you are urged to call one of the following numbers:

*Collier County Sheriff's Office at 239-793-9300*

*The National Center for Missing and Exploited Children at 1-800-THE-LOST*

## **Bryan Dos Santos-Gomes**

Three week old Bryan Dos Santos-Gomes was abducted from Fort Myers, Florida on December 1, 2006. He, his mother, and his mother's friend were waiting at a bus stop when a woman drove up and asked for directions. The women and Bryan got on the bus, but the woman in the vehicle followed the bus until they got off and again asked for help. Bryan, his mother, and his mother's friend got into the vehicle to give her directions. Shortly thereafter, the woman demanded $500 and threatened to harm the women's families. The abductor eventually dropped the two women off on the roadside in Estero, Florida and then drove away with Bryan.

His abductor is described as being Hispanic, between twenty-eight and thirty years of age, heavyset and approximately 5'4", with straight black hair partially pulled up in a bun. She was wearing blue jeans and a black shirt. She spoke Spanish. She is believed to have been driving a black two-door 1998 - 2003 Ford Explorer with peeling window tint. Bryan's mother told police that there was a diaper bag and a car seat in the vehicle, indicating that the abduction was planned. Authorities note that his abductor should be considered armed and dangerous.

After Bryan's abduction, a Fort Myers woman informed the police that she and her infant grandchild had been approached by a woman in a black SUV asking for directions, in the same vicinity where Bryan was taken. According to the woman, it occurred only hours after Bryan's abduction. The woman's and Bryan's mother's descriptions of the woman in the SUV were very similar.

Investigators believe the woman who abducted Bryan wanted to raise him as her own, possibly after suffering a miscarriage or stillbirth, and that he was chosen at random. They believe the abductor may have been from South America or Mexico originally, or possibly a second-generation immigrant. And that English may be her first language, although she spoke Spanish during the abduction.

*(Age Progression to 6)*

At the time of his disappearance, Bryan Santos-Gomes had black hair, was 24", and weighed 12 pounds. He is Hispanic and of Brazilian descent with brown eyes. As of this writing, he is eleven years old.

If you have any information regarding this case, you are urged to call one of the following numbers:

*Fort Myers Police Department at 877-667-1296*

*The National Center for Missing and Exploited Children at 1-800-THE-LOST*

## Jonathan Mordoche, Mario Antonio Mordoche & Yakelin Llanes

Eight year old Jonathan Mordoche, his brother, eleven year old Mario Antonio Mordoche, and their mother, twenty-nine year old Yakelin Llanes were last seen in Miami, Florida on August 28, 1999. They planned to travel to Tampa, Florida to visit the boys' father, although it is unclear if they actually left on their journey before they disappeared or not.

They were driving a rented brown 1999 Chevrolet Malibu with Florida plates GH830M. It has never been located. They never arrived at the father's home and have never been heard from again.

*(Jonathan, Mario and Yakelin at the time of their disappearances)*

At the time of his disappearance, Jonathan Mordoche had black hair, stood between 4'7" - 4'8", and weighed 85 pounds. He is Hispanic with brown eyes. As of this writing, he is twenty-six years old.

At the time of his disappearance, Mario Mordoche had black hair, stood between 5' - 5'4", and weighed 100 pounds. He is Hispanic with brown eyes. As of this writing, he is thirty years old.

At the time of her disappearance, Yakelin Llanes had black hair, stood 5'6", and weighed 120 pounds. She is Hispanic with brown eyes. As of this writing, she is forty-eight years old.

If you have information regarding this case, you are urged to call the Miami-Dade County Police Department at 305-471-8477 or 305-418-7201.

## Andrew Lee Brown

One year old Andrew Lee Brown was last seen playing in the front yard of his family's residence in Colquitt, Georgia on July 24, 1987. Authorities believe he was abducted. Few details are available in his case.

*(Age Progression to 31)*

At the time of his disappearance, Andrew Brown had black hair, stood 2', and weighed 25 pounds. He is African-American with brown eyes. As of this writing, he is thirty-two years old.

If you have any information regarding this case, you are urged to call one of the following numbers:

*Colquitt Police Department at 912-758-3421*

*The National Center for Missing and Exploited Children at 1-800-THE-LOST*

## Teresa Melissa Dean

Eleven year old Teresa Melissa Dean was last seen walking down Lawrence Street near her family's home in Macon, Georgia at approximately 8pm on August 15, 1999. She said she was going to visit a friend's house and see some puppies. She never arrived and has never been seen or heard from since. Authorities believe she may have met with foul play.

*(Age Progression to 19)*

At the time of her disappearance, Teresa Dean had brown hair, stood 4'10", and weighed 75 pounds. She was last seen wearing a blue and white striped button-down short-sleeve shirt, orange pink or rust-colored knit pants, clear plastic gel sandals, and gold ball earrings. She is Caucasian with blue eyes, a speech impediment, and pierced ears. As of this writing, she is thirty years old.

If you have any information regarding this case, you are urged to call one of the following numbers:

*Twiggs County Sheriff's Department at 912-945-3357*

*Georgia Bureau of Investigation at 912-987-4545*

*Federal Bureau of Investigation (FBI) Atlanta Office at 770-216-3000*

## Desmond Santonio Dix

Sixteen year old Desmond Santonio Dix was last seen in Atlanta, Georgia on January 30, 1996 when he was abducted at gunpoint by at least two unknown individuals. He has never been heard from again. Few details are available in his case.

*(Age Progression to 37)*

At the time of his disappearance, Desmond Dix had brown hair, stood 5'6", and weighed 135 pounds. He is African-American. His left eye is brown and his right eye is gray. As of this writing, he is thirty-eight years old.

If you have any information regarding this case, you are urged to call one of the following numbers:

*Atlanta Police Department at 404-546-5699*

*The National Center for Missing and Exploited Children at 1-800-THE-LOST*

## Raymond Lamar Green

Five day old Raymond Lamar Green was abducted from his home in Atlanta, Georgia on November 6, 1978 by a woman his mother thought she could trust. His mother left him with the woman and the baby's uncle while she took a shower. When she finished her shower and walked back into the room, the woman and Raymond were gone. The baby's uncle, who had been napping, said that the baby had started crying and she had taken him outside to calm him. When his mother went outside to find them, a neighbor informed her that the woman and baby Raymond had gotten into the passenger side of a brown vehicle and left. Neither the woman nor Raymond has been seen again.

Authorities determined the identity and all the information the woman had given to Raymond's mother was false. The woman has never been identified. Investigators believe Raymond may have been sold for adoption outside of the United States.

*(Age Progression to 38. Photos from the time of his disappearance are not available.)*

At the time of his disappearance, Raymond Green had black hair and was wearing a blue sleeper. He was wrapped in a green and white hospital blanket. He is African-American with brown eyes. No length and weight measurements from the time of his disappearance are available and neither are any photographs. As of this writing, he is forty years old.

If you have any information regarding this case, you are urged to call one of the following numbers:

*Atlanta Police Department at 404-658-6666*

*The National Center for Missing and Exploited Children at 1-800-THE-LOST*

## Alisha Smiley

Three year old Alisha Smiley was last seen at approximately 1:45pm on June 6, 1985 in Atlanta, Georgia. She was sitting on a bench outside the Omni International Hotel on Techwood Drive. Alisha's aunt left her and her four year old cousin unattended for a moment while she tried to buy wrestling tickets a short distance away. When her aunt returned, Alisha was gone. An extensive search of the area turned up no clues as to her whereabouts. She has never been seen or heard from again.

*(Age Progression to 28)*

At the time of her disappearance, Alisha Smiley had black hair, stood 3', and weighed 30 pounds. She had a gap between her lower front teeth and a slight discoloration in the corner of her right eye. She was last seen wearing a red and white A-line sundress with small checks, white sandals with silver buckles, lilac hair ribbons, and possibly gold earrings. She is African-American with brown eyes. As of this writing, she is thirty-six years old.

If you have any information regarding this case, you are urged to call one of the following numbers:

*Atlanta Police Department at 404-853-3434*

*The National Center for Missing and Exploited Children at 1-800-THE-LOST*

## Madeline Teresa Ponds

Seventeen year old Madeline Teresa Ponds was last seen working alone at PJ's One-Stop convenience store on southbound Highway 82 in Columbus, Mississippi on November 20, 1986. Her mother brought her some dinner, and then went back home. Less than five minutes later, a customer found the store unattended and called police. Madeline has never been seen or heard from again.

Police found her car still parked in the parking lot with her purse, keys, and hairbrush inside. Her mother believes she was abducted, and says her daughter would not have gone without a fight. Madeline was a high school senior at the time, and planned to join the armed forces after graduation.

*(Madeline at the time of her disappearance)*

At the time of her disappearance, Madeline Ponds had reddish-blonde hair, stood 5'1", and weighed 105 pounds. She was last seen wearing a bright orange and blue sweater, straight-leg blue jeans, and white high-top sneakers. She is Caucasian with green eyes and pierced ears. Her nickname is Midge. As of this writing, she is forty-nine years old.

If you have any information regarding this case, you are urged to call one of the following numbers:

*Lowndes County, Mississippi Sheriff's Office at 601-328-6788*

*Pickens County, Alabama Sheriff's Office at 205-367-2000*

## Daffany Sherika Tullos

Seven year old Daffany Sherika Tullos was last seen walking away from her grandparents' residence on Azalea Circle in north Jackson, Mississippi between 7pm and 8pm on July 26, 1988. She has never been seen or heard from again. Few details are available in her case.

*(Age Progression to 34)*

At the time of her disappearance, Daffany Tullos had medium-length black hair styled in a Jheri curl, stood 3'7", and weighed 55 pounds. She was last seen wearing a blue and white checkered or striped sleeveless shirt, blue and white shorts, and no shoes or socks. All of her clothing had her name on the inside. She is African-American with brown eyes and pierced ears. She has epilepsy and requires daily medication. As of this writing, she is thirty-seven years old.

If you have any information regarding this case, you are urged to call one of the following numbers:

*Jackson Police Department at 601-960-1234*

*Federal Bureau of Investigation (FBI) at 1-202-324-000*

## Mark Steven Martin & Carolyn Sue Martin

Two year old Mark Steven Martin and his mother, twenty-four year old Carolyn Sue Martin, were last seen on August 31, 1981 in Madison Heights, Michigan. Their family and friends went to their home that day to help them pack for a move to San Antonio, Texas with Mark's father, Hamparsoum Kirezian. He claimed to have gotten a job in Texas and wanted Carolyn and Mark to join him. Later that evening, Carolyn and Mark stopped by her mother's home in Hazel Park, Michigan to say goodbye. Neither Mark nor Carolyn have ever been seen or heard from again. They were reported missing the following spring.

When questioned by police, Hamparsoum said Carolyn had changed her mind about going to Texas, so he gave her $4,000 in cash and left them on the side of the road near Toledo, Ohio. He said he continued on his way to Texas, but changed his mind when he had car trouble. He then returned to Michigan. He is considered a person of interest in their disappearances, but there is no evidence to tie him to any crime. Carolyn and Mark's social security numbers have not been used since 1981. Foul play is suspected.

*(Carolyn & Mark at the time of their disappearances)*

At the time of his disappearance, Mark Martin had sandy light brown hair, stood 2', and weighed 30 pounds. He is Caucasian with brown eyes. His nickname is Markie. As of this writing, he is thirty-nine years old.

At the time of her disappearance, Carolyn Martin had brown hair, stood 5'5", and weighed 110 pounds. She is Caucasian with blue eyes and pierced ears. As of this writing, she is sixty-one years old.

If you have any information regarding this case, you are urged to call the Madison Heights Police Department at 248-585-2100.

## Nadine Jean O'Dell

Sixteen year old Nadine Jean O'Dell was last seen in Inkster, Michigan on John Daly Road at 9:30am on August 16, 1974. She was on her way to babysit at her boyfriend's house in Taylor, Michigan. She never arrived and has never been heard from again.

*(Nadine at the time of her disappearance)*

At the time of her disappearance, Nadine O'Dell had blonde hair, stood 5'1", and weighed 105 pounds. She was last seen wearing faded baggy blue jeans, a white t-shirt, and her boyfriend's Taylor High School Class of 1976 ring on a necklace. The ring is white gold with a blue stone, a ram's head, and the number 76 or

1976. She is Caucasian with green eyes. As of this writing, she is sixty years old.

If you have any information regarding this case, you are urged to call the Inkster Police Department at 313-563-9850.

## Aaron Mitchell Anderson

One year old Aaron Mitchell Anderson was last seen playing in his family's yard in Pine City, Minnesota at approximately 4:30pm on April 7, 1989. His mother left him unattended for a couple of minutes and he disappeared. An extensive search turned up no signs of him. He has never been seen again.

*(Age Progression to 26)*

At the time of his disappearance, Aaron Anderson had an enlarged head with light brown hair, stood 2'4", and weighed 32 pounds. He was last seen wearing a Pampers diaper, a half-red half-yellow sweatshirt with a puffy dinosaur on the front, light gray corduroy pants with red checkered flannel lining inside and cuffs, a gray ski jacket with red and green tabs, a white knit hat with green snowflakes and green earflaps, brown plastic snowmobile boots with nylon tops and liners, and gray socks. He is Caucasian with brown eyes and a small white-colored birthmark on the lower right side of his abdomen. As of this writing, he is thirty-one years old.

If you have any information regarding this case, you are urged to call the Pine County Sheriff's Office at 320-629-3930.

## Melissa Diane McGuinn

Seven month old Melissa Diane McGuinn was last seen on March 6, 1988 on Lamberton Street in Trenton, New Jersey. Her family lived with two roommates, Wanda Reed and her common-law husband. Wanda is mentally disabled and functions at the level of a four to seven year old child. On March 6th, she asked Melissa's mother for permission to take the baby girl for a walk. Her mother consented and the two left. Just eight minutes later, Wanda returned without Melissa. The child has never been seen again.

Wanda told multiple stories to explain Melissa's disappearance. First, she said an unidentified African-American man jumped out of a car, knocked her down, and took Melissa. Later, she claimed she dropped or threw the baby into the Delaware River. And then, she implicated a neighbor woman as having bought Melissa in exchange for drugs.

An extensive search of the river turned up no signs of the child, and it would have been difficult for Wanda to have walked the distance there and back in the eight-minute time frame. The neighbor that Wanda claimed to have bought Melissa denied any involvement and was cooperative with the investigation, as were Melissa's parents.

The night before Melissa's disappearance, there was a party at the house and several of the guests paid more attention to Melissa than to Wanda's two month old son. Because of this, some believe she may have harmed Melissa out of jealousy.

Two days after the little girl was last seen, Wanda was charged with kidnapping. She was found incompetent to stand trial, and the charges were dropped in December 1989. She was then sent to live in a facility for the mentally disabled.

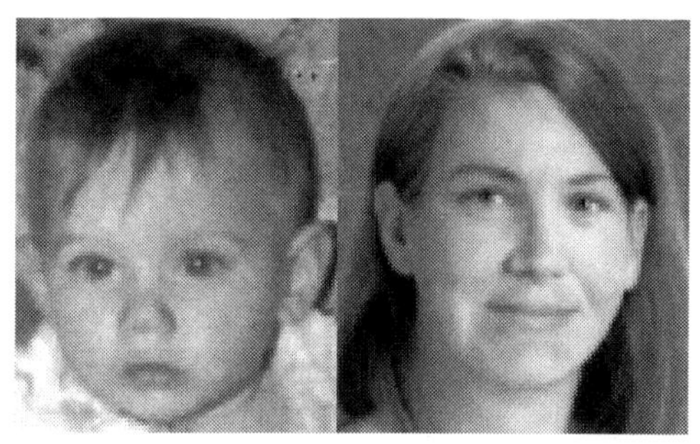

*(Age Progression to 24)*

At the time of her disappearance, Melissa McGuinn had blonde hair, was 28", and weighed 16 pounds. She was last seen wearing a dark hooded sweater, white floral quilted overalls, and pink socks. She is Caucasian with blue eyes and a pigmentation mark on her right tri-cep. As of this writing, she is thirty-one years old.

If you have any information regarding this case, you are urged to call the Trenton Police Department at 609-989-4144.

**Curtis MacKeever Fair**

Two year old Curtis MacKeever Fair was last seen playing in his neighbor's yard on 15th Avenue north in Nampa, Idaho at 12pm on November 15, 1980. He disappeared from the yard and has never been seen or heard from again. Few details are available in his case.

*(Age Progression to 33)*

At the time of his disappearance, Curtis Fair had light blonde hair, stood 2', and weighed 35 pounds. He was last seen wearing a blue hooded sweater, blue pants, and brown boots. He is Caucasian with green eyes, a half-inch scar under his chin, and a two-and-a-half inch scar running vertically up the small of his back. His nickname is Mack. As of this writing, he is thirty-nine years old.

If you have any information regarding this case, you are urged to call the Nampa Police Department at 208-465-2257.

## Jason Keith Cannon

Two year old Jason Keith Cannon was last seen on the front porch of his residence in Boise, Idaho at 2pm on March 16, 1983. His mother stepped inside only long enough to grab his jacket. When she came back out, he was gone. An extensive search turned up no sign of him, and he has never been seen again. Authorities believe he was abducted by a nonfamily member.

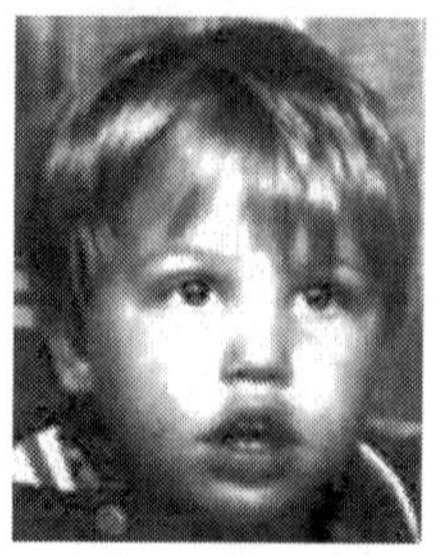

*(Jason at the time of his disappearance)*

At the time of his disappearance, Jason Cannon had dark blonde hair, stood 3', and weighed 37 pounds. He was last seen wearing a blue and yellow shirt, blue bib overalls, and black sneakers. He is Caucasian with brown eyes, a one-inch scar over his eye, and two moles on his neck. As of this writing, he is thirty-eight years old.

If you have any information regarding this case, you are urged to call the Boise Police Department at 208-377-6606 or 208-377-6500.

## Sarah Elizabeth Avon

Six year old Sarah Elizabeth Avon was last seen with her sister at the end of Richards Street in Joliet, Illinois on July 21, 1981.The girls met friends at that location, but Sarah walked away from the group after having an argument with another child. Her family reported her missing at approximately 9pm that night. She has never been seen or heard from again.

*(Age Progression to 38)*

At the time of her disappearance, Sarah Avon had blonde hair, stood 4', and weighed 75 pounds. She was last seen wearing a Joliet District Soccer t-shirt, blue jogging pants with red and white stripes, and blue sneakers with a white stripe. She is Caucasian with brown eyes. As of this writing, she is forty-three years old.

If you have any information regarding this case, you are urged to call the Will County Sheriff's Office at 815-727-8574.

## Tricia J. Kellett

Eight year old Tricia J. Kellett left her family's Uptown apartment in Chicago, Illinois after school on May 7, 1982 and went to play with friends in the street. She was last seen talking to an unidentified man shortly before she went missing.

Witnesses told investigators that they saw the man pull Tricia into a blue four-door 1979 Dodge or Pontiac car. The vehicle was described as having a damaged front passenger door with a license plate beginning with the letters Q and R.

Her mother realized she was missing at 4pm, and the family started looking for her. Her mother called police a few times that evening, but they didn't join in on the search until 10pm. Tricia has never been seen or heard from again. The man has never been identified.

*(Age Progression to 36)*

At the time of her disappearance, Tricia Kellett had blonde hair, a space between her upper front teeth, stood 4', and weighed 70 pounds. She was last seen wearing a blue long-sleeve sweater, blue jeans, and brown shoes. She is Caucasian with hazel eyes. She had previously broken her left wrist and fractured her skull. As of this writing, she is forty-five years old.

If you have any information regarding this case, you are urged to call the Chicago Police Department at 312-744-8266.

## Diamond Yvette Bradley & Tionda Z. Bradley

Three year old Diamond Yvette Bradley and her sister, ten year old Tionda Z. Bradley, were last seen at their home on South Lake Park Avenue in Chicago, Illinois on July 6, 2001. When their mother left for work at approximately 6:30am, the girls were at home. When she returned home around 11am, they were gone.

Tionda had left a note saying they were going to walk to school and to the store. Tionda was enrolled in summer classes at Doolittle Elementary School, but was absent that day. Neither Diamond nor Tionda have ever been seen or heard from again.

The girls' mother is not being called a suspect, although authorities say she has not been cooperative with the investigation. Their grandmother took a polygraph and passed. Police believe Tionda would have contacted her loved ones by now if she could. They think both children are either deceased or have been taken out of the country.

*(Diamond's Age Progression to 19)*

At the time of her disappearance, Diamond Bradley had black hair braided in the back with four ponytails, stood 3', and weighed 40 pounds. She was last seen wearing violet and purple ponytail holders in her hair. She is African-American with brown eyes and a scar on the left side of her hairline. As of this writing, she is twenty years old.

*(Tionda's Age Progression to 26)*

At the time of her disappearance, Tionda Bradley had brown hair worn in long ponytails, stood 4'2", and weighed 70 pounds. She is African-American with brown eyes and a quarter-size burn scar on her left forearm. As of this writing, she is twenty-seven years old.

If you have any information regarding this case, you are urged to call one of the following numbers:

*Chicago Police Department at 312-745-6007*

*Federal Bureau of Investigation (FBI) Chicago Office at 312-431-1333*

## Timothy Jacob Davison

Four year old Timothy Jacob Davison lived with his aunt and two brothers on north Charles Street in Decatur, Illinois in 1985. His parents lived in Winter Haven, Florida and were going through a divorce. His aunt stated she took Timothy and three other children to the Brentwood Shopping Center on north Water Street on October 15, 1985. She left him unattended and asleep in her unlocked red 1981 Dodge Omni at approximately 12pm and took the other children with her inside the Kroger grocery store to shop. When they returned to the parking lot half an hour later, Timothy was gone.

Later, a witness said they thought they saw him getting into a black two-door 1978 or 1979 Oldsmobile Cutlass with Indiana plates. Timothy has never been seen or heard from again.

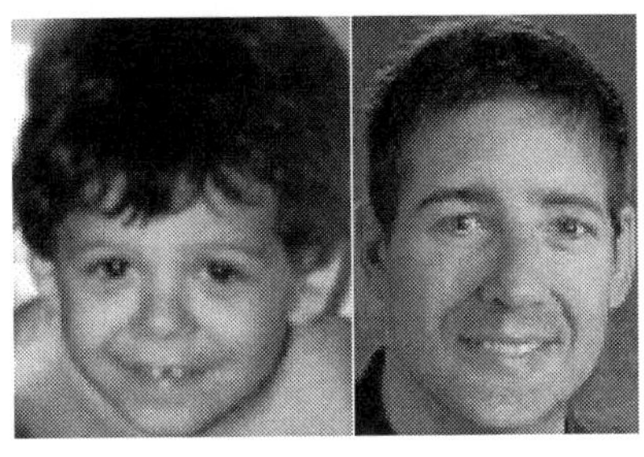

*(Age Progression to 31)*

At the time of his disappearance, Timothy Davison had brown hair, was missing his two upper front teeth, stood 3'4", and weighed 40 pounds. He had a speech impediment at the time. He was last seen wearing a light blue windbreaker, blue jeans, white sneakers, and a black baseball cap. He is Caucasian with brown eyes. His nickname is TJ. As of this writing, he is thirty-seven years old.

If you have any information regarding this case, you are urged to call the Decatur Police Department at 217-424-2738.

**Kelly Juanita Staples**

Six year old Kelly Juanita Staples was last seen walking to her elementary school in the area of 73rd Street and Merrill Avenue during the morning hours of January 8, 1980 in Chicago, Illinois. The school was only a few blocks away from her home, but she never arrived and has never been heard from again. Authorities believe she was abducted.

*(Age Progression to 41)*

At the time of her disappearance, Kelly Staples had black hair, stood 3', and weighed 42 pounds. She was last seen wearing a brown and white striped cap, a brown scarf, a red plaid coat, blue jeans, and blue rubber boots. She is African-American with brown eyes and a birthmark on the left side of her chest. As of this writing, she is forty-five years old.

If you have any information regarding this case, you are urged to call the Chicago Police Department at 312-744-8385.

## Vinyette Trudy Teague

One year old Vinyette Trudy Teague was last seen playing in the seventh-floor hallway of the apartment building where her family and her grandparents lived. Her parents went out to a drive-in movie and left her in the care of her grandmother at 9pm on June 25, 1983. At approximately 9:30pm, her grandmother left her alone in the hallway and went inside her apartment to answer the phone. When she returned, Vinyette was gone. When her parents returned at 3am, they called the police. Vinyette has never been seen or heard from again, and investigators believe she was abducted.

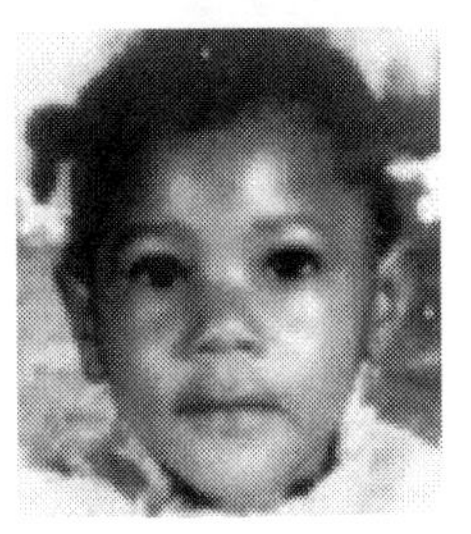

*(Vinyette at the time of her disappearance)*

At the time of her disappearance, Vinyette Teague had black hair styled in short braids, stood 2'8", and weighed 27 pounds. She was last seen wearing a multicolored striped tank top, brown and yellow floral pants, and no shoes or socks. She is African-American with brown eyes. Her nickname is Yinny. As of this writing, she is thirty-six years old.

If you have any information regarding this case, you are urged to call the Chicago Police Department at 312-744-8385.

## Tanner Lucas Skelton, Alexander William Skelton & Andrew Ryan Skelton

Five year old Tanner Lucas Skelton and his brothers, seven year old Alexander William Skelton and nine year old Andrew Ryan Skelton, were with their father, John Skelton, for a court-ordered visitation over Thanksgiving 2010. On November 26th, John attempted to hang himself, but survived and was hospitalized. He stated he gave the boys to a woman named Joann Taylor, whom he had met on the internet several years before. He claimed to have instructed her to return the boys to their mother. He said he did this because he planned to commit suicide, and he didn't want the boys to see it. He said that Joann was married to a pastor named Mark, drove a white or silver minivan, and lived in either Hillsdale or Jackson County, Michigan.

An Amber Alert was issued for the boys. Investigators could find no evidence that Joann Taylor even existed. They announced that they believed the boys were in 'grave danger', and that John's story about Joann was false and something else had caused the boys' disappearances. Later, they stated they were investigating the boys' disappearances as homicides, although none of their remains have been found.

John has always been the prime suspect. His blue Dodge Caravan with Michigan plates 9JQH93 was seen on the Ohio Turnpike, along the Michigan-Ohio border, between 4pm and 7am on November 26th. Anyone who saw his van there that day is urged to call authorities.

Following John's release from the psychiatric hospital, he was immediately arrested and jailed under suicide watch. He was eventually extradited to Michigan and charged with three counts of felony parental kidnapping, three counts of kidnapping, and three counts of false imprisonment. At a court hearing in December 2010, John changed his story and said that his sons were in the care of an organization, which he refused to name.

The boys' parents were in the middle of a bitter custody battle at the time of their disappearances. John had asked the court to sever their mother's rights, but the judge refused to do so. John claimed their mother was abusing them, but authorities could find no evidence of abuse.

In July 2011, John took a plea deal with prosecutors and pleaded no contest to three counts of false imprisonment. The kidnapping charges were dropped. He was sentenced to ten to fifteen years in prison. He stated his children are alive but will never be returned as long as their mother has custody of them. His relatives do not believe he would have harmed his sons.

*(Tanner's Age Progression to 11)*

At the time of his disappearance, Tanner Skelton had blonde hair, stood 3'6", and weighed 40 pounds. He was last seen wearing camouflage pajama pants and a Scooby-Doo shirt. He is Caucasian with blue eyes. As of this writing, he is twelve years old.

*(Alexander's Age Progression to 13)*

At the time of his disappearance, Alexander Skelton had brown hair, wore eyeglasses, stood 3'9", and weighed 45 pounds. He was last seen wearing black pajama pants and a gray shirt. He is Caucasian with brown eyes and scars on his chin and near his hairline. His nickname is Alex. As of this writing, he is fourteen years old.

*(Andrew's Age Progression to 15)*

At the time of his disappearance, Andrew Skelton had brown hair, stood 4'1", and weighed 57 pounds. He was last seen wearing brown pajamas with orange trim. He is Caucasian with brown eyes. As of this writing, he is sixteen years old.

There is a large reward for information leading to the brothers' whereabouts. If you have any information regarding this case, you are urged to call the Morenci Police Department at 517-458-7104.

## Kaylah Neveah Hunter & Kristian Dejuan Justice

Six year old Kaylah Neveah Hunter, her half-brother, seven month old Kristian Dejuan Justice, and their mother, Alicia Fox, disappeared from Detroit, Michigan on May 24, 2014. They had been living with Kristian's father, Erin Justice, on Ardmore Street, but had moved out shortly before they went missing. On June 6th, they were reported missing after Kaylah missed her kindergarten graduation.

On June 9th, Alicia's badly decomposed body was found wrapped in a blanket and dumped in the basement of a vacant house on Penrod Street on the west side of Detroit. She had been shot twice in the head.

Erin was arrested in Atlanta, Georgia on June 11th and charged with first-degree murder in Alicia's case. Authorities found a bullet hole in the wall and blood splatter on the ceiling of an upstairs bedroom inside the Ardmore Street residence. They also determined that Erin had rented a U-Haul and drove it 300 miles between May 27th and 29th, without ever leaving Detroit. He then took a flight to Atlanta. He also sold Alicia's Chevrolet Impala at a junkyard in Taylor, Michigan. The family's white pit bull, that was very protective of the children, was found running loose on West End and Vanderbilt Streets in Detroit on June 19th. It had strangulation marks around its neck and cigarette burns on its face and chest. It was picked up by Southwest Animal Group, given veterinary treatment, and placed in a foster home.

Erin reached a plea deal with the prosecution in September 2015, pleading guilty to second-degree murder in Alicia's case and a felony weapons charge. He was sentenced to forty-five to eighty years in prison.

Due to the circumstances, Kaylah and Kristian are considered to be in grave danger. It is possible they are somewhere in the Atlanta area.

*(Kaylah at the time of her disappearance)*

At the time of her disappearance, Kaylah Hunter had brown hair, stood 4'5", and weighed 65 pounds. She is African-American with brown eyes. She may wear her hair in cornrows. As of this writing, she is ten years old.

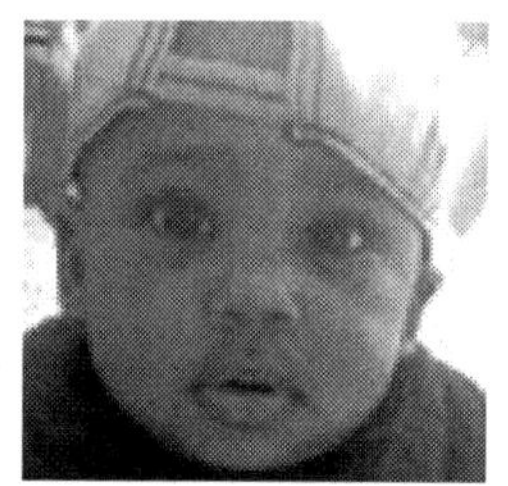

*(Kristian at the time of his disappearance)*

At the time of his disappearance, Kristian Justice had brown hair, was 24", and weighed 17 pounds. He is African-American with brown eyes. As of this writing, he is four years old.

If you have any information regarding this case, you are urged to call the Detroit Police Department at 313-596-5600.

## Tangena Hussain

Two year old Tangena Hussain was last seen at a Marathon gas station on Greenfield Road in Detroit,

Michigan on October 2, 2008. She was with her mother's boyfriend, who had stopped there to buy some juice and gum. He left Tangena in his red four-door 1997 Geo Prism and went into the store at 9:02pm. He came out at 9:06pm and the little girl was gone. Surveillance video from inside the store confirmed the times, but there were no cameras outside where the car had been parked.

The boyfriend said the car had been locked when he left Tangena inside. He didn't call the police or search for her at the time, however. Instead he drove to the nearby Northland Mall to pick up her mother from work. The couple then returned to the store and filed a missing person report with police at 9:30pm. Tangena has never been seen again.

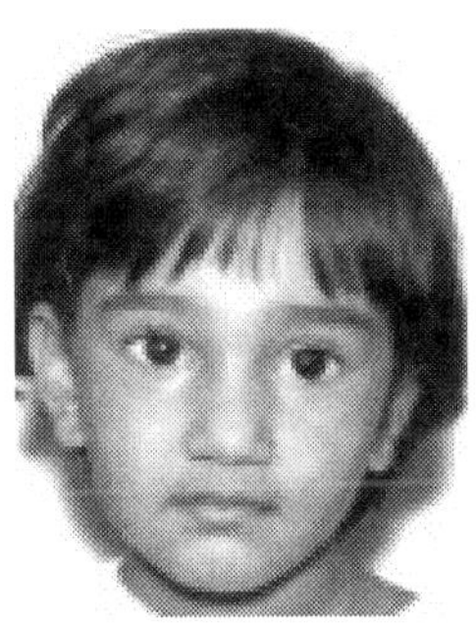

*(Tangena at the time of her disappearance)*

At the time of her disappearance, Tangena Hussain had black hair, stood 3'2", and weighed 34 pounds. She was last seen wearing a long-sleeve brown shirt with a cartoon character on the front, white nylon cargo pants with multiple pockets, and gold-colored sandals. She is Asian with brown eyes and a scar on her upper lip. She is of Bangladeshi descent. As of this writing, she is twelve years old.

If you have any information regarding this case, you are urged to call the Detroit Police Department at 313-596-1800.

## Shannon Marie Sherrill

Six year old Shannon Marie Sherrill was last seen at her family's mobile home on Plum Street in Thorntown, Indiana on October 15, 1986. She was playing hide-and-seek with ten other children at approximately 1:30pm. She went behind the mobile home and has never been seen or heard from again.

An extensive search of the area turned up no clues as to her whereabouts. No one saw her leave the yard. Bloodhounds tracked her scent to a nearby cornfield and cemetery, but then lost the trail.

She lived with her mother and younger brother and was a kindergarten student at Thorntown Elementary School at the time. Both her parents passed polygraph tests and are not considered suspects in her case.

*(Age Progression to 30)*

At the time of her disappearance, Shannon Sherrill had brown hair, stood 3', and weighed 30 pounds. She was last seen wearing a white sundress with blue trim and no socks or shoes. She is Caucasian with blue eyes, pierced ears, and a four-inch scar on her abdomen. As of this writing, she is thirty-eight years old.

If you have any information regarding this case, you are urged to call one of the following numbers:

*Thorntown Police Department at 317-436-7677*

*Federal Bureau of Investigation (FBI) at 1-202-324-3000*

## Beverly Ward

Thirteen year old Beverly Ward was last seen at her home on west 11th Street in Junction City, Kansas on July 4, 1978. Her friend was staying the night and was sleeping in another bed in the same room. In the early morning hours, the household and Beverly's friend woke up to watch a disturbance across the street. Once the commotion was over, they realized Beverly was gone.

The screen in the bedroom window had been cut and removed. None of her clothes or the money she had been saving was gone. Authorities believe someone abducted her from her bedroom between 3am and 5am. She has never been heard from again.

*(Beverly at the time of her disappearance)*

At the time of her disappearance, Beverly Ward had black hair, stood 4'8", and weighed 54 pounds. She was last seen wearing a green nightgown. She is African-American with brown eyes. As of this writing, she is fifty-three years old.

If you have any information regarding this case, you are urged to call the Junction City Police Department at 785-762-5912.

## Marc James-Warren Allen II

Thirteen year old Marc James-Warren Allen II was last seen in Des Moines, Iowa on March 29, 1986. He told his mother he was going to walk to a friend's house down the street and possibly go see a movie. He asked her to save some pizza for him to eat when he got back. He never arrived at his friend's house, but his mother didn't realize he was missing until the next morning. After she called his grandmother and his friends and none of them had seen him, she called the police. But thinking he was a runaway, they refused to investigate until forty-eight hours had passed. He has never been seen or heard from again. His case is now classified as an abduction.

*(Age Progression to 43)*

At the time of his disappearance, Marc Allen II had brown hair, stood between 4'11" - 5', and weighed 90 pounds. He was last seen wearing a light blue t-shirt, blue denim shorts, white socks, and gray sneakers with Velcro fastenings. He is Caucasian with blue eyes and a small scar on the top of his head. As of this writing, he is forty-six years old.

If you have any information regarding this case, you are urged to call the Des Moines Police Department at 515-283-4811.

## Guy Howard Heckle

Eleven year old Guy Howard Heckle was reported missing to the Linn County Sheriff's Office in Cedar Rapids, Iowa late on February 3, 1973, after disappearing while on a Boy Scout camp-out near the Duane Arnold Energy Center. He was last seen at approximately 8pm while playing a game of Capture the Flag with other troop members. He wasn't missed until bed-check that evening. Then troop members spent ninety minutes searching for him before contacting police.

On February 4th, a searcher found his blue parka snagged on a log along the river's east bank. That same day, about 500 people searched on foot for Guy, along with others via helicopter, airplane, all-terrain vehicles, and on horseback. On February 5th, bloodhounds and a special search and rescue team from California joined in on search efforts. Investigators theorized he could have slipped into the river and drown, but admitted it was possible that something else led to his disappearance. His family believes foul play may have been involved.

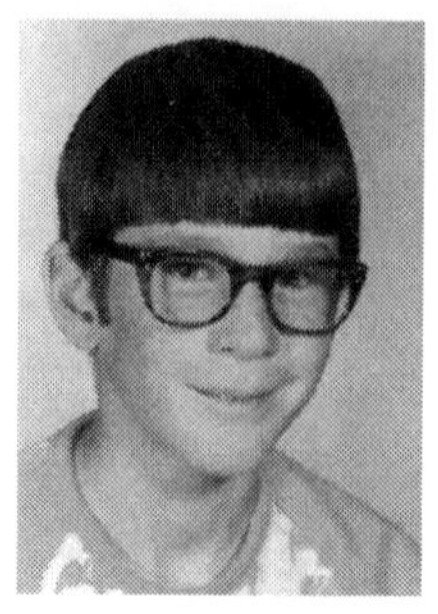

*(Guy at the time of his disappearance)*

At the time of his disappearance, Guy Heckle had brown hair, stood 4'5", and weighed 80 pounds. He was last seen wearing a light blue nylon quilted parka, a Boy Scouts shirt, striped multicolored jeans, and Chukka boots. He is Caucasian with hazel eyes. As of this writing, he is fifty-six years old.

If you have any information regarding this case, you are urged to call one of the following numbers:

*Linn County Sheriff's Office at 319-892-6100*

*Des Moines Police Department at 515-283-4800*

## Jackie Dene Hay

Five year old Jackie Dene Hay was last seen walking away from the Colfax and Golf Park in Topeka, Kansas at 4pm on September 12, 1981. Her family discovered she was missing shortly thereafter. She has never been seen again. Authorities did not start searching for her until four hours had passed. It is now believed she was most likely abducted.

*(Jackie at the time of her disappearance)*

At the time of her disappearance, Jackie Hay had blonde hair cut in a Dutch-boy style, freckles across the bridge of her nose, a small cavity between her upper front teeth, stood 3'6", and weighed 45 pounds. She was last seen wearing blue pants and a white knit shirt with orange and lavender flowers. She is Caucasian with blue eyes and a small scar along her right eyebrow. As of this writing, she is forty-two years old.

If you have any information regarding this case, you are urged to call the Topeka Police Department at 785-368-9551.

## Sidney Keara Smith, Monique Rae Smith & Jennifer Dawn Lancaster

One year old Sidney Keara Smith, her one month old sister, Monique Rae Smith, and their mother, eighteen year old Jennifer Dawn Lancaster, were last seen at approximately 8pm in Topeka, Kansas on May 12, 2000. They left their home to go to a male acquaintance's home, but never arrived and have never been heard from again. Their vehicle was found abandoned at an apartment complex a week later.

*(Sidney's Age Progression to 18)*

At the time of her disappearance, Sidney Smith had black hair, was 2'6", and weighed 22 pounds. She is Biracial (African-American/Caucasian) with brown eyes. As of this writing, she is nineteen years old.

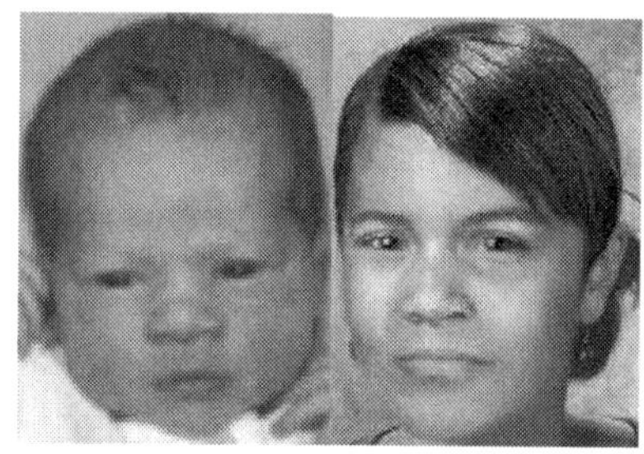

*(Monique's Age Progression to 16)*

At the time of her disappearance, Monique Smith had black hair, was 22", and weighed 9 pounds. She is Biracial (African-American/Caucasian) with brown eyes. As of this writing, she is eighteen years old.

*(Jennifer at the time of her disappearance)*

At the time of her disappearance, Jennifer Lancaster had blonde hair, stood 5'5", and weighed 100 pounds. She was last seen wearing a blue and white shirt, denim shorts, sandals, diamond stud earrings, and gold hoop earrings. She is Caucasian with blue eyes, double-pierced ears, a piercing in her right eyebrow, a tattoo of the words low rider in green and black ink on her left upper arm, and another unknown tattoo on her lower back. As of this writing, she is thirty-seven years old.

If you have any information regarding this case, you are urged to call the Topeka Police Department at 785-368-9400.

## Eugene Wade Martin

Thirteen year old Eugene Wade Martin was last seen between 5:30am and 6am on August 12, 1984 in Des Moines, Iowa. He was preparing to begin his morning paper route at the time. He normally delivered the papers with his older stepbrother, but the older boy was not with him that day. Witnesses saw Eugene carrying on a friendly conversation with a man in his thirties between 5am and 5:15am at southwest 12th Street and Highview Drive. The man has never been identified. Eugene's boss called his home at approximately 7:15am to report that his newspaper sack had not been retrieved from the corner of southwest 14th and Highview Streets. His boss called back fifteen minutes later to report that the papers were still unclaimed. Eugene's father then called police. Eugene has never been seen or heard from again.

*(Age Progression to 39)*

At the time of his disappearance, Eugene Martin had brown hair, stood 5', and weighed 110 pounds. He was last seen wearing a gray and white striped t-shirt with red sleeves, blue jeans, and blue Trax sneakers with white diagonal stripes. He is Caucasian with brown eyes and a scar on his right knee. One of his wrists has a healed fracture. His nickname is Gene. As of this writing, he is forty-eight years old.

If you have any information regarding this case, you are urged to call the Des Moines Police Department at 515-283-4864.

## Rachel Geraldine Pratt

Fifteen year old Rachel Geraldine Pratt was last seen watching a movie inside her home in Garden City, Kansas at approximately 1am on January 16, 1995. She disappeared under suspicious circumstances and has never been heard from again.

She left all her personal belongings and clothes behind. Only her coat was missing. She was supposed to be a witness against her boyfriend, who was being prosecuted for unlawful sexual relations with her. He was nineteen at the time. Because Rachel disappeared before she could testify, the charges were dropped. She was pregnant and in her first trimester at the time. Authorities believe foul play was involved. Her boyfriend has never been ruled out as a suspect, but he maintains his innocence.

*(Age Progression to 35)*

At the time of her disappearance, Rachel Pratt had brown hair, wore contact lenses, stood 5'7", and weighed 125 pounds. She is Caucasian with brown eyes. As of this writing, she is thirty-nine years old.

If you have any information regarding this case, you are urged to call the Garden City Police Department at 620-276-1300.

## Jaquilla Evonne Scales

Four year old Jaquilla Evonne Scales was last seen in her bed in her Wichita, Kansas home on north Volutsia Street at approximately 12:30am on September 5, 2001. She was discovered missing at 3am. She has never been seen or heard from again.

There were no signs of forced entry, however, the back door could not be locked at the time due to a broken knob. The family's dog had not barked during the time Jaquilla went missing.

She lived with her mother, her two year old half-brother, two uncles, and her maternal grandmother at the time. Authorities are not sure if she was abducted or what exactly happened to her. Her mother believes she is still alive.

*(Age Progression to 15)*

At the time of her disappearance, Jaquilla Scales had black hair, decaying upper front teeth, stood 3', and weighed 40 pounds. She was last seen wearing a knee-length floral nightgown with tan hair barrettes. She is African-American with brown eyes, a brown birthmark on the left side of her face, and a scar on her upper right leg. As of this writing, she is twenty-one years old.

If you have any information regarding this case, you are urged to call the Wichita Police Department at 316-268-4646.

## Denise El-Mansura

Fifteen year old Denise El-Mansura was last seen in New Orleans, Louisiana on January 10, 1978. She was supposed to have lunch with her aunt, but never showed up. She has never been seen or heard from again.

Another girl from Denise's neighborhood went missing about six months before she did, and was later found murdered. But it is not known if the two cases are related or not.

*(Denise at the time of her disappearance)*

At the time of her disappearance, Denise El-Mansura had black hair, stood 5'4", and weighed 115 pounds. She is African-American with brown eyes. Her nickname is Dee Dee. As of this writing, she is fifty-six years old.

If you have any information regarding this case, you are urged to call the New Orleans Police Department at 504-658-5300.

## Corey Gilbert

Six year old Corey Gilbert was last seen at the Ten-to-Ten grocery store on Jefferson Highway in Jefferson, Louisiana at 12:30pm on December 16, 1984. He and another boy were playing an arcade game. The other boy looked away for a moment, and when he turned back around Corey was gone. He has never been seen again.

It was theorized that he may have fallen into the Mississippi River and drown, but his body has never been located. It is also possible he was abducted.

*(Corey at the time of his disappearance)*

At the time of his disappearance, Corey Gilbert had short black hair, was missing two bottom teeth, stood 4', and weighed 55 pounds. He was last seen wearing a royal blue muscle shirt or tank top, blue jeans, and either white sneakers with red and blue stripes or blue sneakers with red stripes. He is African-American with brown eyes. As of this writing, he is thirty-nine years old.

If you have any information regarding this case, you are urged to call the Jefferson Parish Sheriff's Office at 504-364-5300 or 504-349-5322.

## George Barksdale

Four year old George Barksdale was last seen playing on the steps of the United Church House of Prayer at Preston Street and Argyle Avenue in Baltimore, Maryland between 8pm and 9pm on April 21, 1969. He has never been seen or heard from again, and authorities believe he was abducted.

*(Age Progression to 48)*

At the time of his disappearance, George Barksdale had black hair, stood 2'6", and weighed 35 pounds. He was last seen wearing a red white and blue pullover polo shirt, red or blue corduroy pants, and black sneakers with red stripes on the bottom. He is African-American with brown eyes and a birthmark on his left calf. His nickname is Sputnik. As of this writing, he is fifty-three years old.

If you have any information regarding this case, you are urged to call the Baltimore City Police Department at 443-984-7385, 443-984-7386, 443-984-7387, or 410-396-2359.

## Bob Louis Richard Boyes

Ten year old Bob Louis Richard Boyes was last seen in Port Republic, Maryland on December 26, 1968. He left a friend's house with his pet deer. The deer returned to their own home, but Bob has never been seen or heard from again.

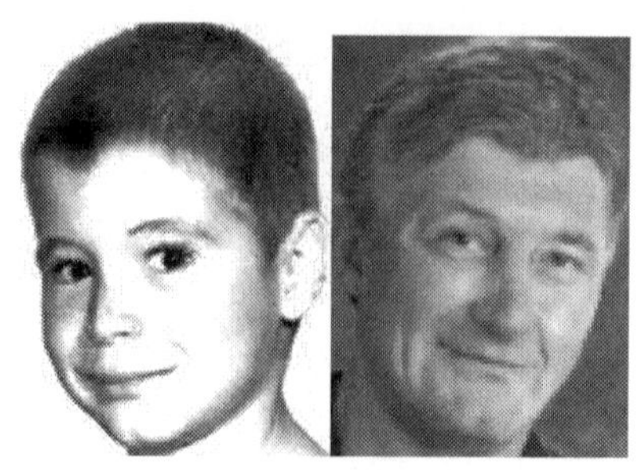

*(Age Progression to 52)*

At the time of his disappearance, Bob Boyes had brown hair, stood 4', and weighed 80 pounds. He was last seen wearing a dark blue hooded coat, dark-colored pants, a plaid shirt, and brown leather boots. He is Caucasian with brown eyes and a scar on his upper lip. As of this writing, he is sixty years old.

If you have any information regarding this case, you are urged to call the Maryland State Police Prince Frederick Barracks at 410-535-1400.

## Tiffany Michele Goines

Twelve year old Tiffany Michele Goines was last seen entering a red convertible near her family's apartment complex in Frederick, Maryland on December 5, 1987. She left her home at John Hanson Apartments on north Bentz Street that morning to visit a friend and run some errands for her neighbors. She has never been seen or heard from again, and the driver and vehicle have never been identified.

She was supposed to return home by 5pm, but she did not. Her mother began searching the neighborhood at 9pm, but due to procedures in place at the time she had to wait twenty-four hours to file a missing person report. Her mother believes she was abducted but is still alive.

*(Age Progression to 32)*

At the time of her disappearance, Tiffany Goines had black hair, wore large brown wire-framed eyeglasses, stood 5', and weighed 78 pounds. She was last seen wearing a blue jacket, a white sweatshirt, blue pants, brown gloves, a white belt, white socks, and white shoes without laces. She is African-American with brown eyes and has a lazy eye that drifts inward. As of this writing, she is forty-three years old.

If you have any information regarding this case, you are urged to call the Frederick Police Department at 301-600-2100.

## Douglas Charles Chapman

Three year old Douglas Charles Chapman was last seen playing in a sand pile approximately twenty-five yards in front of his family's mobile home on Alfred Gore Road in Alfred, Maine at 10:30am on June 2, 1971. His mother was inside talking on the telephone. When she went outside to check on him, he was gone. He has never been heard from again.

Police dogs tracked his scent through a field, past an apple orchard, onto a farm, and down the driveway to the main road. It is believed he was put into a vehicle at that location. No one in his family is considered a suspect in his case.

*(Age Progression to 48)*

At the time of his disappearance, Douglas Chapman had sandy brown hair, stood 3', and weighed 35 pounds. He was last seen wearing a red and blue plaid shirt, red or blue pants, and loafers. He is Caucasian with blue eyes and a mole on his right shoulder. His nickname is Dougie. As of this writing, he is fifty years old.

If you have any information regarding this case, you are urged to call the Maine State Police at 207-657-3030.

## Kurt Ronald Newton

Four year old Kurt Ronald Newton was last seen at the Natanis Point Campground in Chain of Ponds, Maine on September 1, 1975. He was camping with his parents, his older sister, and three other families from their hometown of Manchester, Maine. Kurt was riding his Big Wheel tricycle near the family's campsite when he disappeared between 10am and 10:30am. He has never been heard from again.

Later that morning, his tricycle was found at a dump site eight-tenths of a mile from his family's campsite. An extensive search of the surrounding woods involving bloodhounds and military helicopters turned up no clues as to his whereabouts. He is presumed to have been abducted.

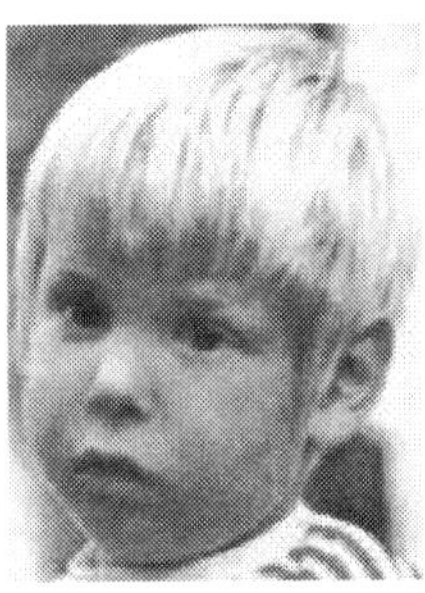

*(Kurt at the time of his disappearance)*

At the time of his disappearance, Kurt Newton had blonde hair, was 3'8", and weighed 45 pounds. He was last seen wearing a navy blue jacket with baseball emblems, a navy blue sweatshirt, a red jersey, red and black speckled corduroy pants, mismatched white socks, and dark brown high-top shoes. He is Caucasian with blue eyes. As of this writing, he is forty-seven years old.

If you have any information regarding this case, you are urged to call the Maine State Police at 207-289-2155.

## Jacob Gabriel Hoggle & Sarah Grace Hoggle

Two year old Jacob Gabriel Hoggle and his sister, three year old Sarah Grace Hoggle, were abducted by their non-custodial mother, Catherine Hoggle. Jacob was last seen at 4pm on September 7, 2014 when he and his mother supposedly went to get pizza. Catherine returned two hours later without her son, and claimed she had left him at a friend's house. Her family believed her, but the story was later determined to be false. The children's father arrived home from work at midnight and noticed Jacob wasn't in his bed, but assumed he had gotten in bed with one of his siblings. The next morning, their father realized only he and his oldest son were home. Sarah had last been seen at 9:30pm the night before. He started to call the police, but changed his mind when he saw Catherine drive up. She said she had taken their two youngest children to a day care center in Germantown, Maryland. He then took her to her day treatment program, where she was enrolled for treatment of being paranoid schizophrenic. She had been diagnosed before the children were born, and she was not supposed to be left alone with them. However, at the time of their youngest children's disappearances she had been showing signs of improvement in managing her illness.

Jacob and Sarah's father picked up their mother from the day treatment program at 2pm and suggested they pick up the children from day care. Catherine began to be evasive in answering his questions, and he told her he was going to the police. A few minutes later, they stopped at a Chick-fil-A restaurant and Catherine disappeared.

Four days later, Catherine was found alive, but alone, walking down the street in Germantown, Maryland, wearing the same clothes she had been wearing when she left. When police asked where Sarah and Jacob were, she first said she left them with a high school friend named Erin, but then she lead them to a playground in Germantown and said she abandoned both children there. She was arrested and charged with two counts of parental abduction, neglect, and hindering a police investigation. She was then committed to a maximum-security psychiatric hospital in Jessup, Maryland.

Doctors there found her incompetent to stand trial. In September 2017, Catherine was charged with two counts of murder, but she has to be deemed competent before she can stand trial. Police believe she murdered her children, but their remains have never been found. She has told the hospital staff that her children are safe, but continues to refuse to reveal their location.

*(Jacob's Age Progression to 4)*

At the time of his disappearance, Jacob Hoggle had light brown hair, stood 3', and weighed 30 pounds. He was last seen wearing a white shirt and blue shorts. He is Biracial (African-American/Caucasian) with brown eyes. As of this writing, he is six years old.

*(Sarah's Age Progression to 6)*

At the time of her disappearance, Sarah Hoggle had brown hair, stood 3'6", and weighed 40 pounds. She was last seen wearing a pink tank top and blue shorts. She is Biracial (African-American/Caucasian) with brown eyes. As of this writing, she is seven years old.

If you have any information regarding this case, you are urged to call one of the following numbers:

*Montgomery County Police Department at 301-279-8000*

*Federal Bureau of Investigation (FBI) at 240-773-5400*

## Melody McCoy

Twelve year old Melody McCoy was last seen on Fremont Avenue in Baltimore, Maryland in an apartment in a now-demolished high-rise at approximately 7pm on December 1, 1991. She left her own coat behind and borrowed her male friend's coat. Her bicycle, which had a flat tire, was also left behind at her friend's home. She has never been seen or heard from again.

Her mother initially thought she was staying with an aunt, but realized she was missing when she did not show up for school on December 2$^{nd}$. She is believed to have been abducted.

She resided on north Mount Street in west Baltimore at the time. She was a sixth grader at Harlem Park Elementary School.

*(Age Progression to 36)*

At the time of her disappearance, Melody McCoy had shoulder-length brown hair, stood 5', and weighed 100 pounds. She was last seen wearing a boy's waist-length sky blue coat with puffy sleeves, blue jeans, a blue sweatshirt, yellow socks, and either red Reebok sneakers or white sneakers. She is African-American with brown eyes and a mole on her right cheek. As of this writing, she is thirty-eight years old.

If you have any information regarding this case, you are urged to call the Baltimore City Police Department at 443-984-7114 or 410-396-2359.

## Solomon Gomile Rose III

Three year old Solomon Gomile Rose III was last seen at the Mondawmin Shopping Center in Baltimore, Maryland on April 1, 1972. His mother had taken him and her seven year old niece to the shopping center and left them unattended for a few minutes while she went to cash a check. When she returned, she found her niece watching television at Sears, but Solomon was gone. He has never been seen or heard from again.

*(Age Progression to 48)*

At the time of his disappearance, Solomon Rose III had black hair cut in a short Afro, stood 3', and weighed 38 pounds. He was last seen wearing a navy blue turtleneck, a dark brown smooth faux fur coat, blue and white checkered pants, and tan buck shoes. He is African-American with brown eyes. His nickname is Poon. As of this writing, she is forty-nine years old.

If you have any information regarding this case, you are urged to call the Baltimore City Police Department at 410-396-2640.

## Jesus De La Cruz

Six year old Jesus De La Cruz was last seen at approximately 6pm on September 28, 1996, walking with a nine year old male friend on Park Street in the Commons area of Lynn, Massachusetts. Jesus was pushing his pink Huffy bicycle, which had two flat tires. He was on his way home from playing in Bennett Circle. Jesus never returned home and has never been seen again.

His friend told police they were approached by a Caucasian man in his twenties or thirties with shoulder-length black hair walking a shepherd/collie dog with one white eye and one brown eye. His friend said the man lured Jesus away by promising him a new bicycle.

Authorities later identified the man as a twenty-six year old who lived just around the corner from Jesus' home in 1996. He owned a dog named Peaches that matched the description. The man called in sick to work on the evening of Jesus' abduction, and duct tape and handcuffs were found inside his apartment. In mid-October, the man was charged with a parole violation, motor vehicle offenses, and possession of stolen property. But he has never been charged in connection with Jesus' abduction.

The Massachusetts Department of Social Services accused Jesus' mother of neglect in the weeks following his disappearance. The agency said that it was because she did not report her son as a missing child until six hours after his apparent abduction. Others speculated that the child was abducted as the result of theorized drug use by his family members. His mother, however, has denied any wrongdoing, and maintains that the claims were the result of racism against Hispanics.

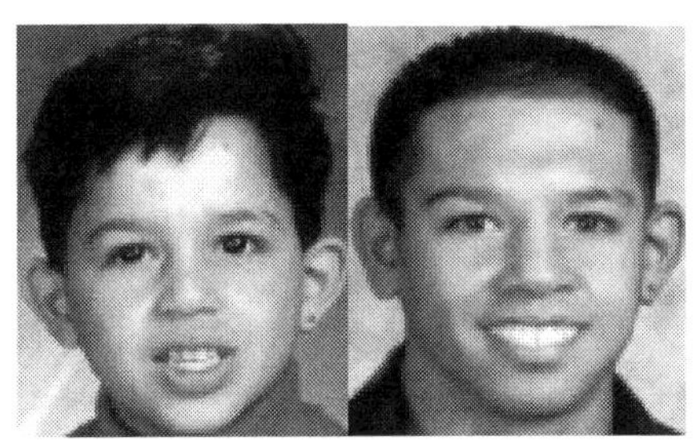

*(Age Progression to 19)*

At the time of his disappearance, Jesus De La Cruz had short brown hair, stood 4'6", and weighed 60 pounds. He was last seen wearing a white t-shirt, blue jeans, and either brown and yellow boots or high-top shoes. He is Hispanic with brown eyes, a scar above his left eye, birthmarks on his left calf and on the left side of his forehead, and his left ear is pierced. As of this writing, he is twenty-eight years old.

If you have any information regarding this case, you are urged to call of the following numbers:

*Lynn Police Department at 781-595-2000*

*Massachusetts State Police at 781-396-0100*

## Giovanni Ernesto Gonzalez

Five year old Giovanni Ernesto Gonzalez was dropped off in the area of Brightwood Terrace in Lynn, Massachusetts at 4pm on August 15, 2008 for a scheduled weekend visitation with his father, Ernesto Gonzalez Jr. He had a Transformers backpack with clothes and toys inside it. He has never been heard from again.

His mother was unable to reach either Giovanni or Ernesto by phone all weekend. When she went to pick up her son, no one answered the door at Ernesto's apartment. She called the police, who came and got inside. Ernesto was there, but Giovanni was not. His toys were inside the apartment, but his backpack and clothes were gone.

The last known sighting of Giovanni was at the Lynn Behavioral Clinic on Union Street between 11am and 12:30pm on August 16th, when he accompanied his father to a doctor's appointment.

When questioned, Ernesto said he wasn't aware of any scheduled visit with his son and had not seen him since August 10th, which was false. Ernesto's neighbors said they had heard a child's voice coming from his apartment later in the day of August 16th.

On August 18th, Ernesto was arrested and charged with child endangerment. Several days later, police searched his apartment and seized several items, including knives, a bloodstained bottle of household cleaner, and a bloodstained mop that had been cleaned with bleach. However, testing later determined the blood was not Giovanni's.

In November 2008, in an interview with the Boston Globe, Ernesto claimed he had stabbed his son to death, dismembered the body, and disposed of the parts in trash bins around Lynn. Authorities, however, do not believe his confession. There was no evidence in his apartment to corroborate his story.

In December 2008, the child endangerment charge against Ernesto was dropped, and he was instead charged with parental kidnapping and misleading police. The parental kidnapping charge was dismissed in June 2011, but restored a year later. In November 2011, he was additionally charged with assaulting a cellmate in jail. Ernesto was declared incompetent to stand trial in October 2013. Both Giovanni's mother and police believe Giovanni is still alive and that his father hid him.

*(Age Progression to 12)*

At the time of his disappearance, Giovanni Gonzalez had brown hair, stood 4'1", and weighed 40 pounds. He was last seen wearing a red t-shirt, blue jeans, black Spiderman sandals, and a braided silver chain necklace. His is Hispanic with brown eyes, a small scar above his right eyebrow, a small birthmark on the inside of his left ankle, and a faded skin pigmentation mark on the lower right side of his chest. He is of Puerto Rican descent. As of this writing, he is fifteen years old.

If you have any information regarding this case, you are urged to call the Lynn Police Department at 781-595-2000.

## Susan Rhonda Labbe

Seventeen year old Susan Rhonda Labbe was last seen on August 8, 1974 on Andover Street in Lawrence, Massachusetts. She had visited her family there; and she decided to hitchhike back home to Lowell, Massachusetts, where she lived in an apartment with her boyfriend. She never arrived home and has never been heard from again.

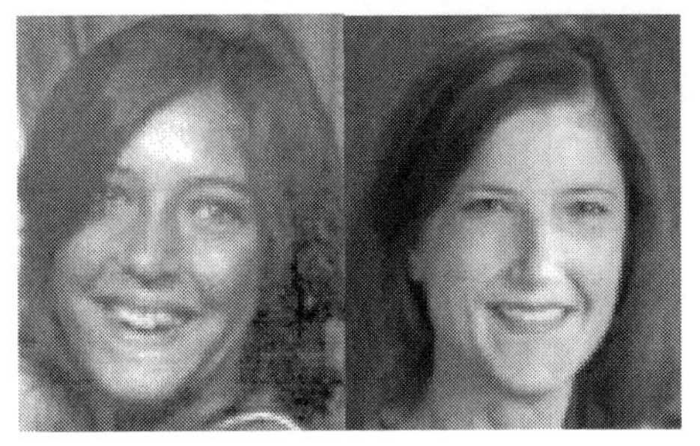

*(Age Progression to 60)*

At the time of her disappearance, Susan Labbe had brown hair, stood 5'5", and weighed 120 pounds. She was last seen wearing a white blouse and blue dungarees. She was carrying a black suede handbag. She is Caucasian with green eyes. She goes by her middle name. As of this writing, she is sixty-one years old.

If you have any information regarding this case, you are urged to call the Billerica Police Department at 978-670-6000 or 978-671-0900.

## Wilfredo Torres

Twelve year old Wilfredo Torres was last seen when he went out looking for bottles near his family's apartment on Columbia Road in the Uphams Corner neighborhood of Dorchester, Massachusetts at 6:30pm on May 9, 1983. An extensive search turned up no sign of him, and he has never been heard from again.

*(Wilfredo at the time of his disappearance)*

At the time of his disappearance, Wilfredo had brown hair, stood 4', and weighed 70 pounds. He was last seen wearing a blue jacket, white shirt, and gray pants. His is Hispanic with brown eyes. He is of Puerto Rican descent and speaks Spanish. He has a learning disability. As of this writing, he is forty-eight years old.

If you have any information regarding this case, you are urged to call the Boston Police Department at 617-343-4200.

## Catherine Barbara Davidson

Six year old Catherine Barbara Davidson was last seen on September 1, 1973 at Warren Dunes State Park in Sawyer, Michigan. She and her family had traveled there from Chicago, Illinois for a picnic. While their parents unpacked the car, Catherine and her five older siblings explored Painterville Creek, which empties into Lake Michigan. The other children returned, but Catherine has never been seen again. An extensive search of the area turned up only a pair of green panties, but it could not be established for sure whether or not they were Catherine's.

*(Catherine at the time of her disappearance)*

At the time of her disappearance, Catherine Davidson had black hair braided in tight rows, stood 3'10", and weighed 70 pounds. She was last seen wearing a white blouse, blue shorts, and white sandals. She is African-American with brown eyes. Her nickname is Cathy. As of this writing, she is fifty-one years old.

If you have any information regarding this case, you are urged to call the Michigan State Police at 296-683-4411.

## Brian Grocki

Fourteen year old Brian Grocki was last seen in Trenton, Michigan on October 16, 1990. He has never been heard from again. His friend first claimed Brian left his residence between midnight and 1am to go home. The friend later changed his story and said that he and Brian had planned to run away. His parents do not believe he left of his own accord, however, because he left all of his belongings behind. Foul play is suspected. Authorities have several persons of interest in his case, including some people who were close to his own age in 1990 and are now grown.

*(Brian at the time of his disappearance)*

At the time of his disappearance, Brian Grocki had blonde hair, stood 5'6", and weighed 125 pounds. He was last seen wearing a jacket, a quilted plaid shirt, blue jeans, and white sneakers. He is Caucasian with green eyes, a two-inch scar on his chin underneath his lip, a scar on his right wrist, and a burn scar on his right leg. His right leg was broken when he was a toddler. He has been diagnosed with a developmental disability related to hand-eye coordination. As of this writing, he is forty-two years old.

If you have any information regarding this case, you are urged to call the Huron Township Police Department at 734-753-4400.

## Adele Marie Wells

Seven year old Adele Marie Wells was last seen in Flint, Michigan on November 21, 1958. She had stayed home that morning because she had a cold. In the afternoon, however, she decided to go to school. She stopped at her grandmother's home, which was just a few blocks from her school. She was last seen leaving her grandmother's residence. She never arrived at school and has never been heard from again.

Police stated they had reliable witness statements of a man carrying a young girl to a dirty black Chevrolet, which was near the creek on Lewis Street. The man is described as a light-skinned African-American wearing a gray coat and red socks. He has never been identified. Other children who attended the same school as Adele said the driver of a car fitting that description tried to lure them into the vehicle in the days preceding Adele's disappearance.

*(Age Progression to 63)*

At the time of her disappearance, Adele Wells had black hair styled with waves at the sides and bangs, stood 3'6", and weighed 50 pounds. She was last seen wearing a gray cotton coat, a blue dress with animals along the lower hemline, red knee socks, and black shoes. She is African-American with brown eyes. As of this writing, she is sixty-seven years old.

If you have any information regarding this case, you are urged to call the Flint Police Department at 810-237-6800.

## Olisa Susan Williams

Ten month old Olisa Susan Williams was taken from her mother in Ann Arbor, Michigan in June 1982 by her father, Isiah Williams. Isiah was later brought to court for violating a restraining order and said he would reveal what happened to Olisa if the case against him was dismissed. The judge refused and threatened to jail him. He then said he last saw his baby daughter sometime in June 1982. He said he had been smoking marijuana and drinking alcohol while driving with Olisa in the vehicle. He claimed he parked at Island Park and fell asleep; when he woke up the car door was open and Olisa was gone. He said he did not report her as missing at that time because he believed her mother or one of her mother's relatives had taken the child.

In the weeks after his daughter's disappearance, Isiah allegedly called the child's mother several times and gave multiple stories as to Olisa's fate. He claimed he lost her, that he had killed her, that she had died in the hospital, and that she was across the water. Ann Arbor police searched the Huron River, but turned up no evidence. Authorities theorize Olisa was either killed by her father or given to others to raise. If she is alive, she may not know she is considered a missing person.

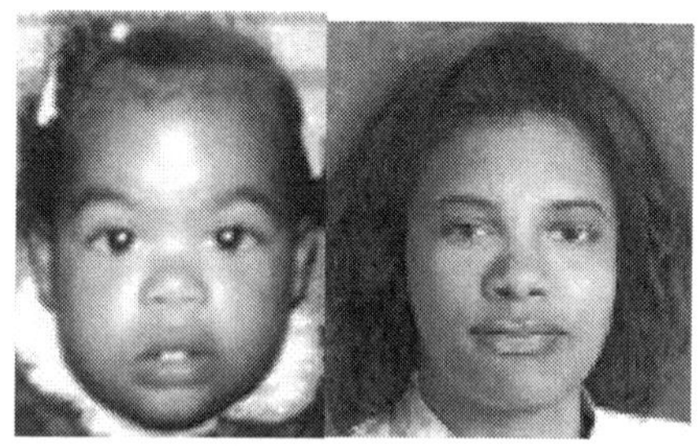

*(Age Progression to 29)*

At the time of her disappearance, Olisa Williams had brown hair, was 24", and weighed 35 pounds. She is African-American with brown eyes. As of this writing, she is thirty-seven years old.

If you have any information regarding this case, you are urged to call the Ann Arbor Police Department at 313-994-2850.

## Kevin Jay Ayotte

Three year old Kevin Jay Ayotte was last seen playing upstairs in his family's summer home in Sugarbush, Minnesota at 4:45pm on September 30, 1982. His mother went outside for a moment, and when she returned, Kevin was gone. His dog, a six month old Springer Spaniel puppy named Flash, disappeared with him. Kevin's older brother was still inside the house.

Kevin had wondered away before, but he always returned after a short time. An extensive search turned up no sign of him. Not even his shoes or his diaper were found and he had a habit of discarding those.

Flash reappeared on October 5th. Police put a tracking collar on the dog and let it go again, hoping it would lead them to Kevin, but it just kept returning home. Some believe Kevin became lost in the woods surrounding their home and died of exposure, but his case is classified as a nonfamily abduction.

*(Age Progression to 36)*

At the time of his disappearance, Kevin Ayotte had blonde hair, stood 4', and weighed 50 pounds. He was last seen wearing a checkered shirt, blue jeans, lace-up sneakers, and a diaper. He is Caucasian with blue eyes, a scar on the right side of his chin, and a cleft chin. He is developmentally disabled and has a hearing impairment. As of this writing, he is thirty-nine years old.

If you have any information regarding this case, you are urged to call the Beltrami County Sheriff's Office at 218-751-9111.

## Victor John "Jackie" Theel

Six year old Victor John "Jackie" Theel attended his first day of school in Paynesville, Minnesota on September 5, 1944. It was a half-day and his older brother was supposed to pick him up. His mother had sent in a note to his teacher giving those instructions. But at 11:30am, Jackie's teacher asked him if he knew how to get home and sent him on his way. His home was on the corner of Lake Avenue south and east Railroad Street in Paynesville. The address is now a vacant lot. He never arrived home and has never been heard from again.

Bloodhounds traced his scent to within a block west of Washburne Street. His home was a block east of Washburne Street. The trail continued to the Crow River. The tracks of a child were found leading west along the river. They went as far as Highway 23 before both the tracks and the scent vanished. Witnesses reported seeing a small boy matching Jackie's description standing along Highway 23 at 1pm that day. Other witnesses claim they saw a small boy getting into a gray car on Highway 23 at 4:45pm. But it has not been confirmed that either child was Jackie. His loved ones believe he became lost and was picked up by a stranger along Highway 23.

In the 1960s, one of Jackie's teachers saw a young man matching his description and calling himself Jackie Theel, getting off a Navy ship in California. The man told the teacher he had been adopted. It has not been confirmed that he was the same Jackie Theel who disappeared in 1944, however.

Jackie is one of fifteen children. One of his sisters and one of his brothers still live in the Paynesville area and are still searching for him. But the police no longer have the case file of the investigation. Their archives go back only to 1960. Jackie Theel has never been declared legally deceased.

*(Jackie at the time of his disappearance)*

At the time of his disappearance, Jackie Theel had blonde hair, stood 3', and weighed 45 pounds. He was last seen wearing a slightly faded navy and blue sailor suit with a square-cut collar that had three stripes, three stripes on each sleeve at the wrist, high front pockets, long pants buttoned at the waist, short brown socks, new black shoes, and no undergarments. One of the buttons in the back of the sailor suit was missing and had been replaced with a safety pin. He is Caucasian with blue eyes and a one-inch scar on the back of his head. As of this writing, he is eighty years old.

If you have any information regarding this case, you are urged to call the Minnesota Bureau of Criminal Apprehension at 651-793-7000.

## LaMoine Jordan Allen & Kreneice Marie Jones

Two year old LaMoine Jordan Allen and three year old Kreneice Marie Jones were last seen playing in front of the Jimmy Jackson Grocery store in Woodville, Mississippi at approximately 4pm on May 10, 1992. They disappeared together and have never been seen or heard from again.

An unidentified blue compact car with a false convertible top, chrome hubcaps, and dark tinted windows was seen in the area at the time of their disappearances, but it is not known if it is connected to their case or not.

LaMoine and Kreneice's families were friends. They were at the store with about twenty other people at the time.

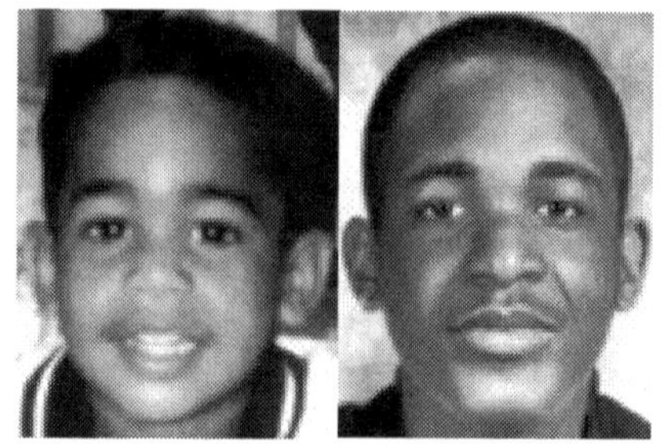

*(LaMoine's Age Progression to 24)*

At the time of his disappearance, LaMoine Allen had black hair, stood 2'11", and weighed 35 pounds. He was last seen wearing a blue and black Hawaiian-style shirt or tank top, light blue shorts, and black and white sandals. He is African-American with brown eyes and a small scar on his left knee. As of this writing, he is twenty-nine years old.

*(Kreneice's Age Progression to 14)*

At the time of her disappearance, Kreneice Jones had black hair braided with ponytails, stood 2'11", and weighed 33 pounds. She was last seen wearing a short multicolored one-piece shorts outfit with a black and white polka-dot tie, a purple and orange bandana, and pink slipper-style sandals. She is African-American with brown eyes, a scar in front of her right ear, and pierced ears. Her nickname is Maw-Maw. As of this writing, she is twenty-nine years old.

If you have any information regarding this case, you are urged to call the Federal Bureau of Investigation (FBI) Mississippi State Office at 601-684-2500.

## Jerry Lee Armstrong

Seventeen year old Jerry Lee Armstrong was last seen in Hernando, Mississippi on December 23, 1977.

That day he borrowed his brother's white two-door 1973 Pontiac LeMans and drove it to his high school prom at the National Guard Armory. He was a senior at Hernando High School and a quarterback on the football team. He disappeared after he took his girlfriend home. He has never been heard from again, and the car he was driving has never been found. The car had red and black racing stripes on the side and the Mississippi plates DAY 485.

One theory is that Jerry was targeted by the local Ku Klux Klan in a case of mistaken identity. His brother James, whose car he was driving, was dating a Caucasian woman, which could have made the Klan angry at him. It's possible that Klan members attacked and murdered Jerry, believing he was James.

James died of a gunshot wound to the chest in 1984. His death was ruled a suicide, but his mother and older brother, Johnny, doubted that explanation. Johnny also criticized the police, saying they failed to thoroughly investigate Jerry's disappearance.

Current officers have said that valuable information and documents were missing from Jerry's case file. Authorities stated they haven't ruled anything out in Jerry's disappearance. They described him as an ordinary teenager, who had no enemies and no reason for anyone to want to hurt him.

*(Jerry at the time of his disappearance)*

At the time of his disappearance, Jerry Armstrong had black hair, stood 5'6", and weighed 145 pounds. He was last seen wearing a green suit and a yellow shirt. He is African-American with brown eyes and a scar over his left eye. As of this writing, he is fifty-eight years old.

If you have any information regarding this case, you are urged to call one of the following numbers:

*Mississippi Bureau of Investigation at 662-934-3029*

*DeSoto County Sheriff's Department at 662-429-1470*

## Ashley Nicole Conroy & Jennifer Lynn Conroy

Seven month old Ashley Nicole Conroy and her mother, fifteen year old Jennifer Lynn Conroy, were last seen in Kansas City, Missouri on December 14, 1993. They lived with Jennifer's grandmother at the time. She told her grandmother they were leaving with a male friend to go to another friend's house and would be back in an hour. She took one diaper and one bottle of baby formula for Ashley. A neighbor saw them get into a pickup truck before leaving. Neither of them has been seen again, and foul play is suspected.

*(Ashley's Age Progression to an unknown age)*

At the time of her disappearance, Ashley Conroy had light brown hair, was 24", and weighed 15 pounds. She is Caucasian with blue eyes. As of this writing, she is twenty-five years old.

*(Jennifer's Age Progression to 36)*

At the time of her disappearance, Jennifer Conroy had brown hair, a chipped upper front tooth, stood between 4'10" - 4'11", and weighed between 120 - 130 pounds. She is Caucasian with blue eyes, a scar under her chin, a Caesarean scar on her abdomen, and a rose tattoo with a ribbon through it on her left ankle. As of this writing, she is forty years old.

If you have any information regarding this case, you are urged to call the Kansas City Police Department at 816-234-5000.

**William Hoag, Joel Hoag, & Edwin Craig Dowell**

Eleven year old William Hoag, his brother, thirteen year old Joel Hoag, and their friend, fourteen year old Edwin Craig Dowell were last seen on the south side of Hannibal, Missouri between 4:20pm and 5pm on May 10, 1967. They were carrying shovels and a flashlight and said they were going to explore Murphy's Cave, near the Highway 79 construction project. Joel and William had been punished the night before for going to the cave without permission and weren't supposed to leave their yard. But they left anyway while their parents weren't home. None of the three boys have ever been seen or heard from again.

That day the construction work resulted in a cave-in at Murphy's Cave. Authorities theorized the boys became trapped inside when it collapsed and were unable to get out. However, extensive search and rescue efforts turned up no sign of any of them. There is speculation that the boys were not trapped in the cave, but that something else had caused their disappearances.

*(William at the time of his disappearance)*

At the time of his disappearance, William Hoag had red hair and freckles. Height and weight measurements are unknown. He is Caucasian with blue eyes. His nicknames are Bill and Billy. As of this writing, he is sixty-two years old.

*(Joel at the time of his disappearance)*

Joel Hoag's distinguishing characteristics from the time of his disappearance are unknown. He was last seen wearing a t-shirt and jeans. He is Caucasian. His nicknames are Joe and Joey. As of this writing, he is sixty-four years old.

*(Edwin at the time of his disappearance)*

Edwin Dowell's distinguishing characteristics from the time of his disappearance are unknown. He is Caucasian. He goes by his middle name. As of this writing, he is sixty-five years old.

If you have any information regarding this case, you are urged to call the Hannibal Police Department at 573-221-3966.

**Lisa Renee Irwin**

Ten month old Lisa Renee Irwin was last seen at her home on Noah Lister Avenue in Kansas City, Missouri on October 3, 2011. Her mother put her to bed in her crib at around 10:30pm. Lisa's two older half-brothers were also in the home, but were asleep in another room. Lisa's mother admitted she drank enough wine to have gotten drunk, along with taking prescription medication for anxiety. Lisa's father came home from work at approximately 4am the next morning, and they then discovered Lisa was gone.

Several lights were on inside the house, the nursery window was open, and three cell phones were reportedly missing. The couple called 911 shortly after 4am to report their daughter missing. An extensive search of the immediate area turned up no sign of baby Lisa.

Three different witnesses said they saw a man walking down the road carrying a baby dressed only in a diaper. However, it is unknown if the man and baby were connected to Lisa's case or not. Authorities have not named any suspects in her disappearance. Her parents believe she was abducted by someone who wanted to raise her as their own.

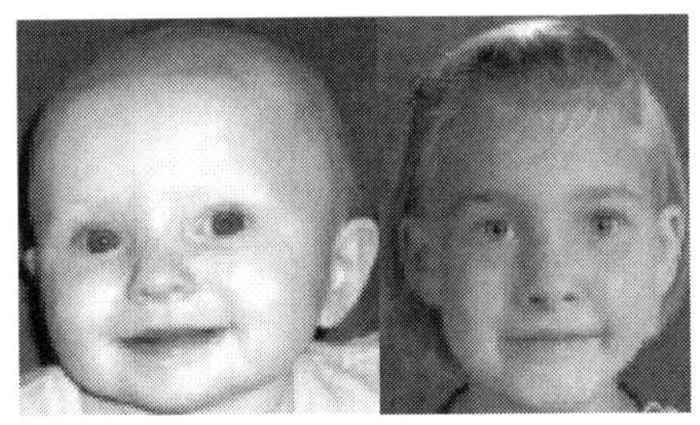

*(Age Progression to 7)*

At the time of her disappearance, Lisa Irwin had blonde hair, was 30", weighed 30 pounds, and had bottom front teeth. She was last seen wearing purple pants or shorts and a purple shirt with white kittens on it. She is Caucasian with blue eyes and a birthmark on her right outer thigh. As of this writing, she is seven years old.

If you have any information regarding this case, you are urged to call the Kansas City Police Department at 816-474-8477.

## Scott Allen Kleeschulte

Nine year old Scott Allen Kleeschulte was last seen at approximately 4:30pm - 5pm in St. Charles, Missouri on June 8, 1988. He left his home on Leverenz Drive and was walking down Ken Drive towards West Adams Street at the time. He has never been seen or heard from again.

Bloodhounds tracked his scent for about five miles northeast on Fox Hill Road, but then lost the trail. An extensive search turned up no clues as to his whereabouts. Authorities and his family believe he was abducted.

*(Age Progression to 32)*

At the time of his disappearance, Scott Kleeschulte had brown hair and freckles across his nose, stood 4’4”, and weighed 60 pounds. He was last seen wearing a black t-shirt that said Rude Dog, khaki pants, and red and black high-top sneakers. He is Caucasian with blue eyes, three small moles on his face, and a small scar on his chin. As of this writing, he is thirty-nine years old.

If you have any information regarding this case, you are urged to call the St. Charles Police Department at 314-949-3300.

## Robyn Ann Pettinato

Fourteen year old Robyn Ann Pettinato went to watch a softball game in Whitefish, Montana on July 5, 1975. She was walking on west Second Street towards the softball field, en route to a house only two residences down from her own when she disappeared.

Neither authorities nor her family believe that she left of her own accord. She wasn't having any problems at home, and she left both her purse and her shoes behind.

Less than a year after Robyn went missing, another teen girl disappeared from a town only ten minutes from Whitefish. She too has never been found. It is theorized that there is some connection between the two cases, but this has not been proven.

*(Robyn at the time of her disappearance)*

At the time of her disappearance, Robyn Pettinato had shoulder-length brown hair, stood 5', and weighed 100 pounds. She was last seen wearing a tan patterned halter top, cut-off denim shorts, and was barefoot. She is Caucasian with blue eyes. As of this writing, she is fifty-seven years old.

If you have any information regarding this case, you are urged to call the Whitefish Police Department at 406-863-2420.

## Bethany Anne Sinclair & Tina Marie Sinclair

Fifteen year old Bethany Anne Sinclair and her mother, thirty-four year old Tina Marie Sinclair, disappeared from their residence on Mountain Road in Chesterfield, New Hampshire in February 2001. They lived there with Tina's boyfriend, Van Bowman Jr. He told authorities that he and Tina had had an argument on February 4th. He claimed he left the house, and when he returned later in the day Tina and Bethany had taken all of their clothes and left. But Tina's vehicle, her pet cat, and all of her and Bethany's personal belongings were left behind.

On February 5th, an unidentified woman called Keene High School and said that Bethany was sick and would not be at school that day. Authorities do not know the identity of the caller.

Bethany and Tina were reported missing on February 10th. The last person known to have heard from them, besides Van, was Bethany's boyfriend, who had had a phone conversation with her from 11:30pm until midnight on February 3$^{rd}$. The two made plans for Valentine's Day.

Tina's sister said she was concerned for Bethany's safety because Van had been charged with molesting his own eight year old daughter. She wanted her niece to come live with her in Connecticut. She and Tina had had an argument regarding the situation in October 2000, and the sisters had not spoken since that time. Tina's sister believes Tina was preparing to leave Van, but she does not believe the two disappeared of their own accord. Van pleaded guilty to the charge of molesting his daughter and served two years in prison after Tina and Bethany went missing.

There has been no activity on Tina's bank account, cell phone, or credit cards since early February 2001. There have been no arrests made in their case. Van has not been named as a suspect, but he is a person of interest. He has since sold the house where the three of them resided. Foul play is suspected.

*(Bethany's Age Progression to 31)*

At the time of her disappearance, Bethany Sinclair had brown hair, wore eyeglasses, stood between 5'2" - 5'7", and weighed between 120 - 135 pounds. She was possibly wearing a crucifix pendant necklace when she went missing. She is Caucasian with brown eyes and a u-shaped scar on her forehead. Her hips and legs are out of alignment and her knees turn inward. Her nickname is Beth, and she may use the last name Deuso. As of this writing, she is thirty-two years old.

*(Tina at the time of her disappearance)*

At the time of her disappearance, Tina Sinclair had blonde hair, long and well-manicured fingernails, stood 5'2", and weighed 120 pounds. She is Caucasian with green eyes, a surgical scar extending downward from her navel, a butterfly tattoo on her right ankle, double-pierced ears, and a previously broken right arm and collarbone. Her previous married name is Mayotte, and her nickname is Tee. As of this writing, she is fifty-one years old.

If you have any information regarding this case, you are urged to call the New Hampshire State Police at 603-271-3636 or 603-358-3333.

## David Edward Williams & Steven Eugene Anderson

Twelve year old David Edward Williams and seventeen year old Steven Eugene Anderson were last seen at the New Lisbon State School off Highway 72 in New Lisbon, New Jersey at approximately 4:30pm on

April 7, 1975. They were students and roommates at the school. They were last seen walking toward their campus residence after playing at a nearby ball field with some staff members. Neither of them have been seen or heard from since.

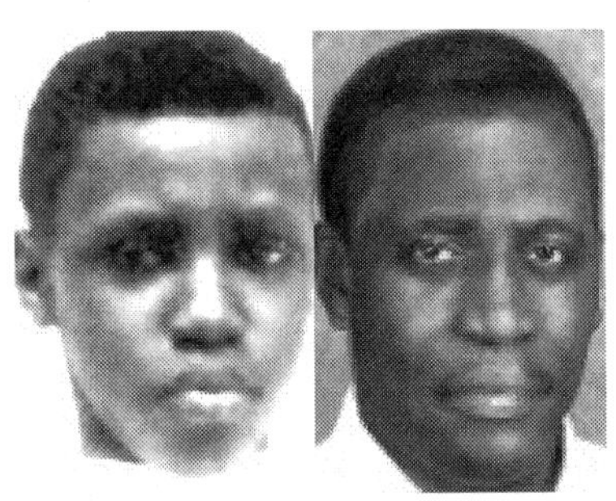

(David at the time of his disappearance)

At the time of his disappearance, David Williams had black hair, stood 5', and weighed 113 pounds. He was last seen wearing a dark-colored polo shirt, a small blue corduroy jacket, striped pants, and a protective seizure helmet. He is African-American with brown eyes and a previously fractured left femur. His is mentally disabled and has epileptic seizures. He is required to take daily medication that he did not have with him when he went missing. As of this writing, he is fifty-five years old.

(Steven at the time of his disappearance)

At the time of his disappearance, Steven Anderson had brown hair, a chipped upper front tooth, stood between 5'7" - 5'9", and weighed 141 pounds. He was last seen wearing a blue shirt, blue pants, and a blue hooded jacket. He is Caucasian with hazel/blue eyes, chicken pox scars on his abdomen, and a previously fractured right clavicle. He is moderately mentally disabled, has trouble communicating, and is not capable of caring for himself. His nickname is Teeve. As of this writing, he is sixty-one years old.

If you have any information regarding this case, you are urged to call the New Lisbon Human Services Police at 609-894-4025.

## Margaret Ellen Fox

Fourteen year old Margaret Ellen Fox was last seen in Burlington, New Jersey on June 24, 1974. She was planning to go to a babysitting job interview at High and west Broad Streets in Mount Holly, New Jersey. The man she was supposed to meet called himself 'John Marshall'. Margaret had advertised for a babysitting job, and the man responded to the ad on June 19th, saying he needed a babysitter for the following weekend. But he postponed meeting her several times. Finally, he said he would meet her in a red Volkswagen and gave her a telephone number to reach him. The number was later traced to a public phone booth at a supermarket in Lumberton, New Jersey. Margaret has never been heard from again, and 'John Marshall' has never been identified.

After news broke of Margaret's disappearance, several other parents in the area said that someone had tried to lure their daughters with fake job offers.

*(Age Progression to 56)*

At the time of her disappearance, Margaret Fox had brown hair and freckles, was missing two of her right front teeth, wore eyeglasses with hexagonal lenses and gold wire frames with broken off nose pieces, stood between 5'2" - 5'3", and weighed 105 pounds. She was last seen wearing a light blue long-sleeve floral blouse squared at the top and flared at the waist, a black and white or blue and white checkered waist-length jacket, a size 34B bra, maroon flared jeans with a yellow patch on one knee, brown sandals with a heel strap, a gold necklace with flowers and a blue stone, and a gold charm bracelet with a round blue stone. She was carrying a brown bag and an eyeglass class with Huckleberry Hound on it. She is Caucasian with blue eyes. As of this writing, she is fifty-eight years old.

If you have any information regarding this case, you are urged to call the Burlington City Police Department at 609-386-3300.

## Mark Joseph Himebaugh

Eleven year old Mark Joseph Himebaugh left his home on Sunray Road in rural Del Haven, New Jersey at approximately 4pm on November 25, 1991 to go watch firefighters put out a brush fire in a marsh a quarter of a mile away. Around the same time, his mother left to go to town to run an errand. When she returned less than an hour later, Mark wasn't home. She assumed he was playing with friends, but by 5pm, she was growing concerned. It was at that time that she contacted the police. Mark has never been heard from again.

There were two unconfirmed sightings of Mark that day. Someone reportedly saw him with a little girl at the entrance to a local park around 3:40pm. The girl was described as being between nine and ten years old in 1991 with blonde hair, almost 4' tall, weighing approximately 70 - 75 pounds, and was wearing a three-quarter length dark blue ski parka with a hunter orange stripe on the back. Authorities believe the little girl could have important information regarding Mark's disappearance, but she has never been identified.

The other witness report placed Mark with a man described as being between thirty and thirty-five years old, between 5'8" - 5'9" tall, and weighing 150 pounds. The man had dark reddish-brown hair in a ponytail and had a scruffy appearance.

Thomas Butcavage Jr. was named as a person of interest in 1995 after a male prostitute came forward with information possibly linking him to Mark's suspected abduction. He resembles the witness description, but he has never been charged in Mark's case. He has served time in prison multiple times for drug offenses and sexual crimes against underage boys, however. In 2015, authorities asked anyone who knew

Thomas Butcavage Jr. in the late 1980s and early 1990s to contact them.

*(Age Progression to 34)*

At the time of his disappearance, Mark Himebaugh had red hair and freckles, stood 4'6", and weighed 85 pounds. He had emotional problems at the time and was taking the antidepressant Prozac. He was last seen wearing a blue U.S.N. sweatshirt, a gray jacket with gray red and blue plaid lining and four outer pockets with Velcro, gray Docker pants, and red and white L.A. Gear sneakers. He is Caucasian with blue eyes. His nickname is Curious George, and he is right-handed. As of this writing, he is thirty-eight years old.

If you have any information regarding this case, you are urged to call the Middle Township Police Department at 609-465-8700.

## William Ebenezer Jones III

Three year old William Ebenezer Jones III was last seen in the backyard of his family's residence on Taylor Avenue in Vineland, New Jersey at 1pm on December 17, 1962. He was playing with his two year old sister and the family dog while his mother watched them through the window from inside. His mother went into a bedroom to check on her other son for a moment. When she came back out, her daughter was standing in the doorway holding a plastic poinsettia. She said William had given her the plant and that a man had taken him. The family immediately searched the neighborhood, to no avail. William has never been seen again. Authorities believe he may have been abducted by someone who wanted to raise a child.

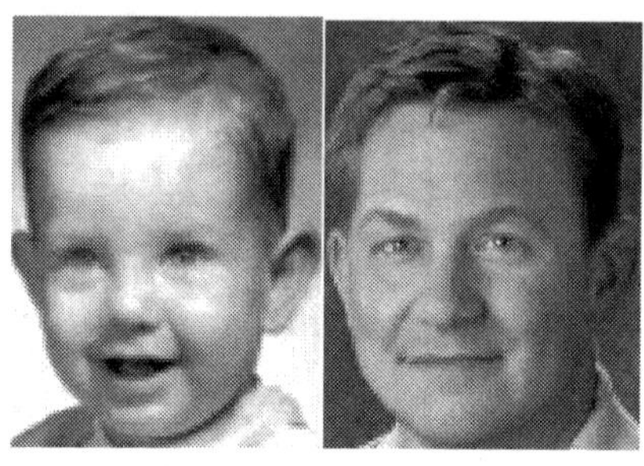

*(Age Progression to 55)*

At the time of his disappearance, William Jones III had light brown hair, stood 3', and weighed 30 pounds. He was last seen wearing a light blue/gray snowsuit with a navy blue collar and large silver buttons, a matching hat, and tan high-top sneakers with yellow laces. He is Caucasian with blue eyes and a giraffe-shaped vaccination scar on the back of his upper left arm. His nickname is Billy. As of this writing, he is fifty-nine years old.

If you have any information regarding this case, you are urged to call the Vineland Police Department at 856-696-1212.

**Anthony Bernard Franko**

Ten year old Anthony Bernard Franko was last seen walking the half-mile to Lemmon Valley Elementary School, where he was in fifth grade, on the morning of May 8, 1983 in Lemmon Valley, Nevada. A witness saw him in a cul-de-sac on the south end of Fremont Street, talking to an unknown individual in a rusted Ford Pinto or Camaro. Anthony never arrived at school and has never been heard from again.

The school didn't notify his family that he was absent, and as a result they didn't realize he was missing until dark that night. Investigators believe he was abducted on his way to school and probably murdered, but his mother continues to hold out hope that he is alive.

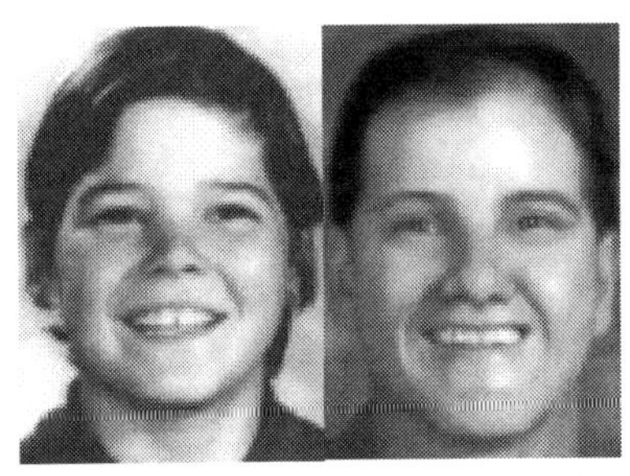

*(Age Progression to 36)*

At the time of his disappearance, Anthony Franko had brown hair, a slight gap between his upper front teeth, stood 4'11", and weighed 85 pounds. He was last seen wearing a red San Francisco 49ers t-shirt, blue jeans, a blue down hooded jacket, and hiking boots. He is Caucasian with brown eyes, small birthmarks above his left eyebrow and on the right side of his neck, two light-colored moles on his cheek and nose, and a scar under his lower lip. His nickname is Tony. As of this writing, he is forty-six years old.

If you have any information regarding this case, you are urged to call the Washoe County Sheriff's Office at 775-328-3001 or 775-328-3369.

## Jennifer Lee Martin

Eleven year old Jennifer Lee Martin was last seen at approximately 3pm in the Lemmon Valley area of Reno, Nevada on June 28, 1987. She bought candy and a soda at a 7-11 convenience store on Lemmon Valley Drive, and then disappeared while walking the few hundred feet back to her home on Surge Street. When twenty minutes passed and she hadn't returned home, her older brother went to the 7-11 to look for her. She has never been seen again. Authorities believe she was abducted, but no suspects have ever been identified in her case.

*(Age Progression to 37)*

At the time of her disappearance, Jennifer Martin had brown hair and freckles, stood 4'6", and weighed 49 pounds. She was last seen wearing a grayish-purple sweatshirt dress and was barefoot. She is Caucasian with blue eyes, pierced ears, two small hairline scars on the underside of her chin, a birthmark on her right hip, and a star-shaped scar on the inside of her upper right arm. As of this writing, she is forty-two years old.

If you have any information regarding this case, you are urged to call the Washoe County Sheriff's Office at 775-328-3001 or 775-328-3369.

## Selah Lee Davis, Sasha Davis & Jarib Bennett

Three month old Selah Lee Davis, her mother, thirty year old Sasha Davis, and her mother's friend, twenty-seven year old Jarib Bennett, left the New York City borough of the Bronx on February 15, 2008 to go to Rochester, New York to visit friends. They planned to return on February 19th, but they did not and have never been heard from again. On February 27th, their rental vehicle was found abandoned on Genesee Street in southwest Rochester. It is uncharacteristic for them to leave without warning.

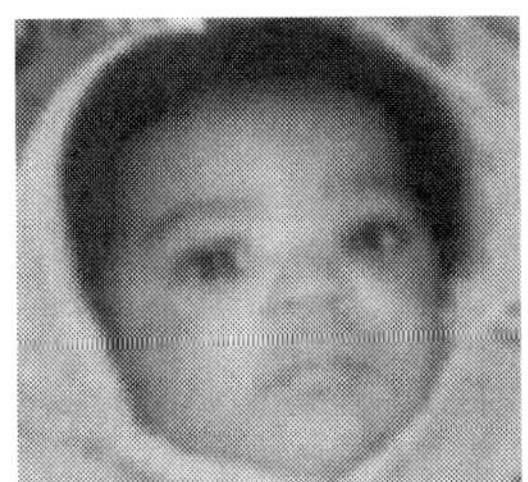

*(Selah at the time of her disappearance)*

At the time of her disappearance, Selah Davis had black hair, was 24", and weighed 20 pounds. She is African-American with brown eyes. As of this writing, she is ten years old.

*(Sasha at the time of her disappearance)*

At the time of her disappearance, Sasha Davis had black hair, stood between 5'5" - 5'7", and weighed 120 pounds. She is African-American with brown eyes, pierced ears, a mole near her right eye, and tattoos on her left breast and right calf. As of this writing, she is forty-one years old.

*(Jarib at the time of his disappearance)*

At the time of his disappearance, Jarib Bennett had black hair, stood 5'11", and weighed between 215 - 230 pounds. He is African-American with brown eyes. His nickname is Griff. As of this writing, he is thirty-eight years old.

If you have any information regarding this case, you are urged to call the New York Police Department at 212-694-7781.

## Andre Terrence Bryant

One month old Andre Terrence Bryant was on a walk with his mother, Monique Rivera, and her two older sons in their Brooklyn, New York neighborhood on March 28, 1989, when two African-American women driving a 1988 or 1989 burgundy Pontiac Grand Am Sports Edition with tinted windows and possibly Maryland plates approached them. One of the women was approximately twenty-two years old and had red hair. Both were about 5'7" and weighed 130 pounds. Monique thought at the time that she had known them back in middle school. The women engaged her in conversation about her children and convinced her to go shopping with them. They bought some clothes and took Monique and her children home.

Monique told her boyfriend's sister, Patricia, that the women used a fraudulent credit card to make their purchases and that she planned to go shopping with them again the following day. Patricia agreed to babysit the children while Monique shopped. On March 29th, Patricia went to Monique's apartment on Madison Street to babysit. The two women did not pick up Monique outside her apartment, but instead called her from a pay phone around the corner and asked her to come and meet them. They insisted she bring Andre with them on the shopping trip as well, so Monique took the baby and left her two older children with Patricia.

On March 30th, Monique's body was found in the woods near City Island Road in the Bronx. She had been struck on the head and strangled. There was no sign of Andre, the women, or their vehicle at the scene. Andre has never been seen again, and the two women have never been identified. Authorities believe Andre may have been sold into an adoption ring.

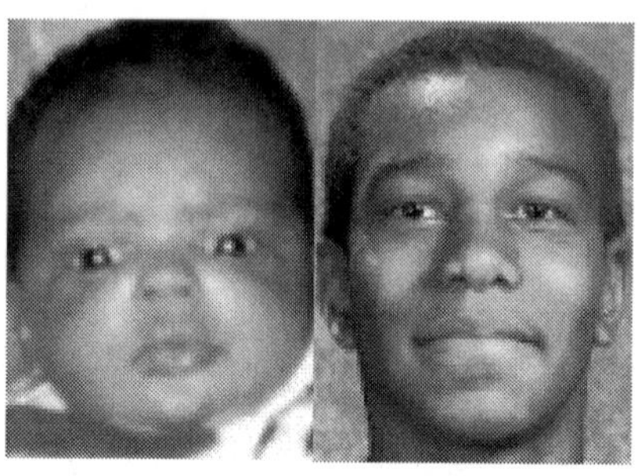

*(Age Progression to 22)*

At the time of his disappearance, Andre Bryant had black hair, was 19", and weighed 10 pounds. He is African-American with brown eyes. As of this writing, he is twenty-nine years old.

If you have any information regarding this case, you are urged to call the New York Police Department at 718-574-1605.

## Sharaun Taree Cole

Twelve year old Sharaun Taree Cole was last seen outside her family's residence on Edgecomb Avenue in Manhattan, New York at 5:30pm on February 25, 1983. She went to play at a nearby park and never returned home. She has never been heard from again.

*(Age Progression to 46)*

At the time of her disappearance, Sharaun Cole had black hair, stood between 5'6" - 5'7", and weighed 115 pounds. She was last seen wearing a beige wool jacket, a gold sweater, blue jeans, and blue and white sneakers. She is African-American with brown eyes and pierced ears. As of this writing, she is forty-seven years old.

If you have any information regarding this case, you are urged to call the New York Police Department at 646-610-6914.

## Cynthia Dawn Constantine

Fifteen year old Cynthia Dawn Constantine was last seen in Oakdale, New York on July 11, 1969. She went to take the dog for a walk along the railroad tracks on the Montauk Branch train of the Long Island Railroad. The dog returned alone, still wearing its collar and leash. Cynthia has never been seen or heard from again. Her family believes she was abducted.

*(Cynthia at the time of her disappearance)*

At the time of her disappearance, Cynthia Constantine had blonde hair, wore eyeglasses, had a discolored front tooth, stood 5'3", and weighed 117 pounds. She was last seen wearing a white blouse, black Bermuda shorts, orange sneakers, and possibly a yellow metal chain with a cross pendant. She is Caucasian with blue eyes, a previously fractured lower right arm, and a mole on her neck. As of this writing, she is sixty-four years old.

If you have any information regarding this case, you are urged to call the Suffolk County Police Department at 631-852-6040.

## Christopher Milton Dansby & Shane Anthony Walker

Two year old Christopher Milton Dansby was last seen at the Martin Luther King Jr. Towers playground located at 113th Street and Lenox Avenue in Harlem in Manhattan, New York on May 18, 1989. His mother was at the park with him but decided to go to the store. Since she didn't have Christopher's stroller with her, she left him in the care of several relatives at the park. When she returned, he was gone. The relatives told her they had seen him playing with a red ball, but he had not brought one with him and she didn't see one in the vicinity. A seven year old neighborhood boy told authorities that he saw Christopher walking on west 111th Street later in the day. He was with an adult male. The man was described as being African-American, between twenty-five and thirty years old, 6' and thin, with dreadlocks. Christopher has never been seen again.

Christopher's case shares striking similarities with the disappearance of one year old Shane Anthony Walker, who disappeared from the same playground on August 10, 1989, three months after Christopher. Shane was also with his mother at the park. A man approached her and began a conversation. She became distracted, and when she looked back, Shane was gone. Authorities believe he too was abducted.

Both Shane and Christopher were last seen by their mothers at the same park playing with the same ten year old girl and her five year old brother. Those children were questioned after Shane's abduction, but it is unknown what, if any, information they were able to give. Both Shane and Christopher lived in the same apartment building, and both disappeared on the same day of the week (Thursday). It was also roughly the same time of day. Shane was abducted at 5pm and Christopher at 7pm. Authorities investigated the possibility that the boys' cases were connected to a black market baby adoption ring, and that Andre Bryant (abducted from Brooklyn in March in 1989) was possibly another victim.

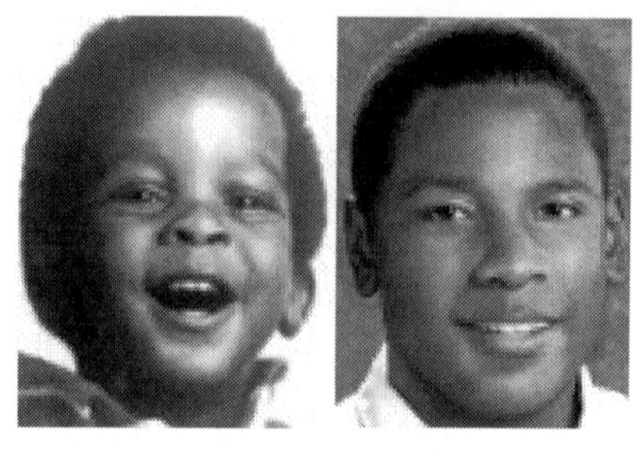

*(Christopher's Age Progression to 26)*

At the time of his disappearance, Christopher Dansby had black hair, was 2'6", and weighed 30 pounds. He was last seen wearing a blue jacket, a floral print shirt, blue jeans, and green and white sneakers. He is African-American with brown eyes, a birthmark shaped like a figure eight on his back, and a burn scar on his thigh. His nickname is Choo-Choo. As of this writing, he is thirty-one years old.

*(Shane's Age Progression to 28)*

At the time of his disappearance, Shane Walker had braided black hair, was 36", and weighed 23 pounds. He was last seen wearing a blue and white shirt, light blue pants, and white L.A. Gear Sneakers. He is African-American with brown eyes and a small scar under his chin. As of this writing, he is thirty years old.

If you have any information regarding this case, you are urged to call one of the following numbers:

*New York Police Department at 646-610-6914*

*New York Housing Police Department at 212-410-8500*

## Tiffany Madia Dixon

Twelve year old Tiffany Madia Dixon was last seen at 8am on October 10, 1991 in Brooklyn, New York. She walked her younger brother to Carroll Elementary School in the Carroll Gardens section of Brooklyn on First Place and Court Street. She saw him through the door and then began walking the three or four blocks to her own junior high school where she was in seventh grade. She was last seen near her school, but she never arrived for class and has never been seen again.

*(Age Progression to 38)*

At the time of her disappearance, Tiffany Dixon had black hair, stood between 4'11" - 5'2", and weighed 105 pounds. She is Hispanic with brown eyes and pierced ears. As of this writing, she is thirty-nine years old.

If you have any information regarding this case, you are urged to call the New York City Police Department at 646-610-6914.

## Sean Wayne Evans

Two year old Sean Wayne Evans was last seen playing with a ball outside his family's home on Water Street in Watertown, New York on May 17, 1984. His baby brother was outside in a playpen. Their mother went back inside to answer the telephone at approximately 5:30pm. She was gone less than two minutes, but when she returned Sean was gone. He has never been heard from again.

The Black River runs near his home, and the ball he had been playing with was on the driveway, which was near the river's bank. Police believe he may have fallen into the river and drown, but his body has never been found. Due to the unclear factors of his disappearance, his case is classified as a nonfamily abduction.

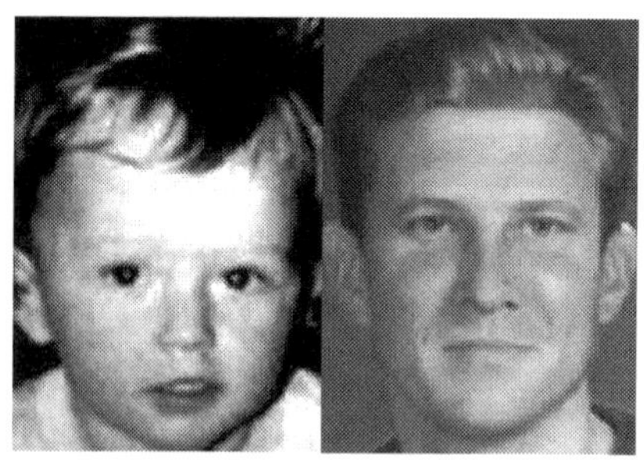

*(Age Progression to 25)*

At the time of his disappearance, Sean Evans had blonde hair, stood between 2'11" - 3', and weighed between 40 - 45 pounds. He was last seen wearing a yellow jacket, red pants, and blue sneakers with white stripes. He is Caucasian with green eyes, a one-inch birthmark between his shoulder blades, a birthmark on his forehead, and a scar on his forehead. He is not circumcised. As of this writing, he is thirty-six years old.

If you have any information regarding this case, you are urged to call the Watertown Police Department at 315-782-2233.

## Timothy Patrick Guthrie Jr., Julie Anne Guthrie & Leslie Anne Guthrie

Three year old Timothy Patrick Guthrie Jr., his sister, six year old Julie Anne Guthrie, and their mother, twenty-nine year old Leslie Anne Guthrie, disappeared from Katonah, New York around 1:30pm on February 5, 1977. Leslie picked up the children at their father's home on Grandview Drive at 1:30pm that day. They left driving a white 1974 300-Series Ford Maverick with a green roof and New York plates 636 - WNA.

Leslie and Timothy Sr. were separated but had an amicable relationship. She had been living with her mother in White Plains, New York. When she and the children didn't return to his home that evening, he assumed they had spent the night in White Plains. He later grew concerned when he hadn't heard from them by afternoon the following day. He reported them missing at 6pm on February 6th. Timothy Jr., Julie, nor Leslie has ever been seen again, and their vehicle has not been located.

Timothy Sr. has been ruled out as a suspect in his family's disappearances, and has gone to great lengths through the years to try and locate them. There were no indications that Leslie had planned to leave; she hadn't taken any clothing or personal belongings for herself or the children, and she hadn't withdrawn any large sums of money from her bank account prior to them going missing.

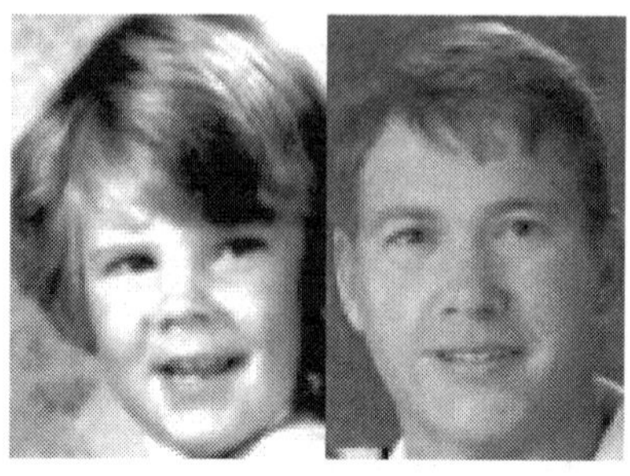

*(Timothy's Age Progression to 40)*

At the time of his disappearance, Timothy Guthrie Jr. had brown hair, stood 3'3", and weighed 30 pounds. He is Caucasian with blue eyes. As of this writing, he is forty-four years old.

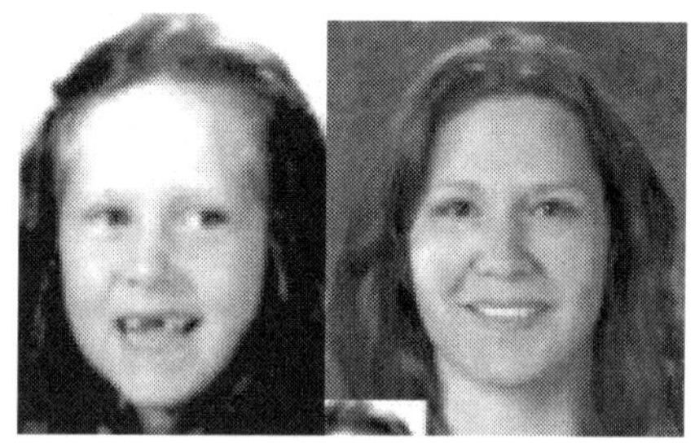

*(Julie's Age Progression to 43)*

At the time of her disappearance, Julie Guthrie had brown hair, stood 4', and weighed 55 pounds. She is Caucasian with blue eyes and strawberry birthmarks on her chin and back. As of this writing, she is forty-seven years old.

*(Leslie's Age Progression to 65)*

At the time of her disappearance, Leslie Guthrie had brown hair, stood between 5'4" - 5'7", and weighed 120 pounds. She was last seen wearing an old ski jacket, jeans, and borrowed boots two sizes two small. She is Caucasian with brown eyes. Her maiden name is Locke. As of this writing, she is seventy-one years old.

If you have any information regarding this case, you are urged to call the Bedford Town Police Department at 914-241-3111.

## Equilla Lynn Hodrick

Eight year old Equilla Lynn Hodrick and her mother were sitting on the front porch of their Briggs Avenue residence in the New York City borough of the Bronx on August 12, 1985. Her mother turned to talk to friends and last saw Equilla running toward the ice cream truck on the corner of Briggs Avenue and 194th Street. Her mother was eight months pregnant at the time and unable to chase after her, but she had always returned quickly before. Equilla's cousin later said she last saw her playing an arcade game on the corner after her mother had last saw her, but since then she has not been since or heard from again.

Her mother called police when she did not return home. An extensive search was launched. Bloodhounds tracked her scent to Webster Avenue in the Bronx, near the tracks of the Metro-North train line, but no other signs of her were found. Her case was recently reopened by a cold case squad in the New York City Police Department.

*(Age Progression to 33)*

At the time of her disappearance, Equilla Hodrick had brown hair, wore eyeglasses, had a gap between her upper front teeth, stood 4'11", and weighed 80 pounds. She was last seen wearing cut-off blue jeans, a white tank top with red and yellow marks, and light blue sneakers. She is African-American with hazel eyes, a scar near her right eye, a scar on her right cheek, discolorations on her buttocks and back, and pierced ears. As of this writing, she is forty-two years old.

If you have any information regarding this case, you are urged to call the New York Police Department at 646-610-6914.

## Frederick Andrew Holmes

One year old Frederick Andrew Holmes was last seen in Grahamsville, New York at 9am on May 25, 1955.

His older siblings were at school and his mother was working in the garden. He was last seen walking down the driveway of his rural home. He has never been seen or heard from again.

*(Frederick at the time of his disappearance)*

At the time of his disappearance, Frederick Holmes had blonde hair, stood 2'6", and weighed 30 pounds. He was last seen wearing faded brown corduroy overalls and a long-sleeve polo-style shirt. He is Caucasian with blue eyes. His nickname is Tookie. As of this writing, he is sixty-five years old.

If you have any information regarding this case, you are urged to call one of the following numbers:

*Sullivan County Sheriff's Office at 845-794-7100*

*The National Center for Missing and Exploited Children at 1-800-THE-LOST*

## Jeremiah George Huger

Four year old Jeremiah George Huger was playing with friends in his family's yard at their residence on LaFontaine Avenue in the New York City borough of the Bronx on June 25, 1985. An unidentified African-

American male called to Jeremiah from the street and when the child approached him, the man grabbed him and disappeared. Neither of them has been since again. Police believe he may have been sold after his abduction, but his mother believes he was taken by an abusive ex-boyfriend of hers who had previously threatened to abduct the child.

*(Age Progression to 36)*

At the time of his disappearance, Jeremiah Huger had brown hair, stood between 3'6" - 3'7", and weighed 45 pounds. He was last seen wearing a light blue shirt, dark blue shorts, and white sneakers. He is African-American with brown eyes, a scar on his left forearm, and his left leg is bowlegged. As of this writing, he is thirty-seven years old.

If you have any information regarding this case, you are urged to call the New York City Police Department at 646-610-6914.

## Russell John Mort

Two year old Russell John Mort was last seen playing in the sandbox in his family's fenced backyard at their residence in Lynch's Trailer Park on River Road in Wheatfield, New York at 12:20pm on May 5, 1982. His mother stepped back inside to repair one of his toys. She was gone less than five minutes, but when she returned she discovered Russell was missing. The gate was still closed and locked from the outside. The fence was four feet high, but one portion of it was shorter than the rest. The day before Russell's disappearance, he had climbed over the fence and went to play in a neighbor's yard. It is possible he climbed over the fence again on the day of his disappearance.

An unidentified Caucasian male and female were spotted in the area of the Mort's home on the day Russell went missing. It is not known if they are connected to the case or not, but investigators would like to question them as possible witnesses, if nothing more. The female had dark brown curly hair and was in her early to mid-twenties in 1982. The male had light brown hair and a mustache and was in his late twenties to early thirties in 1982. The couple were seen in a white 1965 or older Corvette with a black convertible top. There were last seen in the area of Hyde Park Boulevard and Packer Road.

Some believe Russell fell into the Niagara River, which runs about 100 yards from his home. But there is no evidence to support the theory.

*(Age Progression to 34)*

At the time of his disappearance, Russell Mort had light brown hair, a chipped upper left front tooth, stood 3', and weighed 30 pounds. He was last seen wearing a faded brown plaid sun suit over an old shirt and beige knee socks. He is Caucasian with brown eyes, a small cleft in his chin, and a small mole on the left side of his chin. His nickname is Russie. As of this writing, he is thirty-eight years old.

If you have any information regarding this case, you are urged to call the Niagara County Sheriff's Department at 716-439-9327.

## Kirk Quintons

Eleven year old Kirk Quintons left his family's home in the New York City borough of the Bronx at approximately 12pm on September 18, 1983. He was walking to the Top Tomato Supermarket to get his mother a soda. The store was located on Rosedale Avenue, two blocks from his home. He was last seen collecting bottles from a vacant lot near the store. He has never been heard from again.

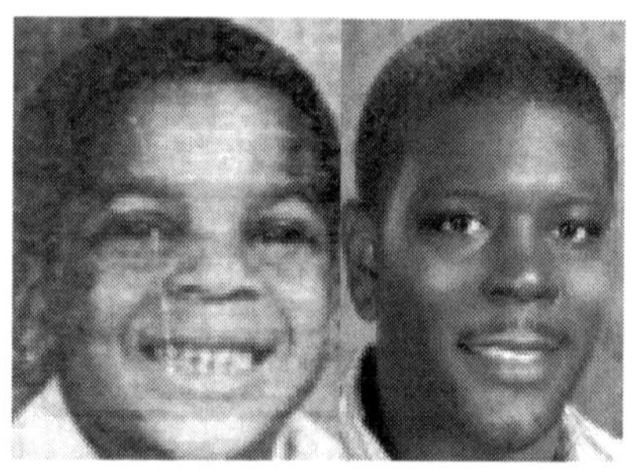

*(Age Progression to 41)*

At the time of his disappearance, Kirk Quintons had black hair, stood 4'9", and weighed 70 pounds. He was last seen wearing Levis jeans and blue and white sneakers. He is African-American with brown eyes and a small scar on the left side of his body. As of this writing, he is forty-six years old.

If you have any information regarding this case, you are urged to call the New York Police Department at 646-610-6914.

## Marlene Santana

Three day old Marlene Santana was abducted at gunpoint by a female suspect in Brooklyn, New York at 9:30pm on October 21, 1985. Her mother had met the abductor three days prior to the abduction at Brookdale Hospital. The woman admired the baby through the nursery window and said she was the prettiest and quietest one. Marlene was kept longer than usual due to jaundice, but was eventually discharged with a clean bill of health. Her mother was leaving the hospital with her when she was kidnapped. The suspect threatened to shoot the baby if her mother did not give her up. Once she had the baby, the kidnapper escaped in a vehicle driven by an accomplice. Marlene has never been seen again.

The abductor is described as being 5'2", 130 pounds, approximately twenty-four to thirty years old in 1985, with dirty blonde or bleached blonde hair, but she may have been wearing a wig, and was Caucasian with some Hispanic features but no accent. The car her accomplice was driving was a white 1976 Chevrolet Malibu with red lettering on the door; it may have been an unlicensed cab.

The week before Marlene was kidnapped a two month old baby was abducted from another New York City hospital. The infant was found unharmed and the abductor arrested. That case is not believed to be related to Marlene's, but the timing was coincidental. It is possible Marlene was sold for adoption, or her abductor may have wanted to raise her as her own.

*(Age Progression to 25. No infant photos are available)*

At the time of her abduction, Marlene Santana had brown hair, was 20", and weighed 7 pounds. She was last seen wrapped in a blue, pink, and yellow swaddling blanket. She is Hispanic with brown eyes and a foot deformity called metatarsus adductus. As of this writing, she is thirty-two years old.

If you have any information regarding this case, you are urged the call the New York City Police Department at 646-610-6914.

## Donna Michele Barnhill

Thirteen year old Donna Michele Barnhill left her home in Lexington, North Carolina on March 18, 1981 at approximately 8:30pm to walk to a nearby friend's house. She was last seen walking on Hemstead Street.

She never arrived at her friend's house and has never been seen again.

Donna's older sister, Anita, died at the age of two in February 1966. Her death was ruled an accident, because her family said she fell out of her high chair and hit her head. However, in 1999 police reopened the investigation into Anita's death while looking into Donna's disappearance, and her death was then reclassified to a homicide by child abuse.

Donna is still listed as missing, and no one has been charged in connection to Anita's murder. In 2004, police searched the family's former residence with ground-penetrating radar but found nothing. Foul play is possible in Donna's case.

*(Age Progression to 49)*

At the time of her disappearance, Donna Barnhill had brown hair, stood 5'7", and weighed 125 pounds. She was last seen wearing a dark blue jacket, an orange sweatshirt, and jeans. She is Biracial (Caucasian/Native American) with brown eyes and a mole or birthmark on her right arm. As of this writing, she is fifty-one years old.

If you have any information regarding this case, you are urged to call one of the following numbers:

*Lexington Police Department at 336-249-8947*

*CUE Center for Missing Persons at 910-343-1131*

## Sherri Lee Truesdale

Fourteen year old Sherri Lee Truesdale left her Pitts Street home about 11:30am on June 13, 1970 to take a bus to downtown Winston-Salem, North Carolina. She told her mother she was going to buy some school supplies, some donuts for her older sister, and make a payment on her mother's charge account at Raylass Department Store. The store clerk later told police that she had saw Sherri about 4:30pm. She has never been seen again. An extensive search turned up no clues as to her whereabouts.

*(Age Progression to 46)*

At the time of her disappearance, Sherri Truesdale had black hair, stood 4'2", and weighed 75 pounds. She was last seen wearing a blue shirt, blue bellbottom pants, a girl's wristwatch with black leather or black plastic band, pentagon-shaped aqua blue earrings, and brown loafers. She is African-American with brown eyes, a mole above her upper lip, a mole on the back of the base of her neck, and pierced ears. As of this writing, she is sixty-two years old.

If you have any information regarding this case, you are urged to call one of the following numbers:

Winston-Salem Police Department at 336-773-7848

CUE Center for Missing Persons at 910-343-1131

## Kathleen Ann Shea

Six year old Kathleen Ann Shea left her home on 14th Street in Tyrone, Pennsylvania at 12pm on March 18, 1965. She had gone to school that morning, came home for lunch, and was on her way back to school at 12pm that day. Her father offered to drive her, but she said she would rather walk. She was last seen walking northbound between 15th and 16th Streets. A crossing guard remembered helping her across 15th Street, and a neighbor spoke to her shortly thereafter. She continued walking after finishing chatting with her neighbor, but never arrived back at school and has never been heard from again. Her school was four blocks from her home.

She was not discovered missing until 4:45pm, when she failed to return home that afternoon. Bloodhounds traced her scent to Garfield Street, just one block from her school, but then lost the trail.

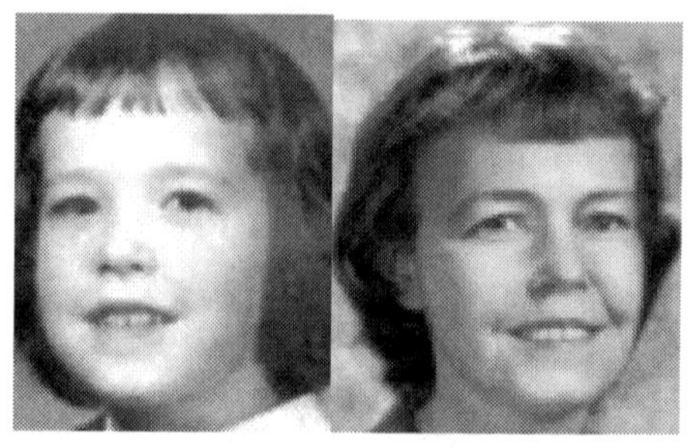

*(Age Progression to 48)*

At the time of her disappearance, Kathleen Shea had blonde hair, stood 3'11", and weighed 47 pounds. She was last seen wearing a dark brown hat with tie-down ear flaps, a beige coat with a fur collar, a red knitted sweater, a brown jumper, earmuffs, red tights, red leather gloves, and yellow boots with a black stripe and black soles. She is Caucasian with blue eyes. Her nickname is Kathy. As of this writing, she is fifty-nine years old.

If you have any information regarding this case, you are urged to call the Pennsylvania State Police at 814-696-6100.

## Louis Anthony Mackerley

Seven year old Louis Anthony Mackerley came home from school on the afternoon of June 7, 1984 and told his babysitter that he was going to walk two doors down, on Chew Street in Allentown, Pennsylvania, to play with friends. Witnesses saw him walking between Forth Street and Gordon Street, about a block from his own home. The owner of Marco's Doggie Shop stated that Louis came in at 4pm and spent approximately forty-five minutes browsing around the store to avoid two teenage boys who were chasing him. Louis left the store at 4:45pm heading east on Gordon Street. Another witness claimed to have seen Louis talking to an unidentified man and woman in a park near Jordan Street at approximately 4:30pm, but that sighting has not confirmed.

His parents did not report him missing until 11:30pm, because his mother had been in the hospital undergoing surgery and Louis had been in the care of an aunt. An extensive search of the area turned up no clues as to his whereabouts. The two boys who had been chasing him that day were later interviewed by police and are not believed to have been involved in his disappearance.

Six months before Louis' disappearance, he had told his parents, his school nurse, and a psychologist that he had been molested by a couple named Frank and Elizabeth. His accounts of the alleged incident differed. Once he said he had been molested on the railroad tracks near Jordan Street and the Lehigh River, and another time he said Frank and Elizabeth had driven him to an apartment in Allentown and molested him there before taking him back to his own neighborhood. There may have been more than one incident, or it may have never happened at all. Louis stated the couple had threatened to hurt him if he told anybody. The Allentown police were notified, but they could not find enough evidence to warrant an investigation. It is not known whether the alleged sexual encounters had anything to do with Louis' disappearance or not.

He is believed to have been abducted. His parents believe he may be alive and just not remember who he is.

*(Age Progression to 40)*

At the time of his disappearance, Louis Mackerley had blondish-brown hair, was missing his four front teeth, stood between 4' - 4'1", and weighed 44 pounds. He was last seen wearing a short-sleeve green-striped or navy and white-striped shirt, long blue pants or jeans with a red stripe on the back pocket that read Doggie, an elastic belt with trim and a buckle shaped like a train, pink socks, and brown shoes. He is Caucasian with blue eyes, and two odd-shaped circular burn scars on the right side of his chest. He has learning and emotional disabilities. As of this writing, he is forty-one years old.

If you have any information regarding this case, you are urged to call the Allentown Police Department at 610-437-7721.

## Lauren Marie Pico Jackson

Five year old Lauren Marie Pico Jackson was last seen digging in the dirt with other children near her mother's apartment complex in Spring City, Pennsylvania on October 4, 1988. When her mother went to check on her later, she was gone. One of her playmates said he saw her walking towards her home, which was about a hundred feet away from where she had been playing. She has never been seen again.

Tracking dogs followed her scent away from her mother's apartment, along Park Road to Route 724, and along there to the Vincent Motel, nearly a mile away from where she was last seen. There, they lost the trail. Investigators believe she was most likely abducted.

*(Age Progression to 29)*

At the time of her disappearance, Lauren Jackson had brown hair, stood 2'6", and weighed 34 pounds. She was last seen wearing a white long-sleeve pullover shirt with a California Raisin printed on the front and back, black knit pants, white socks, and white Reebok sneakers with pink laces. She is Caucasian with brown/hazel eyes, two small surgical scars on her lower abdomen, and surgical scars on the roof of her mouth from an operation to repair a cleft palate. As of this writing, she is thirty-four years old.

If you have any information regarding this case, you are urged to call the East Vincent Police Department at 610-431-6363 or 610-933-0115.

**Michelle Jolene Lakey**

Eleven year old Michelle Jolene Lakey visited her mother at Mercy Hospital in Scranton, Pennsylvania on August 26, 1986. She was last seen walking on north Washington Avenue towards her home. She was planning to spend the night at a friend's house on Myrtle Street. She is believed to have gotten into an unidentified light yellow car approximately one block from her home. She has never been seen again. Authorities believe she was abducted.

Frank Osellanie is considered a possible suspect in her case. He was convicted of kidnapping, raping, and murdering a nine year old Scranton girl in 1990 and has been in prison ever since. He admitted to having known Michelle and said she sometimes visited his auto shop and he would give her rides home. However, he maintains his innocence in her disappearance, and investigators are not sure whether or not he was involved.

*(Age Progression to 43)*

At the time of her disappearance, Michelle Lakey had blondish-brown hair, stood between 4'9" - 5', and weighed 80 pounds. She had long fingernails and a small build at the time; she looked much younger than her age. She wore children's size 14 clothes and size 8 shoes. She was last seen wearing a white shirt with purple trim and tie front, dark blue sweatpants, and brown sandals with straps. She is Caucasian with brown eyes. She goes by her middle name, and her nicknames are Boozer and Boo. As of this writing, she is forty-three years old.

If you have any information regarding this case, you are urged to call the Pennsylvania State Police Troop R at 570-963-3156.

## Kristi Lynn Vorak

Thirteen year old Kristi Lynn Vorak was last seen on October 31, 1982 in Tacoma, Washington. She disappeared that night and has never been heard from again. She had no history of running away. Her mother believes she may be alive and living in the Seattle area, but investigators believe she is deceased.

In May 1993, Kristi was added to the list of probable victims of the Green River serial killer, although her remains have never been found. Foul play is suspected in her case.

*(Age Progression to 43)*

At the time of her disappearance, Kristi Vorak had brown hair, stood 5'3", and weighed 110 pounds. She is Caucasian with hazel eyes and her left middle finger is shorter than the one on her other hand. As of this writing, she is forty-eight years old.

If you have any information regarding this case, you are urged to call the Tacoma Police Department at 253-798-4721.

## Christina Lee White

Twelve year old Christina Lee White went to the Asotin County Fair in Asotin, Washington on April 28, 1979. At 2:30pm, she called her mother from a friend's house to say she was feeling sick from the heat. Her mother could not go get her because she did not have access to a car right then. Instead, her mother told her to put a wet towel on her neck and to lie down and rest. She told her daughter to come home when she felt better. Christina did not call again, and her mother assumed she had gotten to feeling better and returned to the fair. Christina was last seen on 2$^{nd}$ Street sometime between 7pm and 10pm. When her mother went to the fair to pick her up, she was not there. Her friends said she had been on her way home when they saw her last, and she was riding her ten-speed bicycle at the time.

The bicycle had been a birthday gift given to her only eight weeks before. It has a basket in the front and three-inch wing nuts on the front wheels, and is possibly a Schwinn brand. Her bicycle has never been located.

Authorities do not believe she left of her own accord. They do, however, believe that Christina's disappearance may be connected to the 1982 disappearance of thirty-five year old Steven Pearsall and the murders of stepsisters twenty-one year old Kristina Nelson and eighteen year old Brandy Miller, as well as the 1981 murder of Kristin David. Steven, Kristina, and Brandy all disappeared from Lewiston, Idaho on the same night. Kristina and Brandy were last seen walking to the grocery store, and Steven vanished from the Lewiston Civic Theater where he worked. Kristin disappeared while on a bike ride in Idaho and was found dismembered in the Snake River eight days later. Kristina and Brandy's remains were found in a canyon in Kendrick, Idaho in 1984. Steven has never been located, but he is believed to have also been a homicide victim. Authorities believe he may have witnessed the stepsisters' murders and he too was then killed to keep him quiet.

Investigators have a person of interest, but the man has never been publicly identified. He was the last known person to see Christina White before she went missing, and he was employed at the Lewiston Civic Theater where Steven Pearsall was last seen. The man maintains his innocence in all five cases.

*(Age Progression to 44)*

At the time of her disappearance, Christina White had brown hair, stood 5'4", and weighed 135 pounds. She was last seen wearing blue jeans, possibly a tan and pink striped shirt, and red leather sneakers. She is Caucasian with hazel eyes and double-pierced ears. Her nicknames are Chris and Chrissy. As of this writing, she is fifty-one years old.

If you have any information regarding this case, you are urged to call the Asotin County Sheriff's Office at 509-758-2331.

## Hattie Yvonne Jackson

Six year old Hattie Yvonne Jackson was last seen at Rock Creek Park in Washington, D.C. on July 21, 1961. She, her older brother, and some friends were swimming in the creek there when a police officer told them the water was polluted and they could not swim in it. A man sitting nearby offered, after the officer left, to drive them to another place two miles away where the water was clean. The children declined and resumed playing. Then Hattie disappeared. She has never been heard from again.

Several witnesses later reported seeing two young men helping her into a dull blue/gray older model Chrysler, possibly a Plymouth, with yellow license plates. The driver of the car was the same man who had offered to take the children to a cleaner swimming spot. He was described as being Caucasian, between thirty and forty years old in 1961, with a deep tan and dark brown hair brushed straight back. He was wearing a white shirt, gray trousers, a black belt, and sunglasses. He was about 5'9" and had a muscular build. The man has never been identified.

*(Hattie at the time of her disappearance)*

At the time of her disappearance, Hattie Jackson had black hair, was 3', and weighed 45 pounds. She was last seen wearing a white long-sleeve blouse, brown and white checkered shorts, pink sandals, and a blue hair ribbon. She is African-American with brown eyes. As of this writing, she is sixty-three years old.

If you have any information regarding this case, you are urged to call the Washington, D.C. Metropolitan Police Department at 202-727-9099.

## April Nicole Williams

Three month old April Nicole Williams was last seen in Washington, D.C. on December 3, 1983. She and her mother were en route by bus from Suffolk, Virginia to see her mother's boyfriend in Kansas when they had a three-hour layover at a Trailways station in Washington. A woman her mother didn't know asked to hold the baby. Then, still holding April, the woman walked in the direction of a nearby Hardee's restaurant, supposedly to get a soda. The woman never returned, and April has never been seen or heard from again.

Her abductor is described as being African-American in her twenties and 5'3" with red braided hair.

She used the first name Latoya. Investigators believe the woman probably kidnapped April to raise her as her own.

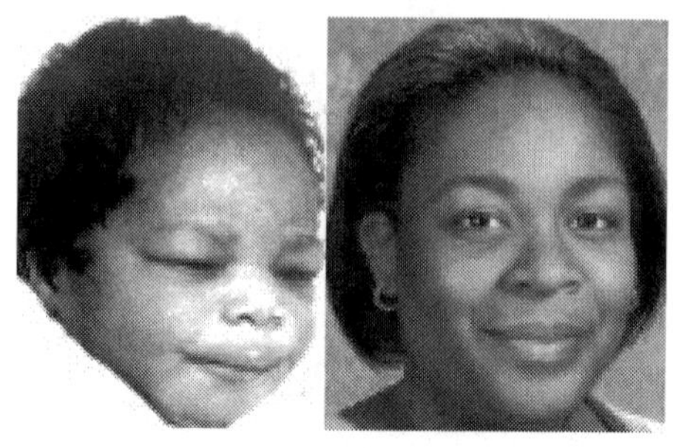

*(Age Progression to 33)*

At the time of her disappearance, April Williams had black hair, was 24", and weighed 11 pounds. She was last seen wearing a blue sleeper with a red number 1 on the left side of the front and a pink and white snowsuit. She is African-American with brown eyes and a one-inch birthmark on her right wrist. Her nickname is Niki. As of this writing, she is thirty-five years old.

If you have any information regarding this case, you are urged to call the Washington, D.C. Metropolitan Police Department at 202-727-9099.

## Victor Dewight Shoemaker Jr.

Five year old Victor Dewight Shoemaker Jr. and his family were visiting his grandfather in Kirby, West Virginia in May 1994. He was last seen playing with his eight and nine year old male cousins in a wooded area behind their grandfather's mobile home near Short Mountain on May 1, 1994. The boys played until approximately 8:30am when Victor got hungry and said he was going back to his grandfather's home to eat. He has never been seen or heard from again.

Investigators believe he became lost in the woods and died of exposure. Victor's father, however, believes his cousins may have harmed him. And as a result, his family has not spoken to the cousins' families since Victor's disappearance.

A dark blue 1990 model pickup truck was seen in the area around the time Victor went missing. It is not known if it is connected to his case, but police are interested in talking to the driver to see what, if anything, he or she may know about the child's disappearance.

*(Age Progression to 24)*

At the time of his disappearance, Victor Shoemaker Jr. had blonde hair, stood 4', and weighed 40 pounds. He was last seen wearing a red Bugs Bunny t-shirt, red shorts, and white X-Men sneakers. He is Caucasian with blue eyes. His Nickname is JR. As of this writing, he is twenty-nine years old.

If you have any information regarding this case, you are urged to call one of the following numbers:

*West Virginia State Police at 304-822-3561*

## Dennis Eugene Johnson

Eight year old Dennis Eugene Johnson was camping with his parents and sisters at Yellowstone National Park in Wyoming on April 12, 1966. His seven year old sister had gotten lost, and he and his father were searching for her when they decided to split up. Dennis was last seen walking away from his father at the Cascade Picnic Area, a quarter-mile north of Canyon Junction, at 1:30pm. His father found his sister, but Dennis has never been seen again.

An extensive two-week-long search turned up clues as to his whereabouts. He is presumed to have become lost or injured in the wilderness, but it is possible he was picked up by a passing motorist on the park road.

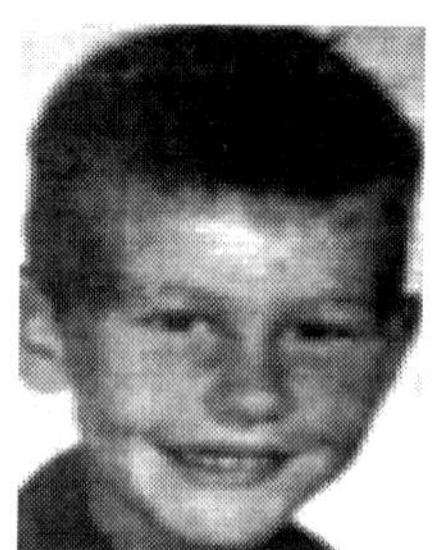

*(Dennis at the time of his disappearance)*

At the time of his disappearance, Dennis Johnson had sandy blonde hair, stood 3’8”, and weighed 60 pounds. He was last seen wearing a dark red long-sleeve shirt, Levis jeans, and a size 8 laced moccasin-type leather hiking boots with crepe soles. He is Caucasian with brown eyes and a six-inch scar on his abdomen. His nickname is Denny. As of this writing, he is sixty years old.

If you have any information regarding this case, you are urged to call the National Park Service at 307-344-2122.

## Deborah Rae Meyer

Fourteen year old Deborah Rae Meyer was last seen leaving a family member's residence near Seventh and Spruce Streets in Rawlins, Wyoming on August 4, 1974. She planned to walk to a local movie theater at the time. She never returned home and has never been seen again. It is not known if she made it to the theater or not. Foul play is suspected.

*(Age Progression to 53)*

At the time of her disappearance, Deborah Meyer had brown hair, stood 5'4", and weighed 115 pounds. She is Caucasian with brown eyes, a small circular growth on her left ear, and wears a full set of dentures. As of this writing, she is fifty-eight years old.

If you have any information regarding this case, you are urged to call the Carbon County Sheriff's Department at 307-324-2776.

## Jessica Delgadillo

Fourteen year old Jessica Delgadillo was last seen walking from her home on north Bolton Street in Amarillo, Texas headed to Palo Duro High School on October 20, 2010. She never made it to school and has never been heard from again. She didn't take any money or clothes with her.

She was originally classified as a runaway, but investigators are no longer pointing in that direction. It is possible she is still in the local area, in Lubbock, Texas, Port Saint Lucie, Florida, or with relatives in Mexico. However, she has had no contact with family or friends since she went missing.

*(Age Progression to 17)*

At the time of her disappearance, Jessica Delgadillo had brown hair, stood 5'6", and weighed 200 pounds. She is Hispanic with brown eyes, a small scar above her eye, and a vertical scar on her abdomen above her appendix. As of this writing, she is twenty-two years old.

If you have any information regarding this case, you are urged to call the Amarillo Police Department at 806-378-3038

## Thomas Estevis

Two year old Thomas Estevis was not yet born when his six older siblings were removed from their parents' home by Texas Child Protective Services (CPS) due to drug use in the household. When Thomas was born on February 20, 2006, he tested positive for cocaine and was immediately taken from his parents and placed in foster care. In December 2007, after the parents had satisfied various CPS requirements, all seven of their children were reunited with them. In November 2010, Thomas' father was arrested for driving under the influence with one of the children in the car. The police went to the family's home to drop off the child and found their mother also under the influence. As a result, CPS took custody of the six children who were present at the house. Thomas wasn't there. His parents said he was in Georgia with a relative. In December 2010, CPS became Temporary Managing Conservator of all the children, including Thomas, and asked his parents again where he was. His parents still claimed he was in Georgia, but gave no evidence to verify it. In January 2011, the children's mother died at the age of twenty-nine. In October 2011, CPS asked the court to dismiss their Temporary Managing Conservator of Thomas because he had never been in their care. CPS filed a missing person report on him in November 2011. Authorities do not know what happened to Thomas, and the exact date he disappeared is unknown.

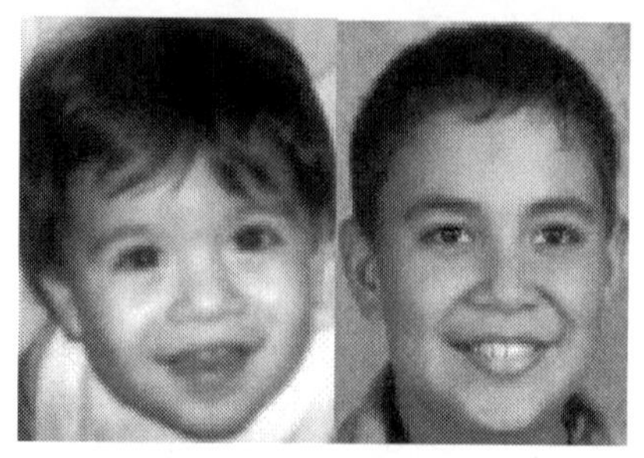

*(Age Progression to 12)*

At the time of his disappearance, Thomas Estevis had brown hair, stood 2'4", and weighed 40 pounds. He is Hispanic with brown eyes and may have scars on his ears. As of this writing, he is twelve years old.

If you have any information regarding this case, you are urged to call the Laredo Police Department at 956-795-2800.

## Karina Michelle Gaitan

Thirteen year old Karina Michelle Gaitan was last seen at her home at the Las Brisas Apartments in San Antonio, Texas at approximately 1am on July 18, 1998. She apparently snuck out of the house in the middle of the night to meet friends at a nearby apartment complex, but they stated she never showed up. She didn't take her purse or any of her personal belongings; and she left the front door unlocked, suggesting she had not planned on being gone long. She has never been heard from again. Foul play is possible in her case.

*(Age Progression to 24)*

At the time of her disappearance, Karina Gaitan had brown hair styled with bangs, painted fingernails and toenails, wore either purple-tinted contact lenses or tortoiseshell-framed eyeglasses with brown or yellow lenses, wore a size 6 or 7 shoe, stood 5'6", and weighed 160 pounds. She was last seen wearing a black mid-calf length t-shirt dress with pearl buttons on the front and cap sleeves, a black skirt or pair of wood shorts with stripes on the side, and black slip-on Reebok beach sandals with white lettering. She is Hispanic with brown eyes and a cross-shaped burn scar on her right hand between the thumb and forefinger. Her nickname is Twiggy. As of this writing, she is thirty-three years old.

If you have any information regarding this case, you are urged to call the San Antonio Police Department at 210-207-7660.

## Megan Elizabeth Garner

Three year old Megan Elizabeth Garner was last seen at a playground near her family's home on Paluxy Drive in Tyler, Texas on March 27, 1991 at approximately 11am. She was accompanied by her brother and cousin at the time. They turned away for a few minutes and Megan disappeared. She has never been seen again.

*(Age Progression to 29)*

At the time of her disappearance, Megan Garner had brown hair, stood 3'2", and weighed 30 pounds. She was last seen wearing a long-sleeve pink blue and green t-shirt with horizontal stripes, pink corduroy pants, blue socks, and blue and white Reebok sneakers with blue trim. She is Caucasian with brown eyes and is right-handed. As of this writing, she is thirty years old.

If you have any information regarding this case, you are urged to call the Tyler Police Department at 903-531-1000.

## Jiovany Gomez

Fourteen year old Jiovany Gomez disappeared from San Marcos, Texas on November 27, 2010. He was last seen with his uncle, forty-three year old Ricardo Gomez, thirty-six year old Luis Manuel Hernandez, forty-eight year old Carlos Ortega-Gonzalez, and thirty-one year old Nicholas Munoz. They had gone to Laredo, Texas that day to pick up some paperwork for a vehicle, and decided to cross the border into Nuevo Laredo, Mexico to go shopping. Luis called his wife at approximately 12pm and said they would be home by 7pm or 8pm. But they were not, and none of them have ever been seen again. The green 2003 Chevrolet Suburban with Texas plates AD98575 they were driving is also missing.

Authorities were notified about their disappearances on November 30th, after Luis and Nicholas failed to show up for their jobs at a concrete company called Heldenfels Enterprises Inc., where they were reliable employees. The circumstances of their disappearances are unknown. They may still be in Mexico. Foul play is considered possible.

*(Jiovany's Age Progression to 17)*

At the time of his disappearance, Jiovany Gomez had black hair, stood 5'5", and weighed 130 pounds. He is Hispanic with hazel eyes. He speaks both English and Spanish and is an American citizen. As of this writing, he is twenty-two years old.

*(Ricardo at the time of his disappearance)*

At the time of his disappearance, Ricardo Gomez had gray hair, stood 5'8", and weighed 250 pounds. He is Hispanic with brown eyes and is a Mexico-born legal U.S. resident. As of this writing, he is fifty-one years old.

*(Luis at the time of his disappearance)*

At the time of his disappearance, Luis Hernandez had black hair, stood 5'7", and weighed 379 pounds. He is Hispanic with brown eyes and is an American citizen. As of this writing, he is forty-three years old.

*(Carlos at the time of his disappearance)*

At the time of his disappearance, Carlos Ortega-Gonzalez had black hair, stood 5'6", and weighed 180 pounds. He is Hispanic with brown eyes and is a Mexico-born legal U.S. resident. As of this writing, he is fifty-five years old.

*(Nicholas at the time of his disappearance)*

At the time of his disappearance, Nicolas Munoz had brown hair, stood 5'7", and weighed 150 pounds. He is Hispanic with brown eyes and is a Mexico-born legal U.S. resident. As of this writing, he is thirty-nine years old.

If you have any information regarding this case, you are urged to call the Hays County Sheriff's Office at 512-753-2108.

## Melissa Suzanne Highsmith

One year old Melissa Suzanne Highsmith was abducted by a woman who called herself 'Ruth Johnson' on August 23, 1971. Melissa's mother had advertised for a babysitter that month. 'Ruth Johnson' responded to the ad and made plans with Melissa's mother to meet at her place of work, but 'Ruth' did not show up. She called later and Melissa's mother hired her sight unseen. 'Ruth' said she had a nice house with a large backyard and cared for other children. At 7:30am on August 23, 1971, 'Ruth' went to the Spanish Gate Apartments on east Seminary Drive in south Fort Worth, Texas where Melissa and her mother lived. Her mother had already left for work, leaving Melissa with their roommate. The roommate later said that 'Ruth' was well-dressed and wore white gloves. She took Melissa, some diapers, a pink dress, and a pair of white sandals. The child has never been seen or heard from again.

When 'Ruth' hadn't brought her daughter back by 8pm that night, Melissa's mother called police. 'Ruth Johnson' has never been located, and authorities are fairly certain that was not her real name. They believe Melissa was taken by someone who wanted to raise a child, but this is only a theory. Her case was reopened in 2005 at the request of her sister.

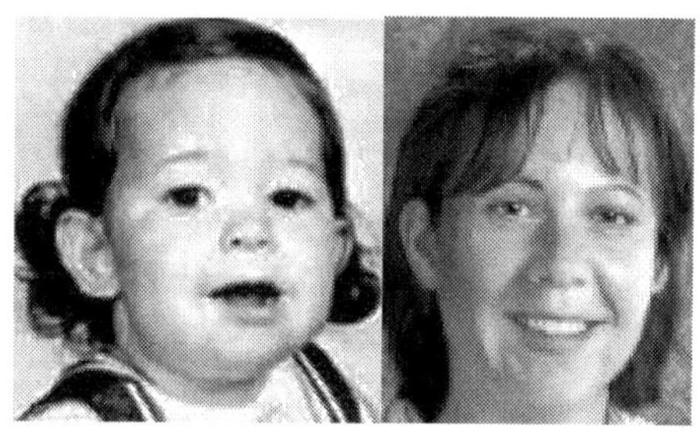

*(Age Progression to 42)*

At the time of her disappearance, Melissa Highsmith had brown hair, stood 2'8", and weighed 27 pounds. She is Caucasian with hazel eyes and a three-inch red-colored birthmark on her back just below her neck. As of this writing, she is forty-eight years old.

If you have any information regarding this case, you are urged to call the Fort Worth Police Department at 817-335-4222.

## Theresa Vernell Jones

Seventeen year old Theresa Vernell Jones was last seen in Alvin, Texas sometime in September 1980. She lived on Highway 6, near the city of Alvin. Her sister, Brenda, was in Houston, Texas and was expecting

Theresa to go give her a ride home. Theresa never arrived and has never been heard from again. She was driving a primer gray late 1960s model Chevrolet Impala or Chevrolet Nova at the time. It has never been located.

Another of the sisters, Gina Ladonna Gibbs, was murdered in Nassau County, Florida on June 2, 1982, at the age of twenty-two. Her murder remains unsolved. Investigators are looking into the theory that Gina's murder and Theresa's disappearance are in some way connected.

*(Theresa at the time of her disappearance)*

At the time of her disappearance, Theresa Jones had brown hair, a slight gap between her upper front teeth, stood between 5'5" - 5'6", and weighed between 110 - 130 pounds. She is Caucasian with brown eyes and a rose tattoo on the back of her right shoulder. Her nickname is Terrie. As of this writing, she is fifty-five years old.

If you have any information regarding this case, you are urged to call one of the following numbers:

*Alvin Police Department at 281-388-4370*

*Brazoria County Sheriff's Office at 979-864-2236*

## Jenna Ray Robbins

Nine year old Jenna Ray Robbins was last seen playing with a six year old friend outside of her family's residence on north 4th Street in Killeen, Texas on May 14, 1989. Her mother went to the store and left the two children playing outside. The six year old child later told authorities that a new-looking light gray or silver two-door Dodge or Plymouth sedan stopped near Jenna's home at approximately 5:30pm. The male driver lured Jenna into his car by saying her would buy her a gift. The man tried to convince her friend to get into the car as well, but she got frightened and ran away. Jenna has never been seen again.

The vehicle was last seen traveling west on Garrison Avenue in Killeen. The driver is described as Caucasian, between twenty and twenty-two years old, with brown slicked back hair. He has never been identified.

Two days before Jenna's abduction a man matching the description of her abductor had tried to lure another child into his vehicle. It has not been proven that the two incidents were the same man, however.

*(Age Progression to 30)*

At the time of her disappearance, Jenna Robbins has brown hair and freckles, stood 4'5", and weighed 50 pounds. She was last seen wearing black spandex pants with florescent green stripes on the sides, a white pullover shirt with a multicolored tree design, and white sneakers. She is Biracial (Asian/Caucasian) with brown eyes and a small scar on her right eyebrow. She is of Korean descent. As of this writing, she is thirty-eight years old.

If you have any information regarding this case, you are urged to call the Killeen Police Department at 817-699-2387.

## Judith Ann Elwell

Five year old Judith Ann Elwell was last seen at her home on north Meta Avenue in Oklahoma City, Oklahoma on the night of July 6, 1967. She has never been seen again. The next day, one of her shoes was found next to an abandoned house half a block away. A short length of braided rope was under the shoe. Authorities believe she was abducted and lost her shoe in the struggle with her kidnapper. No other clues were ever found despite an extensive search.

Almost a month later, on August 3rd, five year old Brenda Lois White disappeared from St. Patrick Drive in Midwest City, Oklahoma. Her remains were found in a shallow grave in a field outside an abandoned house eleven miles from her own home in November 1967. Her murder remains unsolved.

Some believe Judith's abduction and Brenda's murder were the work of the same person. However, the girls did not know one another, and there is no hard evidence to suggest the same person is responsible for both.

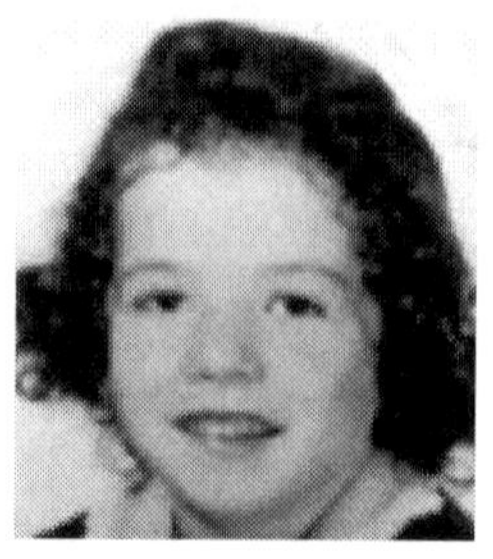

*(Judith at the time of her disappearance)*

At the time of her disappearance, Judith Elwell had black hair. Her height and weight at the time is unknown. She was last seen wearing a blue and white striped pullover shirt, light green shorts, white socks, and blue canvas sneakers. She is Caucasian with dark brown eyes. As of this writing, she is fifty-six years old.

If you have any information regarding this case, you are urged to call the Midwest City Police Department at 405-739-1317.

## Royce Henson & Kathleen Henson

One year old Royce Henson and his mother, thirty year old Kathleen Henson, were last seen in Tulsa, Oklahoma on March 23, 1979 when Kathleen dropped her ten year old son off at his father's place of work. She and Royce were going to a friend's house at approximately 11:30pm that night. They were driving a brown four-door 1969 Chrysler sedan at the time. They never arrived and have never been heard from again.

On March 25$^{th}$, the vehicle was found locked and abandoned at the corner of Ute Street and Peoria Avenue in Tulsa. Kathleen's change purse, her driver's license and Social Security card, a baby bottle, and one credit card were inside the vehicle. But there was no sign of Royce or his mother.

Other than a quick look inside the vehicle and her apartment, the police didn't do any investigating into their disappearances until Kathleen's mother inquired into the status of her daughter and grandson's case in 1984. Foul play is suspected.

*(Royce's Age Progression to 36)*

At the time of his disappearance, Royce Henson had black hair, was 2'9", and weighed 35 pounds. He is Biracial (African-American/ Caucasian) with brown eyes. As of this writing, he is forty years old.

*(Kathleen's Age Progression to 60)*

At the time of her disappearance, Kathleen Henson had brown hair, wore contact lenses, stood 5'7", and weighed 125 pounds. She is Caucasian with blue eyes and pierced ears. Her nickname is Kathy. As of this writing, she is seventy years old.

If you have any information regarding this case, you are urged to call the Tulsa Police Department at 918-596-9122.

## Rita Lorraine Jolly

Seventeen year old Rita Lorraine Jolly left her home on Horton Road in West Linn, Oregon at 7:15pm on June 29, 1973 to go for a walk. She was last seen between 8:30pm and 9pm that day, walking uphill on Sunset Avenue. She never returned home and has never been heard from again.

Some believe she may have been a victim of the serial killer Ted Bundy. He was executed in Florida in 1989. He didn't confess to having any connection to Rita's disappearance, but he is considered a suspect in many deaths and disappearances he did not claim responsibility for. Foul play is suspected in Rita's case.

*(Rita at the time of her disappearance)*

At the time of her disappearance, Rita Jolly had light brown hair, walked with an uneven gait, stood 5'6", and weighed 130 pounds. She was last seen wearing a brown Pendleton shirt, blue jeans or Army fatigue pants, and low-cut blue sneakers with buckskin heels. She is Caucasian with hazel eyes and a previously fractured lower left leg that didn't heal properly. As of this writing, she is sixty-two years old.

If you have any information regarding this case, you are urged to call the Clackamas County Sheriff's Office at 503-723-4949 or 503-557-5811.

## Joan Leigh Hall

Seventeen year old Joan Leigh Hall was last seen walking down Main Street in Warrenton, Oregon between 2pm and 2:30pm on September 30, 1983. She had left a local store and was on her way to Warrenton Grade School. She never arrived and has never been heard from again. She is missing under suspicious circumstances, and her loved ones believe she was murdered.

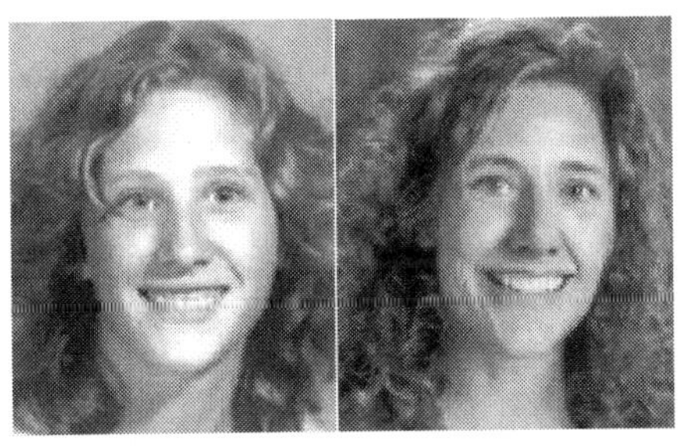

*(Age Progression to 46)*

At the time of her disappearance, Joan Hall had short brown hair that developed blonde highlights in the summer, stood between 5'3" - 5'6", and weighed between 110 - 120 pounds. She was last seen wearing a green hooded sweatshirt, blue jeans, a blue jacket, and maroon and white sneakers. She was carrying a blue and white backpack and a brown purse. She is Caucasian with blue eyes and pierced ears. Her nickname is Joanie. As of this writing, she is fifty-two years old.

If you have any information regarding this case, you are urged to call the Clatsop Sheriff's Department at 503-325-8635.

## Shausha Latine Henson & Shaina Ashley Kirkpatrick

Two month old Shausha Latine Henson and her sister, one year old Shaina Ashley Kirkpatrick left their home in Portland, Oregon with their mother, Kimyala Henson, on April 4, 2001. They planned to travel to British Columbia, Canada with a friend, Christina Mayer, and her husband, Frank Oehring. Frank was wanted in Missouri for allegedly attempting to murder his former wife. It has been established that Kimyala and her daughters spent the night of April 5th at the Shasta Lodge in Redding, California with Christina and Frank. They apparently stopped in Sacramento, California to allow Kimyala to pick up her birth certificate. Christina and Frank may have convinced her she would need it to get into Canada. There has been no sign of the children since that time.

Christina and Frank were discovered at a rest area in Collier County, Florida on April 20, 2001. She had been killed by a gunshot wound to the head. He was critically wounded, also by a gunshot wound to the head, and died on the way to the hospital. Authorities determined their deaths were the result of a murder suicide. Frank left behind letters detailing their plan to steal Kimyala's birth certificate. Christina had assumed her identity in Las Vegas, Nevada. Kimyala's remains were found near Nixon, Nevada on April 28th. She had been struck in the head and shot to death. Authorities believe Frank and Christina were responsible for her murder.

An extensive search of the area turned up no clues as to her daughters' whereabouts. Blood on a hatchet found in Christina and Frank's car was Kimyala's. Authorities believe that Frank and Christina traveled to Florida alone. Motel receipts indicate that the girls were not with them at the time. Their car seats and birth certificates have never been located. Authorities do not know if the couple harmed the children or sold them to someone.

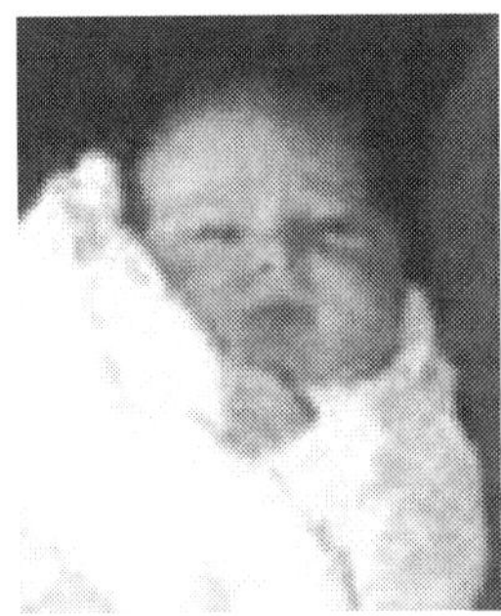

*(Shausha at the time of her disappearance)*

At the time of her disappearance, Shausha Henson had brown hair, was 24", and weighed 16 pounds. She is Caucasian with brown eyes. She suffered from a broken collar bone at birth. As of this writing, she is seventeen years old.

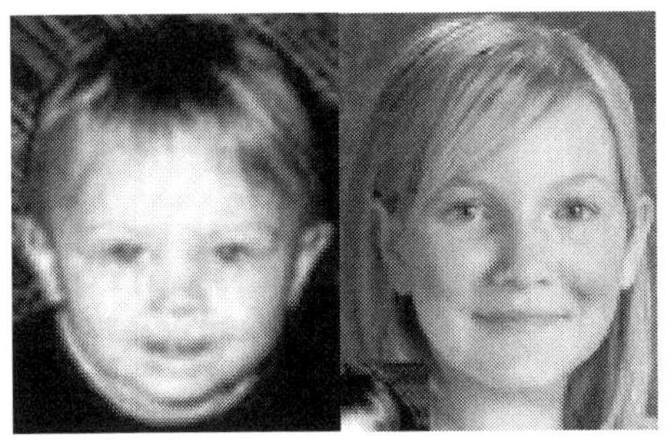

*(Shaina's Age Progression to 14)*

At the time of her disappearance, Shaina Kirkpatrick had blonde hair, stood 3', and weighed 24 pounds. She is Caucasian with blue eyes and a triangle-shaped birthmark on the back of her head. As of this writing, she is nineteen years old.

If you have any information regarding this case, you are urged to call one of the following numbers:

*Portland Police Department at 503-823-0044*

*Federal Bureau of Investigation (FBI) Portland Office at 503-224-4181*

## Kyron Richard Horman

Seven year old Kyron Richard Horman was last seen in Portland, Oregon on June 4, 2010. He usually rode the bus to Skyline Elementary School, but that morning his stepmother, Terri, said she drove him to school so he could set up his exhibit for the science fair. The school is on Skyline Boulevard in a rural area in northwest Portland, about two miles from where he lived with his father and stepmother on Sheltered Nook Road. A witness saw Terri and Kyron together at 8:15am in front of his science exhibit. The bell rang at 8:45am, and Terri said she left at that time. She said Kyron told her he was going to class. He never made it to his classroom and has never been seen or heard from again.

Terri reported him missing at 3:45pm after he failed to arrive home from school at 3:30pm as usual. No one reported seeing him at school after the 8:45am bell. His teacher marked him absent, because she thought he was at a doctor's appointment. Police launched an extensive search immediately. Over the next few days they interviewed all the students and staff at Skyline Elementary and searched the school, school grounds, and the surrounding area. Kyron's loved ones said it would be unlikely for him to leave the school on his own.

Less than two weeks after his disappearance, police stopped the search and said they had upgraded his case from a missing child to a criminal investigation. At the same time, they stated they did not think he had been abducted by a stranger. They focused on Terri, stating cell phone records indicated she was not where she said she was on the day of her stepson's disappearance.

Three weeks after Kyron's disappearance, his father, Kaine, moved out of the home he had shared with Kyron, Terri, and their one year old daughter. During the following days, police released more information to the public. A landscaper, who had worked for the Horman family, told investigators that about six or seven months before Kyron disappeared, Terri had offered him money to kill her husband. When authorities notified Kaine of this, he took his daughter and moved out. He filed for divorce and a restraining order from Terri. A judge barred her from contacting Kaine, Kyron, her baby daughter, or her own teenage son who was being raised by her parents. Kaine sought custody of his daughter and child support from Terri. He accused her of trying to abduct the baby girl from day care two days after the restraining order was granted. In mid-July, Terri moved back to her hometown of Roseburg, Oregon, and Kaine and his daughter moved back into their house on Sheltered Nook Road.

Investigators questioned Terri's friend about her possible knowledge of Kyron's disappearance. They searched the friend's home and asked the public to come forward if they had seen Terri, her white pickup truck, or Terri's friend on June 4th between 9:45am and 1pm. The friend says she knows nothing about Kyron's disappearance, and believes Terri is innocent of any wrongdoing.

Kaine stated that Terri suffered from postpartum depression after the birth of their daughter, and her behavior changed. He said he believed his daughter was not safe with Terri and may have witnessed whatever happened to Kyron on the day of his disappearance. Some of Terri's acquaintances said she was angry at Kaine for making her teenage son move in with her parents in February 2010, four months before Kyron disappeared.

Kyron's biological mother, Desiree, told reporters that she had attempted to get custody of him prior to him going missing, because he had told her several times that he wanted to live with her. In May 2012, she filed a lawsuit against Terri accusing her of kidnapping Kyron and seeking $10 million in damages. She asked the court to order Terri to return Kyron or reveal the location of his remains.

Authorities have not named anyone a suspect in Kyron's disappearance, despite their focus on his stepmother. Kaine theorized that Terri caused Kyron's disappearance, possibly with the help of another person, in order to hurt him. Both Kaine and Desiree continue to hold out hope that their son is alive and will one day be reunited with them.

*(Kyron at the time of his disappearance & age progressions to 11-12 & 14-15)*

At the time of his disappearance, Kyron Horman had brown hair, wore metal-framed glasses, stood 3'8", and weighed 50 pounds. He was last seen wearing a black t-shirt with CSI in green lettering and a handprint on the front, size 7 black cargo pants, white Hanes athletic socks, and size 11 black Sketchers sneakers with orange trim. He is Caucasian with blue eyes. He is allergic to bees. As of this writing, he is fifteen years old.

There is a $50,000 reward for information leading to the resolution of his disappearance. If you have any information regarding this case, you are urged to call the Multnomah County Sheriff's Office at 503-823-3333 or 503-261-2847. You can also email tips to tips@bringkyronhome.org.

## Allen Briscoe Jr. & Christine Green

Sixteen year old Allen Briscoe Jr. was last seen exiting the bus on Woodland Avenue in Philadelphia,

Pennsylvania on December 13, 1985. He and a friend rode the subway around town all day and then returned to their neighborhood by bus. As they exited the bus, Allen told his friend that he was going to see a female friend. Allen has never been seen or heard from again, and authorities do not believe he ran away from home.

Allen's disappearance may be somehow connected to the disappearance of sixteen year old Christine Green, who attended the same high school as he did. She was last seen leaving her home on Greenway Avenue in Philadelphia, Pennsylvania at 8am on April 23, 1985. She was supposed to catch the Woodland Avenue Trolley and go to Bartram High School, but she never arrived and has never been heard from again. There is speculation that she ran away due to a possible pregnancy, but her loved ones stated she had never ran away before and always kept them informed of her whereabouts.

*(Allen's Age Progression to 39)*

At the time of his disappearance, Allen Briscoe Jr. had black hair, a chipped front tooth, stood 5'8", and weighed 140 pounds. He was last seen wearing a black jacket and blue jeans. He is African-American with brown eyes, a lump on his left shoulder, and a scar on his forehead. He is bowlegged, and his nicknames are

Squeak and Squeaky. As of this writing, he is forty-eight years old.

*(Christine's Age Progression to 43)*

At the time of his disappearance, Christine Green had black hair, may have been pregnant, stood 5', and weighed 90 pounds. She was last seen wearing a pink blouse, a blue vest, jeans, and black shoes. She is African-American with brown eyes and a surgical scar on her left side. Her nicknames are Tina and Dinky. As of this writing, she is forty-nine years old.

If you have any information regarding this case, you are urged to call the Philadelphia Police Department at 215-685-1173.

## Corey James Edkin

Two year old Corey James Edkin was last seen at his home on Second Street in New Columbia, Pennsylvania on October 12, 1986. He was asleep when his mother left to go get pizza at 12:10am. She left her son in the care of her roommate, who was awake and watching TV. When his mother returned at approximately 12:40am, the door leading outside was open and Corey was gone. The roommate told authorities that she didn't see Corey leave the house or anyone come in while his mother was gone, and she did not hear any unusual noises. Corey has never been seen or heard from again.

Investigators confirmed that his mother did go to the convenience store just as she said she had, and the roommate passed a polygraph. Several ransom calls were made to different members of the child's family, even as late as January 1991. But the caller(s) have never been identified.

*(Age Progression to 25)*

At the time of his disappearance, Corey Edkin had very light blonde hair, stood 3', and weighed 30 pounds. He was last seen wearing gray pajama pants, a short-sleeve white pajama top with a cartoon beaver on the front, and no shoes or socks. He is Caucasian with blue eyes. As of this writing, he is thirty-four years old.

If you have any information regarding this case, you are urged to call the Pennsylvania State Police at 717-742-8761.

## Mary Ann Verdecchia & Marcella Krulce

Ten year old Mary Ann Verdecchia was last seen on June 7, 1962 in Bloomfield, Pennsylvania. She attended a half-day of classes at Immaculate Conception School, and then went home and changed out of her school uniform. At 12:30pm, she went to the Martinique Apartments on Baum Boulevard in Bloomfield to run errands for a woman who lived there. The woman sent her to the store. Mary Ann was last seen re-entering the apartment complex at 2:45pm. She has never been heard from again. She was reported missing at 10:30pm after her relatives had searched for her to no avail. A few days later, a piece of jewelry believed to have belonged to her was found at the entrance to the Highland Park Zoo, but she could have lost it prior to her disappearance.

In 1991, a man came forward and said that in 1962, when he himself was only nine years old, he witnessed a Presbyterian minister molest and murder a young girl in Pittsburgh, Pennsylvania. Mary Ann was the only reported missing child in the area at the time. The witness's account has never been confirmed and the minister, who maintains his innocence, has never been charged.

Thirty year old Marcella Krulce was also last seen at the Martinique Apartments, three years before Mary Ann disappeared, on November 19, 1959. She lived in the apartments on weekdays and spent weekends at her mother's home in Strabane Township. Marcella failed to show up for work on November 20th and has never been seen again. All of her belongings were left behind in the apartment.

Investigators stated that there is no indication that the two cases are related, other than the Martinique Apartments being the last place they were both seen. Foul play is suspected in both cases.

*(Mary Ann at the time of her disappearance)*

At the time of her disappearance, Mary Ann Verdecchia had black hair, stood 4'10", and weighed 60 pounds. She was last seen wearing a white shirt, red shorts, and white sneakers. She is Caucasian with brown eyes and a scar in the center of her forehead. As of this writing, she is sixty-seven years old.

*(Marcella at the time of her disappearance)*

At the time of her disappearance, Marcella Krulce had brown hair, stood 5'2", and weighed 103 pounds. She was last seen wearing a black coat and black shoes. She is Caucasian with brown eyes and is an insulin-dependent diabetic. Her needles and insulin were left behind. As of this writing, she is eighty-nine years old.

If you have any information regarding this case, are urged to call the Pittsburgh Bureau of Police at 412-323-7800.

## Marjorie West

Four year old Marjorie West was last seen by her eleven year old sister picking wildflowers in the White Gravel area of McKean County, Pennsylvania on May 8, 1938. The girls were there with their parents for a Mother's Day picnic. Her sister left her alone while she spoke to their mother at approximately 3pm. When she returned to the area a few minutes later, Marjorie was gone. She has never been heard from again. Her mother contacted authorities after an initial search by family members turned up no clues as to the child's whereabouts. Hundreds of people joined in on an extensive search for her in the woods, but no trace was ever found.

A taxi driver in Thomas, West Virginia claimed that he saw a crying child matching Marjorie's description and wearing similar clothes riding in a dark green car with an unidentified man in his thirties. The sighting took place at 11:38pm on the night of her disappearance. Investigators determined that if the individual had abducted Marjorie at around 3pm, they would have arrived in Thomas between 11pm and 11:30pm that evening. The driver told the taxi driver that the girl was his daughter and asked where the nearest motel was located. The taxi driver identified Marjorie as the child several days later. A man matching the description of the individual refueled at a gas station outside of Thomas. There an attendant reported seeing a bundle wrapped in a gray blanket in the backseat of the car. The man has never been identified, and authorities are not certain that the child was Marjorie.

*(Marjorie at the time of her disappearance)*

At the time of her disappearance, Marjorie West had red hair and freckles and spoke with a southern accent. Her height and weight at the time are unknown. She was last seen wearing a blue dress, a navy blue mid-length coat with the collar trimmed in pink, a Shirley Temple-type hat, and patent leather shoes. She is Caucasian with blue eyes. As of this writing, she is eighty-five years old.

If you have any information regarding this case, you are urged to call the Pennsylvania State Police at 814-938-0510.

## Kimberly Janis Boyd, Sarah Boyd & Linda McCord

Two year old Kimberly Janis Boyd was last seen with her mother, thirty-two year old Sarah Boyd, and their friend, thirty-one year old Linda McCord, on April 3, 1987 in Waltersboro, South Carolina. They attended a gospel concert that evening, and were returning to their homes in Orangeburg County when they disappeared.

A witness saw their vehicle driving between thirty and forty-five miles per hour along Route 15. Another car was behind them, but the witness was unable to describe the second vehicle or its occupants.

Sarah's husband was initially unconcerned about his wife and daughter because he thought they were with Linda or with relatives; but when they hadn't returned by 6am the following morning, he contacted police. The vehicle they had been traveling in was found disabled and abandoned in Dorchester County near the intersection of Highway 15 and 176 on April 5th. There were no signs of the three in or around the vehicle, and they have never been heard from again.

Sarah's credit card was used at a local mall in 1990, but the signature was barely legible and didn't match her handwriting. The identity of the card user has never been established. Foul play is suspected.

*(Kimberly's Age Progression to 31)*

At the time of her disappearance, Kimberly Boyd had black hair, stood 3'4", and weighed 25 pounds. She is African-American with brown eyes. As of this writing, she is thirty-three years old.

(Sarah at the time of her disappearance)

At the time of her disappearance, Sarah Boyd had black hair, wore eyeglasses, stood between 5'4" - 5'6", and weighed 105 pounds. She is African-American with brown eyes, and she may use the first name Genette. As of this writing, she is sixty-three years old.

(Linda at the time of her disappearance)

At the time of her disappearance, Linda McCord had black hair and wore eyeglasses. Her height and weight at the time are unknown. She is African-American with brown eyes. As of this writing, she is sixty-two years old.

If you have any information regarding this case, you are urged to call the Dorchester County Sheriff's Office at 843-873-5111.

## Charles Hall III

Fifteen year old Charles Hall III was last seen leaving his family's apartment on 40th Avenue North in Nashville, Tennessee at 3pm on December 31, 1981. He was planning to walk to his girlfriend's home, but it is unknown if he made it there or not. He never returned home and has never been seen again. Investigators believe he was abducted.

*(Age Progression to 47)*

At the time of his disappearance, Charles Hall III had black hair, stood 5'8", and weighed between 130 - 140 pounds. He was last seen wearing a black jacket, maroon pants, and sneakers. He is African-American with brown eyes and a birthmark on his right cheek. His nicknames are Charlie and Little Charlie. As of this writing, he is fifty-two years old.

If you have any information regarding this case, you are urged to call the Nashville Police Department at 615-862-7557.

## Jeremy James Grice

Four year old Jeremy James Grice was last seen standing near the mailbox of his family's mobile home on Miller Street in the Bath area of North Augusta, South Carolina on November 21, 1985. He had his bicycle with him and appeared to be waiting for the bus, but he did not have school that day. His disappearance was not discovered until 10am. His stepfather, who had been watching him after his mother left for work, never saw or heard anything suspicious.

Extensive air and ground searches turned up no clues as to his whereabouts. Investigators also drained the local ponds in an effort to locate his remains, to no avail. Authorities believe he was abducted.

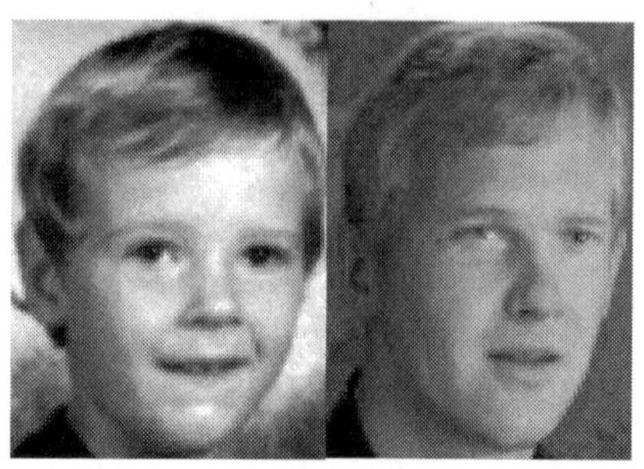

*(Age Progression to 34)*

At the time of his disappearance, Jeremy Grice had blonde hair, stood between 3'8" - 4', and weighed 40 pounds. He was last seen wearing either pajamas or jeans and a t-shirt with no socks or shoes. He is Caucasian with hazel eyes and moles on his scalp and behind his left ear lobe. As of this writing, he is thirty-seven years old.

If you have any information regarding this case, you are urged to call the Aiken County Sheriff's Department at 803-642-1761.

## Zaylee Grace Fryar

Three month old Zaylee Grace Fryar disappeared with her mother, twenty-eight year old Shauna Marie Fryar, from Millersville, Tennessee on May 1, 2011. Shauna's husband left to go to the store at 9pm, and when he returned both his wife and his daughter were gone. Shauna's Honda Accord, her wallet, cell phone, and Zaylee's diaper bag were left behind. Shauna had dropped out of sight on prior occasions and had always come home safely, so her husband did not report her and Zaylee missing until May 5th. Shauna had a history of drug abuse, and authorities believe she may have gone out to look for drugs on the night they went missing.

On May 6th, Shauna's body was pulled out of the Cumberland River near the Jefferson Street Bridge in downtown Nashville, Tennessee. Her remains were positively identified on May 10th. Authorities believe she was murdered in Millersville before her body was dumped in the river, but they have not disclosed her cause of death. They have also stated they have two suspects in Shauna's homicide, but neither has been publicly named. Zaylee has never been located, but she is considered to be in danger due to the circumstances involved.

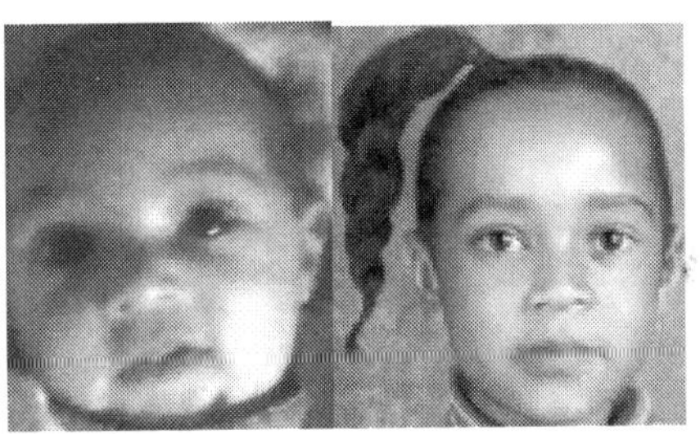

*(Age Progression to 5)*

At the time of her disappearance, Zaylee Fryar had black hair, was 24", and weighed 12 pounds. She is Biracial (African-American/Caucasian) with brown eyes and a brown quarter-sized birthmark on her right leg. As of this writing, she is seven years old.

If you have any information regarding this case, you are urged to call the Millersville Police Department at 615-859-2758.

## Teresa Lynn "Trenny" Gibson

Sixteen year old Teresa Lynn "Trenny" Gibson accompanied forty of her classmates from Knoxville, Tennessee on a field trip to the Great Smoky Mountains National Park on October 8, 1976. The students were hiking to Andrews Bald on the trip and separated into small groups when they reached the trails. Trenny was last seen at approximately 3pm near Clingman's Dome, walking on a moderately steep trail with sharp drop-offs and dense undergrowth on both sides. She has never been seen again.

Extensive searches of the park continued until the end of October 1976, but neither she nor her remains were located. The theory is that she accidentally fell from the trail and was either killed instantly or eventually succumbed to her injuries, but something else may have caused her disappearance. Foul play, however, is not suspected.

*(Trenny at the time of her disappearance)*

At the time of her disappearance, Trenny Gibson had brown hair, stood 5'3", and weighed 115 pounds. She was last seen wearing a blue blouse, a blue and white striped sweater, a borrowed brown plaid heavy jacket, blue jeans, blue Adidas shoes, and a diamond and sapphire ring. She is Caucasian with green eyes. As of this writing, she is fifty-eight years old.

If you have any information regarding this case, you are urged to call the Tennessee Bureau of Investigation (TBI) at 615-744-4000.

## Michael J. Woodward

Nine year old Michael J. Woodward was last seen playing in his yard in Fort Jackson, South Carolina on April 23, 1972, as his father mowed the grass nearby. Sometime between 9am and noon, Michael vanished and has never been seen or heard from again.

*(Age Progression to 50)*

At the time of his disappearance, Michael Woodward had blonde hair, protruding teeth, stood 4'8", and weighed 70 pounds. He was last seen wearing brown striped pants and blue sneakers. He is Caucasian with blue eyes. Prior to his disappearance, he had injured his left eye in a fishing accident and the injury had not healed properly, possibly resulting in blindness in that eye. As of this writing, he is fifty-five years old.

If you have any information regarding this case, you are urged to call the Fort Jackson Army Base Military Police at 803-751-1418.

## Jeremy Lee Bechtel & Erin Leigh Foster

Seventeen year old Jeremy Lee Bechtel and eighteen year old Erin Leigh Foster were last seen outside of Sparta, Tennessee at approximately 10pm on April 3, 2000. They were in Erin's black two-door 1998 Pontiac Grand Am with Tennessee plates 473EJR at the time. They have never been heard from again and the car has never been located. At first investigators believed they may have left of their own accord, but because of the passage of time with no trace of their whereabouts surfacing, that theory now seems unlikely.

*(Jeremy's Age Progression to 29)*

At the time of his disappearance, Jeremy Bechtel had dark brown hair, stood at 5'8", and weighed 150 pounds. He was last seen wearing a dark t-shirt or a plaid shirt, baggy blue jeans, white Fila sneakers, and either a blue baseball cap or a green Army cap. He is Caucasian with blue eyes and multiple piercings in both ears. His nickname is Little C. As of this writing, he is thirty-five years old.

*(Erin's Age Progression to 30)*

At the time of her disappearance, Erin Foster had blonde hair, stood 5'8", and weighed 115 pounds. She was last seen wearing pants, sandals, and three sets of earrings. She is Caucasian with blue eyes. Each of her ears is pierced three times each. As of this writing, she is thirty-six years old.

If you have any information regarding this case, you are urged to call the White County Sheriff's Office at 931-836-2700.

## Tonetta Yvette Carlisle

Fifteen year old Tonetta Yvette Carlisle was last seen walking home from City High School, where she was a freshman, at approximately 2:55pm on March 16, 1989 in Chattanooga, Tennessee. She was headed to her home on Hamilton Avenue at the time. A witness observed Tonetta's abduction approximately one-half block from her home at about 3pm. A woman on Ruth Street near Hamilton Avenue glanced up the hill and watched Tonetta walking down the street. Suddenly, several unidentified individuals jumped out of a tan and yellow vehicle with Tennessee plates LKH 920 and forcibly pulled Tonetta inside and drove away. Her mother filed a missing person report on her eight hours later when her daughter failed to return home.

The plate number of the vehicle involved in the abduction was traced back to Jeffrey Jones. He had previously been convicted of rape and aggravated sexual assault and served eight years in prison. He was released about a year before Tonetta disappeared. Authorities later determined he had also raped another woman who lived in his apartment complex just two months before Tonetta's abduction. He was found deceased from carbon monoxide poisoning by suicide in his van on March 18, 1989, two days after Tonetta had last been seen. There have been rumors that she was possibly taken to California and forced into prostitution.

*(Age Progression to 40)*

At the time of her disappearance, Tonetta Carlisle had black hair styled curly and trimmed short on the top and sides and longer at the back, stood 5'1", and weighed 95 pounds. She was last seen wearing a pink and white striped blouse, a denim skirt, and white sneakers. She is African-American with brown eyes, pierced ears, and several capped teeth. As of this writing, she is forty-five years old.

If you have any information regarding this case, you are urged to call the Chattanooga Police Department at 615-698-9752.

## Dennis Lloyd Martin

Six year old Dennis Lloyd Martin was last seen playing hide-and-seek in Spence Field near the Appalachian Trail in the Great Smoky Mountains National Park in Tennessee at around 4pm on June 14, 1969. He went behind a bush to hide and has never been seen or heard from again. Only five minutes passed before his family began to look for him. The search eventually expanded to more than 1400 people including the National Guard, but no clues as to his whereabouts were ever found. It is believed he became lost and perished inside the park, however, numerous other theories have come to light throughout the years as to what may have happened to him, ranging from the possible to the bizarre.

*(Age Progression to 51)*

At the time of his disappearance, Dennis Martin had wavy dark brown hair and long thick eyelashes, stood between 4' - 4'1", and weighed 55 pounds. He had learning disabilities and was missing one of his upper front teeth at the time. He was last seen wearing a red t-shirt, dark green hiking shorts, white socks, and black low-cut oxford shoes with a simple heel. He is Caucasian with brown eyes. As of this writing, he is fifty-six years old.

If you have any information regarding this case, you are urged to call one of the following numbers:

*Great Smoky Mountain Police Department at 865-436-1230*

*Tennessee Bureau of Investigation (TBI) at 615-744-4000*

## David Clayton Warner

Twelve year old David Clayton Warner was last seen in Jefferson City, Tennessee at 7pm on March 2, 1983. Earlier that day, he said he was going to a church function up the street from his home on Beeler Avenue. He did go to the church, but he did not go inside and instead went to Druther's Restaurant for a hamburger. After eating, he went to a friend's home and they watched television until 7pm. At that time, David said he was going home, which was about thirty yards from his friend's home. He has never been seen or heard from again.

His family did not realize he was not at home until the next morning, and even then they thought he may have spent the night at his friend's house. When his disappearance was reported to police, they believed he may have run away. But now authorities believe he was abducted and murdered, although his remains have never been found, if that was what happened.

*(Age Progression to 42)*

At the time of his disappearance, David Warner had blonde hair, stood between 5'2" - 5'5", and weighed 110 pounds. He was last seen wearing a black and white Pittsburgh Steelers sweatshirt, blue jeans, and sneakers. He is Caucasian with brown eyes and suffers from epilepsy. His nickname is Little David. As of this writing, he is forty-seven years old.

If you have any information regarding this case, you are urged to call the Jefferson City Police Department at 615-475-2002.

## Melissa Alaniz, Marjorie Alice Knox, & Cheryl Lynn Vasquez

Twelve year old Melissa Alaniz was last seen in El Paso, Texas on March 7, 1987. She went to go play video games at a convenience store off Rushing Road and never returned home. She has never been heard from again. Authorities do not believe she left of her own accord.

That same year, several other females disappeared from El Paso, and most of them were later found murdered and buried in the desert. The victims were all small slender young women in the teens and early twenties. Melissa knew at least one of the victims. She lived in the same neighborhood as several of the victims, and her parents worked with the parents of another victim. Melissa and two other girls, fourteen year old Marjorie Alice Knox and nineteen year old Cheryl Lynn Vasquez, are still missing.

Marjorie Knox disappeared between 2am and 3am on February 14, 1987 while she was walking from a friend's house on Chaparral Street in Chaparral, New Mexico to her own home fifteen to twenty minutes away on Byrum Street. She never arrived home and has never been heard from again. Chaparral, New Mexico is only about twenty-five miles from El Paso, where she had attended a Valentine's Day party the day before.

Cheryl Vasquez was last seen at 9:22pm on June 28, 1987 at the Circle K convenience store on McCombs Street in El Paso, Texas. She had gone there to buy cigarettes for a friend and was last seen talking to an acquaintance, David Wood, in the parking lot. She has never been seen or heard from again.

David Wood, a serial rapist who was paroled in January of 1987, was later convicted of murdering six of the El Paso victims, though he maintains his innocence. He was sentenced to death in 1993, but his sentence remains under appeal, because his lawyers claim he is mentally incompetent. The murders of the El Paso girls and women stopped after his October 1987 arrest.

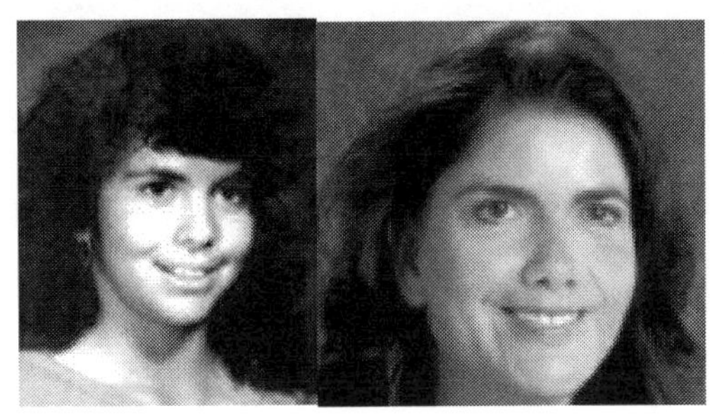

*(Melissa's Age Progression to 41)*

At the time of her disappearance, Melissa Alaniz had black hair, stood 5'2", and weighed 105 pounds. She was last seen wearing a black t-shirt with Iron Maiden on it, black and white checkered jeans, white socks with red and blue stripes on the top, and white sneakers. She is Hispanic with brown eyes. As of this writing, she is forty-four years old.

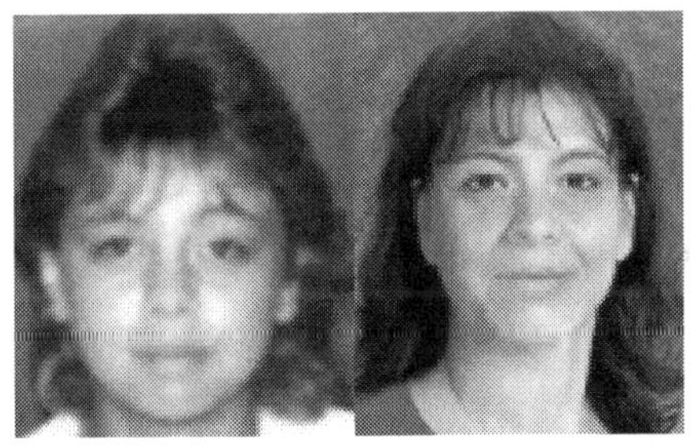

*(Marjorie's Age Progression to 43)*

At the time of her disappearance, Marjorie Knox had brown hair, stood between 5'2" - 5'3", and weighed 115 pounds. She may have been pregnant at the time. She was last seen wearing a purple shirt and blue jeans. She is Biracial (Asian/Caucasian) with brown eyes. She may bleach her hair blonde, and she is of Thai descent. As of this writing, she is forty-five years old.

(Cheryl at the time of her disappearance)

At the time of her disappearance, Cheryl Vasquez had brown hair, stood between 5'6" - 5'9", and weighed 110 pounds. She was last seen wearing a white t-shirt with cartoon characters on it, new jeans, and either white slip-on sandals or high-top sneakers. She is Caucasian with brown eyes and pierced ears. She may use the last names Dismukes and/or Vasquez Dismukes. As of this writing, she is fifty years old.

If you have any information regarding this case, you are urged to call one of the following numbers:

*El Paso Police Department at 915-832-4445 or 915-564-7360*

*Dona Ana County Sheriff's Department at 575-526-0795*

## Emmanuel Kalief Birts

Five week old Emmanuel Kalief Birts was abducted from his grandmother's home in Dallas, Texas on September 14, 1989 by a woman who claimed to be a social worker. The woman, who called herself 'Debra Manning', claimed she had to take the baby to Parkland Memorial Hospital to get him tested for HIV. Emmanuel's mother wanted to go with them, but 'Debra' made up an excuse as to why she could not. Neither Emmanuel nor 'Debra' has been seen again. The family reported him missing at 8pm.

His abductor is described as African-American in her thirties, 5'6" and weighing 145 pounds, with sandy brown hair that may have been a wig. She wore heavy blue eyeshadow and spoke with a foreign accent, possibly African.

Child Protective Services had not authorized Emmanuel's removal from his home for any reason. Investigators believe the abductor may have a history as a con artist. She apparently also had access to the baby's medical records, because she knew he had an eye infection before seeing him or being told.

Both of his parents subsequently tested negative for HIV, meaning Emmanuel could not have had it. The woman who called her herself 'Debra Manning' has never been identified.

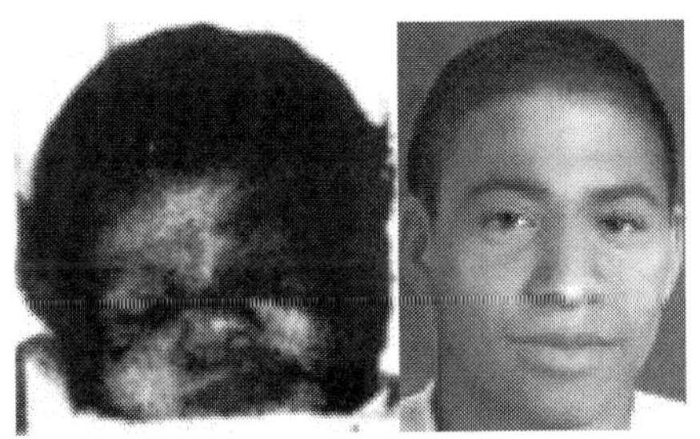

*(Age Progression to 26)*

At the time of his disappearance, Emmanuel Birts had black hair, was 24", and weighed 10 pounds. He was last seen wearing a red white and blue checkered shirt, light blue shorts with red trim, and red and white socks. He is African-American with brown eyes. As of this writing, he is twenty-nine years old.

If you have any information regarding this case, you are urged to call the Dallas Police Department at 214-744-4444.

## Desiree Chaunessy Carroll

Two year old Desiree Chaunessy Carroll was last seen on March 25, 1983 when her mother dropped her and her older sister off near their house a few miles southwest of Kosse, Texas. Her older sister walked to the house, but Desiree followed her mother's truck. She has never been seen or heard from again. Extensive searches turned up no sign of her, and she is presumed to have abducted.

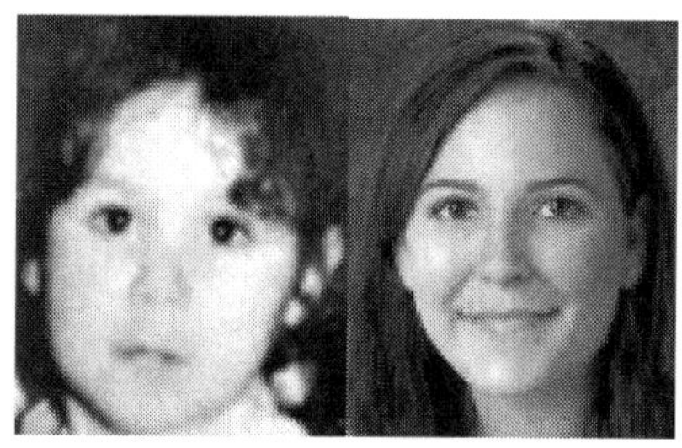

*(Age Progression to 33)*

At the time of her disappearance, Desiree Carroll had brown hair, stood 2'6", and weighed 40 pounds. She was last seen wearing a blue turtleneck sweater, brown coveralls, and sneakers. She is Caucasian with brown eyes and a dog bite scar under her left eye. Her nickname is Desi. As of this writing, she is thirty-eight years old.

If you have any information regarding this case, you are urged to call the Limestone County Sheriff's Office at 817-729-3278.

## David Ezell Blockett

Two week old David Ezell Blockett was taken from his family's residence on 13th Street in Newport News, Virginia on December 11, 1980, by a woman claiming to be a social worker with the State Department of Social Services (DSS). The woman called herself 'Marie Kelly'. She told David's mother that the DSS was sponsoring a function for children at Riverside Regional Medical Center. 'Marie' convinced his mother to let her take David and his two year old brother, Frederick, to the party. Later that afternoon, Frederick was found wandering alone at a shopping center near Old Mallory Road in Hampton, Virginia. He had a piece of paper in his pocket with his name and address on it, and the police returned him to his mother. David was nowhere to be seen and has never been seen again.

His abductor is described as being African-American between thirty-two and thirty-five years old, approximately 5'4" - 5'8" and weighing between 145 - 155 pounds, with a medium complexion and large hips. The woman who claimed to be 'Marie Kelly' has never been identified.

The DSS did not employ a social worker matching the description or the name of the abductor, and there was no Christmas party at the Riverside Regional Medical Center. Authorities believe the abductor may have gotten David's name and address from the local newspaper, which provided a listing of recent births three days before he was taken. Around the same time as David's abduction, a person posing as a social worker approached another nearby family with a newborn. The baby's mother told the person to go away.

As an adult, Frederick can vaguely recall the abduction. He stated that there was a man driving the car, and neither of the adults would look at the children. He remembers them dropping him off in Hampton.

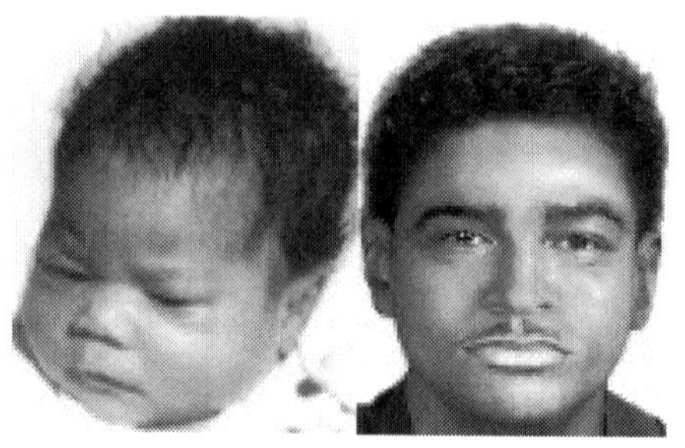

*(Age Progression to 30)*

At the time of his disappearance, David Blockett had black hair, was 20", and weighed 7 pounds. He is African-American with brown eyes, a tiny mole on his right ear, and birthmarks under his arm, on his back, and on his buttocks. As of this writing, he is thirty-seven years old.

If you have any information regarding this case, you are urged to call the Newport News Police Department at 757-926-8706.

## Samatha Lynn Clonch

Thirteen year old Samatha Lynn Clonch was last seen in Henderson, Texas on September 9, 1999. She left her residence en route to Henderson Middle School that morning, but never returned home and has never been heard from again. It is not known whether or not she attended classes that day. Authorities initially believed she had left of her own accord, but due to the passage of time with no trace of her ever surfacing that theory seems unlikely.

*(Age Progression to 27)*

At the time of her disappearance, Samatha Clonch had brown hair, stood 5’6”, and weighed 110 pounds. She was last seen wearing a black shirt, jeans, and white sneakers. She is Native American with brown eyes and a mole on her back. Her left ear lobe is larger than her right one. As of this writing, she is thirty-two years old.

If you have any information regarding this case, you are urged to call the Henderson Police Department at 903-657-3512.

## Joshua Jayvaughn Davis Jr.

One year old Joshua Jayvaughn Davis Jr. was last seen in the kitchen area of his family’s mobile home on Savannah Hills Circle in New Braunfels, Texas between 8pm and 8:20pm on February 4, 2011. He lived with his parents and his older brother. His mother was also eight months pregnant at the time. His parents were hosting a party that night and there were five other people in the house outside of Joshua’s immediate family. He disappeared sometime before 9pm and has never been seen again.

Authorities initially believed he had wandered away because the front door didn’t latch properly. They conducted an extensive search of the neighborhood, but found no sign of him and tracker dogs could not pick up his scent. Soon investigators began to look into other possible causes for his disappearance. His parents said they believed he had been abducted by a family friend who had been in the home that night and left shortly before Joshua was discovered missing. The friend reportedly gave conflicting stories about that night and refused to take a polygraph. Authorities believe one or more of the adults in the house that night are lying or know more than they have disclosed. However, no one has been named as a suspect.

*(Age Progression to 4)*

At the time of his disappearance, Joshua Davis Jr. had black hair, stood 2', and weighed 30 pounds. He was last seen wearing a blue and red plaid long-sleeve button-down shirt over a gray long-sleeve Rocawear shirt, dark blue Rocawear jeans, a beige and white Rocawear onesie, black and white socks, a diaper, and no shoes. He is African-American with brown eyes and a quarter-sized dark brown birthmark above his left knee. He has asthma and required medication to control it. As of this writing, he is nine years old.

If you have any information regarding this case, you are urged to call the New Braunfels Police Department at 830-221-4100.

## Tasha Shante Wright

Ten year old Tasha Shanta Wright walked to a neighbor's home in the Valley Glen Apartment Complex where she lived to deliver a message from her mother between 10:30am and 10:50am on October 14, 1989. The apartment complex was on Hollybush Drive off Ferguson Road in east Dallas, Texas. Tasha did arrive at the neighbor's apartment, but she never made it back to her own. She has never been seen or heard from again, and foul play is suspected.

*(Tasha at the time of his disappearance)*

At the time of her disappearance, Tasha Wright had black hair, stood between 4'3" - 5', and weighed between 70 - 80 pounds. She was last seen wearing a short-sleeve aqua shirt, faded aqua shorts, and brown slip-on leather sandals. Her hair was pulled to the side and held in place with a clip at the time. She is African-American with brown eyes, a mole on one of her fingers, and pierced ears. As of this writing, she is thirty-nine years old.

If you have any information regarding this case, you are urged to call the Dallas Police Department at 214-670-4426.

## Jennifer Lee Klein

Three year old Jennifer Lee Klein was last seen playing in the sand by the river at a campground approximately ten miles north of Moab, Utah on May 25, 1974. Her parents and older brother had been playing with her, but turned to watch a dog fight. While they were distracted, Jennifer disappeared. She has never been seen again. It is possible that she fell into the Colorado River and drown, but her body has never been recovered if that was the case.

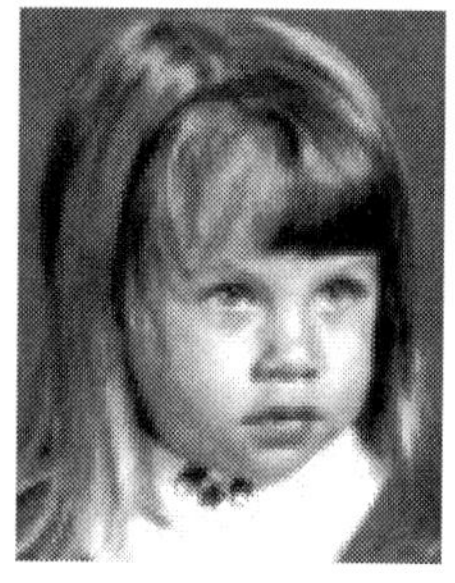

*(Jennifer at the time of her disappearance)*

At the time of her disappearance, Jennifer Klein had light brown hair, stood 3'2", and weighed 35 pounds. She was last seen wearing a swimsuit. She is Caucasian with blue eyes, a cowlick on the right side of her forehead, a birthmark possibly on the left side of her abdomen, a mole in front of her right ear, and a protruding navel. Her nickname is Jenny. As of this writing, she is forty-seven years old.

If you have any information regarding this case, you are urged to call the Grand County Sheriff's Office at 435-259-8115.

## Allyson Kathleen Dalton

Two month old Allyson Kathleen Dalton was last seen at approximately 7:45am on July 27, 1998 in the second-floor apartment she shared with her mother, Sylena Jo Dalton, in Strasburg, Virginia. At 2:25pm that day Sylena was found stabbed to death on a couch inside the residence. Allyson was missing and so were several of her baby bottles. She is presumed to have been abducted by her mother's killer.

Authorities believe Sylena had been killed between 9:15am and 10:30am, but none of her neighbors heard anything usual that morning. The murder weapon had been taken from the scene.

Sylena had petitioned the court for child support from Allyson's father recently, and her mother believes he is responsible for Sylena's murder and Allyson's abduction. However, he nor anyone else has been charged. Baby Allyson has never been seen again.

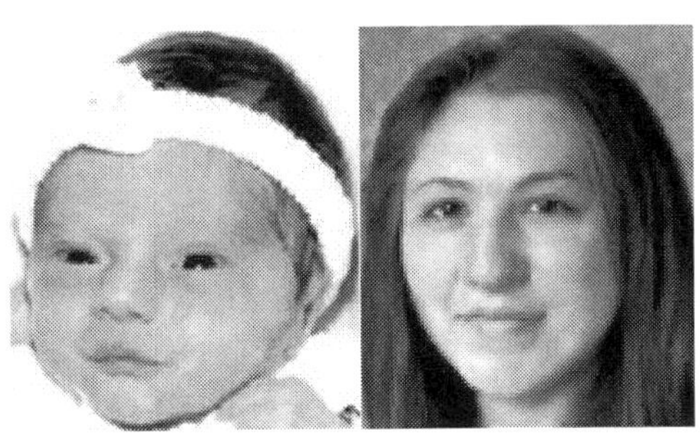

*(Age Progression to 20)*

At the time of her disappearance, Allyson Dalton had brown hair, was 20", and weighed 8 pounds. She is Caucasian with blue eyes. As of this writing, she is twenty years old.

If you have any information regarding this case, you are urged to call the Virginia State Police at 540-829-7766.

## Darren Bruce Hillis

Fourteen year old Darren Bruce Hillis was last seen walking to his school bus stop on Beechwood Avenue in Norfolk, Virginia at 7am on March 12, 1973. He never arrived at school and has never been heard from again.

*(Age Progression to 55)*

At the time of his disappearance, Darren Hillis had brown hair, stood approximately 6'4", and weighed about 150 pounds. He was last seen wearing a green Army jacket, a black and red striped shirt, red bell-bottom pants with white stripes down the legs, a belt, and boots. He is Caucasian with hazel eyes and a round indented chicken pox scar on the bridge of his nose. As of this writing, he is fifty-nine years old.

If you have any information regarding this case, you are urged to call the Norfolk Police Department at 757-664-7046.

## Chloe Johnson & Keir Shante Johnson

Eight month old Chloe Johnson and her mother, thirty-four year old Keir Shanta Johnson, were last seen on Hastings Drive in Hampton, Virginia on April 30, 2017. Keir told her mother she planned to spend the day at Buckroe Beach with Chloe and a friend. They never arrived to meet up with the friend, however. Neither Keir nor Chloe have been seen since. Their family reported them missing the next day.

On May 14th, Keir's black 2013 Kia Optima was found abandoned at a trailer park at Jefferson Avenue and Arch Street in Newport News, Virginia. She has no history of leaving without warning, and it is uncharacteristic for her to be out of touch with her family. Keir's twin sister believes someone they knew is responsible for their disappearances.

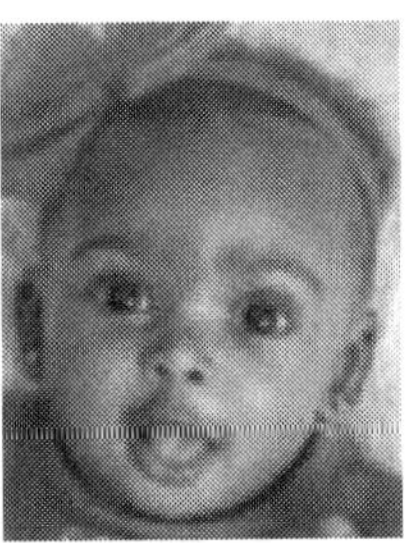

*(Chloe at the time of her disappearance)*

At the time of her disappearance, Chloe Johnson had black hair, was 29", and weighed 20 pounds. She is African-American with brown eyes and pierced ears. As of this writing, she is two years old.

*(Keir at the time of her disappearance)*

At the time of her disappearance, Keir Johnson had black hair, wore eyeglasses, stood 4'11", and weighed 140 pounds. She was last seen wearing a t-shirt, blue jeans, and black slider shoes with Nike in pink letters. She is African-American with brown eyes and pierced ears. As of this writing, she is thirty-six years old.

If you have any information regarding this case, you are urged to call the Newport News Police Department at 888-562-5887.

## Jaisle Elizabeth Thomas

Seventeen year old Jaisle Elizabeth Thomas was last seen in Richmond, Virginia on April 12, 1998. She planned to go to the University of Richmond's school library to do some research. It is unknown if she ever arrived at the university or not.

Her vehicle was found abandoned on the Willey Bridge between Henrico County and Richmond at 3:20pm that day. Her wallet, driver's license, some cash, her work uniform, her paycheck, a camera, her Bible, and her sneakers were still inside the car. Only the keys were missing. There was no sign of her at the scene, and a search of the James River did not turn up any clues as to her whereabouts. Jaisle's family does not believe she ran away. They believe she was abducted by some teens her own age whom were jealous of her.

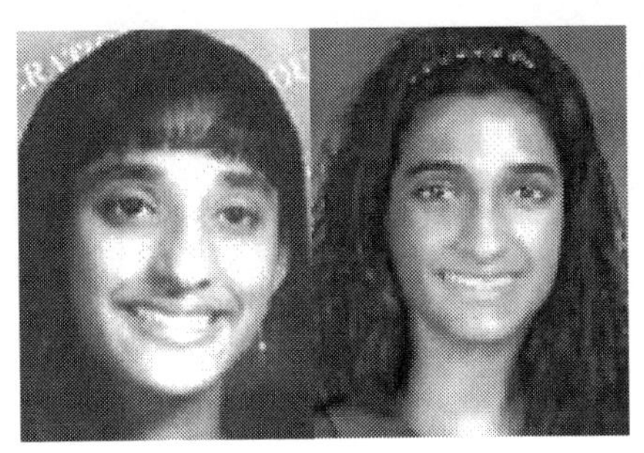

*(Age Progression to 20)*

At the time of her disappearance, Jaisle Thomas had black hair, stood between 5'5" - 5'6", and weighed between 115 - 120 pounds. She was last seen wearing a blue blouse with a dot design, blue pants, and a small chain around her neck. She is Asian with brown eyes, an oval-shaped birthmark on her left shin, a black mole on her left shin just below the knee, and pierced ears. She is right-handed and of Indian descent. As of this writing, she is thirty-seven years old.

If you have any information regarding this case, you are urged to call the Henrico County Police Department at 804-501-5000.

## Sky Elijah Metalwala

Two year old Sky Elijah Metalwala was supposedly last seen in Bellevue, Washington on November 6, 2011. His mother, Julia Biryukova, said he got sick and she was driving him and his four year old sister to Overlake Hospital Medical Center in her brother's silver 1998 Acura when it ran out of gas on 112th Avenue northeast. She claims to have left Sky strapped in his car seat in the unlocked vehicle, took his sister, and walked to a gas station a mile away for help. When she got to the gas station, however, she didn't buy gas. Instead she called a friend, who took her back to the car about an hour after she had left it. By then, according to Julia, Sky was gone. He has never been seen again.

When police arrived to start their investigation, they noticed that she did not have a gas can with her, yet the car had gas in it and was in working order. Witnesses said they had seen the car between 8am and 10am and there was not a child in it. Julia refused to take a polygraph or speak directly to the police about her son's disappearance. She communicated only through her lawyer. The rest of Sky's family, including his father, cooperated with the investigation and have been active in the search for him. Investigators later learned that no one but Julia had seen Sky for at least two weeks prior to when she claimed he disappeared.

In the aftermath of Sky's disappearance, his sister was taken into protective custody and placed in a foster home; but after six weeks, her father was granted custody. He now has custody of both Sky and his sister, even though Sky has been missing since late 2011. Julia has no visitation rights to her daughter.

In the summer of 2015, Julia gave birth to a son by another man. Child Protective Services sought custody of that baby as well, alleging that both Julia and her new husband were unfit parents.

Sky's father believes Julia is responsible for their son's disappearance, and says that she may have given Sky to someone else to hide him. Although no suspects have been named, the investigation has focused primarily on Julia due to her lack of cooperation and the circumstances involved. Authorities believe Sky is still somewhere in Washington, and they say it is possible he went missing some time before his mother reported it.

*(Age Progression to 7)*

At the time of his disappearance, Sky Metalwala had black hair, stood 2'10", and weighed 28 pounds. He was last seen wearing a gray or green hooded sweatshirt, aqua and black striped Carter's sweatpants with an elastic waistband, and white socks. He is Caucasian with brown eyes. He is of Ukrainian and Pakistani descent. As of this writing, he is nine years old.

If you have any information regarding this case, you are urged to call the Bellevue Police Department at 425-577-5656.

## Sofia Lucerno Juarez

Four year old Sofia Lucerno Juarez told her mother she was going to the store five blocks away in Kennewick, Washington, presumably with her grandmother's boyfriend, between 8:15pm and 9:19pm on February 4, 2003. Her mother gave her a dollar to spend at the store and thought she caught a ride from her grandmother's boyfriend. She did not get in the car, however, and he left without her. No one saw her leave the house. When the boyfriend returned at 9:45pm and

Sofia's mother realized she was not with him, she alerted the authorities.

Sofia's disappearance was treated as an abduction from the onset and an Amber Alert was issued. It was canceled after thirty-six hours, even though police continue to believe she was abducted. Her biological father and her grandmother's boyfriend have been ruled out as suspects in her case.

A van similar to a white Ford Tempo panel van was seen in the area around the time of her abduction, as well as a mid-nineties model full-sized faded orange van with a license plate which had a double J in it. The driver of that van was a white male with a thick blonde beard and between thirty-five and forty years old. Police do not know for certain that either van is connected to her disappearance.

Extensive searches of the area have turned up no clues as to her whereabouts. Her mother believed Sofia's kidnapper was someone she knew and trusted, because she was shy and would not have gone with a stranger without a fuss. Her mother passed away of natural causes in January 2009.

*(Age Progression to 17)*

At the time of her disappearance, Sofia Juarez had black hair, was missing her top four front teeth, stood 3', and weighed 33 pounds. She was last seen wearing a red long-sleeve shirt, blue overalls, violet socks, white Converse sneakers, and gold hoop earrings. She is Hispanic with brown eyes, a mole under her eye, and pierced ears. As of this writing, she is twenty years old.

If you have any information regarding this case you are urged to call the Kennewick Police Department at 509-585-4208.

## David William Adams

Eight year old David William Adams was last seen in Issaquah, Washington on May 3, 1968. He had gone to a friend's house to play after school. He was due home at 5pm for dinner, but called his mother and asked if he could stay longer. She told him no and to come on home. He set off on a local trail that was a shortcut to his house, but never arrived. After fifteen minutes had passed, his mother called David's friend's house to see why he had not come home yet, only to find out that he was not there. She then contacted the authorities. An extensive search turned up no sign of him, and he has never been seen or heard from again. Dogs tracked his scent to a neighbor's home.

In 2009, police announced they were looking at that former neighbor as a possible suspect. He would have been twenty years old in 1968, and is believed to have been the last person to see David before his disappearance. Investigators said the man was evasive during questioning, did not have a convincing alibi, and failed a polygraph. The man no longer lives in that neighborhood, and he continues to maintain his innocence.

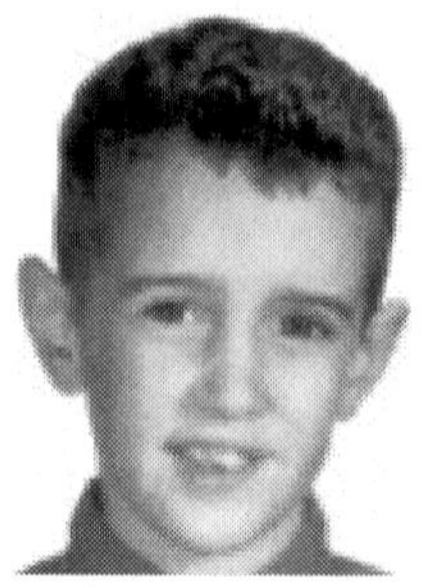

*(David at the time of his disappearance)*

At the time of his disappearance, David Adams had brown hair, stood 4', and weighed 50 pounds. He was last seen wearing a green and brown plaid shirt, jeans, and high-top shoes. He is Caucasian with blue eyes. As of this writing, he is fifty-eight years old.

If you have any information regarding this case, you are urged to call the King County Sheriff's Office at 206-296-0970.

## Catherine Lynne Sjorberg

Sixteen year old Catherine Lynne Sjorberg was last seen leaving her Oconomowoc High School prom at the Concord House dance hall in the early morning hours of June 5, 1974, in Concord, Wisconsin. She got into an argument with her boyfriend at 3am and stepped out for a breath of fresh air. Her never returned to the prom and has never been heard from again. She was supposed to stay the night at a friend's house, so her mother didn't realize she was missing until the next day. Her family does not believe she ran away, because she was happy about upcoming events in her life. In 1995, her mother held a memorial service for her, although her remains have never been found.

*(Age Progression to 55)*

At the time of her disappearance, Catherine Sjoberg had brown hair, stood 5'5", and weighed 120 pounds. She was last seen wearing a light blue formal gown with brown and pink trim and white flowers, a corsage, a gold pin, a gold chain, and high-heeled shoes. She is Caucasian with green eyes, high cheekbones, and pierced ears. She had previously fractured her collarbone. As of this writing, she is sixty-one years old.

If you have any information regarding this case, you are urged to call the Jefferson County Sheriff's Office at 920-674-7300.

## Jeffrey Michael Bratcher

Seven year old Jeffrey Michael Bratcher was visiting his father and stepmother in Ocean Shores, Washington on June 15, 1974. He was playing with five other children in a section of the park separate from where the adults were. They were supposed to return to the picnic area at 7pm for dinner. Jeffrey told the other children that he would take a different trail back to the picnic area, and he separated from the group. He has never been seen or heard from again.

An extensive search of the area turned up no clues as to his whereabouts. Search dogs tracked his scent to the park's entrance, but lost it at the pavement. Authorities believe he was either abducted or fell into the ocean and was swept out to sea.

*(Age Progression to 48)*

At the time of his disappearance, Jeffrey Bratcher had sandy brown hair, stood 3'9", and weighed 45 pounds. He was last seen wearing a blue denim jacket, a white football jersey with the number 33, multicolored plaid pants, a blue denim sailor's cap, and white sneakers with no socks. He is Caucasian with brown eyes. As of this writing, he is fifty-one years old.

If you have any information regarding this case, you are urged to call the Grays Harbor Sheriff's Office at 360-249-3711.

**<u>Ann Marie Burr</u>**

Eight year old Ann Marie Burr was last seen in her home on north 14th Street in Tacoma, Washington on August 31, 1961. She shared a bedroom with her three year old sister, who had a broken arm at the time. In the middle of the night, Ann Marie brought her sister to her parents' room because the cast was bothering her and she was crying. Their parents told them to go back to bed. Ann Marie has never been seen or heard from again. Her mother got up at 5:30am and discovered her missing.

Though locked and chained the night before, she found the front door unlocked from the inside and open. There was a living room window open wider than it had been previously, and it had a piece of red thread stuck in the jam. A garden bench had been taken from the behind the house and put at the open window. A faint footprint was found outside the window that authorities believed to be from a size 6 or 7 Keds sneaker. A similar footprint was found in the back by the basement window. There was no sign of Ann Marie and no evidence of a struggle in her bedroom. Her siblings, who slept in the basement, had not been disturbed, but the family dog had barked that night. Her parents had heard the dog but assumed it was afraid of the storm. Neighbors reported that in the days leading up to Ann Marie's disappearance they had seen someone in their yard peeking in their windows, but they were unable to describe the person.

Her disappearance was treated as an abduction from the beginning. Authorities theorized she may have been taken by someone she knew. A teenage boy, who was a neighbor of the Burr family, failed a polygraph. He passed a second test, but the police never ruled him out as a suspect.

The case went cold and remained that way until the 1970s when Ted Bundy was charged with several murders and suspected in the disappearances of many more. He had lived only a few blocks from the Burr family and knew Ann Marie. He was only fourteen at the time and not looked at as a suspect until his serial killer status came to light over fifteen years later. He denied any involvement in her case when questioned later, but nonetheless, many suspects Ann Marie may have been Ted Bundy's first victim. He was executed in Florida in 1989.

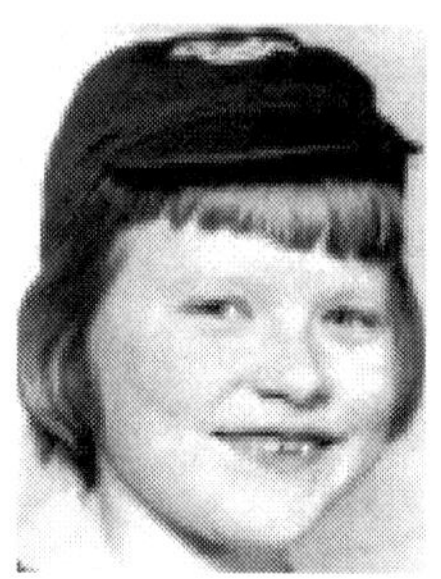

*(Ann Marie at the time of her disappearance)*

At the time of her disappearance, Ann Marie Burr had blonde hair, stood 4'2", and weighed 35 pounds. She was last seen wearing a handmade ankle-length light blue nightgown with blue and white flowers, a small chain necklace with two religious medals engraved with images of Jesus and the Virgin Mary, and a silver identification bracelet with her name address and phone number with the phrase 'Saint Christopher Protect Us'. She is Caucasian with hazel eyes and malformed fingernails. As of this writing, she is sixty-five years old.

If you have any information regarding this case, you are urged to call the Tacoma Police Department at 253-798-4721.

**James William Duffy Jr.**

Two year old James William Duffy Jr. was last seen in Leavenworth, Washington on October 19, 1973. He was camping with his parents and younger sister at Peavine Creek on the Little Wenatchee River. Their parents left the campsite to go collect firewood. When they were about 200 yards away from the camper they heard a scream. When they returned a few minutes later, James' sister was asleep inside the camper and their two cats were there, but the camper door was open and James was gone. He has never been seen or heard from again. An extensive search of the area turned up no sign of him or any clues as to his whereabouts. The theory is that he was kidnapped.

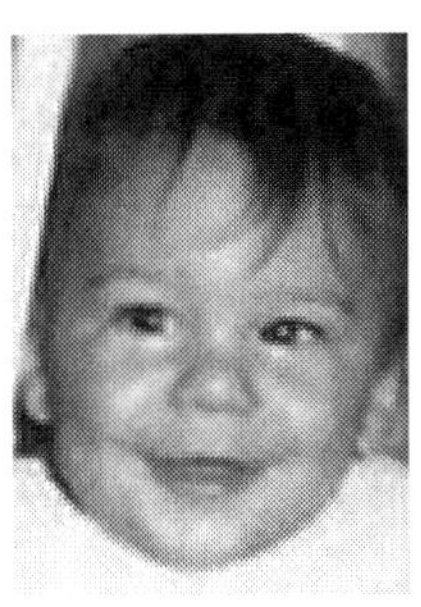

*(James at the time of his disappearance)*

At the time of his disappearance, James Duffy Jr. had brown hair and a very frail build. His height and weight at the time are unknown. He was last seen wearing a dark blue long-sleeve turtleneck over a white t-shirt, light blue jeans, yellow knee-length socks, and white training shoes with smooth soles. He is Caucasian with brown eyes. His nickname is Jimmy. As of this writing, he is forty-seven years old.

If you have any information regarding this case, you are urged to call the Chelan County Sheriff's Office at 509-667-6851.

## Michelle Renee Giusti, Clara Arleen Giusti, & Sharon Louise Giusti

One year old Michelle Renee Giusti, her ten month old sister, Clara Arleen Giusti, and their mother, twenty year old Sharon Louise Giusti, were last seen at their family's farm five miles south of Port Townsend, Washington on March 5, 1963. Sharon's husband said he had been working in the fields all afternoon. When he returned home at the end of the day, his wife and children were gone. A car, some clothing, and some money were also missing from the residence. He reported his family missing on March 9th. The next day, Sharon's vehicle was found beneath a highway overpass more than two miles from their farm. It was unlocked. There was no sign of Sharon or her daughters. They have never been heard from again. Due to the passage of time with no contact, authorities believe they disappeared under suspicious circumstances and are probably deceased.

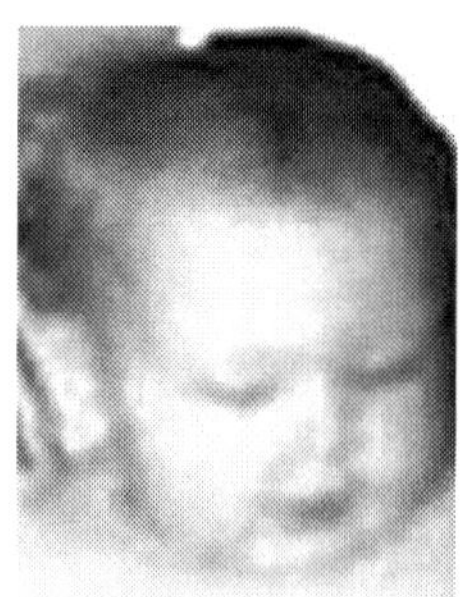

*(Michelle at the time of her disappearance)*

At the time of her disappearance, Michelle Giusti had red hair. Her height and weight at the time are unknown. She is Caucasian with blue eyes. As of this writing, she is fifty-seven years old.

Photographs, height, and weight of Clara Giusti are unavailable. Her birthday is May 4, 1962. She had red hair at the time. She is Caucasian with blue eyes. As of this writing, she is fifty-six years old.

*(Sharon at the time of her disappearance)*

At the time of her disappearance, Sharon Giusti had brown hair, stood 5'5", and weighed between 120 - 130 pounds. She is Caucasian with blue eyes. As of this writing, she is seventy-five years old.

If you have any information regarding this case, you are urged to call the Jefferson County Sheriff's Department at 360-385-3831.

## Tyler Jennings Inman

Three year old Tyler Jennings Inman was last seen in his family's second-floor apartment on east Madison Street in Aberdeen, Washington on the evening of December 21, 1982. His mother's boyfriend was babysitting Tyler and his five year old sister, but left for about twenty minutes to go pull a boat out of the nearby Wishkah River. While he was gone, Tyler apparently ran out of the apartment and never returned. His mother realized he was missing when she came home at 10:20pm. Authorities initially believed he had fallen into the river, but his body has never been found. His case is now classified as a nonfamily abduction.

*(Age Progression to 34)*

At the time of his disappearance, Tyler Inman had blonde hair, warts on his right foot, stood 2'8", and weighed 32 pounds. He was last seen wearing a short-sleeve shirt, blue jeans, and no shoes. He is Caucasian with blue eyes, extra skin on his right ear, and a deformity on his left ear. As of this writing, he is thirty-nine years old.

If you have any information regarding this case, you are urged to call the Aberdeen Police Department at 360-533-3180.

## Dontray Miquel Hunter

One year old Dontray Miquel Hunter was last seen playing with his older sister on the porch of their home near north 18th Street and west Locust Street in Milwaukee, Wisconsin on the morning of August 20, 1975. Their mother was inside dressing their baby brother at the time. Dontray's sister went inside to use the bathroom, and when she returned he was gone. He has never been seen or heard from again. No one who lived in the neighborhood reported seeing or hearing anything suspicious that morning. His mother still lives in Milwaukee and continues to hold out hope for some answers in his case

*(Age Progression to 40)*

At the time of his disappearance, Dontray Hunter had black hair, stood 3', and weighed 30 pounds. He was last seen wearing a white t-shirt, olive green trousers, and white sneakers. He is African-American with brown eyes and a birthmark on the back of his neck. As of this writing, he is forty-four years old.

If you have any information regarding this case, you are urged to call the Milwaukee Police Department at 414-933-4444.

## Alexis S. Patterson

Seven year old Alexis S. Patterson lived with her mother and stepfather in Milwaukee, Wisconsin. Her stepfather walked her to Hi-Mount Boulevard School on West Garfield Avenue near 49th Street at approximately 8am on May 3, 2002. He said he watched her walk towards the playground before he headed back home. She did not attend classes that day, although students reported seeing her crying on the playground both before and after school. She has never been heard from again. Her mother and stepfather were not notified of her absence until school dismissed that afternoon.

It is believed that she refused to attend classes after an argument over homework with her mother the previous evening. She had failed to properly complete her homework, and as a result she wasn't allowed to take cupcakes to her classmates the following day. Authorities believe something caused her disappearance after she was last seen on the playground later in the day. The surrounding areas were searched as soon as she was reported missing, but no clues as to her whereabouts were found.

By May 14th, investigators announced that she had disappeared under suspicious circumstances and reclassified her case from a missing child to a criminal investigation. Some of her classmates told police that they had seen a red truck parked near the school for most of the week before her disappearance. The truck never dropped anyone off or picked anyone up, and they didn't see it anymore after Alexis' disappearance. Neither the truck nor the driver have ever been identified, and it is unknown if it is connected to her case. In September 2002, investigators announced that foul play is suspected in her case.

*(Age Progression to 17)*

At the time of her disappearance, Alexis Patterson had black hair, stood 3'8", and weighed 42 pounds. She was last seen wearing a red hooded pullover jacket with a gray stripe running down each sleeve, a light purple blouse or blue shirt with horizontal stripes, light blue jeans, blue and white high-top Nike sneakers, and cluster-type diamond sunflower-shaped earrings with yellow-gold posts. She was carrying a pink Barbie book bag, and her hair was styled in two French braids which were pulled back into a ponytail. She is African-American with brown eyes, a scar below her right eye, a bump on her left pinky finger, and pierced ears. She is right-handed, and her nicknames are Lexi and Pie. As of this writing, she is twenty-three years old.

If you have any information regarding this case, you are urged to call one of the following numbers:

*Milwaukee Police Department at 414-935-7401 or 414-935-7302*

*Milwaukee County Sheriff's Department at 414-278-4788*

## Timmothy James Pitzen

Six year old Timmothy James Pitzen lived with his parents, James Pitzen and forty-three year old Amy Joan Marie Fry-Pitzen, in Aurora, Illnois at the time of his disappearance. Without telling anyone of her plans, Amy checked Timmothy out of his kindergarten class at Greenman Elementary School on the morning of May 11, 2011. At 10am, she drove to an auto repair shop and dropped off her blue 2004 Ford Expedition SUV. One of the repair shop employees drove Amy and Timmothy to the Brookfield Zoo. When James went to the school to pick up Timmothy when it dismissed for the day, he found out Amy had taken him. He called her cell phone numerous times but got no answer. He then reported his wife and son missing.

At 3pm, Amy and Timmothy returned to the auto repair shop and picked up the repaired vehicle. They then drove to the Key Lime Cove Resort in Gurnee, Illinois, where they spent the night. On May 12th, Amy and Timmothy drove to the Kalahari Resort in Wisconsin Dells, Wisconsin. The following morning at 10am, security camera footage showed them waiting in line to check out. At 1:30pm, Amy made several cell phone calls to her loved ones to say she and Timmothy were fine and not in trouble. He could be heard in the background saying he was hungry but otherwise sounding normal. That was the last time anyone heard from Timmothy.

At 7:25pm on May 13th, Amy was sighted at a Family Dollar Store in Winnebago, Illinois, where she purchased stationary. She was alone at the time. She went to the nearby Sullivan's Foods at 8pm. She then checked into the Rockford Inn in Rockford, Illinois between 11:15pm and 11:30pm. Sometime that night or the next morning, Amy took her own life by slashing her wrists and neck. She had also overdosed on antihistamines. Inn employees found her body at 12:30pm on May 14th. She left a note, as well as sending one to her mother and another one to a friend, saying that Timmonthy was fine and was with people who cared about him, but she did not name those people. One of her notes said no one would ever find him. Timmothy's Spider-Man backpack, his toys and clothes, and the clothes Amy had been wearing when she checked out of the Kalahari Resort have not been found. Her Illinois I-PASS transponder is also missing.

When authorities examined Amy's SUV, they found traces of Timmothy's blood in the backseat, but they couldn't tell how long the stains had been there. One of their relatives said that he had gotten a bloody nose in the vehicle about twelve to eighteen months earlier. The knife Amy had used to commit suicide had only her blood on it. Forensic testing on the undercarriage of the SUV indicated it had stopped for a time on a gravel area just off an asphalt road that had at one time been treated with reflective glass beads used in creating a road. The vehicle had also backed into a grassy meadow or field that had not been cultivated. The field contained Queen Anne's lace and black mustard plants and would have been nearly treeless. Some oak or birch trees would have been in the general area but not in the place where the SUV stopped. Investigators think the meadow or field was probably in Lee County or Whiteside County in northwestern Illinois, but they are also considering Carroll, Ogle, Stephenson, and Winnebago Counties.

Investigators believe Amy may have been planning Timmothy's disappearance for months. In February and March 2011, she took two unexplained trips to the area he would later disappear from.

James is baffled by his son's disappearance and his wife's suicide. He and Amy's mother both stated Amy loved Timmothy and they don't believe she would have harmed him. She suffered from depression and had reportedly left home for extended periods before. All of Timmothy's family members have been cooperative in the investigation and are not considered suspects in his disappearance.

Amy's cell phone, which was missing at the time of her death, was found on the roadside of Route 78 in fall of 3013. However, nothing of interest was on it. Investigators conducted a search of the area where the phone was found, but nothing significant was located.

*(Age Progression to 13)*

At the time of his disappearance, Timmothy Pitzen had brown hair, stood 4'2", and weighed 70 pounds. He was last seen wearing green or blue shorts, a brown t-shirt, white socks, and a Spider-Man backpack. He is Caucasian with brown eyes. His nicknames are Tim and Timmy. As of this writing, he is thirteen years old.

If you have any information regarding this case, you are urged to call the Aurora Police Department at 630-256-5000.

## Laurie Lynn Partridge

Seventeen year old Laurie Lynn Partridge left Ferris High School in Spokane, Washington at 12:30pm on December 4, 1974, because she was suffering from menstrual cramps. She couldn't get a ride, so she decided to walk the two miles to her home on south

Custer Street. She was last seen walking south on Havana Street near 37th Avenue. There were reports of a green Pinto station wagon in the area at the time, possibly following her. Laurie never arrived home and has never been heard from again. Her parents reported her missing when she didn't show up for work at the Lincoln Heights Theater.

The contents of her purse were found on December 6th in the area where she had last been seen. Police initially believed she left of her own accord, but her family never believed that. Authorities have since changed their opinions to believing she was taken against her will.

In 2011, investigators announced they had a new witness who may have saw Laurie at 4:15pm, hours after the last previous known sighting. The witness also placed a Caucasian man in his forties or fifties and a white truck with a dark-colored door and a van rear end in the area at the time of her disappearance. Three people have been questioned as suspects, but no one has been charged.

*(Age Progression to 53)*

At the time of her disappearance, Laurie Lynn Partridge had blonde hair, stood 5', and weighed 110 pounds. She was last seen wearing a long hooded navy blue coat similar to a monk's robe, a tan sweater, tan plaid pants, and blue denim shoes with crepe soles. She was carrying a brown leather purse with a flower design and a beaded shoulder strap. She is Caucasian with blue eyes and a brown mole on her right cheek. As of this writing, she is sixty-one years old.

If you have any information regarding this case, you are urged to call the Spokane County Sheriff's Office at 509-477-4760.

## Diane Nguyen Robbins

Thirteen year old Diane Nguyen Robbins left her home in Kennewick, Washington on June 18, 1985 to visit friends in Seattle, Washington. She joined her friend, twenty-one year old Molly A. Purdin, sometime during the day. Both ladies were seen together in King County, Washington in the late afternoon hours that day. Diane has never been seen or heard from again. She was presumed, at the time, to be a runaway.

In July 1985, Molly's body was found off Index-Galena Road near Milepost 8 in King County. She had been raped and murdered by a blow to the head. There was no sign of Diane at the scene.

No one has been charged in Molly's rape and murder or Diane's disappearance. Foul play is suspected due to the circumstances involved.

*(Age Progression to 40)*

At the time of her disappearance, Diane Robbins had brown hair, stood 5'2", and weighed 90 pounds. She is Biracial (Asian/Caucasian) with brown eyes and a one-inch scar on her forehead. She is of Vietnamese descent. As of this writing, she is forty-six years old.

If you have any information regarding this case, you are urged to call the Benton County Sheriff's Office at 509-735-6555.

## Jesus Alvarado Martinez

Four year old Jesus Alvarado Martinez was last seen at his home in northwest Houston, Texas on October 20, 2004. He was living with his mother, Rocio Alvarado, and his one year old sister at the time. His father, Avelino Martinez, was estranged from the family and had moved in with a roommate, Pedro Vargas, in the Brampton Square Apartments on Witte Road in Houston a few days before. Pedro last saw Avelino, Jesus, and Rocio together at 9am on October 20$^{th}$. Avelino asked to borrow his car so he and Rocio could take their daughter to the doctor. They did visit the doctor and afterwards they planned to buy the children some clothes. Later that day, Rocio's relatives asked police to check on her welfare because they had not seen or heard from her since the previous evening. She wasn't at her apartment, however. At 1am on October 21st, Pedro summoned police to his apartment after he found Rocio stabbed and strangled to death on his bed. The murder weapon had been left behind. She had been covered with blankets, and Pedro thought she was only sleeping until her daughter began to cry and she did not wake up. Her daughter was unharmed, but there was no sign of Jesus or Avelino.

Investigators believe Avelino murdered his wife and abducted Jesus. There was a history of domestic violence in the couple's ten-year relationship. They also believe Avelino took Pedro's brown 1993 Chevrolet Silverado extended-cab pickup truck when he left. It was found abandoned on October 30th on a private dirt road off Interstate 10 and Wilpitz Road near Brookshire, Texas in Waller County. Avelino and Jesus are believed to be either in Nuevo Laredo, Mexico or Laredo, Texas. Due to the nature of charges against his father, Jesus is considered to be in danger. Avelino is considered armed and dangerous, and caution is advised when approaching him.

*(Age Progression to 16)*

At the time of his disappearance, Jesus Martinez had black hair, stood 3', and weighed 30 pounds. He was last seen wearing a gray short-sleeve shirt with white stripes, dark-colored pants, and black Yu-Gi-Oh sneakers. He is Hispanic with brown eyes. His nickname is Nino. As of this writing, he is eighteen years old.

Avelino's birthdate is August 11, 1973. At the time of the abduction, he had black hair, stood 5'8" and weighed between 200 - 215 pounds. He is Hispanic with brown eyes, scars on his stomach, and tattoos of crosses on his right forearm. His nickname is Monsana.

If you have any information regarding this case, you are urged to call the Houston Police Department at 713-308-3600.

## Michael Mayfield & Pamela Mayfield

Six year old Michael Mayfield and his five year old sister, Pamela Mayfield, were walking back to their home from Betsy Ross Elementary School on Bay Street at the Eastex Freeway in northeast Houston, Texas on January 10, 1985. They were both in kindergarten; Pamela was in kindergarten for the first time and Michael was repeating it. Witnesses saw them get into a green vehicle with an unidentified man. They never arrived home and have never been heard from again.

In May 1985, a man called the Houston Police Department to say that Michael and Pamela had not been kidnapped and were living with a grandmother on 75th Street in Los Angeles, California. The Mayfields do have relatives in Los Angeles, but none of them have the children or know where they are. The caller has not been identified, but his voice sounded as if he was an elderly African-American. Police believe the children were abducted by someone they knew, such as a relative or a family friend.

*(Michael's Age Progression to 34)*

At the time of his disappearance, Michael Mayfield had black hair, stuttered, stood 3', and weighed 75 pounds. He is African-American with brown eyes and a burn scar on his right wrist. He may use the last name Gant. As of this writing, he is forty years old.

*(Pamela's Age Progression to 33)*

At the time of her disappearance, Pamela Mayfield had black hair, stood 2'9", and weighed 55 pounds. She is African-American with brown eyes and pierced ears. As of this writing, she is thirty-nine years old.

If you have any information regarding this case, you are urged to call the Houston Police Department at 713-222-3131.

## Allen Michael McPeak & Laura Leticia Ramirez

Four year old Allen Michael McPeak was last seen in Mission, Texas on August 9, 2001. He is believed to be with his mother, twenty-six year old Laura Leticia Ramirez. They may be traveling with forty-one year old Henry Francis Claeys. Some agencies give their disappearance date as November 6, 2001 and say they were last seen in McAllen, Texas. Laura and Allen are missing under suspicious situations, and the circumstances of their disappearances are unclear.

*(Allen's Age Progression to 15)*

At the time of his disappearance, Allen McPeak had light brown hair, stood 3', and weighed 45 pounds. He is Hispanic with brown eyes and a light red birthmark on his forehead. He may go by his middle name. As of this writing, he is twenty years old.

*(Laura at the time of her disappearance)*

At the time of her disappearance, Laura Ramirez had brown hair, stood 5'3", and weighed 110 pounds. She is Hispanic with brown eyes and may use the first name Vicky or the alias name Victoria Claeys. As of this writing, she is forty-one years old.

Henry Francis Claeys surfaced in Texas in 2008. It is not known if he is connected to Allen and Laura's disappearances, knows their current whereabouts, or was simply a companion to Laura.

If you have any information regarding this case, you are urged to call the Hidalgo County Sheriff's Office at 956-383-8114.

## Kimberly Rachelle Norwood

Twelve year old Kimberly Rachelle Norwood was last seen at about 5:15pm by her friends as they were all walking home on May 20, 1989 in Hallsville, Texas. She and her three friends split up approximately one mile from her home. Kimberly has never been seen or heard from again.

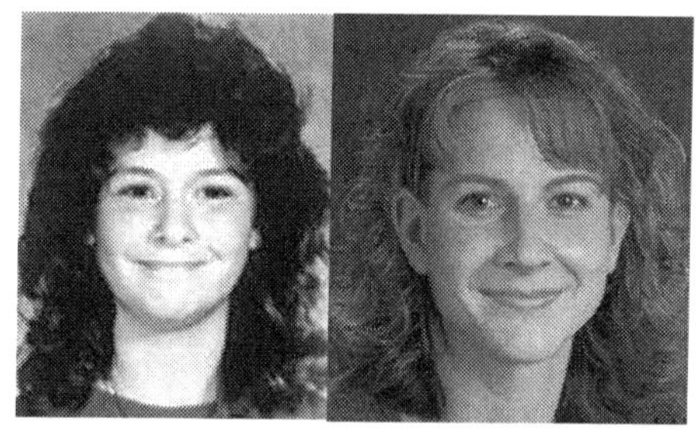

*(Age Progression to 40)*

At the time of her disappearance, Kimberly Norwood had brown hair, stood 5'4", and weighed 110 pounds. She was last seen wearing a white t-shirt with cows and 'Milk Dudes' on it, blue or black jeans, black Keds sneakers, a black bow in her hair, a Swatch watch, and a gold ring with an aquamarine stone. She is

Caucasian with brown eyes, a surgical scar on her abdomen, and pierced ears. Her nicknames are Kim and Kimbo. As of this writing, she is forty-one years old.

If you have any information regarding this case, you are urged to call one of the following numbers:

*Harrison County Sheriff's Office at 903-923-4000*

*The National Center for Missing and Exploited Children at 1-800-THE-LOST*

## Kimberly Abigail Orellana

Twelve year old Kimberly Abigail Orellana disappeared on August 9, 2012 after crossing the United States/Mexico border illegally with other undocumented immigrants. They were walking on Highway 281 between Falfurrias and McAllen, Texas en route to Houston when Kimberly got tired and could not continue. The group left her behind. She has never been heard from again. Her parents reported her missing.

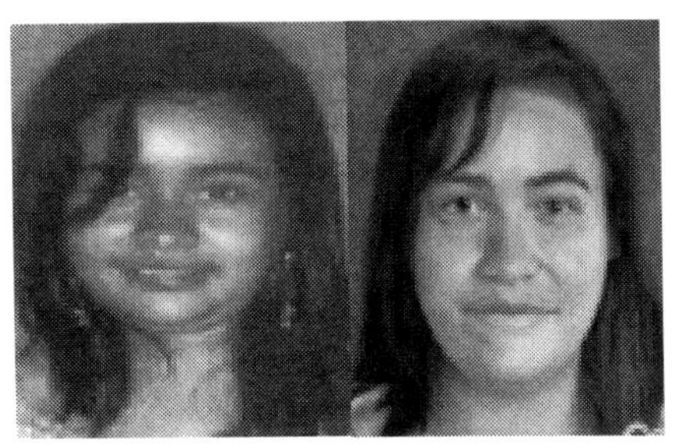

*(Age Progression to 17)*

At the time of her disappearance, Kimberly Orellana had black hair, stood between 5'1" - 5'2", and weighed between 120 - 130 pounds. She was last seen wearing light blue Lacost jeans with no back pockets and dark blue Puma sneakers with a red stripe. She is Hispanic with brown eyes, a small elongated burn scar on her back, an inch-long scar on the inside of her left arm, and pierced ears. She is from El Salvador. As of this writing, she is eighteen years old.

If you have any information regarding this case, you are urged to call the Brooks County Sheriff's Office at 361-325-3696.

## Norman Lamar Prater

Sixteen year old Norman Lamar Prater was last seen in Dallas, Texas on January 14, 1973. At about midnight, he went to the all-night coffee shop where his mother worked and had a soft drink. He was accompanied by an older Hispanic man, whom his mother knew by sight, and two teenage boys with shoulder-length hair, whom she did not recognize. Norman told his mother he was going home, and he agreed to help her move the next day. He apparently never made it home and has never been seen or heard from again.

*(Age Progression to 55)*

At the time of his disappearance, Norman Prater had brown hair, stood 5'8", and weighed 130 pounds. He is Caucasian with blue eyes. As of this writing, he is sixty-two years old.

If you have any information regarding this case, you are urged to call the Dallas Police Department at 214-671-4268.

## Scott Andreas Douglass Sims

Eleven year old Scott Andreas Douglass Sims was last seen in Wichita Falls, Texas on December 9, 1961. He and his older brother were home alone on Stanford Avenue when Scott went outside to play sometime between 12:45pm and 1pm. His mother returned home at 2:30pm and couldn't find him. The family searched without success until finally contacting the police at 8pm. He has never been seen or heard from again.

*(Scott at the time of his disappearance)*

At the time of his disappearance, Scott Sims had blonde hair, wore eyeglasses, stood 4'11", and weighed 90 pounds. He was last seen wearing a black winter coat, a black turtleneck sweater, blue jeans, and a black knitted cap. He is Caucasian with blue eyes. His nickname is Andy. As of this writing, he is sixty-eight years old.

If you have any information regarding this case, you are urged to call the Wichita Falls Police Department at 940-761-7762.

## Jamal Abdul'Faruq

Seven year old Jamal Abdul'Faruq and his eight year old brother, Basil Abdul'Faruq, were dropped off at their mother's apartment on Clarkson Road in Richmond, Virginia by their stepmother on April 16, 1990. Their mother, who had worked the night shift the day before, went to take a nap at 2:30pm, and the boys went outside to play. When she woke up, she searched for her sons but could not find them. She looked for them for forty-five minutes and then contacted the police. Jamal has never been seen or heard from again.

Three days later, investigators discovered Basil's fully-clothed body in a Chesterfield County landfill ten miles from his home. He had been bound, gagged, and stabbed twice in the back. His skull had been fractured postmortem. The killer placed his body in a plastic garbage bag and put it in a dumpster, and from there his remains were taken to the landfill. There was no sign of Jamal, but authorities believe it is possible that he is still alive.

*(Age Progression to 31)*

At the time of his disappearance, Jamal Abdul'Faruq had black hair, a small gap between his upper front teeth, stood 4'5", and weighed 47 pounds. He was last seen wearing a black Batman shirt, blue jeans, a gray and red fleece baseball jacket, and white sneakers. He is African-American with brown eyes, a scar on his right eyebrow, and a mole on his temple above his left ear. As of this writing, he is thirty-six years old.

If you have any information regarding this case, you are urged to call the Richmond Police Department at 804-780-6748.

## Chance Lee Wackerhagen & Lee Herman Wackerhagen Jr.

Nine year old Chance Lee Wackerhagen and his father, forty year old Lee Herman Wackerhagen Jr., disappeared from Lockhart, Texas on December 26, 1993. Chance's parents had divorced three years earlier, and his mother had custody of him. Chance left his mother's house on December 17th to spend Christmas with his father. His mother last spoke to him on Christmas Day, when Chance asked to stay a few extra days. He sounded happy and excited about his Christmas gifts. His mother gave him permission to stay longer and told him to call her later to set up a time to return home. Chance has never been seen or heard from again.

On December 27th, thirty-eight year old Latricia Gail White, Lee's live-in girlfriend, was found murdered in their apartment. Authorities believe she had been killed the previous day. She had been shot in the head six times. There were no indications of a struggle and nothing appeared to have been taken. Neither Lee nor Chance was at the scene.

Three days after the murder, Lee's 1986 Ford pickup truck was found abandoned in east Austin, Texas. Inside the truck, authorities found Lee's hunting rifle (which was not the murder weapon), his checkbook, his wallet, a toolbox, a spare tire, and some bloodstained Christmas gifts. The rifle had not been fired. The blood on the gifts was originally thought to be Latricia's, but testing proved it was not her blood type.

Authorities initially believed Lee had murdered Latricia and fled with Chance, and they kept that belief for the next twenty-five years. But in the spring of 2016, authorities reopened the case and announced that they had evidence to suggest that both Lee and Chance were victims of foul play. Investigators believe Latricia's murder was probably a crime of passion committed by someone who had a close relationship with one or more of the victims. Lee is now considered a missing person and possible homicide victim instead of a fugitive.

*(Chance's Age Progression to 28)*

At the time of his disappearance, Chance Wackerhagen had blonde hair, stood 4'8", and weighed 75 pounds. He is Caucasian with blue/green eyes and a small dimple on his right cheek. He may use the last name Walker. As of this writing, he is thirty-four years old.

*(Lee's Age Progression to 54)*

At the time of his disappearance, Lee Wackerhagen Jr. had dark blonde hair and a mustache, wore eyeglasses, stood between 6' - 6'4", and weighed between 230 - 240 pounds. He is Caucasian with blue eyes, scars on both arms, and a scar on his right leg. His nickname is Dub, and he may use the alias name Doug Walker. As of this writing, he is sixty-four years old.

If you have any information regarding this case, you are urged to call one of the following numbers:

*Kingsville Police Department at 361-593-1700*

*The Federal Bureau of Investigation (FBI) at 1-202-324-3000*

## Tanisha Lorraine Watkins

Two year old Tanisha Lorraine Watkins was last seen playing in a front yard swing at her home on Thrasher Lane in east Austin, Texas on January 5, 1984. A witness reportedly saw her later that day walking eastbound on Riverside Drive with a slender, bearded man wearing an Army hat. She has never been seen again, and the man has not been identified. Foul play is suspected in her case.

*(Age Progression to 32)*

At the time of her disappearance, Tanisha Watkins had black hair, stood 3', and weighed 42 pounds. She was last seen wearing a short-sleeve white pullover shirt, red sweatpants, and white sneakers with velcro fasteners. She is African-American with brown eyes. As of this writing, she is thirty-seven years old.

If you have any information regarding this case, you are urged to call the Austin Police Department at 512-974-0916.

## Shonna Dannette Wesley

Sixteen year old Shonna Dannette Wesley was last seen in Dallas, Texas on May 29, 1981. That day her two year old daughter was found alone at the South Oak Cliff Apartment Complex. The child was not identified immediately and spent a week in foster care before her grandmother came forward and claimed her. During that week, Shonna's boyfriend contacted her mother to say she had disappeared. Her mother reported her missing on June $2^{nd}$. Shonna has never been seen or heard from again.

*(Shonna at the time of her disappearance)*

At the time of her disappearance, Shonna Wesley had black hair, stood 5’5”, and weighed 130 pounds. She was last seen wearing a t-shirt and blue jeans. She is African-American with brown eyes and a scar on her head. As of this writing, she is fifty-three years old.

If you have any information regarding this case, you are urged to call the Dallas Police Department at 214-671-4268.

As of December 31, 2017, the Federal Bureau of Investigation's (FBI) National Crime Information Center (NCIC) had 88,089 active missing persons cases. Those are people from all age groups and nationalities. According to the Canadian Center for Information on Missing Adults (CCIMA), police record over 100,000 missing persons cases in Canada each year.

In the previous sections of this book, I have documented cases involving fires, traveling, and missing children. While those make up a lot of the missing persons cases police departments have on record, they do not account for all.

Sometimes an elderly person (ages 60+) goes missing from their home or someone who is blind disappears. In cases like these, a Silver Alert may be issued. A Silver Alert is a public notification that broadcasts, usually on news stations and radio, about a missing person who has some form of cognitive impairment. Alzheimer's, dementia, autism, blindness, Down Syndrome, cerebral palsy, epilepsy, a person who is insulin-dependent, a patient on kidney dialysis, etc. would be considered reasons for a Silver Alert to be used for the missing person. Different states have different conditions, such as the age of the missing person, and the alert may go by different names. The alerts for the Silver Alert system do not come to your cell phones as an emergency alert like the Amber Alerts do.

Up until recently there was no alert system in the United States for missing adults (ages 18+) who were considered to be in danger or who did not disappear voluntarily, such as in the case of an abduction. However, in September 2018, the United States House of Representatives passed the Ashanti bill. The bill will create a national emergency network for missing adults whose physical safety may be in danger. The bill is named after Ashanti Billie, a nineteen year old woman who went missing from a Virginia military base on September 18, 2017, and was found murdered in North Carolina eleven days later. It is expected to take a year or more to get the alert system up and running. The Ashanti Alert system is expected to send out alerts much like the Amber Alert Program does.

In this last section, all the cases involve missing adults (ages 18+). Hopefully, someone reading this book has that last detail to help bring answers to some of these families. You never know how major some minor detail may be until it is passed onto the right person.

## Thomas Kelly Brown

Eighteen year old Thomas Kelly Brown was last seen in Canadian, Texas on November 23, 2016. His friends dropped him off in the parking lot of the Canadian High School football field where his red 2009 Dodge Durango was parked. His curfew was at midnight and he was rarely late. At 11:36pm, he was seen buying gas at Frank's Oil and Gas on 2nd Street. At 12:03am, his brother sent him a text to ask where he was. The message was never read. His cell phone was last pinged at 12:10am in the vicinity of the football field parking lot. The phone was turned off at 12:22am, and Thomas has never been heard from again.

His parents reported him missing at 1:30am. At 8:45am on November 24th, a search helicopter located his SUV parked under some trees at a wastewater treatment plant on Complex Road. His wallet, keys, laptop computer, and cell phone were missing. There was a very small amount of blood on the driver's side door, but police do not believe it was fresh enough to be related to Thomas' disappearance. Surveillance footage of the area showed that the vehicle had been left there at 6:50am, but the driver could not be identified. Tracker dogs followed Thomas' scent from the SUV for three-quarters of a mile east and southeast before they lost the trail.

In January 2017, his backpack was found in a wooded area four miles from where his vehicle had been left. It was in some brush on the ground off of Lake Marvin Road. His schoolbooks and laptop were inside.

Authorities said the backpack was wet and dirty and appeared to have been in that location for months.

Thomas was a senior at Canadian High School at the time. He was student body president and got good grades. He was well-liked by his friends and classmates, and he had no known enemies. He has not accessed his bank accounts, cell phone, social media, or email accounts since he went missing. Police can find no evidence that he was suicidal or led a secret life. Investigators believe he did not leave of his own accord and may be in danger.

*(Thomas at the time of his disappearance)*

At the time of his disappearance, Thomas Brown had brown hair, wore eyeglasses, stood 6', and weighed between 175 - 195 pounds. He was last seen wearing a black Canadian Wildcats t-shirt, a black pullover windbreaker with an orange Oklahoma State University Cowboys logo on the left side of the chest, faded blue Buckle jeans, gray and black Under Armour sneakers, and possibly an orange beanie hat. He is Caucasian with brown eyes and dimples in his cheeks that show when he smiles. His nickname is Tom. As of this writing, he is twenty years old.

If you have any information regarding this case, you are urged to call the Hemphill County Sheriff's Office at 806-323-5324.

## Robert Dale Casto

Twenty-one year old Robert Dale Casto was last seen driving a blue 1979 Ford Pinto station wagon with Texas plates 907AYJ on November 27, 1983 in Arlington, Texas. He has never been seen or heard from again. Few details are available in his case, but police believe he may have been taken against his will. It is unknown whether or not the vehicle has been located.

*(Robert at the time of his disappearance)*

At the time of his disappearance, Robert Casto had brown hair, stood 6'2", and weighed 175 pounds. He is Caucasian with brown eyes. As of this writing, he is fifty-six years old.

If you have any information regarding this case, you are urged to call the Arlington Police Department at 817-265-8970.

## Margaret Jane Chauncy

Twenty-four year old Margaret Jane Chauncy was last seen in Texarkana, Texas on October 20, 1987. She was driving her red 1983 Pontiac Fiero with Arkansas plates MXB670. Neither she nor her vehicle has ever been seen again. Foul play is suspected in her case.

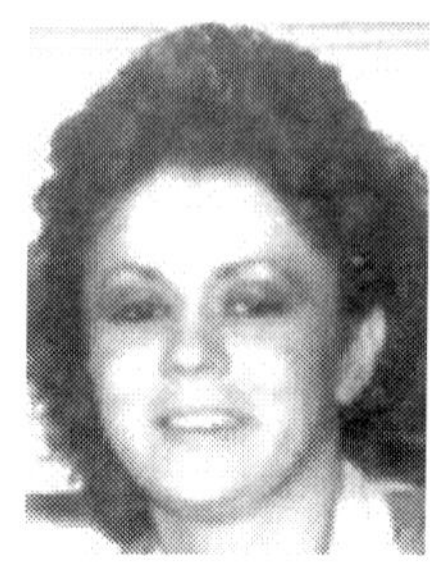

*(Margaret at the time of her disappearance)*

At the time of her disappearance, Margaret Chauncy had blonde hair, stood 5'6", and weighed 125 pounds. She was last seen wearing a blue and white striped blouse with matching skirt or pants, a long gold chain necklace with two attached children's gold bands, and a gold watch with the name Carolyn Sewell engraved on the back. She is Caucasian with hazel eyes. Her four front upper teeth are capped. She may use the last name Latimer. As of this writing, she is fifty-four years old.

If you have any information regarding this case, you are urged to call the Texarkana Police Department at 903-798-3135.

## Donna Kay Cloud

Nineteen year old Donna Kay Cloud was last seen in Splendora, Texas on October 25, 2016. She left home that day to go on a blind date with an unidentified male whom she may have met online. Her father did not realize she did not know the man until she had already left. She later sent her father a text message saying she would probably be back in the morning and if he did not hear from her by 2am to call the police. The following day, she texted him again saying she would see him in the morning and that the date went great. She said she would call him if she needed anything.

Donna and the man were supposed to go eat at the Texas Roadhouse restaurant, but when her father checked the restaurant's surveillance footage, he did not see her. She has never been heard from again. She does not have any credit cards, and she left her car, money, clothes, and identification behind. Her family does not believe she would have disappeared on her own accord.

*(Donna at the time of her disappearance)*

At the time of her disappearance, Donna Cloud had brown hair, stood between 5' - 5'2", and weighed between 95 - 133 pounds. She was last seen wearing a burgundy t-shirt, blue jeans with a hole in the back right side pocket, and white canvas shoes. She is Caucasian with brown eyes, deep dimples, and pierced ears. Her nose is pierced on the right side. She has the following tattoos: a diamond on her right ring finger, a cross on her right index finger, the words Love is Enough on her collarbone, the word Faith in cursive on the inside of her right forearm, a crown on her forearm, and script on her back on the right shoulder blade. As of this writing, she is twenty-one years old.

If you have any information regarding this case, you are urged to call the Montgomery County Sheriff's Department at 936-760-5800.

## Melissa Gail Crabill

Thirty year old Melissa Gail Crabill was last seen at her family's residence in Fort Worth, Texas on April 1, 1995. She told her family that she was meeting a friend during the day. She never returned home and has not been heard from since.

Her vehicle was found abandoned near the Remington Hotel in Houston, Texas several weeks later. There were no clues as to her whereabouts in the vehicle or around it. It is possible she was taken against her will.

*(Melissa at the time of her disappearance)*

At the time of her disappearance, Melissa Crabill had brown hair, stood 5'4", and weighed 130 pounds. She was last seen wearing a blue denim vest, blue jeans, Guess shoes, and possibly hoop earrings. She is Caucasian with hazel eyes and double-pierced ears. Her maiden name is White. As of this writing, she is fifty-four years old.

If you have any information regarding this case, you are urged to call the Fort Worth Police Department at 817-282-6532.

## Mauro Elias Escobar, Jose Guadalupe Gonzalez & Silvia Perez

Twenty-one year old Mauro Elias Escobar, thirty-eight-year old Jose Guadalupe Gonzalez, and twenty-four year old Silvia Perez were last seen together at a Wendy's restaurant in the Greenspoint Mall area of Houston, Texas on April 16, 2004. Jose had a large amount of cash on him, because he was planning to purchase some farming equipment. Silvia, whose boyfriend was friends with both Mauro and Jose, accompanied them to show Jose where some equipment was for sale. None of the three of them have ever been heard from again.

Mauro's 1996 Chevrolet Tahoe with Texas plates TBZ-77X was found stripped and abandoned a few days later in a wrecking yard in Humble, Texas. No clues as to their whereabouts were found in or around the vehicle. Authorities believe foul play may have been involved in their disappearances.

*(Mauro at the time of his disappearance)*

At the time of his disappearance, Mauro Escobar had black hair, stood 5'10", and weighed 300 pounds. He is Hispanic with brown eyes. As of this writing, he is thirty-five years old.

*(Jose at the time of his disappearance)*

At the time of his disappearance, Jose Gonzalez had brown hair and a mustache, stood 5'11", and weighed 180 pounds. He was last seen wearing an orange and blue t-shirt, blue jeans, and black shoes. He is Hispanic with hazel eyes and scars on his abdomen and arm. He wears a removable lower dental bridge. He is a Mexico national. As of this writing, he is fifty-two years old.

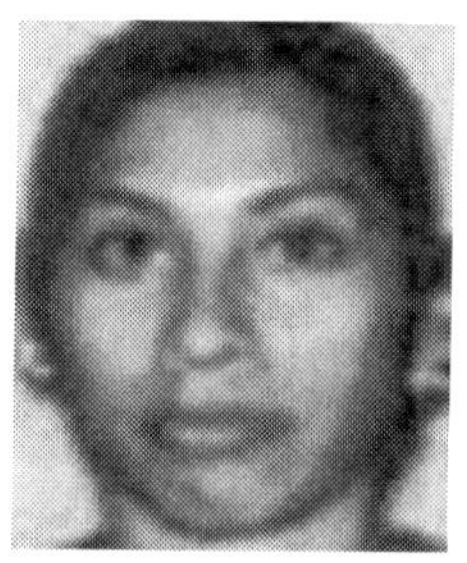

*(Silvia at the time of her disappearance)*

At the time of her disappearance, Silvia Perez had black hair, stood 5'5", and weighed 150 pounds. She was last seen wearing jeans and a t-shirt. She is Hispanic with brown eyes and a tattoo on her left calf. She may use the last name Navarrete. As of this writing, she is thirty-eight years old.

If you have any information regarding this case, you are urged to call the Houston Police Department at 713-731-5223.

## Thomas Flowers

Thirty-one year old Thomas Flowers was last seen in Shiner, Texas on July 1, 2002. He has never been heard from again. Few details are available in his case, but investigators believe he may have been taken against his will.

*(Thomas at the time of his disappearance)*

At the time of his disappearance, Thomas Flowers had black hair, stood at 5'6", and weighed 155 pounds. He is African-American with brown eyes and a scar on his right wrist. He may go by the initials P.T. or attach Jr. to his name. As of this writing, he is forty-seven years old.

If you have any information regarding this case, you are urged to call the Shiner Police Department at 361-594-2831.

## Frank D. Frazier

Eighteen year old Frank D. Frazier was last seen at his home on Caddo Lake Lane in Houston, Texas on October 26, 1990. His sister came home that day and found the house ransacked and a pool of blood on the sofa. Investigators believe Frank was forcibly taken against his will. He has never been heard from again.

His family insists he was not involved in any gang or drug activity. No suspects or persons of interest have been named. He is classified as endangered missing.

*(Frank at the time of his disappearance)*

At the time of his disappearance, Frank Frazier had black hair, stood 5'10", and weighed 170 pounds. He was last seen wearing a t-shirt and size 28 jeans. He is African-American with green eyes and a scar on his cheek. His nickname is Diallo, and he may use the aliases M. Frazier, Franklin Diallo, or Dee Frank Frazier. As of this writing, he is forty-six years old.

If you have any information regarding this case, you are urged to call the Houston Police Department at 713-731-5223.

## Hipolito Sanchez Garcia & Jose C. Molina

Forty-three year old Hipolito Sanchez Garcia and forty-eight year old Jose C. Molina were last seen leaving a club in Dallas, Texas on January 9, 2005. Neither man has ever been heard from again. Their vehicle was found abandoned several weeks later in a residential neighborhood in Dallas.

*(Hipolito at the time of his disappearance)*

At the time of his disappearance, Hipolito Garcia had black hair, stood 6', and weighed 300 pounds. He was last seen wearing a blue/gray western shirt, blue jeans, black leather boots, a black leather belt with this last name on it, and possibly a yellow gold wedding band and chain. He is Hispanic with brown eyes. He has several healed fractures in his left leg. As of this writing, he is fifty-six years old.

*(Jose at the time of his disappearance)*

At the time of his disappearance, Jose Molina had brown hair, stood 5'11", and weighed 190 pounds. He was last seen wearing a faded blue t-shirt, blue jeans, brown high-top lace-up shoes, and a gold chain with a

St. Jude medallion. He is Hispanic with brown eyes. As of this writing, he is sixty-one years old.

If you have any information regarding this case, you are urged to call the Dallas Police Department at 214-671-4242.

## John Allen Giddens

Twenty year old John Allen Giddens was last seen leaving the Long John Silver restaurant where he worked off the Northwest Freeway in Harris County, Texas at 10pm on June 4, 2005. He had cashed his paycheck and probably had a few hundred dollars with him. He drove off in his green 1994 Ford Thunderbird and has never been heard from again. The vehicle was found abandoned on Kiln-Delisle Road in Hancock County, Mississippi about two weeks later. His cell phone and keys were inside it.

*(John at the time of his disappearance)*

At the time of his disappearance, John Giddens had brown hair, stood between 6' - 6'3", and weighed between 170 - 240 pounds. He was last seen wearing a Long John Silver's uniform. He is Caucasian with hazel eyes and a scar on his left thumb. As of this writing, he is thirty-three years old.

If you have any information regarding this case, you are urged to call the Harris County Sheriff's Office at 713-967-5740 or 713-221-6000.

## Elida Mendoza Guzman

Fifty year old Elida Mendoza Guzman was last seen at the bar she owned called Gateway Bar on Pleasanton Road near Division Avenue in San Antonio, Texas on October 23, 2008. She closed the establishment in the early morning hours, and apparently returned to her home on the south side of the city. She disappeared after that and has never been heard from again. Police found her truck parked at her home with her purse locked inside it. Her keys and cell phone disappeared with her and have never been found. Her family does not believe she would have left on her own accord, because she was close to her children and grandchildren.

*(Elida at the time of her disappearance)*

At the time of her disappearance, Elida Guzman had brown hair, stood 5'2", and weighed 140 pounds. She is Hispanic with brown eyes, a mole on her right cheek, a tattoo on her right hand, and pierced ears. As of this writing, she is fifty-nine years old.

If you have any information regarding this case, you are urged to call the San Antonio Police Department at 210-207-7660.

## Stephen Douglas Hamshire

Thirty-six year old Stephen Douglas Hamshire was last seen walking out of his family's Silsbee, Texas home in March 24, 2007. He was going to take his usual walk around town. He has never been heard from again. Dogs tracked his scent to Highway 327 near the Village Creek Bridge, but then lost the trail. His family stated he had a very strict daily routine and would not deviate from it unless something was wrong.

*(Stephen at the time of his disappearance)*

At the time of his disappearance, Stephen Hamshire had brown hair cut in a Beatle-style, stood 5'7", and weighed 190 pounds. He was last seen wearing a dark blue t-shirt with USA on it, blue jeans, and white sneakers with the Texas Longhorn symbol on the back and sides. He is Caucasian with hazel eyes and a birthmark on his right wrist. He is autistic and appears to be much younger than his actual age. As of this writing, he is forty-seven years old.

If you have any information regarding this case, you are urged to call the Silsbee Police Department at 409-385-3714.

## Tot Tran Harriman

Fifty-seven year old Tot Tran Harriman was visiting her family in Texas in the summer of 2001 and had decided to purchase property in the state to be closer to her relatives. She mapped out a route between League City and Corpus Christi, Texas and planned to drive along Highway 35 searching for possible homes. She left her son's residence near League City at approximately 5am on July 12, 2001. She has never been seen or heard from again.

Her cell phone was on, but she did not answer it when a friend called at approximately 8:30am. The phone rang four times and went to voicemail. The friend tried to call again at 10:30am and the call went directly to voicemail, indicating the phone was turned off. Her family reported her missing that evening. Extensive searches between League City and Corpus Christi failed to produce any clues as to her whereabouts. Foul play is suspected.

She was driving her 1995 rose quartz Lincoln Continental with personalized Florida plate reading TOTSY. The vehicle has white leather interior and chrome tailpipes, a small sticker reading PJC on the right side of the rear bumper, and the VIN number 1LNLM97V35Y755926. Her vehicle has not been located.

*(Tot at the time of her disappearance)*

At the time of her disappearance, Tot Harriman had graying black hair, wore eyeglasses, stood 4'11", and weighed 100 pounds. She was last seen wearing a shirt, shorts, sandals, a diamond necklace pendant, and seven gold bracelets on her left wrist. She is Asian with brown eyes and is of Vietnamese descent. She has scars on her abdomen. As of this writing, she is seventy-four years old.

If you have any information regarding this case, you are urged to call the League City Police Department at 281-332-2566.

## Mitchelle Deborah Hicks

Twenty-five year old Mitchelle Deborah Hicks was last seen leaving an address on west Spanish Camp Road in Wharton, Texas on July 12, 2014. She has never been heard from again, and authorities believe she may have been taken against her will. Few details are available in her case.

*(Mitchelle at the time of her disappearance)*

At the time of her disappearance, Mitchelle Hicks had black hair, stood 5'5", and weighed 145 pounds. She was last seen wearing a white floral dress, black tights, and flip flops. She is African-American with brown eyes and scars on her left cheek and abdomen. She has tattoos on her back, neck, right shoulder, and upper right arm. She may use the last name Hector. As of this writing, she is twenty-nine years old.

If you have any information regarding this case, you are urged to call the Wharton Police Department at 979-532-3131.

## Linda Ann House

Twenty-nine year old Linda Ann House was last seen in Dallas, Texas on November 8, 1985. She has never been seen or heard from again, and authorities believe she may have been taken against her will. Few details are available in her case.

*(Linda at the time of her disappearance)*

At the time of her disappearance, Linda House had blonde hair, stood 5'9", and weighed 160 pounds. She was eight months pregnant at the time. She was last seen wearing a violet and white checkered maternity shirt and pants. She is Caucasian with green eyes and gold caps on her back teeth. As of this writing, she is sixty-one years old.

If you have any information regarding this case, you are urged to call the Dallas Police Department at 214-671-4316.

## Dorothy Smith Kelley

Sixty-two year old Dorothy Smith Kelley was last seen near her family's motor home at Balmorhea Lake, Texas during the morning of June 9, 1993. Her husband was away collecting rocks for about ninety minutes. He discovered she was missing when he returned. Search dogs tracked her scent to a picnic table and then lost the trail. Foul play is possible in her case.

*(Dorothy at the time of her disappearance)*

At the time of her disappearance, Dorothy Kelley had gray hair, stood 5'6", and weighed 180 pounds. She was last seen wearing a white button-down blouse underneath a red plaid flannel shirt, jeans, and SAS shoes. She is Caucasian with brown eyes, two small scars on her right cheek, and pierced ears. She has surgical scars on both of her hips and her left knee. As of this writing, she is eighty-seven years old.

If you have any information regarding this case, you are urged to call the Reeves County Sheriff's Office at 432-445-4903.

## Randall Dewayne Lee

Thirty-four year old Randall Dewayne Lee contacted his father on August 15, 1985 to say he was planning to go to Eagle Pass, Texas to look for a job. He was in Del Rio, Texas at the time. Both cities are along the Mexican border and about fifty-five miles apart. It is not known if he ever arrived in Eagle Pass or not. His vehicle, a rust-colored 1977 Chevrolet 210 Series pickup truck with Oklahoma plates 851-1203, disappeared with him and has never been found.

*(Randall at the time of his disappearance)*

At the time of his disappearance, Randall Lee had light brown hair, wore eyeglasses with thick lenses and dark-colored frames, stood between 6' - 6'2", and weighed between 127 - 190 pounds. He had a nervous condition at the time. He is Caucasian with hazel eyes, surgical scars on one of his wrists, a scar on his right eyebrow, and numerous scars on his hands. His nickname is Randy. As of this writing, he is sixty-six years old.

If you have any information regarding this case, you are urged to call the Liberal Police Department at 620-626-0101.

## Maria Jesus Llamas

Sixty-nine year old Maria Jesus Llamas was last seen at the Poteet Flea Market on State Highway 16 south in San Antonio, Texas on November 20, 2016. She told her husband she didn't like the music that was playing and wanted to leave. On the way to the parking lot, he stopped to look at a display and when he turned around she was gone. The surveillance cameras in the area showed her walking towards another exit, through the parking lot, and out the entrance gate to the highway. She has never been heard from again.

Three weeks later on December 10th, her purse was found wrapped around a tree in Leon Creek near the flea market. She had wandered away before, but had always been located within an hour or two. Foul play is not suspected in her case, but there have no sightings of her since that day.

*(Maria at the time of her disappearance)*

At the time of her disappearance, Maria Llamas had graying black hair, wore eyeglasses, stood 5'2", and weighed 120 pounds. She was last seen wearing a black wool coat, a black and white blouse, black pants, black shoes, and a silver necklace. She was carrying a cross-body handbag. She is Hispanic with brown eyes, pierced ears, upper and lower dentures, a vaccination scar on her right arm, and a mole on the left side of her upper lip. Her nickname is Yeya. As of this writing, she is seventy-one years old.

If you have any information regarding this case, you are urged to call the San Antonio Police Department at 210-207-7660.

## German Machuca

Eighteen year old German Machuca was last seen washing his vehicle in Laredo, Texas on March 31, 1990. He left the water running and the soap bucket next to his car. He has never been seen or heard from again, and foul play is suspected.

*(German at the time of his disappearance)*

At the time of his disappearance, German Machuca had black hair, stood 5'7", and weighed 150 pounds. He was last seen wearing a blue t-shirt, multicolored floral blue shorts, and brown deck shoes. He is Hispanic with brown eyes, a chipped front tooth, a pierced left ear, and a quarter-sized scar on his left arm. He has scars between his eyebrows, on his left wrist, and underneath his chin. As of this writing, he is forty-six years old.

If you have any information regarding this case, you are urged to call the Laredo Police Department at 956-795-2800.

## Carmen Magdalena Mares

Thirty-five year old Carmen Magdalena Mares was last seen in San Antonio, Texas on September 2, 2007. She went to the E & G Sports Bar on Zarzamora Street and Woodlawn Avenue with several female friends. She left the bar with a man at 2:30am saying she was giving him a ride home. She called her fiancé at 2:55am to say she was on her way home. She never arrived and has never been heard from again. The man she left the bar with has never been identified, and it is not known whether or not he has anything to do with her disappearance.

Her white four-door 1996 Mitsubishi Galant with Texas plates 686KGV disappeared with her and has never been located. The vehicle had front-end damage, a noisy engine, and no hubcaps on the driver's side.

*(Carmen at the time of her disappearance)*

At the time of her disappearance, Carmen Mares had brown hair, wore purple tinted contact lenses, stood between 5'4" - 5'5", and weighed between 125 - 135 pounds. She was last seen wearing a black t-shirt with crystal studs on it, blue jeans, brown lace-up boots, shrimp-shaped earnings, and a necklace with a gold cross. She is Hispanic with brown eyes, pierced ears, and a tribal tattoo on her lower back. As of this writing, she is forty-five years old.

If you have any information regarding this case, you are urged to call the San Antonio Police Department at 210-207-7660.

## James H. Mayberry Jr. "Jamie Mayberry"

Thirty-five year old James H. Mayberry Jr. "Jamie Mayberry" was last seen leaving her home in Kenedy,

Texas on April 11, 1999. She left with a man who had knocked on her door at 11pm. Although she said she did not know the individual, she left with him anyway, saying she was going to the store and would be right back. Her niece said she appeared frightened and was trembling when she left. She never returned home and has never been seen or heard from again.

At 2:30am the next morning, two men in a truck with a loud muffler tried to get into the home to see Jamie. Her niece told them she was not at home, and they laughed. It is unknown if any of the three men were involved in her disappearance, but foul play is suspected. Her loved ones believe she may have been threatened prior to leaving with the man who knocked on her door that night, and that it was the result of a hate crime.

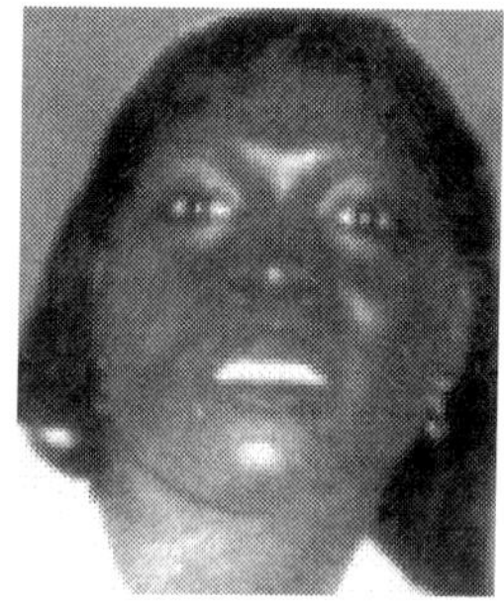

*(Jamie at the time of her disappearance)*

At the time of her disappearance, Jamie Mayberry had shoulder-length black hair with extensions, stood between 5'5" - 5'7", and weighed between 140 - 170 pounds. She was last seen wearing a button-down collarless beige blouse with three-quarter-length sleeves, khaki shorts, size 7.5 or 8 ladies slip-on white sandals or sneakers, a padded forest green Victoria Secret bra, and panties. She was carrying a black leather clutch purse containing $20 or $30 in cash, a black compact, and a pack of Virginia Slims cigarettes. Her hair was pulled back into a ponytail at the time. She is African-American with brown eyes and pierced ears. She is transgender, and although she is biologically male, she chooses to live as a female. She has heart, liver, blood pressure, and respiratory issues. As of this writing, she is fifty-four years old.

If you have any information regarding this case, you are urged to call the Karnes County Sheriff's Office at 830-780-3931.

## Salar Jaafar Mohammed

Twenty-six year old Salar Jaafar Mohammed was working as an Arabic interpreter for the United States Military at the time of his disappearance. He was last seen when his American sponsor dropped him off at the Army National Guard Armory in Denton, Texas on July 21, 2012. Neither his sponsor nor his family have seen or heard from him since. It is believed he may have been taken against his will.

*(Salar at the time of his disappearance)*

At the time of his disappearance, Salar Mohammed had brown hair, stood 5'10", and weighed

150 pounds. He is Asian with brown eyes. He is of Iraqi descent and speaks both Arabic and English. As of this writing, he is thirty-one years old.

If you have any information regarding this case, you are urged to call the Texas Department of Public Safety at 800-346-3243.

## Trung Quang Ngo

Twenty-three year old Trung Quang Ngo was last seen in Katy, Texas on January 12, 2013. He told his family he was going to meet friends. He has never been seen or heard from again.

His gunmetal gray 2004 Nissan Infiniti G35 with Texas plates BP2 L036 disappeared with him and has never been located. His cell phone was found lying along the roadside in front of the Farmington Apartment Complex off north Fry and Franz Roads in Katy. Authorities believe he may have been taken against his will.

*(Trung at the time of his disappearance)*

At the time of his disappearance, Trung Ngo had black hair, stood 5'6", and weighed 140 pounds. He was last seen wearing a sweater, a black shirt, blue jeans, and camel-colored steal-toe work boots. He was possibly carrying a military-style backpack. He is Asian with brown eyes. He has the following tattoos: a fish on the side of his chest, three helmeted Japanese men holding rifles on the other side of his chest, the word Faith on his right forearm, his first name in bamboo-style lettering on his lower left leg, and his last name on his arm. As of this writing, he is twenty-eight years old.

If you have any information regarding this case, you are urged to call the Stafford Police Department at 281-261-3950.

## Carey Mae Parker

Twenty-three year old Carey Mae Parker was last seen in Quinlan, Texas on March 17, 1991. She has never been seen or heard from again. She was driving a blue and gray 1980 or 1981 Buick Skylark with Texas plates. The vehicle disappeared with her and has not been located. Her family does not believe she left of her own accord, because she was in the middle of planning a birthday party for her young son at the time.

*(Carey at the time of her disappearance)*

At the time of her disappearance, Carey Parker had brown hair, stood between 5'7" - 5'10", and weighed between 115 - 125 pounds. She is Caucasian with blue eyes and pierced ears. She has an indentation on the side of her calf and scars on her left arm. She had previously broken her pelvis and chipped her toe bone. She may eyeglasses. As of this writing, she is fifty years old.

If you have any information regarding this case, you are urged to call the Hunt County Sheriff's Office at 903-453-6800.

## Modesto Robles Jr.

Forty-three year old Modesto Robles Jr. and his friends Hilario "Larry" Cardenas and Daniel "Danny" Gonzalez were deep sea fishing off the gulf coast of Matagorda Bay, Texas on September 8, 2000. Neither the men nor the boat returned to shore. The United States Coast Guard launched an extensive search on September 11, 2000. Two of their coolers were found floating in the water, with one of them tied to a shoe. No other evidence was located and the search was called off on September 15$^{th}$.

Ten days after they disappeared, leg bones, including a femur severed several inches above the knee, were discovered on the beach at Mustang Island. Three days later, additional remains were found in Kleberg County, Texas. DNA tests later proved that the remains were those of Larry and Danny. The medical examiner was not able to determine the cause of death, and it is unknown whether or not foul play was involved. Modesto remains missing. Authorities said it was odd that debris from the boat was not discovered, but added that the waters hampered recovery efforts.

The boat is a 25-foot white 1985 Wellcraft with a Bimini top, a cuddy cabin, and twin 115-horsepower Yamaha outboard engines. The boat's hull identification number is 1BTBKRR20D1202790. Its description number is ELA8576M82B248, and its Texas registration number is 4113EF. The boat has never been located.

*(Modesto at the time of his disappearance)*

At the time of his disappearance, Modesto Robles Jr. had brown hair, stood 5'11", and weighed 200 pounds. He is Hispanic/Latino with brown eyes. His nickname is Bud. As of this writing, he is sixty years old.

If you have any information regarding this case, you are urged to call the Texas Department of Public Safety at 800-346-3243.

## Dudley Truett Scott

Fifty-two year old Dudley Truett Scott was last seen walking into a wooded area on Creekwood Drive near his home in Splendora, Texas at 3pm on December 12, 1994. He has never been seen or heard from again.

*(Dudley at the time of his disappearance)*

At the time of his disappearance, Dudley Scott had brown hair, stood 5', and weighed 140 pounds. He was last seen wearing blue short-sleeve coveralls with no shirt, blue boxer shorts, and brown lace-up boots. He was carrying two wallets, a Swiss Army knife, and a homemade identification card. He is Caucasian with blue eyes, a cleft palate, a vertical scar on his abdomen, and he has no teeth. He has Down syndrome and is mute. As of this writing, he is seventy-five years old.

If you have any information regarding this case, you are urged to call the Montgomery County Sheriff's Office at 936-760-5800.

## Jessica Dawn Schreiber

Thirty-one year old Jessica Dawn Schreiber was last seen on November 26, 2003 in Nacogdoches, Texas. She called her mother that day and said she was in Austin, Texas with a friend named Danny. She has never been seen or heard from again. Foul play is possible.

She left behind a young daughter, Sadie Blevins, who went to live with her mother, Eileen Gunter. In August 2006, Eileen shot nine year old Sadie to death at their home in Kirbyville, Texas before taking her own life. It is unknown if the murder-suicide was in any way related to Jessica's disappearance.

*(Jessica at the time of her disappearance)*

At the time of her disappearance, Jessica Schreiber had brown hair, stood 5'7", and weighed 127 pounds. She is Caucasian with brown eyes, a chain tattoo on her left wrist, an eagle tattoo on her right ankle, and a flower tattoo at her navel. As of this writing, she is forty-six years old.

If you have any information regarding this case, you are urged to call the Stephen F. Austin State University Police Department at 936-468-2608.

## Glenn Layne Towery

Fifty-six year old Glenn Layne Towery left home at 7:30am on April 17, 2017 to drive to work on Mockingbird Circle in Victoria, Texas, where he was employed as a chiropractor. He was last seen at a convenience store in Raisin, Texas that morning, which was his usual morning routine. He never arrived at work and has never been heard from again.

His gray 2014 Ford F-150 pickup truck was found abandoned at a rural farm in southeastern Victoria

County on May 7th. It had been there since at least ten days after Glenn was last seen. It was parked along a fence at the end of a private road, about a mile and a half from the nearest public road. There was no sign of Glenn and no clues as to his whereabouts in or around the truck. Authorities believe he was taken against his will.

*(Glenn at the time of his disappearance)*

At the time of his disappearance, Glenn Towery had blonde hair, a gray goatee, stood 5'10", and weighed 160 pounds. He was last seen wearing a black pullover shirt with white stripes and San Antonio Spurs on the front left side, either black cargo pants or black slick-looking shorts, a white cap, either brown hiking boots or black lace-up chukka shoes, white socks, a wedding ring, and a watch on his left wrist. He is Caucasian with green eyes and a burn scar on his left wrist. He may go by his middle name. As of this writing, he is fifty-seven years old.

If you have any information regarding this case, you are urged to call one of the following numbers:

*Goliad County Sheriff's Office at 361-645-3451*

*Victoria County Sheriff's Office at 361-574-8023*

## Ladana Renee Wiley

Twenty-seven year old Ladana Renee Wiley was last seen when her mother dropped her off at her residence in New Boston, Texas at approximately 8:30pm on January 1, 2000. Her mother said she appeared to be nervous as she exited the vehicle. Her mother called her approximately one hour later but there was no answer. Ladana has never been heard from again.

There were no indications of a struggle at her home after her disappearance. All of her personal belongings were left behind. Only a set of keys were missing.

A woman fishing in Wright Patman Lake in June 2000 discovered possible reddish-brown human hair. Authorities searched the area, but no further evidence was located. Investigators stated that they could not determine if the material was in fact human hair.

*(Ladana at the time of her disappearance)*

At the time of her disappearance, Ladana Wiley had brown hair, wore eyeglasses, stood 5’2”, and weighed 155 pounds. She is Caucasian with brown eyes and a scar on her abdomen. As of this writing, she is forty-six years old.

If you have any information regarding this case, you are urged to call the New Boston Police Department at 903-628-3771.

## Richard Keith Call & Cassandra Lee Hailey

Twenty year old Richard Keith Call and eighteen year old Cassandra Lee Hailey, both students at Christopher Newport University, went on their first date together on April 9, 1988. He picked her up at her Grafton, Virginia home, and they planned to spend the day together. They were seen together in Keith's red 1982 Toyota Celica, and then later at a party in Newport News, Virginia at 1:30am on April 10$^{th}$. Neither of them have been seen or heard from since.

Keith's vehicle was discovered abandoned at the York River Overlook on Colonial Parkway in Yorktown, Virginia at 7am on April 10$^{th}$.There was no sign of a struggle inside the vehicle. The keys were on the driver's seat, and a watch and eyeglasses were on the dashboard. Nearly all of the clothing Keith had been wearing, including his underwear, was found in the backseat of the car. Cassandra's undergarments and some other pieces of her clothing were also in the backseat. Her purse and Keith's wallet were missing.

Authorities initially speculated they may have gone swimming and drown, but an extensive search of the river turned up no sign of either of them. And the water temperature was in the forties the night of their disappearance. Foul play is now suspected.

The bodies of three other young couples, all of them college students, were found in areas off the

Colonial Parkway from 1986 - 1989. In all cases, their cars were found abandoned with most of their possessions intact inside. However, if the cases are related, only Keith and Cassandra's remains have never been found.

The Colonial Parkway extends for twenty-three miles and runs through the Virginia cities of Yorktown, Jamestown, and Williamsburg. Authorities have long suspected that a serial killer stalked and killed in the area in the mid to late 1980s. They believe the perpetrator may have impersonated a law enforcement officer in order to approach his victims.

*(Richard at the time of his disappearance)*

At the time of his disappearance, Richard Call had light brown hair, stood 6', and weighed 150 pounds. He was last seen wearing a gray and brown cardigan sweater, a white polo shirt, two-tone brown dress slacks, and leather shoes. He is Caucasian with blue eyes. As of this writing, he is fifty years old.

*(Cassandra at the time of her disappearance)*

At the time of her disappearance, Cassandra Hailey had brown hair, stood 5'7", and weighed 135 pounds. She was last seen wearing a long-sleeve rust-colored jersey turtleneck with a white blouse over it, stonewashed jeans, and a 1987 Tabb High School class ring. She is Caucasian with brown eyes, three piercings in her left ear, and two piercings in her right ear. Her nicknames are Cassie, Sandra, and Sandy. As of this writing, she is forty-eight years old.

If you have any information regarding this case, you are urged to call one of the following numbers:

*Virginia State Police at 757-424-6850*

*Federal Bureau of Investigation (FBI) Norfolk, Virginia Office at 804-455-0100*

## Miller Smith Harlow

Sixty-two year old Miller Smith Harlow was last seen in Louisa, Virginia on August 28, 1991. He regularly walked from his house on Route 33, two miles outside of Gordonsville, Virginia to The Wooden Nickel restaurant for breakfast. He was last seen standing in front of Preddy's Funeral Home in Gordonsville at 1:30pm. He has never been seen or heard from again.

He didn't drive and would get around by using his bicycle, walking, or asking friends or family for rides to where he needed to go. His cousin was supposed to pick him up at the restaurant on the day he went missing, but when he arrived Miller was not there. His cousin went to his house, where he lived alone, and Miller was not there either. He left a note on the door, and then came back the next day. The note was still there. His family reported him missing on August 31st. Authorities stated there is no evidence of a crime in his case and no suspects, but he had predictable habits and no history of leaving without warning. He is considered missing under suspicious circumstances.

*(Miller at the time of his disappearance)*

At the time of his disappearance, Miller Harlow had gray hair, wore eyeglasses with brown rims, stood 5'4", and weighed 200 pounds. He was last seen wearing a red t-shirt, blue jeans, black sneakers, and a blue or black baseball cap with AMC on it. He is Caucasian with brown eyes. As of this writing, he is eighty-nine years old.

If you have any information regarding this case, you are urged to call the Louisa County Sheriff's Office at 540-967-1234.

## Eric Grady Smith

Forty-two year old Eric Grady Smith was last seen in Cedar Bluff, Virginia on November 8, 2013. He left home on foot during the early morning hours to go hunting on his property on west Buggy Road. He is an experienced hunter and was very familiar with the area.

He has never been seen or heard from again. When he failed to return home by evening, his family began searching for him to no avail. They then notified the police. An extensive search turned up no evidence as to his whereabouts. There has been speculation that he met with foul play, but his remains have never been found.

*(Eric at the time of his disappearance)*

At the time of his disappearance, Eric Smith had brown hair, stood 6'1", and weighed 210 pounds. He was last seen wearing camouflage hunting clothes and a titanium Timex watch. He was carrying a Thompson Center .50 caliber muzzleloader with a stainless steel barrel and camouflage stock. He is Caucasian with brown eyes and a brown knot on the front of his left shin. He is blind in one eye. As of this writing, he is forty-seven years old.

If you have any information regarding this case, you are urged to call the Tazewell County Sheriff's Office at 276-988-0645.

## Israel Ray Smith

Twenty-eight year old Israel Ray Smith was last seen on March 10, 2008 in Wytheville, Virginia. He completed his shift at Radio Shack at 8pm, and then went to visit his brother. Later, he spoke to his mother on the phone. He has never been seen or heard from again.

On March 14th, police conducted a welfare check on him and went to his apartment on east Fulton Street. The door was unlocked, the TV was on with a game controller on the floor, and his keys were on the coffee table. There were no signs of a struggle or forced entry. None of his belongings were missing except for his cell phone. There were no indications that he had planned to leave for an extended amount of time. His green 1992 Ford Explorer was parked next to the apartment building. It was unlocked and had clean laundry inside.

He had worked at Radio Shack since September of the previous year and was considered an ideal employee, who never missed work and was never late without calling. His cell phone has not been used since he went missing and all calls have been transferred directly to voicemail. Authorities stated that there is no hard evidence of foul play, but they do not believe he left of his own accord.

*(Israel at the time of his disappearance)*

At the time of his disappearance, Israel Smith had brown hair, stood 5'10", and weighed 160 pounds. He was last seen wearing a black leather jacket, a white dress shirt, blue jeans, and white sneakers. He is Caucasian with blue eyes. As of this writing, he is thirty-eight years old.

If you have any information regarding this case, you are urged to call the Wytheville Police Department at 276-223-3300.

## John William Wingler Sr.

Seventy-four year old John William Wingler Sr. was last seen at this residence in Whitetop, Virginia during the early morning hours of November 12, 2015. He has never been seen or heard from again. His red 2002 Ford Ranger extended cab pickup truck with Virginia plates XDK - 1981 disappeared with him and has never been found.

*(John at the time of his disappearance)*

At the time of his disappearance, John Wingler Sr. had graying red hair, stood 5'9", and weighed 145 pounds. He was last seen wearing a gray t-shirt, a silk and nylon blue coat with white trim and white lining, blue jeans, and a yellow gold wedding band. He is Caucasian with blue eyes and a scar over the left side of his ribcage. He has a heart condition that requires medication. As of this writing, he is seventy-seven years old.

If you have any information regarding this case, you are urged to call the Grayson County Sheriff's Office at 276-773-3241.

## John Allen Akkerman

Twenty-seven year old John Allen Akkerman was last seen in Spokane, Washington on August 7, 1987. He worked as a cabdriver at the time. He picked up a male passenger at Fifth Avenue and Wall Street, near Deaconess Medical Center at 12:20am. He told the dispatcher he was taking the man to the Spokane Valley. He has never been seen or heard from again.

Two hours later, another cabdriver found John's cab at the intersection of Fifth Avenue and Madison Street, just four blocks from where he had picked up his last fare. It was unlocked and parked at an unusual angle. The windows were rolled down and the knife John kept for protection was next to the driver's seat. Both his personal wallet and the one he kept for his cab fares were missing.

He was a good employee. Neither his employer nor his wife believe he left of his own accord. The man he last picked up has never been identified.

*(John at the time of his disappearance)*

At the time of his disappearance, John Akkerman had brown hair with long sideburns and a mustache, wore eyeglasses with brown plastic frames, stood 6', and weighed 160 pounds. He was last seen wearing a white long-sleeve shirt with a red and blue checkered pattern on the cuffs and collar, new blue jeans, blue low-cut sneakers with Velcro fasteners, a gold-colored necklace with a brass ring, and a silver digital wristwatch with a silver band. He is Caucasian with hazel eyes, a birthmark on his penis, and a vertical six-inch scar above his navel. He has the following tattoos: a heart on the inside of his forearm with the initials A.J. inside it and a lightning bolt on the right side and a heart on his left shoulder with a sword through it and a name blacked out. As of this writing, he is fifty-eight years old.

If you have any information regarding this case, you are urged to call the Spokane Police Department at 509-625-4231.

## Beverly Ann Cummings

Fifty-three year old Beverly Ann Cummings was in Federal Way, Washington early in the morning on July 18, 1990 when she went out to run errands at the grocery store and the post office. She said she would be back by 9am to babysit her granddaughter, but she never returned and has never been heard from again. When her family checked the post office and the grocery store, they discovered the mail had not been collected and no one had seen her at the store.

In September 1990, her brown 1977 Toyota Celica hatchback was found abandoned on a forest service road three and a half miles off Highway 410 in Greenwater, Washington. Residents said the car had been there since mid-July.

It is uncharacteristic for her to leave without warning, and neither her bank account nor credit cards have been used since she went missing. Her family can think of no reason why she would have left of her own accord.

*(Beverly at the time of her disappearance)*

At the time of her disappearance, Beverly Cummings had brown hair, wore pink-framed eyeglasses, stood between 5' - 5'1", and weighed between 105 - 115 pounds. She is Caucasian with blue eyes and pierced ears. As of this writing, she is eighty-one years old.

If you have any information regarding this case, you are urged to call the King County Sheriff's Department at 206-205-7810.

## Nancy E. Glovick

Thirty-three year old Nancy E. Glovick was last seen leaving her Aberdeen, Washington residence on January 1, 1977. Her black and green four-door Oldsmobile with Washington plates HCC 459 disappeared with her and has never been located.

*(Nancy at the time of her disappearance)*

At the time of her disappearance, Nancy Glovick had brown hair, stood 5'10", and weighed 155 pounds. She was last seen wearing a brown coat and brown pants. She is Caucasian with hazel eyes. As of this writing, she is seventy-four years old.

If you have any information regarding this case, you are urged to call the Aberdeen Police Department at 360-538-4420.

## Phyllis Ellen Lewellen

Thirty-six year old Phyllis Ellen Lewellen was last seen leaving her home on John Street near Kelso,

Washington in Cowlitz County on December 27, 1996. Her husband said she decided to go for a drive to think during the evening hours. She was accompanied by her female Rottweiler. They were traveling in Phyllis' light blue four-door 1981 Peugeot 505 sedan with Washington plates Q680494. The vehicle disappeared with her and her dog and has never been located.

*(Phyllis at the time of her disappearance)*

At the time of her disappearance, Phyllis Lewellen had reddish-blonde hair, stood between 5'5" - 5'6", and weighed 120 pounds. She was last seen wearing a white sweatshirt, a western-style coat, blue jeans, and rubber-soled slippers. She is Caucasain with blue/green eyes and a distinct southern accent. As of this writing, she is fifty-eight years old.

If you have any information regarding this case, you are urged to call the Cowlitz County Sheriff's Office at 360-577-3092.

## Ramon Castro Moore

Fifty-five year old Ramon Castro Moore was last seen at his workplace, Tacoma Cabinet & Fixture, on east D Street in Tacoma, Washington on April 12, 2012. He had held the same job for ten years prior to his disappearance, and had never missed a day without calling. His coworkers reported him missing after he stopping coming to work. He lived alone in a basement apartment at the time, and usually walked or took the bus where he needed to go. He is considered to be missing under suspicious circumstances.

*(Ramon at the time of his disappearance)*

At the time of his disappearance, Ramon Moore had gray hair, stood 5'5", and weighed 190 pounds. He was last seen wearing a black hooded sweatshirt and a grayish hat. He often wears a green hip-length Army-type jacket. He is Hispanic with brown eyes and a brown birthmark on his cheek. He has scars on his face, right hand, right wrist, and left thigh. He is of Cuban descent. As of this writing, he is sixty-one years old.

If you have any information regarding this case, you are urged to call the Tacoma Police Department at 253-798-4721.

## Nancy Kareen Moyer

Thirty-six year old Nancy Kareen Moyer was last seen in Tenino, Washington on March 6, 2009. She worked as a financial analyst for the State Department of Ecology in Lacey, Washington. She left work at

5:15pm, drove a coworker home, and bought some items at a Triftway Market at 6:45pm. That was the last time anyone saw her. She has never been heard from again.

Her daughters were visiting their father for the weekend, and did not return home until March 8th. When they arrived at their mother's home on State Route 507, Nancy was not there. The front door was ajar, the TV and living room lights were on, a partially consumed glass of wine was on the coffee table, and the bedside lamp in her bedroom was turned on. There were no indications of a break-in or a struggle, however. All of her belongings, including her keys, purse, and cigarettes were in the house. Her car was parked out front. She was reported missing at 5pm on March 8th.

Her bank account and credit cards have not been accessed since March 6th. She had been employed for the Department of Ecology for twelve years, and her employers described her as a reliable worker who would always notify them if she had to be absent. She and her husband were separated, but it was an amicable break up and they had managed to work out a shared custody agreement without involving the courts. He is not considered a suspect in her case. Authorities suspect foul play was involved.

*(Nancy at the time of her disappearance)*

At the time of her disappearance, Nancy Moyer had dark brown hair, smoked cigarettes, stood between 4'11" - 5', and weighed between 105 - 120 pounds. She is Caucasian with brown eyes, a scar on her right knee, a pierced navel, and pierced ears. She has the following tattoos: stars, hearts, and flowers on her upper right arm, a butterfly on her lower back, the words Doublemint and Juicyfruit with flowers and hearts on her upper back, a hibiscus flower on her left hip, a Playboy bunny on her right hip, and cherries with the initials A.S. on her right foot. As of this writing, she is forty-five years old.

If you have any information regarding this case, you are urged to call the Thurston County Sheriff's Office at 360-786-5279.

## William Kermig Summers Jr.

Twenty-two year old William Kermig Summers Jr. was a Petty Officer in the United States Navy in 1982. He was a Machinist Mate Second Class assigned to the U.S.S. Robison, which was in port at the Naval Shipyard in Bremerton, Washington on January 4, 1982. He disappeared that day and has had no contact with anyone since.

*(William at the time of his disappearance)*

At the time of his disappearance, Williams Summers Jr. had brown hair, stood 6'1", and weighed between 150 - 160 pounds. He is Caucasian with blue eyes and two amalgam fillings in his teeth. He may use the first name Andrew, and his nickname is Billy. As of this writing, he is fifty-eight years old.

If you have any information regarding this case, you are urged to call the Naval Criminal Investigative Service (NCIS) Washington D.C. Office at 202-433-9225 or 1-800-479-9685.

## Eugene Bush Wekesa

Twenty-two year old Eugene Bush Wekesa was last seen leaving his apartment on northwest 16th Place in Bellevue, Washington at 9pm on November 24, 2010. He told his mother and brother, whom he lived with, that he was going to walk to the nearby Crossroads Shopping Center. No surveillance footage from the shopping center captured him there that night, however. He left his wallet, keys, and cell phone at home. Although there is no evidence of foul play, it is uncharacteristic for him to leave without warning and his family believes he may have come to harm.

*(Eugene at the time of his disappearance)*

At the time of his disappearance, Eugene Wekesa had black hair, stood between 5'8" - 6'1", and weighed between 140 - 155 pounds. He was last seen wearing a black jacket, a gray t-shirt, black jeans, a black beanie, and brown boots. He is African-American with brown eyes. He was born in Kenya, but he had lived in the United States for five years. His nickname is Musebe. As of this writing, he is thirty years old.

If you have any information regarding this case, you are urged to call the Bellevue Police Department at 425-452-4629.

## Karen Sue Adams

Fifty-four year old Karen Sue Adams was last seen on March 11, 2007. That day she left her home in Aliquippa, Pennsylvania and went to the Mountaineer Gaming Resort in Chester, West Virginia. She used her credit card there. Security cameras showed her leaving the parking lot at 4:31am. At 4:35am, she accessed her cell phone's voice mail. She never arrived home and has never been heard from again. Her maroon two-door 2005 Suzuki Forenza with Pennsylvania plates EDT5587 disappeared with her and has not been located. Her family does not believe she would have left without warning or abandoned her dog, which she cherished.

*(Karen at the time of her disappearance)*

At the time of her disappearance, Karen Adams had brown hair, wore lightly-tinted wire-rimmed eyeglasses, stood between 5'4" - 5'6", and weighed between 110 - 120 pounds. She was last seen wearing a green coat, two dark-colored shirts, blue jeans, and a baseball cap. She is Caucasian with green eyes and pierced ears. As of this writing, she is sixty-five years old.

If you have any information regarding this case, you are urged to call the Independence Township Police Department at 724-378-7774.

## Carlene Brown

Nineteen year old Carlene Brown was last seen in Rawlins, Wyoming on July 4, 1974. She and nineteen year old Christy Gross visited the Little Britches Rodeo that day. Both of them disappeared afterwards. Their car was later found abandoned in Worland, Wyoming. Authorities initially believed they left of their own accord, but as time passed with no one having heard from them, they began to investigate other possibilities.

In October 1983, Christy's remains were found three miles south of Sinclair, Wyoming. She had died from blunt force trauma to the head. There was no sign of Carlene at the scene, and she has never been seen or heard from again.

Carlene and Christy's case is believed to be connected to other disappearances and murders in the surrounding area. Fourteen year old Deborah Meyer disappeared from the Rawlins area on August 4th of the same year as Carlene and Christy. Like Carlene, she too has never been found. Ten year old Jayleen Banker disappeared on August 23, 1974 from Rawlins as well. Her remains were later found in a field.

Royal Russell Long is considered a possible suspect in Carlene and Deborah's disappearances and Christy and Jayleen's murders. He was a truck driver in the 80s. He pleaded guilty to kidnapping twelve year old Sharon Baldeagle of South Dakota in 1984. She, too, has never been found. He was also charged with the murders of thirteen year olds Cinda Pallett and Charlotte Kinsey of Oklahoma City, Oklahoma. But the charges were later dismissed due to a lack of evidence. Authorities believe they are all deceased, but Carlene, Deborah, Cinda, and Charlotte's remains have never been found. Royal lived in the Rawlins area in 1974 and worked at local fairs and carnivals. He died of a heart attack in prison in 1993. He was never convicted in connection to any of the cases besides Sharon's.

*(Carlene at the time of her disappearance)*

At the time of her disappearance, Carlene Brown had brown hair, stood between 5' - 5'3", and weighed between 100 - 120 pounds. She is Caucasian with brown eyes and surgical scars on the big toes of both feet. As of this writing, she is sixty-three years old.

If you have any information regarding this case, you are urged to call the Carbon County Sheriff's Department at 307-328-2782.

## Latoya Brown

Twenty-one year old Latoya Brown was last seen leaving her family's home in Northport, Alabama on April 26, 2011. She left with a friend to go get something to eat that night and never returned. The next day an EF-4 tornado tore through Alabama from Tuscaloosa to Birmingham, killing 65 and injuring approximately 1500. The shopping center where Latoya had planned to go the night before was completely destroyed by the tornado. Her cell phone records place her at the Rosendale Apartments in the Rosendale Court area at 5:30pm on the day of the tornado, and someone placed a call on her cell phone just minutes before the storm hit. Eleven people were confirmed deceased in the Rosendale community alone. After the tornado, 600 people were reported missing, but only four still remain unaccounted for. Latoya is one of them. The other three are twenty-eight year Teresa Marioquen and her two young daughters. Photos and descriptions of the three of them are unavailable. Latoya's mother is holding out hope that her daughter was not a storm victim and is alive. She says she will continue to hope for a miracle until she has proof that her daughter is gone.

*(Latoya at the time of her disappearance)*

At the time of her disappearance, Latoya Brown had black hair and stood 6'1". Her weight at the time is unknown. She is African-American with brown eyes. She has the following tattoos: her nickname Toya on her lower back, angel wings on the back of her neck, and the Virgo astrological sign on the top of her left foot. As of this writing, she is twenty-eight years old.

If you have any information regarding this case, you are urged to call the Tuscaloosa Police Department at 205-349-2010.

## Oscar Lewis Key

Seventy-two year old Oscar Lewis Key was last seen in Centre, Alabama on December 1, 2013. He was driving a blue 2001 Dodge Dakota pickup truck with Alabama handicapped plates F75D and an eagle sticker on the back windshield. The truck disappeared with him and has never been found.

He is originally from Texas and still has family there. He would drive there to visit them occasionally, but it is not known if he went there at the time of his disappearance or not. His route would have taken him along Interstate 59 to Birmingham, Alabama, and then on Interstate 20 to Texas.

*(Oscar at the time of his disappearance)*

At the time of his disappearance, Oscar King had gray hair, wore eyeglasses, stood 6'2", and weighed 195 pounds. He was last seen wearing a blue hooded jacket. He is Caucasian with gray eyes and a tattoo on his right forearm. He may go by his middle name. As of this writing, he is seventy-seven years old.

If you have any information regarding this case, you are urged to call the Cherokee County Sheriff's Office at 256-927-3365.

## Stephen Horace Pearson

Fifty-three year old Stephen Horace Pearson was last seen at his residence in Grand Bay, Alabama on December 27, 2000. The previous day, the postal carrier was having a hard time finding an address to deliver a package. Stephen went to a neighbor's home to help. Because the neighbors were on vacation, he told the postal carrier to just leave the box on the porch. The package contained ten pounds of marijuana and it was delivered to the wrong address. It was actually addressed to someone down the street. Stephen called the post office to report it. When the police came to the neighbor's house to pick up the marijuana, they noticed a significant amount of it was missing. It turned out that the neighbors had sold it. They were angry at Stephen for reporting the incident. He told his daughter he was afraid for his safety. The next day, he called the police to report a burglary at his home. He disappeared before the officer arrived to take the report. He has never been seen or heard from again.

His car was found abandoned several days later parked in the woods near Henderson Camp Road. He is described as a reliable person of habit, and it is uncharacteristic for him to leave without warning. Authorities have not determined whether his disappearance was related to the marijuana or the burglary, but foul play is suspected.

*(Stephen at the time of his disappearance)*

At the time of his disappearance, Stephen Pearson had gray hair, wore eyeglasses, stood 6'1", and weighed 165 pounds. He is Caucasian with blue eyes. He may have a mustache or a beard. He suffers from bipolar disorder. As of this writing, he is seventy years old.

If you have any information regarding this case, you are urged to call the Mobile County Sheriff's Department at 334-574-4775.

## Shanna Genelle Peoples

Nineteen year old Shanna Genelle Peoples was last seen walking near her home on north Morris Drive in Geneva, Alabama on September 8, 2011. She left the front door wide open and did not take her bicycle, which was her only means of transportation. She has never been seen or heard from again. Her family says she has a shy nature and is afraid of the dark and thunderstorms. Her loved ones believe someone she knew took advantage of her. Authorities believe foul play is possible.

*(Shanna at the time of her disappearance)*

At the time of her disappearance, Shanna Peoples had long sandy blonde hair, stood 6', and weighed 120 pounds. She was last seen wearing a blue and green blouse, white pants, and flip flips. She is Caucasian with brown eyes, a dime-sized birthmark on the inside of her leg just above the knee, and a slight speech impediment. She is mildly mentally disabled, and functions at the level of a twelve to fourteen year old. She can not read or write well, can not remember addresses or telephone numbers, and rarely talks. She may use the last name McKee. As of this writing, she is twenty-six years old.

If you have any information regarding this case, you are urged to call the Geneva Police Department at 334-684-2777.

## Reginald Jermaine Short

Forty year old Reginald Jermaine Short left his 12th Avenue residence in Phenix City, Alabama on November 5, 2014. He had had a seizure and hit his head two days prior. He had seemed disoriented at times but refused to seek medical attention. Authorities believe it is possible he is suffering from memory loss and can not recall his identity or how to get home. His mother believes he may be homeless.

*(Reginald at the time of his disappearance)*

At the time of his disappearance, Reginald Short had black hair, stood 5’9”, and weighed 150 pounds. He was last seen wearing a red shirt, black or blue jeans, and white sneakers. He is African-American with brown eyes. His nickname is Reggie. As of this writing, he is forty-four years old.

If you have any information regarding this case, you are urged to call the Phenix City Police Department at 334-482-2800.

## Kierra Stubbs

Twenty-three year old Kierra Stubbs was last seen on April 24, 2014 at 9am when her brother dropped her off on 3rd Avenue west in Birmingham, Alabama. She was meeting a man at Boost Mobile so he could help fix her car's brakes. Surveillance video showed her getting into the man's burgundy 2012 Chrysler 200. She has never been seen or heard from again. Foul play is suspected.

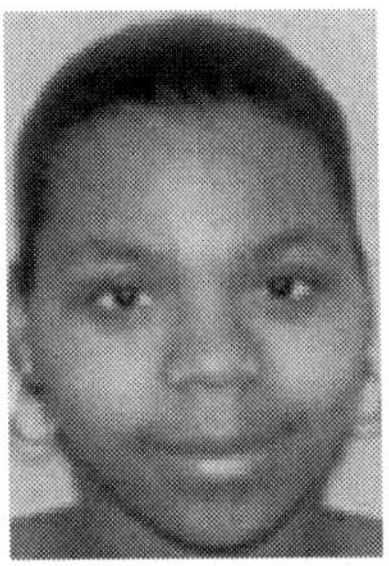

*(Kierra at the time of her disappearance)*

At the time of her disappearance, Kierra Stubbs had black hair, stood 5'3", and weighed 145 pounds. She was last seen wearing gray clothes. She is African-American with brown eyes and pierced ears. As of this writing, she is twenty-seven years old.

If you have any information regarding this case, you are urged to call the Birmingham Police Department at 205-328-9311.

## Erin Marie Gilbert

Twenty-four year old Erin Marie Gilbert was last seen during the evening hours of July 1, 1995 at the

Girdwood Forest Fair in Girdwood, Alaska. She was on a date with a man she had met the night before. At 6pm, the couple went to his car but the vehicle would not start because he had left his lights on. He told her he would walk to a nearby friend's house for help. But after two hours of walking around looking for his friend's residence to no avail, he returned to the car to find Erin gone. He thought she might have returned to the fair. He went back there and searched for her until 1am with no success. At 7am, he called her sister, whom she lived with, and asked if she had made it home. She had not. Her family then drove to Girdwood and had her name announced onstage at the fair. They also searched the fair and nearby woods, all to no avail. They then called the police and reported her missing. An extensive search involving tracker dogs and helicopters turned up no sign of her.

Her date is neither a suspect nor a person of interest in her case. Her loved ones describe her as a responsible person, and stated it is uncharacteristic for her to leave without warning. Her family believes she met with foul play and is deceased, but her remains have never been found if that is the case.

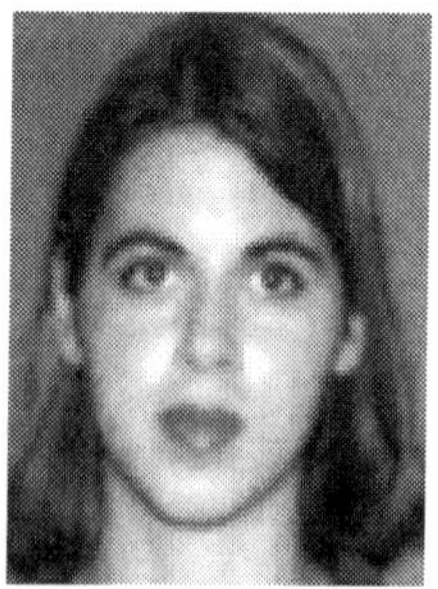

*(Erin at the time of her disappearance)*

At the time of her disappearance, Erin Gilbert had brown hair cut in a short bob, stood 5'11", and weighed 145 pounds. She was last seen wearing a black leather jacket, a black and white striped shirt, black jeans, and mountain boots. She is Caucasian with hazel eyes. As of this writing, she is forty-seven years old.

If you have any information regarding this case, you are urged to call the Alaska State Troopers at 907-428-7200 or 907-269-5497.

## Frank Johnston

Nineteen year old Frank Johnston was last seen hitchhiking northbound on Sterling Highway in Homer, Alaska on September 30, 1980. He planned to hitchhike to California. He has never been seen or heard from again. He is considered to be missing under suspicious circumstances.

*(Frank at the time of his disappearance)*

At the time of his disappearance, Frank Johnston had brown hair, stood 6', and weighed 200 pounds. He is Caucasian with blue eyes and an eight-inch circular tan-colored birthmark on his lower right back. As of this writing, he is fifty-seven years old.

If you have any information regarding this case, you are urged to call the Alaska State Troopers at 907-235-8239 or 907-262-4453.

## Sheila Kathleen McBroom

Forty year old Sheila Kathleen McBroom was last seen in Anchorage, Alaska on October 27, 2008. She left home that morning, supposedly to drive to work. At 8:30am, an Alaska State Trooper stopped her on Seward Highway six miles south of Girdwood, which was not on her route to work. She passed a sobriety test and told him she was tired. He suggested she take a nap before moving on. She has never been seen or heard from again. On October 31st, her truck was found at mile marker 106 on Seward Highway at the place where the trooper had spoken to her. There were no indications of foul play and the vehicle was in operable condition.

Her loved ones do not believe she would have abandoned her family. She worked with the United States Army Corps of Engineers at Elemendorf Air Force Base at the time. She is missing under unclear circumstances, and her family believes she may be in danger.

*(Sheila at the time of her disappearance)*

At the time of her disappearance, Sheila McBroom had brown hair, stood 5'5", and weighed 200 pounds. She was last seen wearing a white hooded jacket. She is Caucasian with blue eyes and pierced ears. Her nickname is Kathy. As of this writing, she is fifty years old.

If you have any information regarding this case you are urged to call the Anchorage Police Department at 907-786-8817.

## Mary Kathleen Thill

Twenty-one year old Mary Kathleen Thill was last seen in Seward, Alaska on July 5, 1975. A friend gave her a ride into town and dropped her off at the bakery. Another friend saw her at the waterfall on Lowell Point Road between 1:30pm and 2pm. She has never been seen or heard from again.

Investigators believe the serial killer Robert Hansen may have been involved in her case. In 1984, he confessed to seventeen murders and thirty rapes over the previous twelve years. He led authorities to the grave sites, but only twelve bodies were found. He admitted he was in Seward the day Mary was last seen, but denied any involvement in her case. Regardless, police still believe she may have been one of his victims. He died in prison in 2014.

*(Mary at the time of her disappearance)*

At the time of her disappearance, Mary Thill had red hair, wore eyeglasses with round pink frames and thick lenses, stood 5'5", and weighed 130 pounds. She was last seen wearing an Army jacket, a gray pullover sweater, Levis blue jeans, leather Tuffy hiking boots, and carrying a small black backpack. She is Caucasian with blue eyes. As of this writing, she is sixty-four years old.

If you have any information regarding this case, you are urged to call the Seward Police Department at 907-224-3338.

## Jose D. Jesus Chavez & Gilberto Gonzalez

Nineteen year old Jose D. Jesus Chavez lived with his relative, twenty-three year old Gilberto Gonzalez, in Tucson, Arizona in 1996. The men lived in an apartment on Irvington Road. They were both employed at a business on South Sixth Avenue at the time. The two were last seen in Tucson on January 20, 1996. Their friends became concerned when they failed to arrive for a scheduled event. Their apartment was checked and the door was discovered unlocked. The keys were inside and their vehicle was parked nearby. There were no signs of a struggle inside the apartment, and all their belongings were left behind. Neither man has been seen or heard from since.

*(Jose at the time of his disappearance)*

At the time of his disappearance, Jose Chavez had black hair, stood 5'7", and weighed 160 pounds. He was last seen wearing a gold chain and a watch. He is Hispanic with blue eyes and pierced ears. As of this writing, he is forty-one years old.

*(Gilberto at the time of his disappearance)*

At the time of his disappearance, Gilberto Gonzalez had black hair and a mustache. His height and weight measurements at the time are unknown. He is Hispanic with brown eyes. As of this writing, he is forty-five years old.

If you have any information regarding this case, you are urged to call one of the following numbers:

*Pima County Sheriff's Department at 520-741-4600*

## Miguel Angel Cisneros

Twenty-seven year old Miguel Angel Cisneros was last seen with a group of people attempting to enter the United States illegally from Mexico on February 23, 2004. They were between Arivaca and Sasabe, Arizona when the group was robbed and two of its members beaten. Miguel disappeared and has never been seen or heard from again. His family in both the United States and Mexico says he was close to them and it is uncharacteristic of him not to contact them for so long.

*(Miguel at the time of his disappearance)*

At the time of his disappearance, Miguel Cisneros had brown hair, stood 5'7", and weighed 150 pounds. He was last seen wearing a black sweater, black jeans, yellow hiking boots, a black jacket with the Raiders logo on the back, a black baseball cap, a wristwatch, a wedding band, and a black rosary. He is Hispanic with brown eyes, a piercing in his left ear, a burn scar on his forearm, and a small scar above his eyebrow. Some missing persons agencies refer to him as Miguel Angel Cisneros Valdovinos. As of this writing, he is forty-one years old.

If you have any information regarding this case, you are urged to call the Pima County Sheriff's Office at 520-741-4600.

## Bobby Davidson

Thirty-one year old Bobby Davidson was last seen on November 12, 1965 in the vicinity of Central Avenue and east Monroe Street in Phoenix, Arizona. He cashed his paycheck after work that day, then went to his apartment near 20th Street and Roosevelt Street where he cleaned up and changed clothes. Later, he went to the Kissel's Cocktail Lounge on east Monroe Street. He had only one drink before leaving at 10pm to go eat dinner. He has never been seen or heard from again. His Mercedes was found abandoned in the lounge parking lot with his work tools, some of which were expensive, in the trunk.

He is a Navy veteran who worked servicing and repairing appliances for Byassee Equipment Co. at the time. His boss described him as an ideal employee. He left all of his belongings behind. He had recently made a car payment and paid his rent in advance. He was divorced and childless at the time, and his boss stated he had no enemies and everyone liked him.

*(Bobby at the time of his disappearance)*

At the time of his disappearance, Bobby Davidson had brown hair, stood between 6' - 6'2", and weighed between 150 - 160 pounds. He is Caucasian with blue eyes. As of this writing, he is eighty-four years old.

If you have any information regarding this case, you are urged to call the Phoenix Police Department at 602-261-8042.

## Ruth T. Doss

Seventy-three year old Ruth T. Doss was scheduled to have breakfast with two acquaintances at the Denny's restaurant at west Indian School Road and west 51st Avenue in Phoenix, Arizona on June 18, 1999. Authorities are not sure whether or not she arrived at the restaurant, however, her son found her white 1997 Dodge Dakota extended cab pickup truck abandoned in the parking lot of the restaurant shortly after she disappeared. There was no sign of Ruth at the scene and she has never been seen or heard from again. She is described as a kind, trusting individual. Foul play is possible in her case.

*(Ruth at the time of her disappearance)*

At the time of her disappearance, Ruth Doss had brown hair, wore eyeglasses, stood 5'8", and weighed

105 pounds. She was last seen wearing a purple blouse, blue green pants, and carrying a gray purse. She is Caucasian with blue eyes, metal implants in both of her knees, and surgical scars on both legs below the knees. As of this writing, she is ninety-two years old.

If you have any information regarding this case, you are urged to call the Phoenix Police Department at 602-262-6141.

## Bruce Allen Evans

Thirty-seven year old Bruce Allen Evans was last seen leaving his home on west Ironwood Hill Drive in Tucson, Arizona at 10am on December 21, 2010. He was reportedly going to Phoenix on business. He has never been seen or heard from again. The white 2009 three-quarter-ton cargo van he was driving disappeared with him and has never been found. He is considered to be missing under suspicious circumstances.

*(Bruce at the time of his disappearance)*

At the time of his disappearance, Bruce Evans had brown hair, stood 6'4", and weighed between 155 - 210 pounds. He is Caucasian with hazel eyes, a birthmark on his right wrist, a tongue piercing, and pierced nipples. He has the following tattoos: a large dragon on his shin, a tribal design on his shin, barbed wire wrapped around his upper right arm, and a skull on the upper left side of his torso. As of this writing, he is forty-five years old.

If you have any information regarding this case, you are urged to call the Pima County Sheriff's Office at 520-351-4900.

## June Goodman

Sixty-six year old June Goodman was last seen buying groceries at Ed's Market in Snowflake, Arizona at 8:25pm on March 28, 2003. She was missed the next morning when she failed to show up for work. Authorities believe she was abducted from her home on the morning of March 29th. The sliding glass door to her residence was found ajar, the outdoor floodlights were on, and so was the TV. All the shoes she owned were left behind, which indicated she would not have gone far barefoot. All of her other personal belongings also remained behind. Her van was parked in its usual place, and there was no sign of a struggle inside her home.

*(June at the time of her disappearance)*

At the time of her disappearance, June Goodman had brown hair, stood 5'2", and weighed 130 pounds. She was possibly wearing a light purple sweat suit when she went missing. She is Caucasian with green eyes. As of this writing, she is eighty-one years old.

If you have any information regarding this case, you are urged to call the Snowflake - Taylor Police Department at 928-536-7500.

## Adela Guzman – Mendoza

Forty-five year old Adela Guzman - Mendoza was last seen in Tucson, Arizona on September 20, 2010. She left her job at the Mountain Oyster Club in the vicinity of Speedway Boulevard and Wilmot Road at 8:30am, just half an hour into her shift. She said she felt sick and was going home. She normally took two buses to get between work and her home in the area of Ruthrauff Road and Interstate 10. She never arrived home and has never been heard from again. Authorities determined she did board the first bus. Her cell phone pinged off a tower about a quarter-mile from her home. Her whereabouts after that are unknown.

According to her family, she is a devoted mother and hard worker who would not have walked out on her life. Since she went missing, her bank account has not been accessed, nor has her prescription medications been refilled. Police suspect foul play was involved.

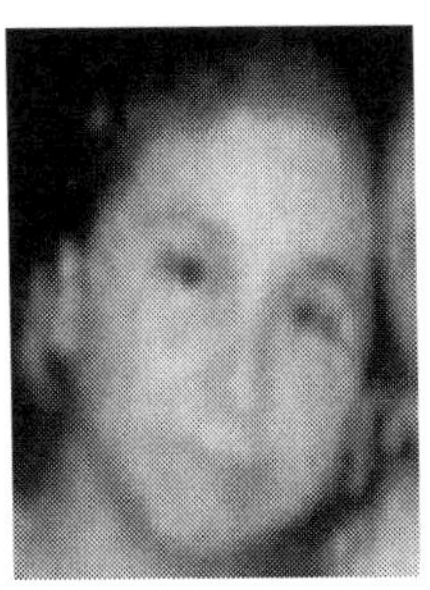

(Adela at the time of her disappearance)

At the time of her disappearance, Adela Mendoza had brown hair, stood 5'3", and weighed between 115 - 140 pounds. She is Hispanic with green eyes. She has several unspecified medical conditions, including diabetes. She requires medication that she does not have with her. As of this writing, she is fifty-three years old.

If you have any information regarding this case, you are urged to call the Pima County Sheriff's Office at 520-351-4900.

## Aleca Renee "Lisa" Manning

Twenty-two year old Aleca Renee "Lisa" Manning was last seen at approximately 10:30pm on February 17, 1975 on north 32nd Street in Phoenix, Arizona. She was attending a concert at the Celebrity Theater with friends and became separated from them. She never returned home and has never been heard from again. Foul play is suspected.

(Lisa at the time of her disappearance)

At the time of her disappearance, Lisa Manning had brown hair, stood 5'2", and weighed 125 pounds. She was last seen wearing a light green blouse, moss-green pants, a dark green floor-length coat, and dark tan-colored shoes. She is Biracial (Caucasian/Native American) with green eyes. As of this writing, she is sixty-six years old.

If you have any information regarding this case, you are urged to call the Phoenix Police Department at 602-261-8042 or 602-262-6141.

## Hurbert Turner

Eighty-five year old Hurbert Turner was last seen near the intersection of Redmont Drive and Sugarloaf Street in Mesa, Arizona on December 24, 2010. He left home at 11am for his daily walk, which normally lasted about twenty minutes. He never returned home and has never been heard from again. An extensive search of the area turned up no sign of him.

*(Hurbert at the time of his disappearance)*

At the time of his disappearance, Hurbert Turner had white hair, wore wire-rimmed eyeglasses, stood 5'6", and weighed 150 pounds. He was last seen wearing a navy blue waist-length jacket, tan pants, white sneakers, a tan baseball cap, a gold ring with his initials, and a gold ring with diamonds. He is Caucasian with blue eyes and a scar above his right knee about four inches in size. He suffers from heart disease. As of this writing, he is ninety-three years old.

If you have any information regarding this case, you are urged to call the Mesa Police Department at 480-644-2014.

## David Allen Lamb

Thirty year old David Allen Lamb was last seen mowing his lawn in Plainview, Arkansas on May 10, 1995. His wife returned home late that evening and found the lawn mower still in the yard, which had only been partially mowed. The lights inside the house were on and David's wallet, checkbook, keys, and other belongings were all inside the house. He has never been seen or heard from again.

*(David at the time of his disappearance)*

At the time of his disappearance, David Lamb had brown hair, stood 5'9", and weighed 150 pounds. He was last seen wearing a blue shirt, blue jeans, work shoes, and a camouflage hat. He is Caucasian with blue eyes, a tattoo of the name Connie on his upper right arm, and scars on his chest, abdomen, left elbow, left wrist, and left forearm. He has a heart condition and wears a pacemaker. As of this writing, he is fifty-four years old.

If you have any information regarding this case, you are urged to call the Yell County Sheriff's Department at 479-495-2811 or 479-229-4175.

## Gloria White Moore McDonald

Sixty-eight year old Gloria White Moore McDonald, her husband, her stepson, and his girlfriend visited Queen Wilhelmina State Park in Polk County, Arkansas on January 26, 2001. The group began hiking along a trail that bordered the Queen Wilhelmina Lodge near Rich Mountain at approximately 12:25pm. They were headed towards the Lovers' Leap area. Several trees blocked the path ahead and Gloria told the others that she was returning to the lodge. She turned back about 150 to 200 yards into the hike. The group continued walking for another twenty minutes before returning to the lodge. Upon their arrival, they discovered Gloria was missing. Their vehicle had not been moved and her purse and other personal belongings were locked inside the car. Extensive searches of the area turned up no clues as to her whereabouts.

*(Gloria at the time of her disappearance)*

At the time of her disappearance, Gloria McDonald had red hair, stood 5'6", and weighed 120 pounds. She was last seen wearing a blue plaid flannel shirt, a glossy bright yellow hooded jacket, blue jeans, sneakers, rose-tinted sunglasses, a gold wedding band, a platinum ring resembling two balls intersecting one another, a three-and-a-half-carat sapphire ring, a necklace with a cross pendant, and possibly a small-sized gold filigree ring. She was carrying a Minolta Riva Zoom 90 camera with the serial number 40907425. She is Caucasian with brown eyes. As of this writing, she is eighty-five years old.

If you have any information regarding this case, you are urged to call one of the following numbers:

*Polk County Sheriff's Office at 501-394-2511*

*Arkansas State Police at 800-553-3820*

*Federal Bureau of Investigation (FBI) at 202-324-3000*

## Mary Jimmie Shinn

Twenty-five year old Mary Jimmie Shinn was last seen in Magnolia, Arkansas on July 20, 1978. She was trying to sell a house on east McNeil Street and had advertised it in the newspaper. Investigators believe she showed the house to an unknown man at 4pm on July 19th. He wanted to trade her house for a parcel of land he owned on Taylor Highway, but Mary did not think the transaction would go through. At 11am on July 20th, however, she got a call from the man and he said he wanted to see the house again. He told her his car was having repairs done and that he needed to take a cab to the house. They agreed to meet at the EZ Mart across the street from the art studio Mary owned on Magnolia Street, and then go together to the house. Mary told a friend to expect her back by 1:30pm. She has never been heard from again.

A carpenter who had been working across the street from the house Mary was trying to sell recalled having seen her there with a man on July 20th between 10:30am and 11:30am. The man is described as Caucasian in his mid-twenties with dark curly hair, approximately 5'8", and weighing between 185 - 200 pounds.

Mary's blue 1976 Buick Special was found unlocked with the keys inside it at Smitty's Grocery the day she was last seen. Two employees at the store said it had been parked there since 1pm. Authorities stated the items inside the car indicated she had not left of her own accord. Her navy blue denim purse was emptied out on the driver's side floorboard and its contents scattered. Her white canvas sneakers were pushed under the gas and brake pedals. Her wallet with some cash inside was there, but her address book was missing. The rear left fender of the Buick had deep scratches in the paint, and seeds and bits of grass were inside it. Police believe it had been driven into a meadow. The man Mary was supposed to meet that day has never been identified. Foul play is suspected.

*(Mary at the time of her disappearance)*

At the time of her disappearance, Mary Shinn had brown hair, stood 5'6", and weighed 118 pounds. She was last seen wearing several jewelry pieces including a custom-designed gold necklace with three diamond pendants. She is Caucasian with brown eyes, a scar on her left cheek, and a birthmark on her forehead. Her nickname is Bobo. As of this writing, she is sixty-five years old.

If you have any information regarding this case, you are urged to call the Columbia County Sheriff's Office at 870-234-5331.

## Terkessa Wallace

Thirty-four year old Terkessa Wallace was last seen in North Little Rock, Arkansas on January 10, 2014. She has never been seen or heard from again. She was driving a white 2009 Toyota Corolla with Arkansas plates 290 RHM. It is unknown whether or not her vehicle has ever been located. Foul play is suspected.

Another African-American woman, Shequenia Bernett, disappeared from North Little Rock on the same day. In December 2015, one of her legs was found floating in the Arkansas River. The rest of her remains have never been found. The two women had known each other since childhood and were friends. Authorities, however, are not sure if the two cases are related or not.

*(Terkessa at the time of her disappearance)*

At the time of her disappearance, Terkessa Wallace had black hair, stood 5'6", and weighed 195 pounds. She is African-American with brown eyes. As of this writing, she is thirty-eight years old.

If you have any information regarding this case, you are urged to call one of the following numbers:

*North Little Rock Police Department at 501-758-1234*

*Little Rock Police Department at 501-771-7117*

## John R. Yates

Eighty-two year old John R. Yates lived in Hot Springs, Arkansas in June 2003. On June 16th, he went to Onyx in Yell County, Arkansas to go fishing. He was last seen at a convenience store in Rover in Yell County. He has never been seen or heard from again. His truck was found abandoned on June 17th on County Road 130 off State Highway 314 in Onyx. He would normally park and then walk to the river to fish. An extensive search of the area turned up no clues as to his whereabouts.

*(John at the time of his disappearance)*

At the time of his disappearance, John Yates had graying red hair, stood 5'9", and weighed 180 pounds. He is Caucasian with blue eyes. As of this writing, he is ninety-seven years old.

If you have any information regarding this case, you are urged to call the Yell County Sheriff's Department at 479-495-2811 or 479-229-4175.

## Robert Vincent Black, Richard Dean Davison, & Patricia Laxer

Sixty-four year old Robert Vincent Black was last seen leaving his Los Angeles, California residence on March 12, 1996. He was going to a doctor's appointment. He never returned home and has never been seen or heard from again.

Robert was reportedly a patient of the same doctor who treated sixty-three year old Patricia Laxer, seventy-five year old Goldie A. Swanger, and seventy year old Richard Dean Davison, all of which disappeared going either to or from their appointments with him. Goldie Swanger's case was closed in 2004, but it is unknown if she was found alive or deceased. The other three have never been located. Authorities think they may be patients in a hospital or nursing home somewhere, but it is strange that none of them have contacted their families. None of them are described as having Alzheimer's, dementia, or prior histories of going missing. Other than all four disappearing within months of each other, having the same doctor, and residing in nearby neighborhoods, it is not known if their cases are otherwise connected. No information on the doctor could be found.

Richard Dean Davison was last seen leaving his Los Angeles, California residence on October 29, 1997. He was en route to a doctor's appointment at the time. He never arrived at his destination and has never been heard from again.

Patricia Laxer was last seen in North Hollywood, California at her residence after returning home from a doctor's appointment on August 21, 1997. Her vehicle was located abandoned in Hollywood shortly after she went missing. She has never been heard from again.

*(Robert at the time of his disappearance)*

At the time of his disappearance, Robert Black had gray hair, wore eyeglasses, stood 6'1", and weighed 170 pounds. He is Caucasian with brown eyes. As of this writing, he is eighty-six years old.

*(Richard at the time of his disappearance)*

At the time of his disappearance, Richard Davison had thinning gray hair, wore eyeglasses, stood 5’10”, and weighed 145 pounds. He is Caucasian with brown eyes. As of this writing, he is ninety years old.

*(Patricia at the time of her disappearance)*

At the time of her disappearance, Patricia Laxer had blonde hair, stood 5’7”, and weighed 145 pounds. She is Caucasian with blue eyes. As of this writing, she is eighty-four years old.

If you have any information about these three cases, you are urged to call the Los Angeles Police Department at 213-485-5381.

## Heather Bloom

Twenty-eight year old Heather Bloom was last seen in Berkeley, California on October 1, 2005 when the police were called to an apartment at Carleton and California Streets to intervene in an argument between her mother and her sister. She and her mother were visiting her sister from Brooklyn, New York. The argument was resolved and the police left. When Heather's mother returned to New York, she left her in her sister's care. The sisters lived in an apartment on Parker Street. Heather has not been seen by anyone other than her sister since. Her mother contacted police in June 2009 and said she hadn't heard from either of her daughters since the argument in October 2005. She asked them to check on Heather's welfare. Her sister had moved away from the Parker Street apartment in 2007, and it took months for law enforcement to track her down. Police went to her new apartment in March 2010, but she refused to open the door. She answered questions through the window and said Heather was fine, but she declined to let anyone see her.

Authorities learned in 2016 that Heather's sister moved to Norway on a student visa. All attempts to locate Heather have been unsuccessful. Investigators are unsure what happened to her. They don't necessarily believe she is in danger or deceased, but they need to be able to see her and confirm her well-being to close her case. It is possible her sister placed her in a home or with another caregiver in the San Francisco Bay area.

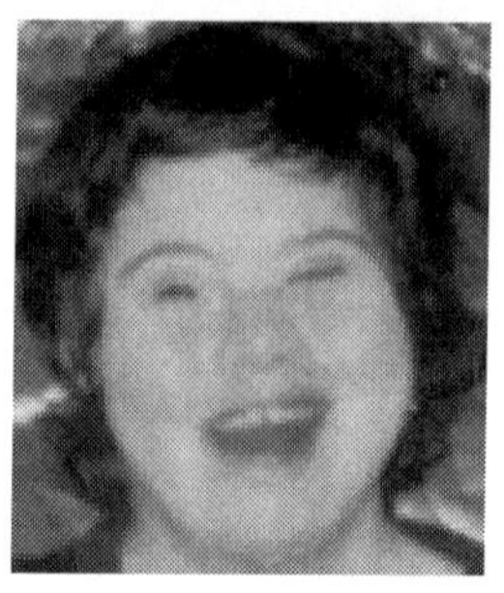

*(Heather at the time of her disappearance)*

At the time of her disappearance, Heather Bloom had brown hair, stood between 5' - 5'7", and weighed between 140 - 160 pounds. She is Caucasian with blue eyes, a vertical surgical scar on her chest, and a lump on the back of her neck near her hairline. She has Down Syndrome, a heart condition, and congenital hypothyroidism. She needs daily medication. She is mentally disabled and wheelchair-bound. She requires constant care and supervision. She is non-verbal but does know some sign language. She may wear eyeglasses. As of this writing, she is forty-one years old.

If you have any information regarding this case, you are urged to call the Berkeley Police Department at 510-981-5938.

## Agnes Bross

Eighty-three year old Agnes Bross was last seen at approximately 10:30am on April 2, 2001 in Daly City, California. She was en route to her apartment in Westlake Village at the time. She never arrived home and has never been heard from again.

She does not drive and relies on public transportation to get around. She was in good physical and mental condition at the time. Her family said it is uncharacteristic of her to leave without warning.

*(Agnes at the time of her disappearance)*

At the time of her disappearance, Agnes Bross had gray hair, walked with a slight limp, stood 4’11”, and weighed between 83 - 100 pounds. She was last seen wearing a baseball cap or hat with a visor, a waist-length windbreaker, and slacks. She is Caucasian with hazel eyes and pierced ears. As of this writing, she is one hundred years old.

If you have any information regarding this case, you are urged to call the Daly City Police Department at 650-991-8147, 650-991-8119, or 650-992-1225.

## John Stewart Campbell

Eighteen year old John Stewart Campbell was a student at Humboldt State University in Arcata, California in 1985. He disappeared from the campus on February 16th and has never been seen again. He was reported missing by a resident hall advisor. A park ranger later found his vehicle in a wooded area. There were no signs of robbery, but he did disappear under suspicious circumstances. Investigators believe he may have been taken against his will.

(John at the time of his disappearance)

At the time of his disappearance, John Campbell had blonde hair, freckles, a facial skin discoloration, light-colored skin on his neck near his left shoulder, stood between 5'11" - 6", and weighed 160 pounds. He was last seen wearing a knee-length gray/green trench coat and was carrying his wallet. He is Caucasian with blue eyes. His nickname is Jonathan. As of this writing, he is fifty-one years old.

If you have any information regarding this case, you are urged to call the Humboldt State University Police Department at 707-826-3456.

## John Darwin Chesley

Eighty-one year old John Darwin Chesley was last seen at his residence on Peak View Drive in Oroville, California at 1pm on February 24, 2014. He was outside doing yard work when he left home on foot and disappeared. He has never been heard from again. An extensive search of the area turned up no clues as to his whereabouts, and authorities believe he may have been picked up by a passing motorist. Foul play is not suspected in his case, but due to his age and state of health there is concern for his safety.

*(John at the time of his disappearance)*

At the time of his disappearance, John Chesley had gray hair, stood 5'8", and weighed 143 pounds. He was last seen wearing a long-sleeve blue flannel button-up shirt, a white tank top, blue jeans, dark-colored sneakers, a large Black Hills gold ring, and a wedding band. He is Caucasian with blue/green eyes and a large mole on his back. He suffers from dementia and is hearing-impaired. As of this writing, he is eighty-five years old.

If you have any information regarding this case, you are urged to call the Butte County Sheriff's Department at 530-538-7434 or 530-538-3828.

## Le Tung Dinh

Thirty-eight year old Le Tung Dinh was last seen at his apartment in San Diego, California on February 4, 1996. He was standing in the doorway looking outside. His mother left the room for a few minutes and when she returned he was gone. He has never been heard from again.

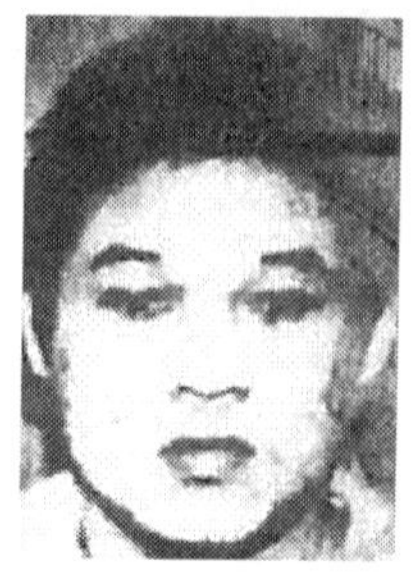

*(Le Tung at the time of his disappearance)*

At the time of his disappearance, Le Tung Dinh had black hair, stood between 5'4" - 5'8", and weighed between 140 - 150 pounds. He was last seen wearing a black t-shirt and light blue jeans. He is Asian with brown eyes. He is mentally disabled and incapable of caring for himself. He is of Vietnamese descent. As of this writing, he is sixty years old.

If you have any information regarding this case, you are urged to call the San Diego Police Department at 619-531-2277.

## John Carl Goodman

Fifty-two year old John Carl Goodman was last seen on east Whittier Boulevard in La Habra, California on June 26, 2007. His mother reported him missing on June 29th. When police went to his residence, they discovered the front door open, a back window broken out, and the rear window of John's truck broken out. His white 1997 Chevrolet Suburban with California plates 4GWV182 was missing. He has never been heard from again, and it is believed that his vehicle is still missing as well. Because of the circumstances and the condition of his home, he is believed to be in danger. His neighbors stated that he is a quiet person who keeps to himself.

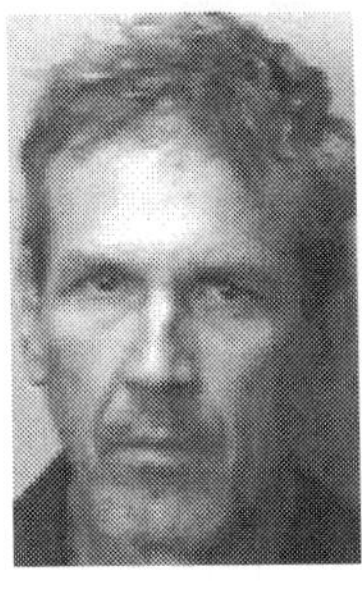

*(John at the time of his disappearance)*

At the time of his disappearance, John Goodman had brown hair, stood 5'10", and weighed 160 pounds. He is Caucasian with brown eyes. As of this writing, he is sixty-three years old.

If you have any information regarding this case, you are urged to call the La Habra Police Department at 562-905-9756.

## Roger Her

Twenty-eight year old Roger Her was last seen on McAlexander Road in Hayfork, California at 1:24pm on March 26, 2017. When relatives when to his home to check on him, they found the fireplace lit and the TV on. His wallet was also there, but there was no sign of Roger and he has never been seen or heard from again. Rumors have circulated that he was abducted, but authorities have not named any suspects or persons of interest.

*(Roger at the time of his disappearance)*

At the time of his disappearance, Roger Her had black curly shoulder-length hair, braces on his teeth, stood 5'7", and weighed 160 pounds. He was last seen wearing a hooded sweatshirt, a t-shirt, gray sweatpants, and Croc shoes. He is Asian with brown eyes, the Thoj tattooed on his upper left arm, and his last name tattooed on his upper right arm. As of this writing, he is twenty-nine years old.

If you have any information regarding this case, you are urged to call the Trinity County Sheriff's Department at 530-623-2611.

## Jorge Cruz Hernandez

Twenty-four year old Jorge Cruz Hernandez was last seen in Corona, California on January 18, 2011. He has never been seen or heard from again. Authorities believe he was taken against his will.

*(Jorge at the time of his disappearance)*

At the time of his disappearance, Jorge Hernandez had black hair, stood 5'5", and weighed 160 pounds. He is Hispanic with brown eyes and a tattoo of the name LA Hernandez on his left arm. As of this writing, he is thirty-one years old.

If you have any information regarding this case, you are urged to call the Corona City Police Department at 951-739-2330.

## Johnnie Joe Herrera

Twenty year old Johnnie Joe Herrera was last seen at a bachelor party on west Cedar Street in Oxnard, California on August 27, 1971. He has never been heard from again. His light blue 1969 Volkswagen Beetle with California plates ZWM775 disappeared with him and has never been found.

He was married at the time and had an infant son. He was happy with his life, and his loved ones can think of no reason why he would have wanted to walk out on his life. His twin brother had him declared legally dead in 1978, but his remains have never been found.

*(Johnnie at the time of his disappearance)*

At the time of his disappearance, Johnnie Herrera had black hair, a chipped right front tooth, stood between 5’5” - 5’6”, and weighed 137 pounds. He was last seen wearing a purple shirt and white pants. He is Hispanic with brown eyes, a scar on the bridge of his nose, a black mark on one of his feet between the big toe and the second toe, and a burn scar on his elbow. As of this writing, he is sixty-seven years old.

If you have any information regarding this case, you are urged to call the Oxnard Police Department at 805-385-7646.

## Jeanette Kamahele

Twenty year old Jeanette Kamahele was hitchhiking on the Cotati on-ramp off Highway 101 in Santa Rosa, California on April 25, 1972. A friend of hers was going to stop and pick her up but before the friend could, another vehicle pulled over. She was last seen getting into a faded brown 1970 - 1972 Chevrolet pickup truck driven by a twenty to thirty year old Caucasian male with an Afro-type hairstyle. She has never been seen or heard from again.

Around the time of Jeanette's disappearance, seven females disappeared and were later found murdered. They were all between the ages of twelve and twenty-three years old and all of them were habitual hitchhikers. Jeannette is the only one to have never been found. Authorities believe a serial killer was operating in the area. Both Ted Bundy and the Zodiac Killer were considered possible suspects at the time, but Ted was later cleared.

*(Jeannette at the time of her disappearance)*

At the time of her disappearance, Jeannette Kamahele had black hair, stood 5'5", and weighed 120 pounds. She was last seen wearing a dark brown blouse or sweater, Levis jeans, sandals, and gold post-type earrings. She is Pacific Islander with brown eyes and a large birthmark beneath her right breast. She is of Hawaiian descent and wears a dental bridge. As of this writing, she is sixty-six years old.

If you have any information regarding this case, you are urged to call the Sonoma County Sheriff's Office at 707-565-2185.

**Barbara Ann Larkin**

Forty year old Barbara Ann Larkin was last seen in San Bernardino, California on March 3, 2001. She has never been seen or heard from again. She was reported missing when she failed to show up for work at Riverside Community Hospital, where she was the supervisor of the administration staff. All of her belongings were left behind in her apartment, and there were no signs of a struggle. Her loved ones stated that she had a long-established routine and an excellent work history, and it is uncharacteristic for her to leave without warning.

At the time of her disappearance, she was pregnant by her ex-boyfriend, who was unhappy about the pregnancy. Prior to her going missing, she had prepared documents that released him from all legal responsibility towards the baby. The ex-boyfriend has been interviewed by police and is not considered a suspect in her disappearance. Although police have been unable to verify his alibi, they say he has cooperated in the investigation and they found no evidence in his home or his vehicle to implicate him.

*(Barbara at the time of her disappearance)*

At the time of her disappearance, Barbara Larkin had blonde hair, stood 5'8", and weighed 130 pounds. She was five months pregnant at the time. She is

Caucasian with blue eyes. As of this writing, she is fifty-seven years old.

If you have any information regarding this case, you are urged to call the San Bernardino County Sheriff's Department at 909-384-5742.

## Bryce David Laspisa

Nineteen year old Bryce David Laspisa was last seen in Castaic, California on August 30, 2013. He was attending Sierra College in northern California at the time. He called his mother at 2:30am, saying he was too tired to drive and was going to stop his car and sleep. He said he would call her when he woke up. He has never been heard from again. His beige 2003 Toyota Highlander was found lying on its side in a ravine off Lake Hughes Road near Castaic Lake, a few hours after he spoke to his mother. The rear window was smashed. His cell phone, wallet, laptop, and other belongings were inside the vehicle, but there was no sign of Bryce. An extensive search of the area turned up no clues as to his whereabouts.

*(Bryce at the time of his disappearance)*

At the time of his disappearance, Bryce Laspisa had red hair, stood 5'11", and weighed 170 pounds. He was last seen wearing a blue and white checkered shirt, white cargo shorts, and a size 12 red and white Nike shoes. He is Caucasian with green eyes, pierced ears, and a tattoo of a Taurus bull head and his birthday in Roman numerals on his upper left arm. As of this writing, he is twenty-four years old.

If you have any information regarding this case, you are urged to call the Los Angeles County Sheriff's Office at 323-890-5500.

## Donnie Dale Lee & Aleksey Leonidvich Shelest

Sixty-one year old Donnie Dale Lee was last seen in the vicinity of Squaw Valley Road and Sand Creek Road in Squaw Valley, California on November 1, 2016. He disappeared under suspicious circumstances and has never been heard from again.

Authorities theorize that his disappearance may be related to the disappearance of another Squaw Valley man. Thirty-three year old Aleksey Leonidvich Shelest was last seen in Squaw Valley, California on May 18, 2016. His landlord asked him to move out of his residence. When the landlord went to check to see if he had moved out or not, Aleksey was gone, but his pets and personal belongings were left behind. He has never been seen or heard from again. He was reported missing on May 29th.

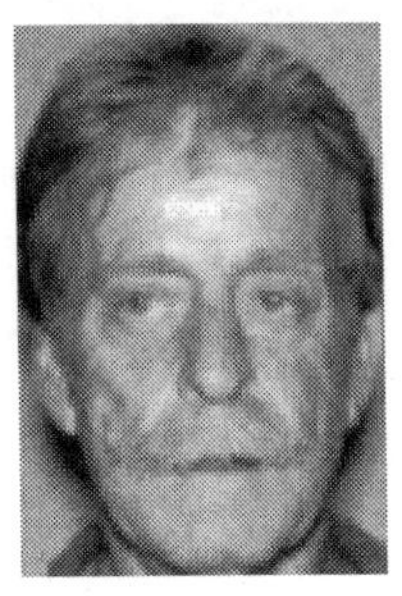

*(Donnie at the time of his disappearance)*

At the time of his disappearance, Donnie Lee had gray hair, stood between 6' - 6'1", and weighed between 170 - 180 pounds. He is Caucasian with blue eyes. He has a scar on his right hand, a tribal tattoo on his upper right arm, and a tattoo of a heart and arrow on his left calf. He also has tattoos on both shoulders and both upper arms. As of this writing, he is sixty-three years old.

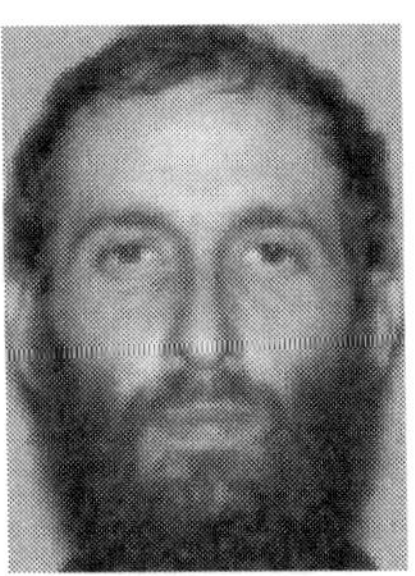

*(Aleksey at the time of his disappearance)*

At the time of his disappearance, Aleksey Shelest had black hair, was clean shaven, stood 5'10", and weighed 150 pounds. He is Caucasian with brown eyes and a scar on his left arm. As of this writing, he is thirty-five years old.

If you have any information regarding these two cases, you are urged to call the Fresno County Sheriff's Department at 559-600-8403 or 559-600-3111.

## Cindy Lee Mellin

Nineteen year old Cindy Lee Mellin was last seen on January 20, 1970 in the parking lot of the Buenaventura Shopping Center where she worked as a sales clerk at Broadway Department Store in Ventura, California. She left work shortly after closing and was last seen standing next to her car at 9:40pm. She was accompanied by an unknown Caucasian man between thirty and forty years old. The man drove a light-colored vehicle. According to witnesses, he was assisting in changing Cindy's left rear tire. She never arrived home and has never been seen or heard from again.

At 7am the next day, her father went to the shopping center and found her car up on the jack with the flat tire still on. The spare tire was lying on the ground nearby. There was no sign of Cindy. She is missing under suspicious circumstances, and the man has never been identified.

*(Cindy at the time of her disappearance)*

At the time of her disappearance, Cindy Mellin had brown hair, wore contact lenses, stood 5'6", and weighed 105 pounds. She was last seen wearing a navy blue dress with red buttons, a brown corduroy three-quarter-length coat, blue shoes with gold buckles, a gold ring set with a single pearl, and a red hair ribbon. She is Caucasian with blue eyes. As of this writing, she is sixty-seven years old.

If you have any information regarding this case, you are urged to call the Ventura Police Department at 805-339-4462.

## Audrey Louise Moran & Jonathan David Reynoso

Twenty-six year old Audrey Louise Moran and her boyfriend, twenty-eight year old Jonathan David Reynoso, were last seen in Coachella, California on May 10, 2017. They left her mother's home so she could drive him to his residence in Palm Desert, California. They never arrived at his home and have never been heard from again.

At 9am on May 12th, their gray 2010 GMC Terrain was found on the roadside on westbound Interstate 10, west of Oak Valley Parkway in Beaumont, California. It had gas in it and was in working order. There was no sign of Audrey or Jonathan at the scene. Dogs tracked their scents from the vehicle, but lost the trail after twenty yards. Their cell phones, Jonathan's wallet, and Audrey's purse disappeared with them and have never been found. There has been no activity on their financial accounts since they went missing. Their loved ones say the couple had a good relationship prior to their disappearances, and it is completely uncharacteristic of them to leave without warning. Their families fear they may have met with foul play.

*(Audrey at the time of her disappearance)*

At the time of her disappearance, Audrey Moran had brown hair, stood 5'10", and weighed 130 pounds. She is Hispanic with brown eyes and scars on her back and left thigh. She has the following tattoos: the phrase My Little Piece of Heaven in red ink on the left side of her chest, a dove with the word Faith on one hip, and a dove with the word Hope on the other hip. As of this writing, she is twenty-seven years old.

*(Jonathan at the time of his disappearance)*

At the time of his disappearance, Jonathan Reynoso had brown hair and a goatee, stood 5'11", and weighed 190 pounds. He is Hispanic with brown eyes, a small extra nipple on the left side of his chest, a mole on the right side of his nose, and scars on his right knee and above his right eyebrow. He has the following tattoos: an open book with the phrase Son of God on the inside of his left arm, the number 760 on his left arm, ethnic flags on the inside of his right arm, a skull on his right arm, and an Asian symbol on the left side of his chest. He may us the last name Darling. As of this writing, he is twenty-nine years old.

If you have any information regarding this case, you are urged to call one of the following numbers:

*Riverside County Sheriff's Department at 760-836-1600*

*Indio Police Department at 760-391-4051*

## Arnel Nagal Narvaiz

Thirty-six year old Arnel Nagal Narvaiz was last seen in Stockton, California on July 1, 1994. He left home to go to work in the fields at the Delta Island Ranch in the Twin Cities Road area of Sacramento County, California. He never arrived and has never been heard from again. His beige 1988 Toyota Cressida with California plates 2HTD233 disappeared with him and has never been located. Authorities say he is missing under suspicious circumstances.

*(Arnel at the time of his disappearance)*

At the time of his disappearance, Arnel Narvaiz had black hair, stood 5'7", and weighed 160 pounds. He was last seen wearing a black jacket with the word

Alaska on the back and Levis jeans. He is Asian with brown eyes. He is of Filipino descent. As of this writing, he is fifty-nine years old.

If you have any information regarding this case, you are urged to call the Stockton Police Department at 209-937-8377.

## Myoung Keun Noah

Sixty year old Myoung Keun Noah was last seen in San Bruno, California at approximately 7pm on May 1, 2007. He told his teenage son he was going to pick up a customer for his private car service, E - Limousine Services. His car is a black 2007 Lincoln Town Car with the transportation number TCP 18525 printed on the back bumper. He did not say who he was picking up or where. Myoung has never been seen or heard from again. His vehicle disappeared with him and has not been located. Authorities consider his disappearance suspicious, as he has no history of leaving without warning.

*(Myoung at the time of his disappearance)*

At the time of his disappearance, Myoung Noah had black hair, stood 5'8", and weighed 165 pounds. He was last seen wearing a black suit and a white tie. He is

Asian with brown eyes. He may spell his last name Noh. His nickname is Mike. He is of Korean descent. As of this writing, he is seventy-one years old.

If you have any information regarding this case, you are urged to call the San Bruno Police Department at 650-616-7100.

## Vidal Reyes Orobio

Sixty year old Vidal Reyes Orobio was last seen in El Cajon, California on December 27, 2013. He lived in Tijuana, Mexico and worked across the border in the United States. He was reported missing after he didn't show up for work for seven days. He was a reliable employee, and it is uncharacteristic for him to miss work without calling.

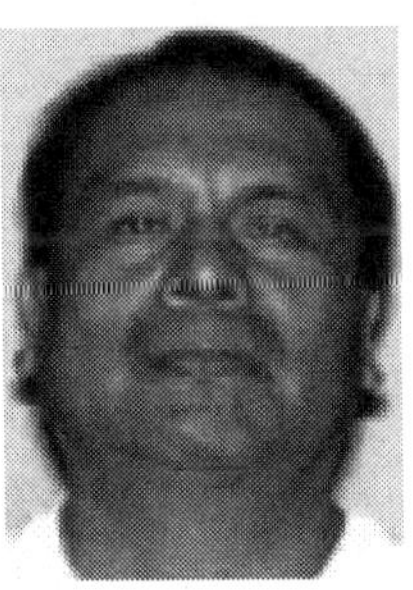

*(Vidal at the time of his disappearance)*

At the time of his disappearance, Vidal Orobio had black hair, stood 5'7", and weighed 135 pounds. He is Hispanic with brown eyes. As of this writing, he is sixty-five years old.

If you have any information regarding this case, you are urged to call the San Diego Police Department at 619-531-2277.

## Edrel Mae Pierce

Fifty-six year old Edrel Mae Pierce was last seen in Honeydew, California on May 17, 1981 as she walked down her driveway to mail some letters. She disappeared under suspicious circumstances and has never been heard from again.

*(Edrel at the time of her disappearance)*

At the time of her disappearance, Edrel Pierce had brown hair, stood 5'6", and weighed 150 pounds. She was last seen wearing a light blue London Fog raincoat, dark blue slacks, a multicolored blouse, tan Kinney calf-high boots with new soles, a one-carat diamond ring with diamonds surrounding the band, and a small white gold Bulova watch with a gray face and black hands with three diamonds on each side. She has an unspecified mental disorder and was in poor health at the time. She is Caucasian with blue eyes. She has an appendectomy scar on her abdomen and has had a partial hysterectomy. As of this writing, she is ninety-three years old.

If you have any information regarding this case, you are urged to call the Humboldt County Sheriff's Department at 707-445-7439.

## Leslie Ann Porter

Twenty-four year old Leslie Ann Porter was last seen by her husband at their West Covina, California residence on January 19, 1984. She was supposed to take her truck in for repairs at 10am, and then call her mother for a ride from the repair shop. She was also scheduled to work that day at Robinson's Store in the Puente Hills Mall. Her shift started at 1pm. But Leslie never took her truck to the repair shop, called her mother, or showed up for work. When her husband came home, he found her truck still parked undisturbed where it had been that morning. Their apartment door was unlocked. All of her personal belongings, including her purse and keys were still inside the residence. There were no indications of a struggle, but a pair of her cherished gold earrings was on the living room floor. Authorities believe she is missing under suspicious circumstances and may have been abducted.

*(Leslie at the time of her disappearance)*

At the time of her disappearance, Leslie Porter had brown hair, stood between 5'4" - 5'5", and weighed between 122 - 160 pounds. She was last seen wearing a red hooded sweatshirt with two rainbow and heart buttons. She is Caucasian with hazel eyes, a mole just above the right side of her mouth, and a mole underneath the right side of her chin. As of this writing, she is fifty-eight years old.

If you have any information regarding this case, you are urged to call the West Covina Police Department at 626-814-8540.

## Isabel Maria Quair

Twenty-two year old Isabel Maria Quair left her residence on Roosevelt Street in Salinas, California at approximately 8:30pm on November 3, 1986. She was headed to a nearby store to purchase milk. She never returned home and has never been heard from again.

*(Isabel at the time of her disappearance)*

At the time of her disappearance, Isabel Quair had black hair, stood between 5' - 5'1", and weighed 120 pounds. She was six months pregnant at the time. She was last seen wearing a brown plaid jacket, a yellow or white blouse, and brown or green corduroy pants. She is Hispanic with brown eyes, a scar on her right elbow, and skin graft scars on her outer right left and left arm. Her nickname is Chavela. As of this writing, she is fifty-three years old.

If you have any information regarding this case, you are urged to call the Salinas Police Department at 831-758-7250.

## Charles Anthony Radice

Seventy-six year old Charles Anthony Radice was last seen near his home in downtown Lancaster, California on May 15, 1995. He was visiting a neighbor in the vicinity of 10th Street West and Avenue J4. He has never been seen or heard from again. He lived with his adult grandson at the time, but it was not he who reported Charles missing. He stated he was puzzled by his grandfather's disappearance, but he did not think to go to the police. A friend reported Charles as missing to police. Authorities believe he is missing under suspicious circumstances.

*(Charles at the time of his disappearance)*

At the time of his disappearance, Charles had brown hair, wore wire-rimmed eyeglasses, stood 5'9", and weighed 150 pounds. He is believed to have been wearing a baseball cap when he went missing. He is Caucasian with hazel eyes. His nickname is Charlie. As of this writing, he is ninety-nine years old.

If you have any information regarding this case, you are urged to call the Los Angeles County Sheriff's Department at 323-890-5500.

## Wallace Arthur Manasseh Richards III

Twenty-three Wallace Arthur Manasseh Richards III was last seen between 11am - noon on November 10, 2005 when he dropped off a friend at work in the vicinity of Kearney Street in San Francisco, California. He was supposed to return to pick up his friend at the end of her shift at 7:30pm, but he never arrived and has never been heard from again. He was driving his friend's gold four-door 2003 Mercedes - Benz C240 at the time. She had lent it to him because he promised to have the oil changed for her.

On November 15th, authorities activated the vehicle's security tracking device and located it undamaged in the vicinity of Embers Way and Hesperian Boulevard in San Lorenzo, California. There was no sign of Wallace at the scene and no indications of foul play. His cell phone, credit cards, and debit card have not been used since he went missing. His loved ones stated he does not know anyone in the area where the car was found, and they do not believe he stole his friend's vehicle. He had a car of his own that he took good care of. His family says he does not use drugs and rarely drinks alcohol. They fear he met with foul play.

*(Wallace at the time of his disappearance)*

At the time of his disappearance, Wallace Richards III had black hair, stood 6'3", and weighed 235 pounds. He was last seen wearing a white t-shirt, blue jeans, a lightweight hunter green and dark gray North Face jacket, and a gold Figaro link chain necklace with a bracelet attached to it to make it longer. He is African-American with brown eyes, a large dark-colored scar on the top of his wrist, large scars on both knees, scars on his back and left side, and acne on his cheeks. He had previously fractured his arm. His nicknames are Walle and Little Wallace. As of this writing, he is thirty-five years old.

If you have any information regarding this case, you are urged to call the Berkeley Police Department at 510-981-5900.

## Hector Noel Rivera

Twenty-one year old Hector Noel Rivera was last seen in Santa Ana, California on January 27, 2000. He was driving his black 1999 Chevrolet S-10 pickup truck with standard cab and California plates 6B31169. He has never been seen or heard from again and his vehicle has never been located. There has been no activity on his cell phone since January 2000.

*(Hector at the time of his disappearance)*

At the time of his disappearance, Hector Rivera had brown hair, wore gray contact lenses, stood 5'5", and weighed 140 pounds. He was last seen wearing a silver Century High School class ring, a silver Guess watch, a white t-shirt, black underwear, jeans, white New Balance shoes, and either a black hooded sweatshirt or a long-sleeve red Abercrombie shirt. He is Hispanic with brown eyes. As of this writing, he is thirty-nine years old.

If you have any information regarding this case, you are urged to call one of the following numbers:

*Santa Ana Police Department at 714-245-8700*

*Los Angeles County Sheriff's Department at 310-855-8850*

## Anne Marie Robinson

Forty-one year old Anne Marie Robinson was last seen on January 3, 1972. She disappeared after leaving work at the Pacific Telephone Company Office on south Vermont Avenue in Gardena, California between 11:15pm and 11:30pm. She never arrived home on College Park Drive in Long Beach, California and has never been heard from again. Her car was found abandoned with a flat tire two blocks from her place of employment. The vehicle was unlocked and its contents undisturbed. She usually either went directly home after work or called her husband to say she would be late. She is considered to be missing under suspicious circumstances.

*(Anne Marie at the time of her disappearance)*

At the time of her disappearance, Anne Marie Robinson had blonde hair, stood 5'2", and weighed 115 pounds. She was last seen wearing a royal blue three-quarter-length velvet coat, a red knit suit with a three-quarter-length jacket with white lines, and red patent leather shoes. She is Caucasian with blue eyes. She may use the last names Luoma and/or Takaluoma. As of this writing, she is eighty-eight years old.

If you have any information regarding this case, you are urged to call the Long Beach Police Department at 562-570-7201.

## Kristine Grace Rodrigo

Twenty-three year old Kristine Grace Rodrigo was last seen in Oxnard, California sometime in 2003. She planned to fly to the Carolinas to meet someone she had met on the internet. She has never been heard from again, and it is unknown whether or not she left California.

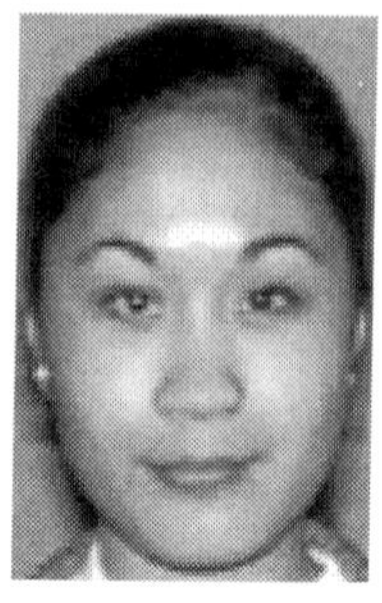

*(Kristine at the time of her disappearance)*

At the time of her disappearance, Kristine Rodrigo had brown hair, stood 5'1", and weighed 95 pounds. She is Asian with dark brown eyes. Her nickname is Ting Ting, and she may use the middle name Maraville. As of this writing, she is thirty-eight years old.

If you have any information regarding this case, you are urged to call the Oxnard Police Department at 805-385-7656.

## Diana Raquel Rojas

Twenty-seven year old Diana Raquel Rojas resided in an apartment on Ackerfield Avenue in Long Beach, California in 2000. She was in the midst of divorcing her husband, who lived in the same apartment complex. She dropped her young daughter off at his residence on October 19, 2000 for a court-ordered visitation. She returned to her own apartment with her boyfriend afterwards. Her boyfriend left between 12:15am and 12:30am on October 20th. He told authorities that Diana was asleep on the couch when he left. She never showed up for work that day and has never been heard from again. Her boyfriend tried to call her at approximately 9am, but she didn't answer. It was later discovered that her black 1992 Nissan extended-cab pickup truck with Texas plates BY3242 was also missing from the parking lot. The vehicle has never been located. Diana's family suspect foul play was involved in her disappearance. They do not believe she would have willingly abandoned her daughter.

*(Diana at the time of her disappearance)*

At the time of her disappearance, Diana Rojas had brown hair, stood 5'2", and weighed between 115 - 127 pounds. She was last seen wearing a beige tank top or a pink spaghetti-strap shirt, blue sweatpants with a Winnie the Pooh logo imprinted on the left leg, a blue zip-up jacket with a medical insignia on the left side, and a ring on her left hand. She is Hispanic with brown eyes, a mole on her back between her shoulder blades, and acne scars on her face and back. She is of Filipino descent, and she may use the last name Cortez. As of this writing, she is forty-five years old.

If you have any information regarding this case, you are urged to call the Long Beach Police Department at 562-570-7244 or 562-570-7288.

**Pushpinder Kaur Sangha**

Twenty-seven year old Pushpinder Kaur Sangha was last seen leaving her family's residence on North Butte Road in Live Oak, California on February 11, 2000 at approximately 11:49am. She was driving her black 1997 Chevrolet Lumina. She has never been heard from again. Her husband reported her missing nine days later. Shortly thereafter, her vehicle was discovered abandoned, but there was no sign of her at the scene. She missed an appointment on February 23rd with the United States Immigration and Naturalization Service in Sacramento. Authorities believe she is missing under suspicious circumstances.

*(Pushpinder at the time of her disappearance)*

At the time of her disappearance, Pushpinder Sangha had brown hair, stood 5'4", and weighed 135 pounds. She is Asian with brown eyes. Her nickname is Jatinder, and she is of Indian descent. As of this writing, she is forty-five years old.

If you have any information regarding this case, you are urged to call the Sutter County Sheriff's Office at 530-822-7313.

**Doris Catherine Scandalis**

Thirty year old Doris Catherine Scandalis was last seen in Carmichael, California on November 7, 1960. She left her home to go shopping at the mall and then see a movie. She was driving her white 1959 Mercury. She has never been heard from again. On November 10th, her vehicle was found parked at a beauty salon on Balmoral Drive. There was no sign of Doris. Authorities believe she is missing under suspicious circumstances.

*(Doris at the time of her disappearance)*

At the time of her disappearance, Doris Scandalis had brown hair, stood 5'6", and weighed 135 pounds. She was last seen wearing a purple sweater, a skirt, and a blue hooded coat. She is Caucasian with blue eyes. She may use the last name Peterson. As of this writing, she is eighty-eight years old.

If you have any information regarding this case, you are urged to call the Sacramento County Sheriff's Department at 916-874-5370.

## Chandra Marie Taylor

Twenty-eight year old Chandra Marie Taylor was last seen at a gas station on Watt Avenue and Auburn Boulevard in Sacramento, California on May 7, 2017. She was supposed to meet a man in a charcoal-gray van to hang out. She has not been heard from since. She has not used her cell phone or social media accounts since that day. She was involved with drugs and prostitution at the time of her disappearance, and the area where she was last seen is a known hangout for sex workers. Although police can find no evidence that she was taken for sex trafficking, her family believes that may be what happened.

*(Chandra at the time of her disappearance)*

At the time of her disappearance, Chandra Taylor had dyed her naturally brown hair blonde, stood 5'3", and weighed between 90 - 125 pounds. She is Caucasian with blue eyes and pierced ears. She has a tattoo of a compass and the phrase Be the One to Guide Me and an anchor with the phrase But Never Hold Me Down. She may use the alias names Chandra Marie Freitas, Mariah Freitas, or Marie Taylor. As of this writing, she is twenty-nine years old.

If you have any information regarding this case, you are urged to call the Sacramento County Sheriff's Department at 916-874-5115.

**Donald William Tobin**

Fifty-two year old Donald William Tobin was last seen in Riverside, California on July 7, 2010. He left his home on Redwood Drive to go put some items in a storage unit and never returned. He has never been heard from again. On July 11th, his silver 2007 Toyota Corolla was found abandoned at Carlson Dog Park on Mission Inn Avenue, less than a mile from his home. The items he had planned to put in the storage unit were still inside the car, as were his wallet and cell phone. He has not accessed his bank account since he disappeared, and he never picked up his last paycheck. His family believes he is deceased. Investigators do not believe he committed suicide or left of his own accord, but they do not know what caused him to go missing.

*(Donald at the time of his disappearance)*

At the time of his disappearance, Donald Tobin had graying brown hair and a mustache, wore metal wire-rimmed eyeglasses, stood between 5'8" - 5'9", and weighed 160 pounds. He is Caucasian with green eyes. As of this writing, he is sixty years old.

If you have any information regarding this case, you are urged to call the Riverside Police Department at 951-353-7104.

## Arlene Kazuko Tsuji

Twenty-five year old Arlene Kazuko Tsuji was last seen during her daily walk in the Vienna Woods neighborhood near Cabrillo College in Aptos, California on the evening of October 24, 1991. She was seen talking to a man on Haas Drive at approximately 7pm. She never returned home and has never been heard from again.

Authorities believe she was abducted. Searchers found what they believed to be a piece of plastic from her headphones on Haas Drive, about a mile from her home. Investigators believe she may have known her attacker, because it would be uncharacteristic of her to go anywhere with a stranger. She worked as a clerk for a travel agency at the time, and is described as a private person and a dependable employee who was close to her family. Foul play is suspected in her case.

*(Arlene at the time of her disappearance)*

At the time of her disappearance, Arlene Tsuji had black hair, stood 5', and weighed 103 pounds. She was last seen wearing a long-sleeve pullover, black shorts, and Walkman headphones. She is Asian with brown eyes, three piercings in her left ear, and two piercings in her right. She was born in Japan. As of this writing, she is fifty-two years old.

If you have any information regarding this case, you are urged to call the Santa Cruz Sheriff's Office at 831-454-2311 or 831-471-1121.

## Kenneth Anthony Chacon

Forty-nine year old Kenneth Anthony Chacon was last seen between 8pm and 9pm on March 5, 2005 at his home on west Main Street in Montrose, Colorado. He was reported missing when he failed to show up for work at the Russell Stover candy factory. He had held the same job for fifteen years and was a reliable worker. All of his belongings were left behind, including his vehicle. He had no known financial problems that would have made him want to walk on out his life. He had paid off his house just prior to his disappearance, and he was planning to go visit members of his extended family. Although there is no evidence of foul play, he has never left without warning before and authorities are calling his case suspicious.

*(Kenneth at the time of his disappearance)*

At the time of his disappearance, Kenneth Chacon had graying black hair that he usually wore pulled back into a long braid, wore wire-framed glasses, smoked cigarettes, stood between 5'6" - 5'8", and weighed between 140 -180 pounds. He was possibly wearing the following when he went missing: a white t-shirt, a flannel shirt or jacket, jeans, a baseball cap turned backwards, and white sneakers. He is Hispanic with brown eyes. His nickname is Tony. He speaks both English and Spanish fluently. As of this writing, he is sixty-two years old.

If you have any information regarding this case, you are urged to call the Montrose Police Department at 970-252-5200.

## Patricia Ann Cordova

Forty-six year old Patricia Ann Cordova was last seen between 7pm and 9pm on February 15, 2005, leaving a family member's house on Clay Street in Westminster, Colorado to go to the store. She has never heard from again, and is missing under unknown circumstances.

*(Patricia at the time of her disappearance)*

At the time of her disappearance, Patricia Cordova had brown hair, drew on her eyebrows, stood 5'4", and weighed between 100 - 120 pounds. She was possibly wearing the following at the time: a purple and gray Champs sweater, black jeans, black socks, and white shoes. She may have been carrying a black purse. She is

Caucasian with hazel eyes, a scar above her eyebrows, a scar on the tip of her nose, and double-pierced ears. She had previously fractured her left arm. As of this writing, she is sixty years old.

If you have any information regarding this case, you are urged to call the Adams County Sheriff's Department at 720-322-1215.

## Andy Joe Lepley

Eighteen year old Andy Joe Lepley was last seen at the Texaco station at Interstate 25 and Colorado 165 in Colorado City, Colorado on May 30, 1976. He had worked there part time for two years. He had begun his shift at 6:15am. Only fifteen minutes later, customers discovered the station unattended. The manager and police found his 1967 pickup truck in the parking lot with the keys in the ignition. Inside the station, the manager's CB radio had its microphone ripped out and the cash register was empty. Andy has never been seen or heard from again.

Authorities stated that a middle-aged Caucasian male with graying sandy-colored hair and blue eyes, about 5'11" and 175 pounds was seen at the station between 6:30am and 7:30am on the morning Andy disappeared. He is the prime suspect in Andy's presumed abduction. The man drove a two-door late model car, possibly a Pontiac Grand Prix that was either silver or white with maroon trim and a maroon landau top. He was pulling an unusual four- or five-foot-long tarp-covered handmade plywood trailer. The man may have been en route to Wyoming. He has never been identified.

Foul play is suspected in Andy's case. He was a senior and honor student at Rye High School at the time, and he was only days before graduation when he went missing. He had planned to join the Air Force after high school. His mother believes he was abducted after he surprised someone burglarizing the gas station. Although he went missing during the daylight hours in a high-traffic area on Memorial Day weekend, no one reportedly saw or heard anything suspicious.

*(Andy at the time of his disappearance)*

At the time of his disappearance, Andy Lepley had collar-length brown hair, a coppery complexion, stood 5'9", and weighed 150 pounds. He was last seen wearing a green Texaco shirt, a coat with his middle name on it, blue jeans, and lace-up hiking boots. He is Caucasian with brown eyes, a scar, and a deformed right hand. His nickname is Taco, and he goes by his middle name. As of this writing, he is sixty years old.

If you have any information regarding this case, you are urged to call the Pueblo County Sheriff's Office at 719-583-6400.

## Richard Stanley Meyer

Thirty-nine year old Richard Stanley Meyer was last seen in Nederland, Colorado on July 29, 1989. He was en route to his residence at the Columbine Campground near Central City, Colorado at the time. He was driving a red 1978 Dodge Monaco with expired Florida plates FDL - 30J. The vehicle disappeared with him and has never been found.

*(Richard at the time of his disappearance)*

At the time of his disappearance, Richard Meyer had dark brown hair, a mustache, wore eyeglasses, stood at 5'10", and weighed between 180 - 250 pounds. He is Caucasian with blue eyes, a large scar on his abdomen, and a strawberry birthmark on the back of his neck. His shoe size is 11E, and his nickname is Dick. As of this writing, he is sixty-eight years old.

If you have any information regarding this case, you are urged to call the Colorado Bureau of Investigation (CBI) at 303-239-4211.

## Rebecca Sue Morris

Fifty-nine year old Rebecca Sue Morris was last heard from on February 1, 2017. She said she was somewhere in Colorado and was en route to El Paso, Texas. She has never been heard from again, and authorities believe she may have been taken against her will.

*(Rebecca at the time of her disappearance)*

At the time of her disappearance, Rebecca Morris had brown hair, stood 5'10", and weighed 180 pounds. She is Caucasian with blue eyes and pierced ears. As of this writing, she is sixty years old.

If you have any information regarding this case, you are urged to call the Texas Department of Public Safety at 1-800-346-3243.

## Jose Ortiz

Nineteen year old Jose Ortiz was last seen in New Haven, Connecticut on December 28, 2005. He was riding his bicycle at the time. He was reported missing on January 1st. The day he disappeared, a firefighter reported seeing a young man being abducted from the intersection of Poplar Street and Lombard Street near the firehouse. Three men, approximately between the ages of fifteen and twenty-one years, were observed pulling another man off his bicycle and into a silver 1990s model Ford Taurus. Jose lived with his mother near the abduction site on Lombard Street. Authorities believe he was involved with drugs, but his family does not. They said he lived a quiet life and dreamed of becoming a police officer. Foul play is suspected.

*(Jose at the time of his disappearance)*

At the time of his disappearance, Jose Ortiz had brown hair, stood 5'10", and weighed 140 pounds. He was last seen wearing a black hooded sweatshirt, a bandana, and blue jeans. He is Hispanic with brown eyes. His nickname is Bin Laden. As of this writing, he is thirty-two years old.

If you have any information regarding this case, you are urged to call the New Haven Police Department at 203-946-6316.

## John Jay Ashley Jr.

Eighteen year old John Jay Ashley Jr. was last seen walking home from his school basketball practice in Wilmington, Delaware on December 14, 1971. He has never been heard from again.

A seventeen year old boy also disappeared from Wilmington that same night. He was located deceased from drowning in February 1972, but it has not been proven that the two cases are related.

*(John at the time of his disappearance)*

At the time of his disappearance, John Ashley Jr. had black hair, stood 5'4", and weighed 130 pounds. He is African-American with brown eyes and a congenital defect to his right hip. As of this writing, he is sixty-four years old.

If you have any information regarding this case, you are urged to call the Wilmington Police Department at 302-576-3670.

## Nefertiri Trader

Thirty-three year old Nefertiri Trader was last seen being dragged from her home by a man at 4am in the Saddlebrook area of New Castle, Delaware on June 29, 2014. A neighbor witnessed it but assumed the man was taking the woman to the hospital, so the police were not called. At 6pm, after she was supposed to have returned home from work, her mother went to her home. She discovered cigarettes, coffee, and a single unopened condom on a chair on the porch. A smashed loaf of bread was lying on the ground in the front yard. Nefertiri's flip flops were next to the front door, and the house was deserted. Her mother reported her missing. Her family believes she left the house to purchase some items at a nearby convenience store and was abducted from her porch and forced into her own vehicle when she returned home. Her vehicle, a silver 2000 Acura RL with Delaware plates 404893, disappeared with her and has never been found.

*(Nefertiri at the time of her disappearance)*

At the time of her disappearance, Nefertiri Trader had brown hair, stood 5'6", and weighed 125 pounds. She was last seen wearing a pink sweat suit. She is African-American with brown eyes, pierced ears, and tattoos on her left arm, lower back, and the right side of her chest. Her nickname is Neffie. As of this writing, she is thirty-seven years old.

If you have any information regarding this case, you are urged to call the New Castle County Police Department at 302-395-2781.

## Judith Dunton Osteen

Sixty year old Judith Dunton Osteen was last seen in Old Town, Florida on December 15, 2007. She shared a home with her sixty-four year old developmentally disabled sister off State Road 349. Her sister stated that they went to sleep in separate bedrooms that night, and when she woke up there was a strange man in her room. The man shoved her to the floor. At that point, Judith walked into the room and the man grabbed her and forced her from the home. She has never been heard from again. Her sister stayed in her room for several hours without contacting the police because she was afraid for her life. Their housekeeper reported the abduction the next morning.

Her sister was able to provide a vague description of the abductor, saying that he was Caucasian with short gray hair and a receding hairline. The man has never been identified. Authorities found no sign of forced entry to the sisters' house, and the rain quite possibly washing away any tire tracks or footprints the abductor had left behind. Judith's purse and shoes were still inside the home.

Judith was a frequent computer user and knew many people over the internet. Police searched her hard drive for clues to her case and spoke to some of her online friends, but it is unknown if her abduction was related to her online presence or not.

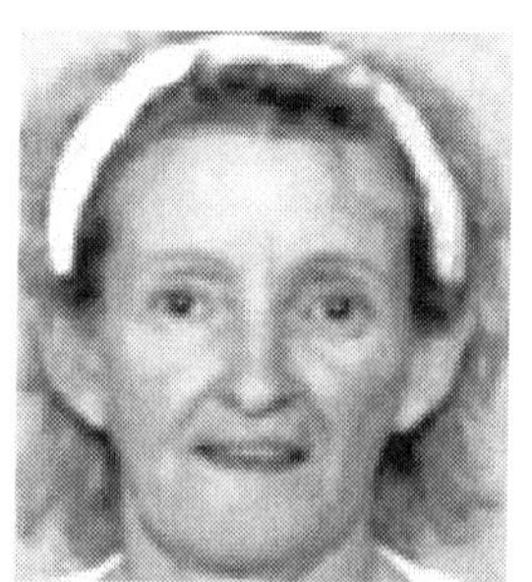

*(Judith at the time of her disappearance)*

At the time of her disappearance, Judith Osteen had brown hair, smoked 305 brand cigarettes, stood 5'2", and weighed 120 pounds. She is Caucasian with a scar on her face. Her eye color is unknown. As of this writing, she is seventy-one years old.

If you have any information regarding this case, you are urged to call the Dixie County Sheriff's Office at 352-498-1231.

## Annie Ruth Paul

Seventy-two year old Annie Ruth Paul was last seen standing on the porch at Rosa's Caring Heart, an assisted living facility on northwest U.S. Highway 221 in Greenville, Florida at 2:30pm on February 8, 2015. An extensive search turned up no clues as to her whereabouts.

*(Annie at the time of her disappearance)*

At the time of her disappearance, Annie Paul had black hair, stood 5'5", and weighed 140 pounds. She was last seen wearing a long-sleeve white shirt, blue jeans, and black slippers with a pink stripe. She is African-American with brown eyes. She has dementia and needs medication. As of this writing, she is seventy-five years old.

If you have any information regarding this case, you are urged to call the Madison County Sheriff's Office at 850-973-4001 or 850-973-4151.

## Albert Lee Baker

Thirty-four year old Albert Lee Baker was last seen when his uncle dropped him off at the emergency room at Wuesthoff Memorial Hospital on Longwood Avenue in Rockledge, Florida on May 2, 1988. He was disoriented at the time and having chest pains. When his uncle returned to the hospital an hour later, he was told Albert had left without being seen by a doctor. He has never been heard from again.

*(Albert at the time of his disappearance)*

At the time of his disappearance, Albert Baker had brown hair and a mustache and goatee, stood 5'10", and weighed 170 pounds. He was last seen wearing a white t-shirt, green or navy blue work pants, and black size 10 or 10.5 shoes. He is African-American with brown eyes. As of this writing, he is sixty-four years old.

If you have any information regarding this case, you are urged to call the Rockledge Police Department at 321-690-3988.

## Delia Bacarisas Baxter

Thirty-seven year old Delia Bacarisas Baxter was last seen leaving her workplace and entering the parking lot on March 17, 2000 in Melbourne, Florida. She was employed as an assembler for Dictaphone. A coworker saw her getting into her vehicle, a four-door 1988 Chevrolet Corsica at 4:30pm. The witness noticed an SUV in the parking lot at the same time, and stated that it followed Delia's vehicle out of the parking lot as she left. She had promised to bring home pizza for her three daughters that day, but she never returned home and has never been seen again.

Four months later, her vehicle was found abandoned at an apartment complex in Melbourne, not far from the Palm Bay city line. It is uncharacteristic for her to leave without warning, and foul play is suspected.

*(Delia at the time of her disappearance)*

At the time of her disappearance, Delia Baxter had black hair, stood 5'6", and weighed 120 pounds. She was five months pregnant at the time. She is Asian with brown eyes. She was born in the Philippines and is of Filipino descent. Her nickname is Dee. As of this writing, she is fifty-five years old.

If you have any information regarding this case, you are urged to call the Melbourne Police Department at 321-259-1211.

**<u>Robert Gene Harrison</u>**

Eighty year old Robert Gene Harrison was last seen at his home on Milwaukee Street in West Melbourne, Florida on May 25, 2014. He went to bed at 9pm. His wife of seventeen years woke up at 3am and the lights were on, but Robert was gone. After going to bed he had apparently gotten back up, dressed in the same clothes he had worn the night before, put in his dentures, put on one shoe, and left. He has never been heard from again.

A police dog tracked his scent for five blocks before losing the trail. An extensive search turned up no clues as to his whereabouts. He had never wandered away from his home before. He was carrying his Florida driver's license and about $40 in cash in his wallet, but no credit cards at the time. He left his eyeglasses and one of his shoes behind. He was born and raised in Red House, West Virginia, and he had previously lived in Indian River County, Florida for twenty years. His family believes he may have tried to return to one of those places.

*(Robert at the time of his disappearance)*

At the time of his disappearance, Robert Harrison had gray hair, wore an upper denture, stood between 5'11" - 6', and weighed 150 pounds. He is believed to have been wearing a green and white Western-style shirt with snaps, a white t-shirt, jeans, and one shoe. He is Caucasian with green eyes. He suffers from high blood pressure and Alzheimer's disease, both of which require medication that he does not have with him. His nickname is Bob. As of this writing, he is eighty-four years old.

If you have any information regarding this case, you are urged to call the Brevard County Sheriff's Office at 321-264-5217.

## Robert David Helphrey

Thirty-four year old Robert David Helphrey closed the restaurant he managed at 12:30am on May 22, 2006 and joined his friends at Peggy O'Neill's Irish Pub and Eatery in Palm Harbor, Florida. At approximately 1:30am, he left the pub driving his blue/gray Mitsubishi Outlander hatchback with Florida plates G83NYD. He was supposed to meet a friend at a nearby residence, but spoke to them on the phone at 2am instead. He never returned to his apartment and has never been heard from again. His vehicle disappeared with him and has not been located.

Robert is a military veteran who served in Operation Desert Storm. His loved ones describe him as a hardworking dependable person and a devoted father, who would not have left without warning. He left behind all his belongings, and there has been no activity on his bank accounts since he went missing.

*(Robert at the time of his disappearance)*

At the time of his disappearance, Robert Helphrey had blonde hair, stood 5'11", and weighed between 190 - 220 pounds. He was last seen wearing a polo shirt with the words Thirsty Marlin on it, shorts, and a leather necklace with a brown stone. He is Caucasian with blue eyes, a fence tattooed around his arm, a Tasmanian devil tattooed on his ankle, and possibly a fish tattooed on the back of his shoulder. He takes medication for high blood pressure. His nickname is Bob. As of this writing, he is forty-six years old.

If you have any information regarding this case, you are urged to call the Pinellas County Sheriff's Office at 727-582-6200.

## Deborah Deann Poe

Twenty-six year old Deborah Deann Poe was employed at the Circle K convenience store near Hall Road and Aloma Avenue in Orlando, Florida in 1990. On February 4th, her boyfriend saw her inside the store at 1am. A friend who drove by at 3am saw her standing behind the counter. Between 3:15am and 3:30am, a customer came into the store and saw a Caucasian male behind the counter. He was described as being between nineteen and twenty-five years of age with long black hair and dark eyes, wearing a black Megadeth t-shirt, a skull ring on his finger, and a cross earring in his right ear. He appeared to be the only one in the store and the customer assumed he was the clerk. The customer bought cigarettes and the man rang it up on the cash register and gave her back her change. The man has never been identified, and it is possible he was just another customer. But investigators would still like to question him to see if he can give any more insight into Deborah's disappearance.

The store was discovered unoccupied at 4am, and customers called the police. A cup of coffee and a carton of chocolate milk were on the floor behind the counter, and Deborah's smock was left inside the store. Her car was in the parking lot with her purse, paycheck, and keys inside. There was no sign of a struggle inside or outside the store. The cash register was locked and there was no evidence of a robbery. Tracker dogs followed her scent to the rear of the store, over a fence, and to a road. They then lost it, suggesting that she got into a vehicle. She has never been heard from again.

*(Deborah at the time of her disappearance)*

At the time of her disappearance, Deborah Poe had curly streaked dark blonde hair, stood between 5'2" - 5'3", and weighed 100 pounds. She is Caucasian with blue eyes, triple pierced ears, and a burn scar on her left shoulder. As of this writing, she is fifty-four years old.

If you have any information regarding this case, you are urged to call the Orange County Sheriff's Office at 407-836-3700.

## Yekaterina Gennadyevna Belaya

Forty-seven year old Yekaterina Gennadyevna Belaya was last seen near her home on Rock Springs Drive in Melbourne, Florida on September 28, 2014. She was driving a white 2003 Honda Odyssey with Florida plates A43-1CR with peeling paint around the windshield. She told her daughter she was going to the store and would be back in half an hour. She never returned home and has never been heard from again. It is unknown whether or not the vehicle has been located.

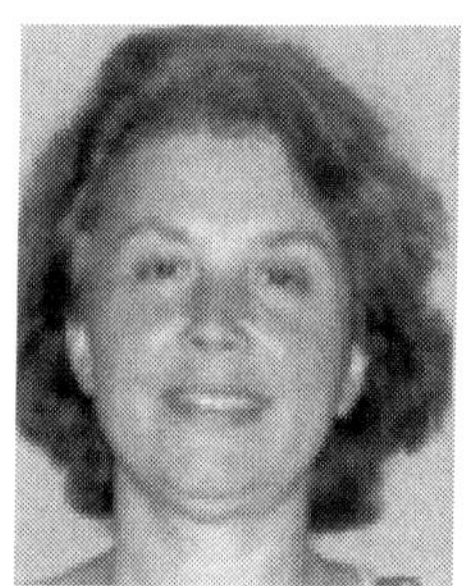

*(Yekaterina at the time of her disappearance)*

At the time of her disappearance, Yekaterina Belaya had brown hair, stood 5'4", and weighed 155 pounds. She was last seen wearing a long-sleeve white shirt and a long skirt with a blue and white floral design. She is Caucasian with brown eyes and scars on her abdomen and left calf. Her nicknames are Kat and Katie.

Prior to her disappearance, she had been experiencing blackouts. As of this writing, she is fifty-one years old.

If you have any information regarding this case, you are urged to call the Brevard County Sheriff's Office at 321-633-8419.

## Barry Alan Block, David George Rhodes, Mark Douglas Jackson, Jason Rodney Galehouse, James Mark Shumaker, Bradley Lee Williams, Mark Allen Thompson

Twenty-four year olds Barry Alan Block and David George Rhodes shared an apartment in Drake Towers on north Andrews Avenue in Fort Lauderdale, Florida. They were last seen there together on June 22, 1988. Neither man has ever been heard from again.

Sixteen years later, thirty-five year old Mark Douglas Jackson, also a resident of Drake Towers, disappeared from the building on June 27, 2004. There is speculation that these three disappearances are connected to the murder of twenty-six year old Michael Wayne Wachholtz, the presumed murder of twenty-six year old Jason Rodney Galehouse, and the disappearances of thirty year old James Mark Shumaker, thirty year old Mark Allen Thompson, and thirty-one year old Bradley Lee Williams.

All eight men are Caucasian and gay, all were within roughly the same age group at the time, and all disappeared from the gulf side of Florida. Barry Block, David Rhodes, and Mark Jackson disappeared from Fort Lauderdale. Mark Thompson disappeared from Clearwater. James Shumaker, Jason Galehouse, Michael

Wachholtz, and Bradley Williams all disappeared from Tampa. Only Michael Wachholtz's remains have been found, all other seven men remain missing.

In May 2004, Steven Lorenzo and Scott Schweikert were charged with drugging Michael Wachholtz and Jason Galehouse. Neither man has been connected to the other six disappearances.

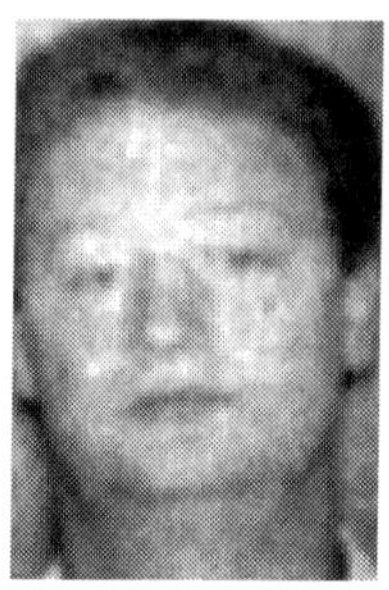

*(Barry Block at the time of his disappearance)*

At the time of his disappearance, Barry Block had brown hair, stood 5'9", and weighed 160 pounds. He is Caucasian with blue eyes. As of this writing, he is fifty-four years old.

*(David Rhodes at the time of his disappearance)*

At the time of his disappearance, David Rhodes had brown hair, stood 5'8", and weighed 150 pounds. He is Caucasian with blue eyes. As of this writing, he is fifty-four years old.

*(Mark Jackson at the time of his disappearance)*

At the time of his disappearance, Mark Jackson had light brown hair, stood between 6' - 6'2", and weighed between 170 - 180 pounds. His wallet, passport, and credit cards disappeared with him and have never been found. He is Caucasian with blue eyes and scars on his nose and between his eyes. As of this writing, he is forty-nine years old.

*(Jason Galehouse at the time of his disappearance)*

At the time of his disappearance, Jason Galehouse had brown eyes, stood 5'10", and weighed between 180 - 185 pounds. He was last seen wearing a red sweater, blue jeans, white sneakers, a silver ring, and a watch with a silver face and a dark leather band. He is Caucasian with green eyes. As of this writing, he is forty years old.

*(James Shumaker at the time of his disappearance)*

At the time of his disappearance, James Shumaker had blonde hair, stood between 5'9" - 5'11", and weighed between 150 - 160 pounds. He was last seen wearing a green purple and black vest, green surgical pants, black Reebok sneakers, and a silver neck chain. He is Caucasian with hazel eyes. He may go by his middle name or the name Marcus. As of this writing, he is fifty-three years old.

*(Bradley Williams at the time of his disappearance)*

At the time of his disappearance, Bradley Williams had brown hair, stood 6'2", and weighed 170 pounds. He is Caucasian with brown eyes. As of this writing, he is forty-eight years old.

*(Mark Thompson at the time of his disappearance)*

At the time of his disappearance, Mark Thompson had brown hair, stood between 5'10" - 5'11", and weighed 160 pounds. He was last seen wearing knee-length khaki shorts and a pink or blue or white and blue striped shirt with a drawstring collar. He has bipolar disorder and required medication. He is Caucasian with brown eyes. As of this writing, he is forty-seven years old.

If you have any information regarding these cases, you are urged to call one of the following numbers:

*Fort Lauderdale Police Department at 954-828-5529*

*Tampa Police Department at 813-276-3503*

*Clearwater Police Department at 727-562-4365*

## Diane Hollins

Thirty-one year old Diane Hollins and her fourteen year old daughter Tammy disappeared together from Daytona Beach, Florida on June 11, 1979. A neighbor saw them walking down the street away from their home that morning at 6am. Diane never showed up for work that day, and Tammy never arrived at school. They left all of their belongings behind, and the money in their banking account has not been touched.

Tammy's skeletal remains were found in rural Screven County, Georgia in 1986, but were not identified until July 2013. No trace of Diane has ever been found.

*(Diane at the time of her disappearance)*

At the time of her disappearance, Diane Hollins had black hair, stood 5'6", and weighed 135 pounds. She is African-American with brown eyes. As of this writing, she is seventy years old.

If you have any information regarding this case, you are urged to call the Daytona Police Department at 386-671-5100.

## Charles Franklin Huff

Seventy-six year old Charles Franklin Huff was last seen at his Lakeland, Florida home at 8am on November 25, 2004. He is believed to have left his house to go on a hunting trip. His wife came home from work and found him gone and a package of chicken spoiled in the sink. By 6pm when he still had not returned home, she became worried. At 1am on November 26th, she reported him missing. That day, his white 1994 pickup truck was found on Tanic Grade Road, six miles inside of the

50,000-acre Green Swamp Wildlife Management area, which was also Charles' favorite hunting spot. There was no sign of him at the scene, but his sneakers were inside the truck. His loved ones theorize that he possibly met with foul play after being robbed. However, there is no evidence to support the theory.

*(Charles at the time of his disappearance)*

At the time of his disappearance, Charles Huff had gray hair, wore yellow-tinted eyeglasses with wire frames, stood 6', and weighed 200 pounds. He was last seen wearing a Rolex watch, a ring with a large diamond, blue jeans, a camouflage shirt and jacket, an orange vest, a camouflage hat reading The Gun Shed, and hunting boots. It is believed that he was probably carrying a 22-gauge rifle. He is Caucasian with brown eyes and a tattoo on his left forearm. He is borderline diabetic and has arthritis in his left knee. He needs medication that he does not have with him. As of this writing, he is ninety years old.

If you have any information regarding this case, you are urged to call the Sumter County Sheriff's Office at 352-793-0222.

**<u>Tammy Lynn Huston</u>**

Twenty-five year old Tammy Lynn Huston was last seen in Jacksonville, Florida on November 19, 1984. Her boyfriend, Larry Butts, forced his way into her home on east 25th Street and abducted her. She has never been seen or heard from again. Larry's body was found floating in the St. Johns River near the Jacksonville Naval Air Station five weeks later.

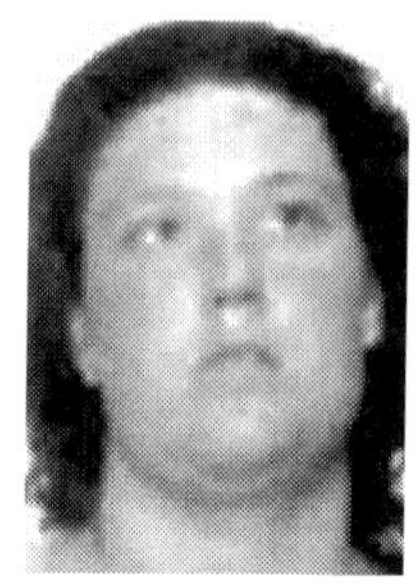

*(Tammy at the time of her disappearance)*

At the time of her disappearance, Tammy Huston had brown hair, stood 5'5", and weighed 160 pounds. She was last seen wearing pajamas. She is Caucasian with blue eyes. As of this writing, she is fifty-nine years old.

If you have any information regarding this case, you are urged to call the Jacksonville Sheriff's Office at 904-630-0500.

## Dennis Lee Brown

Forty-three year old Dennis Lee Brown was last seen on November 24, 1983 at his home on Slater Road in North Fort Myers, Florida. He left a note on his front door saying he was going to run an errand and would be back soon. His green four-door 1973 Ford LTD sedan with Florida plates disappeared with him and has never been located. Foul play is suspected.

*(Dennis at the time of his disappearance)*

At the time of his disappearance, Dennis Brown had black hair with gray sideburns and a mustache, wore upper and lower dentures, stood 5'11", and weighed 190 pounds. He was seen wearing a watch. He is Caucasian with hazel eyes. His nickname is Denny. As of this writing, he is seventy-seven years old.

If you have any information regarding this case, you are urged to call the Lee County Sheriff's Department at 239-477-1000.

## Kristine May Bruce

Thirty-eight year old Kristine May Bruce was last seen at her home on Wellington Loop in Kissimmee, Florida at 10:30am on September 6, 2013. She walked away from her home without her cell phone, medication, or personal belongings. She has never been heard from again.

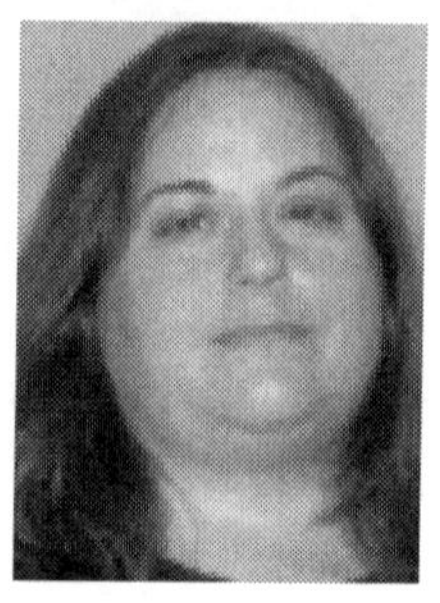

*(Kristine at the time of her disappearance)*

At the time of her disappearance, Kristine Bruce had brown hair, wore contact lenses, stood 5'4", and weighed 210 pounds. She was last seen wearing a shirt or tank top, pajama bottoms, and a white summer robe with no belt. She is Caucasian with brown eyes. She has the following tattoos: a Goth rabbit on her upper right arm at the shoulder, a mechanical owl on her side, a black heart filled in with red ink on her right forearm, a blue star with a black outline on her finger, and a blue dotted background with two birds, a crown, a circle with the number 17 inside, clouds, and a bomb on her upper chest. Her nickname is Kris. As of this writing, she is forty-three years old.

If you have any information about this case, you are urged to call the Osceola County Sheriff's Office at 407-344-5230 or 407-344-5226.

## Tommie Eugene Jackson

Forty-nine year old Tommie Eugene Jackson was last seen in St. Augustine, Florida on January 11, 2007 dropping his young daughter off at Cathedral Parish School on St. George Street. His usual routine was to drop his daughter off at school, and then return home to do chores until time to leave for his 2pm to 10pm shift at a rest area off Interstate 95. There is evidence that he did return home after dropping off his child at school, but he never arrived at work. When his wife called him at 4pm as usual the call went straight to voicemail. He has never been heard from again. His gray four-door 1989 Pontiac 6000 with license plates X20EXQ disappeared with him and has not been located. He is described as a dependable, reliable man who had never left without warning in the past. Foul play is suspected.

*(Tommie at the time of his disappearance)*

At the time of his disappearance, Tommie Jackson had black hair, stood 6'1", and weighed 250 pounds. He is African-American with brown eyes. As of this writing, he is sixty years old.

If you have any information regarding this case, you are urged to call the St. Johns County Sheriff's Office at 904-824-8304.

## Doris Wade Carter

Sixty-one year old Doris Wade Carter and her girlfriend, thirty-eight year old Kelly Moriarty, were last seen at Doris' home on McLean Drive, in Plant City, Florida on December 16, 2011. On December 20th, Kelly's car was found abandoned on State Road 62 in

Parish, Florida. On December 27th, a severed leg washed ashore in St. Petersburg, Florida. Authorities believe it had only been in the water a couple of days. Kelly was reported missing on January 27, 2012 and Doris on January 29th. There were no signs of a struggle at the home.

In March of 2012, the severed leg was positively identified as belonging to Kelly. The rest of her remains have never been found, and investigators are not sure what caused her death or how her leg was removed from her body. No sign of Doris has ever been found.

*(Doris at the time of her disappearance)*

At the time of her disappearance, Doris Carter had brown hair, stood 5'1", and weighed 110 pounds. She is Caucasian with hazel eyes and a tattoo of a cross with wings on the back of her neck. She has a surgical scar on the right side of her abdomen, and her ears are pierced. Her nickname is Pat. As of this writing, she is sixty-eight years old.

If you have any information regarding this case, you are urged to call the Hillsborough County Sheriff's Office at 813-247-8703.

**Philistin Saintcyr**

Sixty-six year old Philistin Saintcyr had an unspecified medical emergency and was transported via helicopter to the North Naples Hospital in Naples, Florida on April 26, 2006. He stayed overnight and was released the next morning. The hospital gave him a voucher to pay for a cab back to his home in Immokalee, Florida. Once in that city, however, he was unable to provide the cab driver with his address, so the driver took him back to the hospital. The hospital staff then told him how to take the bus home. He was last seen at the bus stop on 7th Street north. He never arrived home and has never been heard from again.

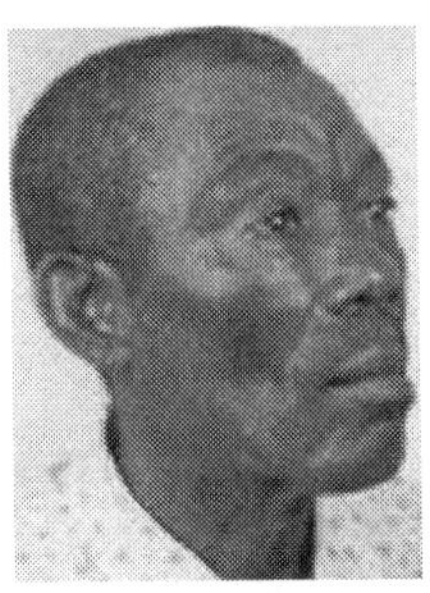

*(Philistin at the time of his disappearance)*

At the time of his disappearance, Philistin Saintcyr had black hair, stood 5'5", and weighed 135 pounds. He was last seen wearing a red and white striped shirt, green pants, a green baseball cap, and black shoes. He is African-American with brown eyes. He is missing several teeth. He suffers from high blood pressure and possibly dementia. He speaks only Haitian Creole. As of this writing, he is seventy-eight years old.

If you have any information regarding this case, you are urged to call the Collier County Sheriff's Office at 239-793-9300.

## Douglas Harlan Selby

Thirty-seven year old Douglas Harlan Selby was last seen leaving the Caribbean Club in Key Largo, Florida on August 22, 1989. He has never been heard from again. His 1980 Dodge pickup truck was later found abandoned outside the Twin Harbors Campground by mile marker 104. Police believe he may have been taken against his will.

*(Douglas at the time of his disappearance)*

At the time of his disappearance, Douglas Selby had brown hair, stood between 6' - 6'2", and weighed 190 pounds. He is Caucasian with brown eyes, a scar on his chest, and scars on his back. As of this writing, he is sixty-six years old.

If you have any information regarding this case, you are urged to call the Monroe County Sheriff's Office at 305-289-2430.

## Sandra Lee Lemire

Forty-seven year old Sandra Lee Lemire left her grandmother's home near Interstate 4 and John Young Parkway in Orlando, Florida on May 8, 2012. She was driving her grandmother's red 2004 Ford Freestyle minivan with Florida plates J36-8ZE. She was going to Kissimmee, Florida to meet a man she had been communicating with through an online dating service. She called her grandmother to say she had arrived in Kissimmee, and promised to call before she began the journey back home, but she never did. She has never been heard from again. She was last seen leaving a McDonald's restaurant in Kissimmee. Authorities interviewed the man she had gone to visit, but he had an alibi. He had worked an overnight shift during the time she disappeared. Her disappearance is considered suspicious, and investigators believe foul play may have been involved. It is unknown whether or not the vehicle has ever been found.

*(Sandra at the time of her disappearance)*

At the time of her disappearance, Sandra Lemire had bleached blonde hair, wore eyeglasses with black frames, stood 5'4", and weighed 130 pounds. She was last seen wearing a gray blouse, blue jeans, and sandals. She is Caucasian with blue eyes. She has diabetes and requires insulin, which she does not have with her. As of this writing, she is fifty-three years old.

If you have any information regarding this case, you are urged to call the Orlando Police Department at 407-246-3946.

## Steven James MacKrell

Twenty-five year old Steven James MacKrell was last seen buying snacks at a Valero gas station on north Dixie Highway in Pompano Beach, Florida at 2:32am on July 30, 2015. He had left Lucky's Tavern in Fort Lauderdale at 1:30am, and he was supposed to be going to meet friends but he never arrived. Outside the gas station, he got into an altercation with an unidentified African-American man who was a passenger in a silver sedan. That car was seen following Steven as he drove away. He has never been heard from again. His white four-door 2013 Ford Fusion with a missing hubcap on the front driver's side and plate number WJ70L disappeared with him and has never been found. His cell phone has not been turned on since he disappeared, and his debit card has not been used. Foul play is possible in his case.

*(Steven at the time of his disappearance)*

At the time of his disappearance, Steven MacKrell had brown hair with a mustache and goatee, stood 5'10", and weighed 165 pounds. He was last seen wearing a short-sleeve gray t-shirt with a circular design on the front, khaki pants, and black shoes. He is Caucasian with brown eyes, a scar on the back of his head, a scar on the right side of his forehead, and the letters DTF tattooed on the inside of his lip. As of this writing, he is twenty-eight years old.

If you have any information regarding this case, you are urged to call the Fort Lauderdale Police Department at 954-828-5700.

## William Ronnie Staggs

Fifty-three year old William Ronnie Staggs was last seen at approximately 1:30am on February 6, 2007 at his residence on Fietzway Road in Dover, Florida. He told his wife he had heard a noise and thought someone was outside. He took a shovel and went out to investigate. He never returned and has never been heard from again. His house slippers, cigarettes, and eyeglasses were later found in his yard.

*(William at the time of his disappearance)*

At the time of his disappearance, William Staggs had graying brown hair, stood 5’11”, and weighed 165 pounds. He was last seen wearing a tan and green striped shirt and tan pants. He is Caucasian with blue eyes and a large surgical scar in his groin area. He is missing the tip of his left middle finger down to the second knuckle. He goes by his middle name. As of this writing, he is sixty-four years old.

If you have any information regarding this case, you are urged to call the Hillsborough County Sheriff's Office at 813-247-8200.

## Stephanie Edwards

Fifty year old Stephanie Edwards was last seen in Winter Park, Florida on May 24, 2010. At 10pm that day, she walked to a friend's home six blocks from her own residence. She stayed about ten minutes, and then left to go back to her own home. She never arrived and has never been heard from again. Her mother reported her missing a week later. Authorities do not believe she left of her own accord.

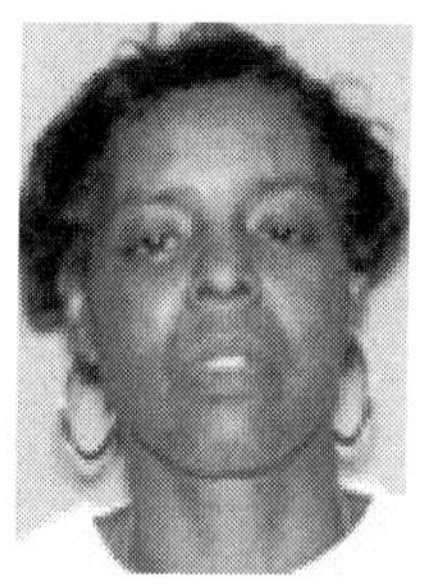

*(Stephanie at the time of her disappearance)*

At the time of her disappearance, Stephanie Edwards had graying black hair, stood 5'4", and weighed 140 pounds. She was last seen wearing a red t-shirt and blue jeans. She is African-American with brown eyes, a mole on her lower left leg, and pierced ears. She is missing her two upper front teeth. As of this writing, she is fifty-eight years old.

If you have any information regarding this case, you are urged to call the Winter Park Police Department at 407-644-1313.

## Carol Joan McHugh

Seventy-two year old Carol Joan McHugh was last seen on east Lenox Court in Inverness, Florida at 3:30pm on June 8, 2017. She left her home on east Regency Row in the Seven Lakes Subdivision to go for a walk and never returned home. An extensive search turned up no sign of her, and she has not been heard from since.

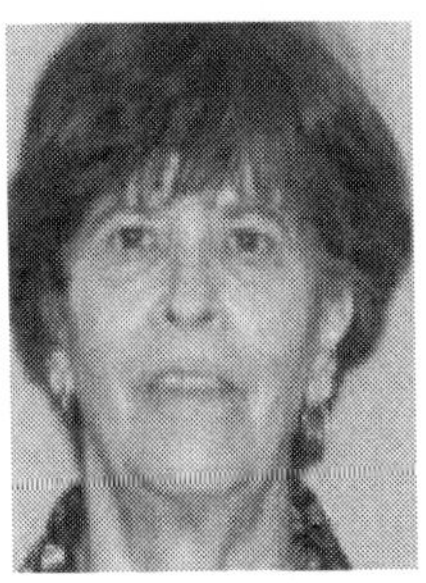

*(Carol at the time of her disappearance)*

At the time of her disappearance, Carol McHugh had brown hair, stood 5’2”, and weighed 113 pounds. She was in the early stages of dementia at the time. She was last seen wearing a tan short-sleeve button-down shirt with brown stripes and a large collar and dark-colored pants. She is Caucasian with brown eyes, a scar on her abdomen, and pierced ears. She needs medication that she does not have with her. As of this writing, she is seventy-three years old.

If you have any information regarding this case, you are urged to call the Citrus County Sheriff's Office at 888-269-8477.

## Richard James Estrada

Thirty-eight year old Richard James Estrada was last seen leaving the Hibiscus Golf Club where he was employed in Naples, Florida on May 5, 2000. His blue two-door 1990 Oldsmobile Toronado with Florida plates D70AZ disappeared with him and has never been found. Three days after he disappeared, his house burned down. However, it is not known whether or not the fire was related to his disappearance. He was considered a reliable employee in 2000 and had no problems with drugs, alcohol, or gambling. Authorities do not believe he left voluntarily.

*(Richard at the time of his disappearance)*

At the time of his disappearance, Richard Estrada had black hair, stood 5'4", and weighed between 185 - 190 pounds. He is Hispanic with brown eyes and a scar on his chest. He may use the alias first names: Richardo, Ricardo, Tony, Antonio, and/or Joe. He may use the alias last name Perez. As of this writing, he is fifty-six years old.

If you have any information regarding this case, you are urged to call the Collier County Sheriff's Office at 941-793-9300.

## Newton Humphrey Whidden

Eighty-five year old Newton Humphrey Whidden was last seen at a pharmacy on 10th Street in Sarasota, Florida on August 20, 2012. He left his cell phone behind at the pharmacy and disappeared. He has never been heard from again. His white 2000 Dodge Caravan was found abandoned in a ditch in a rural area outside of Okeechobee, Florida, nearly 100 miles from where he was last seen. No clues as to his whereabouts were found inside or around the vehicle. His keys, wallet, checkbook, and identification disappeared with him and have not been found. Although his daughter says that he sometimes gets confused, he was in good health at the time.

*(Newton at the time of his disappearance)*

At the time of his disappearance, Newton Whidden had gray hair, wore eyeglasses for reading, stood 5'9", and weighed 135 pounds. He was last seen wearing a long-sleeve plaid button-down shirt, tan corduroy pants, and suede sneakers. He is Caucasian with hazel eyes, a large mole in the middle of his back, a scar on his abdomen, and a scar on his thumb. His right pinky finger has a tendon contraction and is bent as a result. He may use the nickname Newt or his initials W.H. As of this writing, he is ninety-one years old.

If you have any information regarding this case, you are urged to call the Sarasota County Sheriff's Office at 941-861-5800.

## Noemi Gonzalez

Fifty-four year old Noemi Gonzalez was last seen sleeping in her bedroom in the duplex she shared with her adult son at northwest 136th Street and northwest 4th Avenue in North Miami, Florida at 2am on February 12, 2014. When her son woke up at 8am, she was gone. Her bed was unmade and the front door was unlocked. She left behind her purse, keys, cell phone, and medication. She has never been heard from again. Tracker dogs were unable to pick up her trail. Her family says it would be very uncharacteristic for her to leave the house without her belongings and without telling anyone where she was going. She has no history dropping out of sight.

*(Noemi at the time of her disappearance)*

At the time of her disappearance, Noemi Gonzalez had gray hair, wore eyeglasses, stood 5'1", and weighed 160 pounds. She was last seen wearing a white t-shirt and navy blue pants. She is Hispanic with brown eyes and birthmarks on her face and arm. She has epilepsy and needs daily medication to prevent seizures. She also has cardiogenic syndrome, which is a heart problem that can cause her to pass out. As of this writing, she is fifty-eight years old.

There is a reward being offered for information that leads to locating Noemi. If you have any information regarding this case, you are urged to call the North Miami Police Department at 305-471-8477.

## Lottie Albertha Wise

Ninety-one year old Lottie Albertha Wise was last seen at her residence on Venus Drive in Titusville, Florida at 9:25pm on January 10, 2006. She was living with her daughter, who had set an alarm to go off when the door was opened. Lottie walked out the front door while her daughter was in the shower and has never been heard from again. When her daughter heard the alarm, she got dressed and went outside to look for her mother but not find her. She then reported her disappearance to the police. An extensive search of the area turned up no clues as to her whereabouts. Due to being in the advanced stages of Alzheimer's disease, she may be confused and not ask for help.

*(Lottie at the time of her disappearance)*

At the time of her disappearance, Lottie Wise had graying black hair, stood at 5'4", and weighed 130 pounds. She was last seen wearing a brown zip-up jacket with a beige leaf design, a white blouse, green pants, and tan-colored shoes. She had her hair braided at the time. She is African-American with brown eyes. As of this writing, she is one-hundred-and-three years old.

If you have any information regarding this case, you are urged to call the Titusville Police Department at 321-264-7874.

Blaine County on November 17, 1996. He called his mother to say his pickup truck had stalled and he was going to get help. His truck was later discovered near the Laidlaw Corral area north of Rupert, Idaho. He has never

## Aram Wade Dowell

Thirty-six year old Aram Wade Dowell was last seen in Boundary County, Idaho on December 16, 2015. He disappeared shortly after getting into a domestic dispute with his father-in-law, who fired several shots in his direction. Aram sold his truck before he went missing, so if he left of his own accord his family and authorities do not known what means of transportation he used. Although police have no evidence of foul play, his family believes someone caused his disappearance. His mother said it is completely out of character for him to leave without warning.

*(Aram at the time of his disappearance)*

At the time of his disappearance, Aram Dowell had brown hair, stood 5'9", and weighed 140 pounds. He is Caucasian with hazel eyes, a scar near his left eye, tattoos on both upper arms, and missing a finger on his right hand. As of this writing, he is thirty-eight years old.

If you have any information regarding this case, you are urged to call the Boundary County Sheriff's Office at 208-267-3151.

## Daniel Glennon

Thirty-two year old Daniel Glennon was last seen at the Bank of America in Sandpoint, Idaho on December 5, 1995. He has never been heard from again. He left behind all his belongings. Authorities believe he may have been taken against his will.

*(Daniel at the time of his disappearance)*

At the time of his disappearance, Daniel Glennon had blonde hair and a full beard, stood 6'3", and weighed 220 pounds. He is Caucasian with blue eyes. As of this writing, he is fifty-four years old.

If you have any information regarding this case, you are urged to call the Banner County Sheriff's Office at 208-263-8417.

## Steven R. Asplund

Thirty-two year old Steven R. Asplund was last seen at a friend's house in Moline, Illinois on January 9, 1994. He had gone there to borrow a caulking gun for a remodeling project he was working on. He left going home that evening but never arrived. When he wasn't home by 6am, his fiancée began searching for him. He has never been heard from again.

His red Ford Mustang was found abandoned in a parking lot at the base of the Interstate 74 bridge in Bettendorf, Iowa. Steven was nowhere to be seen. Unspecified forensic evidence was discovered inside the car, but test results on it were inconclusive.

Several months after his car was found, his driver's license was found on a bridge at the Loud Thunder Forest Preserve in Rock Island County, Illinois. Police searched the river below but found nothing relating to his case.

In January 2014, authorities announced they had a person of interest in the twenty-year cold case. They also stated they now believe that there was more than one individual involved in Steven's disappearance, but no names have been released. Both authorities and his family believe foul play was involved in his disappearance.

*(Steven at the time of his disappearance)*

At the time of his disappearance, Steven Asplund had blonde hair, stood 6', and weighed 180 pounds. He was last seen wearing a Chicago Bears pullover jacket, a white sweatshirt, gray sweatpants, and sneakers. He is Caucasian with blue eyes. His nickname is Steve. As of this writing, he is fifty-six years old.

If you have any information regarding this case, you are urged to call one of the following numbers:

*Moline Police Department at 309-797-0401*

*Crime Stoppers at 1-800-724-9500*

## Anthony Keith Klama

Thirty-six year old Anthony Keith Klama was last seen walking into the Foxfire Apartment Complex's main entrance shortly after midnight on November 5, 1998 in Palatine, Illinois. He was accompanied by an unidentified male. The man was described as being about 5'9", weighing 190 pounds, with dark hair and a mustache. The two had just exited a light-colored car in the parking lot. Anthony has never been heard from again.

He had played darts with an unidentified individual at Splinter's Sports Bar on north Rand Road in Palatine on the day of his disappearance. He had left the bar alone between 11:30pm and midnight, walking back to his apartment. It is not known whether or not the man he played darts with at the bar was the same person he was seen with at the apartment complex.

There were no indications of a struggle inside his apartment, but the handset of his new cordless phone was missing. His bicycle was inside his apartment and his car sat undisturbed in the parking lot. He kept in touch with his parents and siblings, and was known to be a responsible worker. He had made appointments to get more tattoos and was excited about a work promotion. His loved ones said he had no debts or enemies, and he wasn't involved with drugs, gambling, or any other illegal activity at the time. He had given no indication that he planned to take a trip. There is no evidence of foul play, but authorities do think his disappearance is puzzling.

*(Anthony at the time of his disappearance)*

At the time of his disappearance, Anthony Klama had brown hair and a mustache, stood 6'1", and weighed 160 pounds. He was last seen wearing a blue and white plaid flannel shirt, a baseball cap, dark-colored jeans, and a blue plaid flannel jacket. He had a set of keys hooked to his belt loop, and was carrying approximately $40 from an ATM withdrawal earlier that evening. He was known to be a heavy drinker at the time. He is Caucasian with green eyes. He has several Native American-type tattoos across his shoulders and chest. His nickname is Tony. As of this writing, he is fifty-five years old.

If you have any information regarding this case, you are urged to call one of the following numbers:

*Palatine Police Department at 847-359-9000*

*Illinois State Police at 217-785-3327*

## Jerrica Lizette Laws

Twenty-four year old Jerrica Lizette Laws was last seen when she left her residence to go for a walk on a trail behind her house on Lee Street in Park Forest, Illinois at 7pm on August 17, 2015. She left her purse and identification behind. She has never been heard from again. Her family described her as a homebody and said it was very uncharacteristic for her to leave without warning.

*(Jerrica at the time of her disappearance)*

At the time of her disappearance, Jerrica Laws had black hair, stood between 5’1” - 5’2”, and weighed 140 pounds. She was last seen wearing a dark-colored shirt. She is African-American with brown eyes and pierced ears. Her nickname is Ric Ric. As of this writing, she is twenty-six years old.

If you have any information regarding this case, you are urged to call the Park Forest Police Department at 708-748-1309 or 708-748-4701.

## Hiep T. Luu

Twenty-one year old Hiep T. Luu was last seen in Berwyn, Illinois on the morning of December 15, 2003. He left home to go to his job at Storm Products in Woodridge, Illinois. He never arrived at work and has never been heard from again. His dark gray 1992 Nissan Maxima with Illinois plates 335 6037 disappeared with him and has never been found.

*(Hiep at the time of his disappearance)*

At the time of his disappearance, Hiep Luu had black hair, stood between 5'4" - 5'6", and weighed between 125 - 160 pounds. He is Asian with brown eyes. As of this writing, he is thirty-six years old.

If you have any information regarding this case, you are urged to call the Berwyn Police Department at 708-795-5600.

## Mark Allen Miller

Forty-eight year old Mark Allen Miller was last seen in Rockford, Illinois on March 12, 2009. He left his job at the Clock Tower Resort and Conference Center and was believed to have gone home. He and a roommate lived on Whitman Avenue. He has never been heard from again. Three days later, his silver 1998 Chrysler New Yorker was found abandoned on Harlem Boulevard, about a mile from his home.

The day he disappeared, Mark told a friend that he was going to ask his roommate of two years to move out. It is not known what his reasoning for the change was. Later, he called his friend and said he had done it and that it had gone better than he had expected. His roommate, Manuel Vasquez Rivera, was the last person known to have seen Mark. Authorities are interested in locating Manuel so they can find out what, if anything, he knows about Mark's disappearance.

*(Mark at the time of his disappearance)*

At the time of his disappearance, Mark Miller had dark brown hair, stood between 5'10" - 6', and weighed between 170 - 180 pounds. He is Caucasian with green eyes. As of this writing, he is fifty-seven years old.

If you have any information regarding this case, you are urged to call the Rockford Police Department at 815-987-5824.

## Karen L. Schepers

Twenty-three year old Karen L. Schepers was last seen at approximately 1am on April 16, 1983 in Carpentersville, Illinois. She had gone to a bar with about twenty coworkers to celebrate her recent promotion at work. Karen was the last in the group to leave, and it is not known where she went after she left the bar. Nor is it known if she ever made it home. She has never been heard from again. Her bright yellow 1980 Toyota Celica hatchback with red accent stripes and Illinois plates XP8919 disappeared with her and has never been found. The vehicle's VIN number is RA42326350.

*(Karen at the time of her disappearance)*

At the time of her disappearance, Karen Schepers had brown hair, stood 5'7", and weighed 125 pounds. She was last seen wearing a tan hooded corduroy coat and a Wittenauer watch. She is Caucasian with brown eyes. As of this writing, she is fifty-eight years old.

If you have any information regarding this case, you are urged to call the Elgin Police Department at 847-289-2700.

## Janet Lollisa Tillman

Forty-seven year old Janet Lollisa Tillman was last seen getting into a dark red car with an African-American male in the vicinity of Ninth Street and Exchange Avenue in East Saint Louis, Illinois on October 28, 2007. She has never been heard from again. Her family reported her missing November 5th.

*(Janet at the time of her disappearance)*

At the time of her disappearance, Janet Tillman had black hair, wore eyeglasses, stood 5’7”, and weighed 185 pounds. She is African-American with brown eyes. She is mentally handicapped and classified as disabled. She has a tracheotomy scar on her neck and a scar on her left eyebrow. As of this writing, she is fifty-eight years old.

If you have any information regarding this case, you are urged to call the Belleville Police Department at 618-234-1218.

## Marina Pearl Boelter

Eighteen year old Marina Pearl Boelter was last seen leaving the parking lot of the IGA where she worked in Bloomfield, Indiana at 6pm on December 31, 2014. She got into a light-colored Mercury Milan with multi-spoke rims, a spoiler, and a shark fin antenna at the top. The vehicle was driven by a middle-aged Caucasian man with glasses. They drove off in the direction of her apartment. When she failed to show up for work the next day and missed a visitation with her young son, who was in foster care, she was reported missing.

Her ex-boyfriend and father of her son, D.J. Lockhart, was stabbed to death six weeks after her disappearance. However, authorities stated they had no evidence to suggest that his murder was related to Marina's case.

*(Marina at the time of her disappearance)*

At the time of her disappearance, Marina Boelter had blonde hair, smoked Marlboro cigarettes, stood 5'3", and weighed between 95 - 120 pounds. She was last seen wearing a black and purple plaid coat, jeans with rhinestones on the back pockets, pink and white Nike Shocks shoes with a purple swoosh outlined in black, and a cross necklace. She was carrying a purse with LOVE written on the side. She is Caucasian with blue eyes. She may wear non-prescription glasses and dye her hair reddish-brown. Her ears are pierced, she is right-handed, and she has a tattoo of a star with butterfly wings on her foot. As of this writing, she is twenty-two years old.

If you have any information regarding this case, you are urged to call one of the following numbers:

*Indiana State Police at 812-384-4624*

*Bloomfield Police Department at 812-332-4411*

*Federal Bureau of Investigation (FBI) at 1-202-324-3000*

## Eva Mae Hale

Seventy-nine year old Eva Mae Hale left her Terre Haute, Indiana residence on October 15, 1996 and went to visit her brother's grave in the Marco Cemetery on a remote rural road in Greene County, Indiana. She has never been heard from again. Her 1983 Chrysler New Yorker was found at the cemetery with her purse and money locked inside. Her spare set of car keys were laying on the ground nearby. Foul play is suspected.

*(Eva at the time of her disappearance)*

At the time of her disappearance, Eva Hale had brown hair, wore glasses, stood 4'10", and weighed 98 pounds. She is Caucasian with blue eyes and pierced ears. As of this writing, she is one-hundred-and-one years old.

Eva's family is offering a reward for information leading to the arrest and conviction of any person or persons involved in her disappearance. If you have any information regarding this case, you are urged to call one of the following numbers:

*Greene County Sheriff's Department at 812-384-4411*

*Indiana State Police at 812-384-4624*

## Danyel Pauley

Twenty-nine year old Danyel Pauley was last seen getting into a red Chevrolet Suburban with an unidentified African American male on July 20, 2012. She has never been heard from again.

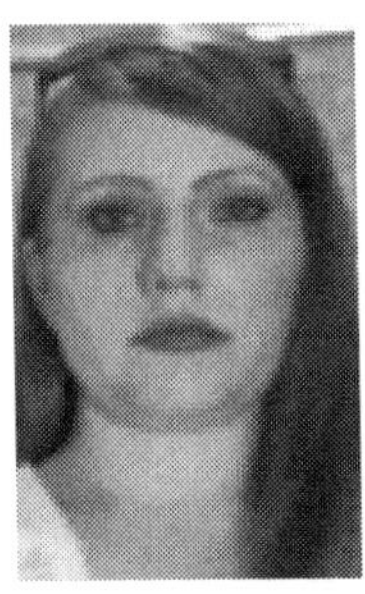

*(Danyel at the time of her disappearance)*

At the time of her disappearance, Danyel Pauley had long red hair down to the middle of her back, stood 5'6", and weighed 110 pounds. She is Caucasian with green eyes and a tattoo of a rose on her left shoulder. As of this writing, she is thirty-five years old.

If you have any information regarding this case, you are urged to call the Indianapolis Police Department at 317-327-6915.

## Daniel Reaves

Twenty-five year old Daniel Reaves was last seen in Madison, Indiana on May 3, 2008. He was watching TV with his girlfriend at her house. She fell asleep at about 2am. When she awoke, Daniel and his car were gone. At 4am, he sent her a text message saying, "I love you". She tried to call him five minutes later, but he didn't answer. He has never been heard from again.

Ten days later, his gold 1999 Chrysler Sebring convertible was found unlocked and abandoned on Green Hills Road in Madison. It had been there for about a week. His wallet with money inside, identification, and credit cards were all left in the vehicle. His loved ones said it was uncharacteristic of him to leave his vehicle unlocked, and that he had no reason to disappear. His cell phone has not been used since the day he went missing.

*(Daniel at the time of his disappearance)*

At the time of his disappearance, Daniel Reaves had dark brown hair, stood 5'11", and weighed 145 pounds. He was last seen wearing a white or light blue t-shirt, long tan shorts, light brown suede steel-toe sneakers, and possibly a black leather jacket. He is Caucasian with blue eyes. As of this writing, he is thirty-five years old.

If you have any information regarding this case, you are urged to call one of the following numbers:

*Jefferson County Police Department at 812-265-2648*

*Indiana State Police at 812-689-5000*

## Larissa Marie Sam

Twenty-two year old Larissa Marie Sam was last seen on south Mount Street in Indianapolis, Indiana at 4:30am on June 21, 2015. She had finished her shift at work and stopped at her uncle's house for drinks afterwards. At 4:30am, she left. She has never been seen or heard from again.

Police found her gold 2006 Dodge Stratus backed into the driveway of an abandoned house on Lyons Avenue in the Mars Hill area. The driver's window was down, the keys were in the ignition, and one of the front tires was flat. Her cell phone, some cash, her purse, and her shoes were inside the car. But there was no sign of Larissa at the scene. Surveillance footage in the area showed a man running away from the vehicle after it was parked in the driveway. Some believe she could have become a sex trafficking victim.

*(Larissa at the time of her disappearance)*

At the time of her disappearance, Larissa Sam had black hair with red extensions, wore glasses with black frames, stood 5'7", and weighed 135 pounds. She was last seen wearing a black tank top with the words Weed is my Spirit Animal and a lime green marijuana leaf inside a dream catcher on the front and matching lime green shorts or a skirt. She is Caucasian with brown eyes. Her hair is normally dark brown. She has the following tattoos: a cross on her lower back, stars across the back of each shoulder, candles, a cupcake, an ice cream cone, musical notes, and the word Princess across her upper chest. His nickname is Rissa. As of this writing, she is twenty-five years old.

If you have any information regarding this case, you are urged to call the Indianapolis Metropolitan Police Department at 317-327-6539.

## Mark D. Tomich

Twenty-eight year old Mark D. Tomich was last seen in Indianapolis, Indiana on March 4, 1992. He worked as an organic chemist for the Eli Lilly Pharmaceutical Company at the time, and was last seen leaving home to go to work. His brother, whom he lived with, stated that Mark took a shower as usual that morning, said goodbye and left at his normal time, between 6:15am - 6:30am. He never arrived at work and has never been heard from again. Later, his 1990 BMW was found locked and abandoned in the company parking lot.

Authorities learned he had withdrawn a four-figure sum of cash from his company savings account about a month before he went missing. They do not know why or whether it was related to his disappearance. According to his family, he was not having any personal or work problems, and it is uncharacteristic for him to leave without warning.

*(Mark at the time of his disappearance)*

At the time of his disappearance, Mark Tomich had brown hair, stood 5'9", and weighed 165 pounds. He is Caucasian with brown eyes, and scars on his left arm and upper lip. He has hair implants at his temples. As of this writing, he is fifty-five years old.

If you have any information regarding this case, you are urged to call the Indianapolis Police Department at 317-327-6613.

## Dora Maria Villarrea-Tolx

Seventy-three year old Dora Maria Villarrea-Tolx was last seen sitting on the back porch of her daughter's home on South Brandywine Court in Greenfield, Indiana at 11pm on June 2, 2007. She disappeared without any money or identification. She has never been heard from again. She had moved in with her daughter the week before. She had previously lived in Florida with her husband, who had recently passed away. Authorities believe she may have accepted a ride from a passing motorist near her daughter's home. She may have been trying to return to Florida. Her family says it is uncharacteristic for her to leave without warning or to be out of touch with them.

*(Dora at the time of her disappearance)*

At the time of her disappearance, Dora Villarrea-Tolx had black hair, stood 5'2", and weighed between 150 - 170 pounds. She was last seen wearing an orange shirt and shorts. She is Hispanic with brown eyes. She suffers from depression and dementia, and she may be withdrawn and confused as a result. As of this writing, she is eighty-four years old.

If you have any information regarding this case, you are urged to call the Hancock County Sheriff's Department at 317-477-1144.

## Wanda Elaine Washington

Twenty-five year old Wanda Elaine Washington was last seen at approximately 5am in Fort Wayne, Indiana on July 12, 1993. Her mother saw her get into a late model blue Chevrolet Camaro outside their home on south Hanna Street. But she did not take note of the vehicle's driver or license plate, because at the time nothing seemed amiss. Wanda has never been heard from again.

*(Wanda at the time of her disappearance)*

At the time of her disappearance, Wanda Washington had black hair, stood 5', and weighed 125 pounds. She was last seen wearing a white shirt, black pants, and black shoes. She was carrying a black purse. She is African-American with brown eyes, pierced ears, scars on the center of her forehead, and scars on her left earlobe. As of this writing, she is fifty years old.

If you have any information regarding this case, you are urged to call the Fort Wayne Police Department at 219-427-1230.

## Jodi Sue Huisentruit

Twenty-seven year old Jodi Sue Huisentruit was abducted from the parking lot of her apartment complex at around 4am on June 27, 1995 in Mason City, Iowa. She was an anchor/producer for KIMT-TV in Mason City at the time. She spoke to a coworker at the station at approximately 4am and said that she would be to work shortly. She has never been heard from again. Her coworkers became concerned when she had not shown up or called back to say she was running late. They contacted the police.

A pair of red dress shoes, a can of hair spray, a pair of earrings, and her key cars were found scattered around her red Mazda Miata in the apartment complex's parking lot. The inside of her apartment showed no signs of a struggle, however. Witnesses reported hearing a scream from the parking lot shortly after 4am. Authorities have followed numerous leads, but none of them have yet to lead to information as to her whereabouts.

In 2015, two witnesses came forward with details that form a connection between Jodi and a convicted serial rapist, who was living in the area at the time. Another witness came forward to say that as they were jogging past the apartment complex that morning, they saw a car speed away with its lights off. She was declared legally deceased in May 2001, although her remains have never been found.

*(Jodi at the time of her disappearance)*

At the time of her disappearance, Jodi Huisentruit had blonde hair, stood between 5'3" - 5'4", and weighed between 110 - 120 pounds. She is Caucasian with brown eyes. As of this writing, she is forty-nine years old.

If you have any information regarding this case, you are urged to call one of the following numbers:

*Mason City Police Department at 515-421-3636*

*Federal Bureau of Investigation (FBI) at 1-202-324-3000*

## Ethan Bert Kazmerzak

Twenty-two year old Ethan Bert Kazmerzak was last seen at a party on 190th Street in Hampton, Iowa in the early morning hours of September 15, 2013. He had gone out with friends to watch the Iowa State football game at a local bar, and then he went to a small party. He called his mother that evening and told her of his plans to go help his grandfather the next day between his shifts at the Windsor Theater, where he worked. He did not normally call his mother late at night, but the night he went missing he called her shortly after midnight. Her cell phone was on vibrate, however, and she did not get it. He did not leave a message. She awoke early the next morning and called him back but there was no answer. When she found out he did not show up for work, she began to get concerned. It was uncharacteristic for him to miss work and not call to say he was going to be late or absent.

Nothing was disturbed at his apartment, but his car was not there. It is a 2006 Volkswagen Jetta with Iowa plates AUZ 382. It is believed that the vehicle remains missing as well.

The last call that he made to his mother was traced to near the intersection of 190th Street and Olive Avenue. Aerial, land, and water searches in the following days and weeks offered no leads as to his whereabouts. His credit and debit cards have not been used since he went missing, nor has his cell phone.

*(Ethan at the time of his disappearance)*

At the time of his disappearance, Ethan Kazmerzak had blonde hair and a reddish-brown beard, wore eyeglasses, stood 5'5", and weighed between 150 - 185 pounds. He was last seen wearing a white/teal printed shirt with orange or peach-colored shorts. He is Caucasian with blue eyes and a red and blue Grateful Dead tattoo on his upper left arm. As of this writing, he is twenty-six years old.

If you have any information regarding this case, you are urged to call the Hampton Police Department at 641-456-2529.

## Jane M. Bousley

Seventy year old Jane M. Bousley was last seen at Angie's Hair Design in Winchester, Kentucky on October 19, 2001. She went to the salon to get her hair done, and the hair dresser said she seemed distracted. She may have been en route to Walmart or Lowe's when she left. She has never been heard from again. Her 1997 Mercury Tracer with Kentucky plates 157-BXR disappeared with her and has never been found.

*(Jane at the time of her disappearance)*

At the time of her disappearance, Jan Bousley had black hair, wore eyeglasses, stood 5'4", and weighed between 125 - 140 pounds. She is Caucasian with brown eyes, scars on her chest from open heart surgery, and scars on her scalp from a craniotomy. She has had a mitral valve replacement. She previously had two strokes and is susceptible to blood clots. She may be confused and disoriented due to her conditions. As of this writing, she is eighty-six years old.

If you have any information regarding this case, you are urged to call the Clark County Sheriff's Office at 859-744-4390.

## Albert Gary Mitchell

Sixty-five year old Albert Gary Mitchell was last seen on August 26, 2004 in Middletown, Kentucky. He has never been heard from again. His tan 1992 GMC minivan with Kentucky plates 270KDN disappeared with him and has never been found. He had been assaulted inside his home three weeks prior to his disappearance, although it is not known if is related to him going missing or not.

*(Albert at the time of his disappearance)*

At the time of his disappearance, Albert Mitchell had black hair, wore eyeglasses, stood between 6' - 6'2", and weighed 205 pounds. He was last seen wearing blue jeans, a blue denim shirt, black cowboy boots, a brown leather belt, and a gold horseshoe ring with one carat on his right ring finger. He is Caucasian with blue eyes and a partial denture plate. He has high blood pressure and a heart condition that requires medication that he does not have with him. He may go by his middle name or his initials A.G. As of this writing, he is seventy-nine years old.

If you have any information regarding this case, you are urged to call one of the following numbers:

*Bluegrass Crime Stoppers at 859-253-2020*

*Bourdon County Sheriff's Department at 859-987-2130*

*Kentucky State Police at 859-428-1212*

## Melvia Kaye Roarx

Twenty-eight year old Melvia Kaye Roarx was last seen on a grocery store security camera four miles from her home in Horse Branch, Kentucky on June 4, 2013. She went out to get cigarettes and cold drinks. The cameras filmed her buying drinks and then driving away in the direction of her home, but she never arrived and has never been heard from again. The white 2000 Dodge Caravan she was driving was later found abandoned eighty miles away at the 109 mile marker off Interstate 65 in Bullitt County, Kentucky. The driver's seat was pushed back as far as it would go, indicating that someone tall or large had been driving. Melvia, at under five-and-a-half foot, could not have reached the pedals. The windows were rolled down and her purse was inside, but her wallet was gone. The ignition key was broken and found in two pieces in different parts of the van. Her credit cards have not been used since she went missing. Her family does not believe she would have abandoned her four children.

*(Melvia at the time of her disappearance)*

At the time of her disappearance, Melvia Roarx had blonde hair, stood between 5' - 5'4", and weighed 100 pounds. She was last seen wearing a bright green tank top, patchwork denim shorts, black or blue flip flops, a gold ring with an opal, and a silver ring with a diamond cluster. She is Caucasian with blue eyes, pierced ears, a scar on her abdomen, and a scar on her upper right arm. She has the following tattoos: two dolphins in a heart shape on her lower back, Winnie the Pooh on her right forearm, the name Jamie on the base of her neck, and the letter L in Old English writing on her right leg. As of this writing, she is thirty-three years old.

If you have any information regarding this case, you are urged to call the Grayson County Sheriff's Office at 270-259-3024.

## Claude Shelton & Martha Sue Shelton

Thirty-seven year old Claude Shelton and his wife, twenty-seven year old Martha Sue Shelton, were last seen in Corbin, Kentucky on May 21, 1971. They put their three children to bed at their home in Gerry's Trailer Park on 18th Street and then left. Neither of them has ever been heard from again. Their white 1967 Ford Galaxie 500 with Kentucky plates 937 944 disappeared with them and has never been found.

It was originally thought they were headed for King's Truck Stop, around five miles from their home, but no one there reported seeing the couple or their vehicle the night they went missing. Their loved ones say it would be very unlike them to have abandoned their children. Foul play is suspected.

*(Claude and Martha at the time of their disappearances)*

At the time of his disappearance, Claude Shelton had brown hair, stood 5'6", and weighed 170 pounds. He is Caucasian with brown eyes. As of this writing, he is eighty-four years old.

At the time of her disappearance, Martha Shelton had light brown hair, stood between 5'2" - 5'4", and weighed between 125 - 135 pounds. She was last seen wearing a wedding band and a braided silver ring set with a blue stone. She is Caucasian with blue eyes. As of this writing, she is seventy-four years old.

If you have any information regarding this case, you are urged to call the Kentucky State Police at 606-878-6622.

## Robbin Lewis Slaughter

Thirty-six year old Robbin Lewis Slaughter was last seen by his wife on November 14, 1993 at their home on west 10th Street in Owensboro, Kentucky. He left to walk to Franey's Food Mart, five or six blocks away. Surveillance cameras do not show him inside the store, although an acquaintance reportedly saw him in the parking lot. He did not drive at the time and normally walked wherever he wanted to go. He was a regular customer at Franey's, coming in several times a week. His wife stated he had been acting normal prior to his disappearance, was in good health, and not having any problems that she knew of. Authorities do not believe he left of his own accord.

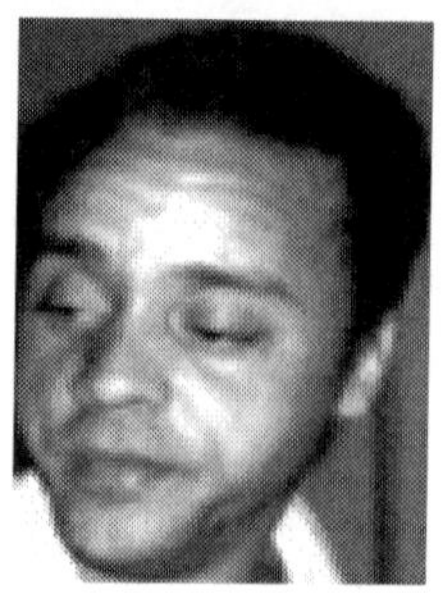

*(Robbin at the time of his disappearance)*

At the time of his disappearance, Robbin Slaughter had black hair cut above his ears, stood 5'7", and weighed 130 pounds. He was last seen wearing a short sleeve gray sports shirt with a black collar, jeans, a gray and blue sweater, and white tennis shoes. He is African-American with brown/hazel eyes. As of this writing, he is sixty-one years old.

If you have any information regarding this case, you are urged to call the Owensboro Police Department at 270-687-8888.

## Sharon Rose Sons

Twenty-eight year old Sharon Rose Sons was last seen in Lexington, Kentucky on October 20, 1993. She lived with her boyfriend on Cane Run Road. He stated she left to use the telephone at a laundromat in the Russell Cave Plaza and never returned. She has never been heard from again. Authorities suspect foul play.

*(Sharon at the time of her disappearance)*

At the time of her disappearance, Sharon Sons had blonde hair, stood 5'1", and weighed 98 pounds. She was last seen wearing a knee-length denim skirt, tennis shoes, a plain gold chain with a cross, a gold necklace that said Willie, and three or four rings. She is Caucasian with green eyes, a torn earlobe, a Caesarean section scar on her abdomen, a scar on the top of her head, and poison ivy scars on her arms and legs. She has a small partially-colored rose tattoo on her right ankle. Her nickname is Susie. As of this writing, she is fifty-three years old.

If you have any information regarding this case, you are urged to call one of the following numbers:

*Lexington – Fayette Urban County Division of Police at 859-258-3563*

*Kentucky State Police at 502-564-5230*

## Barbara Ann Blount

Fifty-eight year old Barbara Ann Blount was last heard from at 11:30am on May 2, 2008, when a neighbor spoke to her on the telephone at her residence on State Highway 1036 in rural Livingston Parish, Louisiana. She said she was cleaning out her kitchen cabinets. She has never been heard from again. When her nephew checked her house, the front door was open and Barbara's phone was lying on the floor with the battery pulled out. Her silver four-door 2006 Toyota Camry was found abandoned about a quarter of a mile from her home, on a dirt road twenty-five to thirty yards off the main road and hidden by trees.

She is a widow, who lived alone at the time, but she kept in touch with relatives and would not have disappeared on her own accord. Her family describes her as a cautious person who did not open her door to strangers and carried a gun when she went out to milk the cows. Investigators believe she was taken against her will, and foul play is suspected.

*(Barbara at the time of her disappearance)*

At the time of her disappearance, Barbara Blount had brown hair, wore eyeglasses, stood between 5'5" - 5'7", and weighed between 135 - 150 pounds. She was last seen wearing shorts and a tank top. She is Caucasian with hazel eyes. Her maiden name is Barber. As of this writing, she is sixty-seven years old.

If you have any information regarding this case, you are urged to call the Livingston Parish Sheriff's Office at 225-938-4323.

## Jim William "JW" Delaney

Seventy-eight year old Jim William "JW" Delaney was last seen in Pollock, Louisiana on February 21, 2012. He went duck hunting near a friend's home in the Flagon Creek area and never returned. An extensive search turned up no clues as to his whereabouts, and he has never been heard from again.

*(JW at the time of his disappearance)*

At the time of his disappearance, JW Delaney had white hair, stood 6'4", and weighed 250 pounds. He was last seen wearing a camo jacket, moccasin-style house shoes, and blue jeans. He was carrying a sixteen-gauge shotgun with the serial number 40493. He is Caucasian with green eyes. He suffers from Alzheimer's disease. He has had two previous strokes and takes medication. As of this writing, he is eighty-four years old.

If you have any information regarding this case, you are urged to call the Grant Parish Sheriff's Office at 318-627-3261.

## Donna Christine O'Banion

Twenty-five year old Donna Christine O'Banion was last seen leaving her waitressing job after finishing her shift at Southern Comfort on Airport Highway in Baton Rouge, Louisiana on the morning of October 23, 1985. When she did not arrive home, her mother reported her missing. She has never been heard from again.

*(Donna at the time of her disappearance)*

At the time of her disappearance, Donna O'Banion had brown hair, stood 5'6", and weighed 125 pounds. She was last seen wearing a cut-off tank top, jeans, and sandals. She is Caucasian with blue eyes, a tattoo of an eagle on her right shoulder blade, and a tattoo of a sun a cloud and a lightning bolt on her upper right arm. As of this writing, she is fifty-seven years old.

If you have any information regarding this case, you are urged to call the East Baton Rouge Sheriff's Office at 225-389-3800.

## Adrian Juan Planells

Twenty-three year old Adrian Juan Planells was last seen at Luc Eddie's Lounge on Mississippi Avenue in Kenner, Louisiana on September 24, 1989. He had gone to the lounge with friends, but after having only a couple of beers he told them he was going home. He was seen exiting the lounge, crossing the street, getting into his car and driving away. He never arrived home and has never been heard from again. His rusty bluish-green 1968 Chevrolet Camaro with Louisiana plates 816B554 disappeared with him and has never been found.

He had never been in trouble with the law, and still lived at home with his parents. He left behind all his clothes and other personal belongings, and his bank account has not been touched since he went missing. Authorities believe he met with foul play after leaving the lounge.

*(Adrian at the time of his disappearance)*

At the time of his disappearance, Adrian Planells had long brown hair, stood 5'4", and weighed 130 pounds. He is Hispanic with brown eyes. As of this writing, he is fifty-one years old.

If you have any information regarding this case, you are urged to call the Kenner Police Department at 504-466-4606.

**David Edward Carter**

Thirty-six year old David Edward Carter was last seen between 2pm and 3pm on December 14, 2004 leaving his place of work in Whiteford, Maryland. He got into a white 1993 Nissan pickup with two Caucasian males and has never been seen or heard from again. Foul play is suspected.

*(David at the time of his disappearance)*

At the time of his disappearance, David Carter had light brown hair and a mustache, stood 5'7", and weighed 175 pounds. He was last seen wearing a red sweatshirt under a short-sleeve orange shirt, blue jeans, white socks, and tan work boots. He is Caucasian with blue eyes, an H-shaped scar in the center of his chest, and a gap between his upper front teeth. He had previously fractured his left wrist. His nickname is Dave. As of this writing, he is fifty years old.

If you have any information regarding this case, you are urged to call the Maryland State Police at 410-838-4101.

## Marilyne Chamberlain

Sixty-five year old Marilyne Chamberlain was last seen riding on the Washington Metropolitan Area Transit Authority subway near Landover, Maryland on

November 2, 1998. She had been to the Pentagon Federal Credit Union in Washington, D.C., and then she paid a bill at a nearby Sears store. She has never been heard from again. Investigators believe she disappeared under suspicious circumstances.

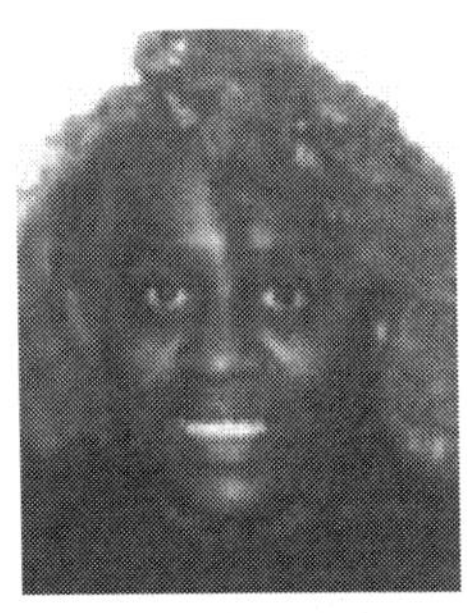

*(Marilyne at the time of her disappearance)*

At the time of her disappearance, Marilyne Chamberlain had gray hair, wore round brown/burgundy-framed eyeglasses, stood 5’3”, and weighed 145 pounds. She is African-American with brown eyes, pierced ears, and a scar on her upper left arm. Two of her upper molars are missing. As of this writing, she is eighty-five years old.

If you have any information regarding this case, you are urged to call the Prince George County Police Department at 301-699-2601.

## James Arthur Cole

Twenty-one year old James Arthur Cole was last seen in Severna Park, Maryland early on the morning of April 11, 1994. The previous evening, he and his brother went to the Shangri La restaurant and cocktail lounge, and then to the Gingerbread Man restaurant. His brother eventually went home, and James returned to the

Shangri La restaurant on Ritchie Highway. He left on foot at 1:30am, alone and visibly intoxicated, probably en route to the home he shared with his parents on Hodges Lane four blocks away. He never arrived at home and has never been heard from again. His family reported him missing twenty-four hours later after they searched for him in the neighborhood without success.

His loved ones do not believe he left of his own accord. He left behind all of his belongings. He was in a happy three year relationship with his girlfriend, and was employed at K & J Maintenance at the time. He never picked up his last paycheck.

*(James at the time of his disappearance)*

At the time of his disappearance, James Cole had shoulder-length brown hair, stood between 5'6" - 5'7", and weighed 140 pounds. He was last seen wearing a burgundy and green baseball shirt, blue jeans, a green Loyola baseball cap, and new low-cut beige and black hiking boots. He is Caucasian with brown eyes and a tattoo of a black widow spider on his right forearm. His nickname is Jimmy. As of this writing, he is forty-five years old.

If you have any information regarding this case, you are urged to call the Ann Arundel County Police Department at 410-222-3588.

## Mason Armani Gomez

Nineteen year old Mason Armani Gomez was last seen on Wilson Avenue not far from his apartment on Glenshannon Court in Baltimore, Maryland on February 13, 2016. He has never been heard from again. He left behind a baby girl and a girlfriend of six years. His family stated it is very uncharacteristic for him to leave without warning, and they believe he met with foul play.

*(Mason at the time of his disappearance)*

At the time of his disappearance, Mason Gomez had black hair and a mustache, stood 6', and weighed between 130 - 160 pounds. He was last seen wearing a black North Face jacket, a gray North Face sweater, gray North Face pants, and red and white Nike sneakers. He is African-America with brown eyes. As of this writing, he is twenty-one years old.

If you have any information regarding this case, you are urged to call the Baltimore County Police Department at 410-887-3943.

## Mary Kathryn Greene

Thirty-four year old Mary Kathryn Greene was last seen in Dundalk, Maryland at 6:30pm on December 10, 1966 when she went to the store. She never returned home and has never been heard from again. Her blue and white 1957 Ford station wagon with Maryland plates EX-7023 disappeared with her and has never been found. Foul play is suspected.

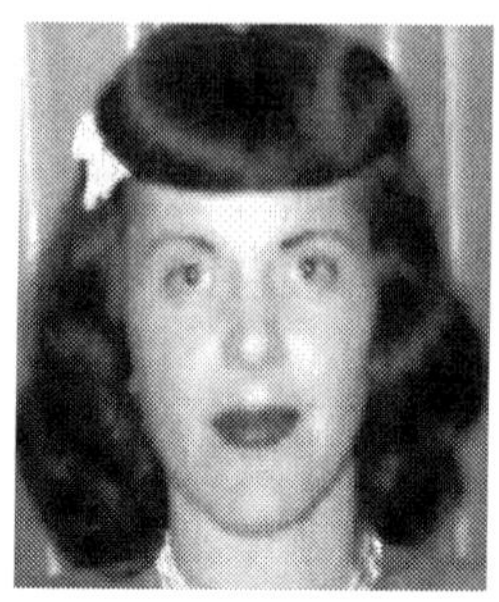

*(Mary at the time of her disappearance)*

At the time of her disappearance, Mary Greene had brownish-red hair, a fair complexion, a slender build, stood 5'8", and weighed 126 pounds. She was last seen wearing a blue or green waist-length lumber jacket with two breast pockets and a zipper and low-heeled shoes. She was carrying a two-tone brown purse. She is Caucasian with hazel eyes. As of this writing, she is eighty-six years old.

If you have any information regarding this case, you are urged to call one of the following numbers:

*Baltimore County Police Department at 410-887-3943*

*Metro Crime Stoppers at 1-866-7-LOCKUP or email a tip at www.metrocrimestoppers.org*

**John James Morris Jr.**

Thirty-seven year old John James Morris Jr. was last seen at approximately 11pm on July 30, 2007 in the driveway of his and his ex-boyfriend's residence on Whites Ferry Road in Dickerson, Maryland. The men had recently ended their relationship, and his ex-boyfriend was staying in a condo in Washington, D.C. John spoke to his mother on the telephone that day and sounded angry and distressed. He told her someone was coming to pick him up. A neighbor, who is believed to be the last person to see him, said he was in the driveway and appeared to be waiting on a ride. He has never been seen or heard from again. His family reported him missing on August 23th after he uncharacteristically missed several of his weekly telephone calls to them.

All of his belongings, his truck, and his beloved dog were left behind at his home. Neither his cell phone nor his credit card has been used since he went missing. He is considered to be missing under suspicious circumstances, and foul play is suspected. The theory that he was a victim of a hate crime has been ruled out.

*(John at the time of his disappearance)*

At the time of his disappearance, John Morris Jr. had graying brown hair, stood 6', and weighed 175 pounds. He was last seen wearing a gold chain, a watch, a red fleece jacket, and jeans. He is Caucasian with brown/hazel eyes, a cosmetically reconstructed nose, a piercing in his left ear, and a cap on a front tooth. He had previously broken his ankle. He has degenerative bone disease in one of his toes, ADHD, depression, and possibly bipolar disorder. He has a tattoo of a panther on his right forearm and a tattoo of a scorpion on his left shoulder. As of this writing, he is forty-eight years old.

If you have any information regarding this case, you are urged to call the Montgomery County Police Department at 301-840-2407.

## Tu Thi - Cam Tran

Twenty-four year old Tu Thi - Cam Tran was last seen on the evening of November 26, 1990 as she left the fine arts building at 8:30pm on the University of Maryland campus. She finished class at 6:45pm and had a conversation with another student in the university center. She appeared to be in good spirits at the time. She apparently never made it to her car and has never been heard from again. An extensive search of the university's 500-acre campus turned up no clues as to her whereabouts.

*(Tu Thi – Cam at the time of her disappearance)*

At the time of her disappearance, Tu Thi - Cam Tran had brown hair, stood 4'9", and weighed 90 pounds. She was last seen wearing a blouse, jeans, sneakers, and a scallop design necklace with white pearl beads and blue stones. She is Asian with brown eyes and is missing a toe. As of this writing, she is fifty-two years old.

If you have any information regarding this care, you are urged to call the UMBC Police Department at 410-455-3133.

## Lynn Burdick

Eighteen year old Lynn Burdick worked part-time as a clerk at The Barefoot Peddler Company Store in Florida, Massachusetts in 1982. The store was located on the corner of Route 2 and Central Shaft Road, just a few hundred yards from the Burdick family's residence. Lynn had been working at the store for three years. The owner called the store at approximately 8pm on the night of April 17, 1982 to check on Lynn, who was scheduled to close the store within an hour. She told the owner that a customer had just come in and she had to hang up to attend to them. She has never been heard from again.

Another customer entered the store approximately forty minutes later and found it abandoned with the door left open. He knew the Burdick family and called them to report her missing. Her open book and a half-empty soda were still on the counter, but her jacket and purse were gone. Cash underneath the counter was untouched, but $187 was missing from the cash register. Lynn would have been aware of the extra money, but an intruder would not have been. Authorities never believed she had been responsible for her own disappearance. One lead focused on an unidentified male who had attempted to abduct a girl from the Williams College Campus near Florida, Massachusetts approximately forty-five minutes before the store owner last spoke to Lynn.

*(Lynn at the time of her disappearance)*

At the time of her disappearance, Lynn Burdick had brown hair, wore eyeglasses, stood 5'4", and weighed 115 pounds. She was last seen wearing a McCann Vocational Technical High School class ring with a blue stone and either her name or her initials engraved on it. She is Caucasian with blue eyes. As of this writing, she is fifty-four years old.

If you have any information regarding this case, you are urged to call the Massachusetts State Police at 413-499-1112.

## Jennifer Kabura Mbugua

Thirty-one year old Jennifer Kabura Mbugua was last seen by a neighbor outside her apartment building on south Main Street in Fall River, Massachusetts on May 27, 2014. She was inside her car, shuffling through some papers, at the time. She left all her belongings behind, including her wallet and driver's license. She has never been seen or heard from again.

On May 28th, her gray Toyota Camry was found abandoned behind a Shell gas station off Route 1 in North Attleboro, Massachusetts. It had been left there between midnight and 3am. Her keys and one of her sandals were in a nearby dumpster.

*(Jennifer at the time of her disappearance)*

At the time of her disappearance, Jennifer Mbugua had black hair, stood 5'3", and weighed 140 pounds. She is African-American with brown eyes. She was born in Kenya. As of this writing, she is thirty-five years old.

If you have any information regarding this case, you are urged to call one of the following numbers:

*North Attleboro Police Department at 508-695-1212*

*Fall River Police Department at 508-676-8511*

**Charlita Sonya Harris**

Twenty-four year old Charlita Sonya Harris was last seen in Detroit, Michigan on Thanksgiving Day, November 28, 1991. She left to go to the store at 8pm that day and never returned. She has never been heard from again.

*(Charlita at the time of her disappearance)*

At the time of her disappearance, Charlita Harris had brown hair, stood 4'11", and weighed 110 pounds. She is African-American with brown eyes. Her nickname is Lita. As of this writing, she is fifty-one years old.

If you have any information regarding this case, you are urged to call the Detroit Police Department at 313-596-2221.

## Margie Ann Ranshaw

Twenty-nine year old Margie Ann Ranshaw was last seen in Barryton, Michigan on May 17, 1987. She left home to go buy a gallon of milk and never returned. A few weeks later, her vehicle was found abandoned at a hotel off Interstate 96 in Howell, Michigan.

*(Margie at the time of her disappearance)*

At the time of her disappearance, Margie Ranshaw had blonde hair, stood between 5'2" - 5'6", and weighed between 130 - 140 pounds. She is Caucasian with blue eyes and a small scar near her eyebrow. As of this writing, she is sixty years old.

If you have any information regarding this case, you are urged to call the Mecosta County Sheriff's Office at 231-592-0154.

## Robert Louis Vance

Thirty-nine year old Robert Louis Vance was last seen at 6:30am on June 12, 2003 at an acquaintance's residence on Burlingame Street in Detroit, Michigan. He left there en route to his own home to change clothes for work. He never arrived and has never been heard from again. His white four-door 1996 Cadillac DeVille with Michigan plates XCU341 disappeared with him and has never been found.

*(Robert at the time of his disappearance)*

At the time of his disappearance, Robert Vance was bald with a goatee, stood 5'10", and weighed 185 pounds. He was last seen wearing a round silver diamond stud earring set. He is African-American with brown eyes and a horizontal scar just above his left eyebrow. He may use the name Roscoe. As of this writing, he is fifty-four years old.

If you have any information regarding this case, you are urged to call the Detroit Police Department at 313-596-1040.

## Lisa Walton

Twenty-two year old Lisa Walton was last seen at her home on Pacific Avenue in Detroit, Michigan on January 21, 1986. That same day, her eleven month old son was found abandoned, but unharmed, in an alley on Pelkey Street. He was identified after his grandmother saw him on a news broadcast. It was at that time that they realized Lisa was missing.

*(Lisa at the time of her disappearance)*

At the time of her disappearance, Lisa Walton had brown hair, was pregnant, stood between 5'6" - 5'9", and weighed 160 pounds. She is African-American with brown eyes and pierced ears. As of this writing, she is fifty-four years old.

If you have any information regarding this case, you are urged to call the Aberdeen Police Department at 605-626-7003.

## Carla Beth Anderson

Twenty-three year old Carla Beth Anderson was last seen in Wadena, Minnesota on November 13, 1987. She was employed at a Hardee's restaurant and had just found out she had been named employee of the month. Her mother and stepfather took her out to eat that evening to celebrate. After dinner, they picked up some movies for her to watch, and then dropped Carla off at her apartment in the Greenwood Apartments. It has been established that she did make it safely inside her apartment. A cup of soda from the restaurant was found inside and one of the videos she had rented was in the VCR. Nothing was amiss, but her keys were gone. The door was locked from the outside. She has never been heard from again.

On the night of her disappearance, there had been a fire burning in a swamp on the outskirts of Wadena. She would have been able to see the fire from her window. Investigators theorize that she left home to get a better look at the fire and someone attacked and/or abducted her. However, there is no evidence to prove or disprove the theory.

That same evening, a brown Plymouth Horizon was stolen a couple of blocks from Carla's apartment building and it has never been recovered. But it is not known if the car theft is related to her going missing or not.

Carla's family stated that people in the area sometimes harassed her or attempted to take advantage or her, because she is mildly mentally disabled. However, she tried to lead a normal life and was proud to be independent enough to have a job and her own home. She also had a boyfriend, who lived in Lake Park, Illinois. Her family and her boyfriend have been ruled out as suspects in her case. Foul play is suspected.

*(Carla at the time of her disappearance)*

At the time of her disappearance, Carla Anderson had blonde hair, stood between 4'11" - 5', and weighed 80 pounds. She was last seen wearing a brown and orange Hardee's jacket, a white Pepsi and Mountain Dew sweatshirt with three bears on it, blue jeans, and pink sneakers. She is Caucasian with brown eyes and a half-inch scar over her right eye. As of this writing, she is fifty-four years old.

If you have any information regarding this case, you are urged to call the Wadena Police Department at 218-631-7700.

## Dawn Joy Carlson

Forty-three year old Dawn Joy Carlson was last seen in Karlstad, Minnesota at 10am on October 2, 2013.

She may have been en route to Badger or Brainerd, Minnesota at the time. She was driving a black four-door 2001 Mercury Sable with a dent in the passenger side door and Minnesota plates 743-ECY. The vehicle disappeared with her and has never been found. She left behind all of her belongings and her five pet dogs. Authorities are concerned for her safety.

*(Dawn at the time of her disappearance)*

At the time of her disappearance, Dawn Carlson had blonde hair, stood 5'6", and weighed 220 pounds. She was last seen wearing a black jacket, a sweatshirt, blue jeans, and a small pin with an angel. She is Caucasian with green eyes and a small scar on one of her knees. She suffers from Lyme disease, and her family believes the condition had been impairing her thought processes at the time she went missing. As of this writing, she is forty-seven years old.

If you have any information regarding this case, you are urged to call the Kittson County Sheriff's Department at 218-843-3535.

## Lucia Chilel Perez

Forty year old Lucia Chilel Perez was last seen in Worthington, Minnesota in late June 2011. She left with a Hispanic man who has a history of sexual and physical violence. The two were stopping at various businesses and applying for jobs. When the man returned to Worthington from Iowa on June 26th, he had a large scratch on his face. He said that Lucia had been detained in Hull, Iowa due to an immigration problem, but his story turned out to be false. Authorities processed her vehicle but could find no evidence pertaining to her disappearance. Investigators believe she may be in danger.

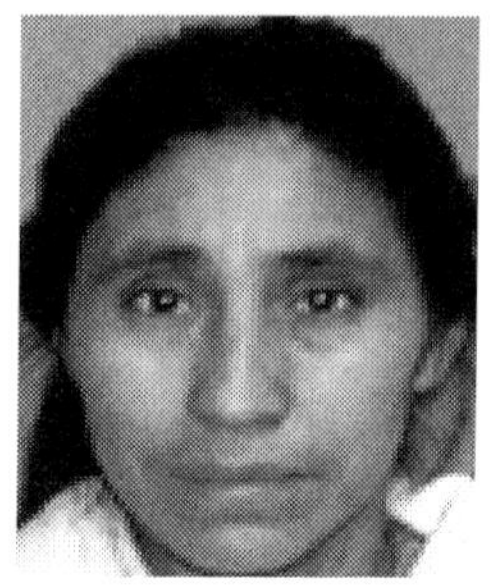

*(Lucia at the time of her disappearance)*

At the time of her disappearance, Lucia Perez had black hair, stood 5'1", and weighed between 120 - 140 pounds. She was last seen wearing a short sleeve black blouse with a white design and an ankle-length denim skirt. She was carrying a black backpack. She is Hispanic with brown eyes. She may use the alias name Mary Rodriquez Figueroa. As of this writing, she if forty-seven years old.

If you have any information regarding this case, you are urged to call the Worthington Police Department at 507-372-2136.

**Kelly L. Allen**

Twenty year old Kelly L. Allen was last seen at a female friend's apartment on Frost Avenue in Berkeley, Missouri on March 13, 2007. She was staying there for a few days. When her friend left for work, Kelly was there but she was gone by the time she came back. All of her belongings were left behind, including a tax return check for $2,000. On the day of her disappearance, she went to a job interview at a telemarketing company on Watson Road and made an appointment for a second interview. Authorities believe she is missing under suspicious circumstances and may be in danger.

*(Age Progression to 25)*

At the time of her disappearance, Kelly Allen had brown hair with micro-braided blonde extensions, stood 5'4", and weighed 165 pounds. She was last seen wearing a blue blazer, apple-bottom jeans, and sparkly silver shoes. She is African-American with hazel eyes and pierced ears. She has a tattoo of two brown eyes and a rose on her left shoulder and a tattoo of a half-moon behind her left ear. As of this writing, she is thirty-one years old.

If you have any information regarding this case, you are urged to call the St. Louis Metropolitan Police Department at 314-444-5338.

## Diana Jane Braungardt

Eighteen year old Diana Jane Braungardt was last seen leaving the Venture store in the Twin City Mall, where she worked part-time as a clerk, in Crystal City, Missouri on March 11, 1987. She was walking toward her family's yellow 1982 Ford Escort in the parking lot after finishing her shift at 10pm. She had told her coworkers that she needed to get home and study for a test. She never arrived home and has never been seen or heard from again. The car was still in the parking lot, but there was no trace of Diana. Authorities do not believe she ever made it to the vehicle.

Witnesses saw a man talking to her in the store parking lot before she disappeared. He is described as being Caucasian in his early twenties in 1987, about 5'10" with a medium build, and brown or black hair. The man has never been identified.

*(Diana at the time of her disappearance)*

At the time of her disappearance, Diana Braungardt had dark brown hair, stood between 5'6" - 5'7", and weighed 108 pounds. She was last seen wearing a Venture smock, bright turquoise pants, and a short black boy's coat. She is Caucasian with hazel eyes. As of this writing, she is forty-nine years old.

If you have any information regarding this case, you are urged to call the Crystal City Police Department at 314-937-4601.

## Byron Lee Davis

Fifty-three year old Byron Lee Davis was last seen leaving his residence in the vicinity of 57th Street and Bales Avenue in Kansas City, Missouri on May 18, 1993. He has never been heard from again. Authorities do not believe he left of his own accord, and both his family and investigators suspect foul play.

At the time of his disappearance, Byron Davis had black hair and a beard, stood 5'9", and weighed 175 pounds. He was last seen wearing a blue t-shirt, blue slacks, black shoes, and a navy blue cap. He is African-American with brown eyes. He is mentally disabled and is missing most of his teeth. His nickname is Joe. As of this writing, he is seventy-eight years old.

If you have any information regarding this case, you are urged to call the Kansas City Police Department at 816-234-5136.

## Cheryl Ann Kenney

Thirty year old Cheryl Ann Kenney was last seen at her job at the Quality Convenience Store on Business 71 Highway in Nevada, Missouri on the evening of February 27, 1991. She usually worked until midnight, but it was a slow night and she decided to close the store early. Her time card shows that she clocked out at 10pm and set the store alarm at 10:17pm. She never arrived at home and has never been heard from again. Her white Chevrolet was later found where she had parked it when she first arrived at work that day. The store's janitor left a few minutes before Cheryl had closed up. He said there were not any customers' cars in the parking lot when he left, but there was a male customer inside the store whom he did not recognize. The customer has not been identified and it is unknown whether or not he had anything to do with Cheryl's disappearance. Two witnesses in the area reported hearing a woman scream around the time she would have been leaving the store. But the witnesses did not go to the police until they read about the possible abduction. Her family, along with authorities do not believe she left of her own accord.

It is possible that Cheryl's disappearance is related to the abduction of two other Missouri women. Angela Hammond was abducted from a convenience store parking lot while talking to her boyfriend in a telephone booth on April 4, 1991. She has never been heard from again.

Trudy Darby was abducted from the convenience store where she worked in Macks Creek on January 19,

1991. In her case, $220 was stolen from the store. Two days later, her nude body was found in the Little Niangua River. She had been shot twice in the head. Two half-brothers were later convicted of Trudy's rape and murder, but no one has ever been charged in connection with Angela's abduction or Cheryl's disappearance.

*(Cheryl at the time of her disappearance)*

At the time of her disappearance, Cheryl Kenney had light brown hair bleached blonde at the tips, wore glasses with tan frames, stood between 5'6" - 5'7", and weighed 117 pounds. She was last seen wearing a blue pullover sweatshirt, a blue denim jacket, blue jeans, and white L.A. Gear sneakers. She is Caucasian with green eyes, a unique tooth pattern, mole removal scars on her chest and upper left arm, and a scar on her wrist. As of this writing, she is fifty-seven years old.

If you have any information regarding this case, you are urged to call the Nevada, Missouri Police Department at 417-448-2710.

## Cheryl Ann Scherer

Nineteen year old Cheryl Ann Scherer was last seen working her shift at Rhodes Pump-Ur-Own Station self-service gas station in Scott City, Missouri on April

17, 1979. She disappeared from the station sometime between 11:40am - 11:50am. She has never been seen or heard from again. Approximately $480 was also taken from the cash register. Authorities believe that Cheryl was abducted during a robbery. There were no witnesses to the robbery or her apparent kidnapping. Her car with the keys inside was still in the parking lot, and her purse and checkbook were still inside the station. While authorities thought she could have fallen victim to one or both serial killers Otis Toole and Henry Lee Lucas, there was never enough evidence to convict either in her case.

*(Age Progression to 58)*

At the time of her disappearance, Cheryl Scherer had red hair, stood between 5' - 5'1", and weighed 100 pounds. She was last seen wearing a light blue pullover sweater with white trim, a dark blue zip-up windbreaker with a thin white lining and the hood trimmed in white, brown corduroy pants, earrings, a silver ring with a tiny diamond, and a yellow gold necklace with a one-inch cross pendant. She is Caucasian with blue eyes, a mole half an inch from her navel, a dime-sized dark brown birthmark between her shoulder blades, and pierced ears. As of this writing, she is fifty-eight years old.

If you have any information regarding this case, you are urged to call the Scott County Sheriff's Office at 573-545-3525.

## Jonathan Williams

Twenty-eight year old Jonathan Williams was last seen at his home on Paseo Parkway in Kansas City, Missouri on June 6, 1994, just two days after he got married. The day before, he had hosted a small party at his house. He left to take a friend home and never returned. He called his wife in the early morning hours of June 6th, but what he said in the phone call is unknown. He has never been seen or heard from again. His black 1994 Ford Tempo with Missouri plates N3C885 disappeared with him and has never been found. He did not have anything with him, not even his wallet. His wife reported him missing that afternoon.

He was employed as a correctional officer at the Leeds County Jail and was a member of the United States Army Reserve. He had custody of his young daughter, and his family does not believe he would have left without warning. Foul play is suspected.

*(Jonathan at the time of his disappearance)*

At the time of his disappearance, Jonathan Williams was bald, stood 6', and weighed 200 pounds. He is African-American with brown eyes and a scar on his abdomen. His nicknames are Joe and Joey. As of this writing, he is fifty-two years old.

If you have any information regarding this case, you are urged to call the Kansas City Police Department at 816-234-5136.

## Dorothy Geneva Freeman

Twenty-six year old Dorothy Geneva Freeman was last seen in Missoula, Montana on September 7, 1970. She left her apartment at 9:30pm en route to her student teaching job in Hamilton, but never arrived. Her green and white 1960 Ford Fairmont with Montana plates 91315 disappeared with her and has never been found. Her family describes her as a responsible and deeply religious woman who would not have left without warning.

*(Dorothy at the time of her disappearance)*

At the time of her disappearance, Dorothy Freeman had brown hair, stood 5'8", and weighed 140 pounds. She is Caucasian with blue eyes. As of this writing, she is seventy-three years old.

If you have any information regarding this case, you are urged to call the Ravalli County Sheriff's Office at 406-375-6282.

## Jose Concepcion

Thirty-three year old Jose Concepcion was last seen in the vicinity of 57th Street and Kennedy Boulevard in West New York, New Jersey on June 24, 2002. He went to work that morning, and called his wife to check-in at 11:45am. He has never been heard from again. He was self-employed as a tow truck driver at the time. His black 2000 Chevrolet tow truck with red decals and New Jersey plates X8823G disappeared with him and has never been found.

*(Jose at the time of his disappearance)*

At the time of his disappearance, Jose Concepcion had brown hair, stood 5'9", and weighed 230 pounds. He is Hispanic with brown eyes and a scar on his forehead. He may use the last name Diaz. As of this writing, he is forty-eight years old.

If you have any information regarding this case, you are urged to call the West New York Police Department at 201-295-5011.

## William Joseph Jamison

Thirty-three year old William Joseph Jamison was last seen in Linden, New Jersey on March 27, 1981. He left his home in the Colfax Manor Apartments on St. George Avenue driving his company car, and went to a bowling alley on Stiles Street. Later, he went to St. George's dinner. He left the diner at approximately 1:30am and has never been seen or heard from again. The vehicle is a dark blue 1981 Ford LTD station wagon with New Jersey plates 861-PKY. It disappeared with him and has never been found.

*(William at the time of his disappearance)*

At the time of his disappearance, William Jamison had dark brown hair, stood 5'9", and weighed 220 pounds. He was last seen wearing a dark brown suede coat, a blue or white Oxford dress shirt, dress slacks, dress shoes, and a watch. He is Caucasian with green eyes, a half-inch scar on his right ear, and a one-inch scar under his chin. He wears a size 6.5 shoes. His nickname is Bill. As of this writing, he is seventy years old.

If you have any information regarding this case, you are urged to call the Roselle Park Police Department at 908-245-2300.

## Patrick Francis Carnes

Eighty-six year old Patrick Francis Carnes was last seen with his eight year old brown Akita Mix named Lucky in Wells, Nevada on April 13, 2011. He was driving his green Subaru Forester with Nevada plates when the Nevada Highway Patrol stopped him for a traffic violation at 9pm. He had been visiting relatives in Toledo, Ohio and was on his way back home to Reno, Nevada. When he spoke to the trooper, he indicated he was following a truck driver and that the trucker was going to Elko, Nevada. Patrick has never been heard from again, and the truck driver he claimed to be following has never been identified. Around 6am the following day, his vehicle was found abandoned in a rural area at the Pumpernickel Valley exit ramp off Interstate 80 near Winnemucca, Nevada. There was no sign of Patrick or Lucky. The vehicle had gas in it and was in operable condition, but it was stuck in some sagebrush and facing the wrong direction. His belongings, including his checkbook, were still inside it. There were no signs of a struggle and only one set of footprints leading away from the vehicle.

Strangely, Patrick's vehicle was found in the same place as sixty-two year old Judith Ellen Casida's 1991 Mazda pickup had been found when she disappeared on February 14, 2006. However, authorities have no evidence to suggest that the two cases are related.

*(Patrick and Lucky at the time of their disappearances)*

At the time of his disappearance, Patrick Carnes had gray hair, wore eyeglasses, stood between 5'11" - 6', and weighed 180 pounds. He was last seen wearing a tan jacket, a blue plaid shirt, tan or beige pants, tan canvas shoes, and a Toledo Mud Hens baseball cap. He is Caucasian with blue eyes. His nickname is Pat. As of this writing, he is ninety-three years old.

If you have any information regarding this case, you are urged to call the Humboldt County Sheriff's Office at 775-623-6419.

## Opal Marie Parsons

Eighty-one year old Opal Marie Parsons was last seen by her daughter at the residence they shared on Sir David Way in Las Vegas, Nevada at approximately 5am on August 30, 2007. She was supposed to have lunch with friends at 12:30pm that day, but she never arrived. When her daughter returned home from work at 2pm, her mother was gone. Her vehicle was still there with the keys inside it, and none of her personal belongings were missing besides her purse. There was no sign of forced entry into their home. Opal had left the television on and the door unlocked, with her key inserted in the lock.

She did not leave a note indicating where she had gone. She has never been heard from again.

According to her family, Opal did not normally walk anywhere, but instead preferred to drive her car where she wanted to go. It was also uncharacteristic for her to go somewhere without leaving a note. She was in good health at the time, and is described as an active social woman with several friends. She kept a strict routine at the time.

Opal's debit card was used at Sam's Town Casino in Las Vegas the day after she went missing. Her driver's license and Social Security card were found lying on the floor inside the casino. Authorities do not believe she used the card herself, however, because she was not seen on any of the casino's surveillance cameras. Investigators identified the man who used the card, but he is not considered a suspect in her disappearance. He said he had found her purse in a trash bin. Investigators believe Opal was lured away or abducted from her home by someone she knew and trusted.

*(Opal at the time of her disappearance)*

At the time of her disappearance, Opal Parsons had dyed blonde hair, stood 5'4", and weighed between 125 - 130 pounds. She was last seen wearing a diamond and ruby ring, a heavy gold chain with a gold nugget and a diamond pendant, and possibly a floor-length silky black and tan robe with abstract designs. She is Caucasian with brown eyes, surgical scars on her abdomen from a hysterectomy and a colon operation, and pierced ears. She wears an upper denture. She had previously broken her arm. As of this writing, she is ninety-two years old.

If you have any information regarding this case, you are urged to call the Las Vegas Metropolitan Police Department at 702-828-2907 or 702-828-5678.

## Abraham Romero Jimenez & Raquel Lucina Rodriguez

Seventy-four year old Abraham Romero Jimenez and his live-in girlfriend, fifty-four year old Raquel Lucina Rodriguez, were last seen at their residence in Roswell, New Mexico on April 19, 2015. Neither of them has been heard from since. They left their dogs at home without food or water, which is uncharacteristic of them. The couple's van was found abandoned and in working condition on the street about a mile from their home. Raquel's son stated that neither she nor Abraham had any enemies and that he could think of no one who would have wanted to hurt them. Authorities consider their disappearances suspicious and are concerned for their safety.

*(Abraham at the time of his disappearance)*

At the time of his disappearance, Abraham Jimenez had black hair, stood between 5'7" - 5'10", and weighed between 175 - 190 pounds. He is Hispanic with brown eyes. As of this writing, he is seventy-seven years old.

*(Raquel at the time of her disappearance)*

At the time of her disappearance, Raquel Rodriguez had black hair, stood 5'3", and weighed 160 pounds. She is Hispanic with brown eyes and pierced ears. As of this writing, she is fifty-seven years old.

If you have any information regarding this case, you are urged to call the Chaves County Sheriff's Office at 575-624-6500.

## **Pernell Lloyd Tewangoitewa**

Twenty-one year old Pernell Lloyd Tewangoitewa was last seen on May 29, 1998 driving his sister's 1988 Pontiac Subaru station wagon away from Gator's Bar & Grill in Farmington, New Mexico. He worked there as a bouncer. He only lived ten miles away but he never arrived home and has never been heard from again. On June 18th, the vehicle was found in a dry river wash in Choke Cherry Canyon, five miles northwest of Farmington. It had been burned. There was no sign of Pernell. Authorities believe he may have been the victim of a homicide, but his remains have not been found. No arrests have been made in his case.

*(Pernell at the time of his disappearance)*

At the time of his disappearance, Pernell Tewangoitewa had black hair, stood 6'2", and weighed 175 pounds. He was last seen wearing a blue shirt and blue jeans. He is Native American with brown eyes. He is of Navajo and Hopi Indian descent. As of this writing, he is forty-one years old.

If you have any information regarding this case, you are urged to call one of the following numbers:

*Farmington Police Department at 505-599-1010*

*San Juan County Sheriff's Department at 505-334-6108*

## Corrie Lynn Anderson

Thirty-six year old Corrie Lynn Anderson was last seen at Lake City Dodge on Washington Street in Jamestown, New York on October 28, 2008. She had stopped there to visit her boyfriend. She left the dealership at 1:10pm driving her dark blue 2005 Dodge Caravan. She missed a meeting at 3:15pm, and she also failed to pick up her son from school. Items found at her home suggest she returned there before she disappeared. Her van was found abandoned on October 30, in a rural wooden area off of Kortwright Road. It was parked out of view of the road and was about two miles from her home. Her purse disappeared with her and has never been found.

Corrie was in the process of divorcing her second husband at the time. They had been separated for approximately two years, and there was an order of protection against him after he had allegedly put a tracking device on her vehicle. Police searched his home and questioned him, but he is not being called a suspect or a person of interest in her case. Her boyfriend has been ruled out as well, because he was at work at the time. Her cell phone had been turned off since she went missing.

(Corrie at the time of her disappearance)

At the time of her disappearance, Corrie Anderson had blonde hair, wore small wire-rimmed glasses, stood 5'11", and weighed 170 pounds. She was last seen wearing a black leather jacket and black corduroy pants. She is Caucasian with green eyes, double-pierced ears, a scar in the center of her abdomen, and a surgical scar on her knee. As of this writing, she is forty-five years old.

If you have any information regarding this case, you are urged to call the New York State Police Troop A at 716-665-3113.

## William Anderson

Sixty-five year old William Anderson was last seen at approximately 7am on December 5, 2000 in Brooklyn, New York. He left from Venice Marina in his 23-foot blue and white Wellcraft boat, the Mary C, for a day of fishing. He spoke to his fiancée on the telephone and said he would return to shore at 3pm. He has never been heard from again. His boat disappeared with him and has never been found. An extensive search turned up no sign of him or the boat.

(William and his boat at the time of his disappearance)

At the time of his disappearance, William Anderson had graying brown hair and a mustache, wore eyeglasses, stood 6'1", and weighed 190 pounds. He was last seen wearing a blue jacket, a gray hooded sweatshirt, jeans, white sneakers, and a black plastic watch. He is Caucasian with brown eyes. As of this writing, he is eighty-three years old.

If you have any information regarding this case, you are urged to call the New York Police Department at 646-610-6914.

## Catherine Chiang

Fifty-eight year old Catherine Chiang was last seen near her apartment on Dudley Avenue in the Middletown section of the New York City borough of the Bronx on June 6, 1997. She has never been heard from again. Authorities searched her residence and found all her belongings, including her purse and credit cards. Foul play is suspected.

*(Catherine at the time of her disappearance)*

At the time of her disappearance, Catherine Chiang had black hair, wore eyeglasses, stood 5'7", and weighed 110 pounds. She was last seen wearing a black leather jacket or coat, blue jeans, and black shoes. She was carrying a black handbag. She is Asian with brown eyes. She is a native of Taiwan. As of this writing, she is seventy-nine years old.

If you have any information regarding this case, you are urged to call the New York Police Department at 646-610-6914.

## Bethanie Lynne Dougherty

Forty year old Bethanie Lynne Dougherty was last seen by her son between 10pm - 11pm on April 1, 2008. At around 6am the following morning, he noticed her missing. Her car and all of her belongings were left behind. Her clothes were laid out for work, and it appeared she had left wearing only pajamas.

Neighbors heard a woman screaming in the area between 3am and 3:30am and called police, but the responding officers could find nothing amiss. And her son had been in the house all night and had not heard or seen anything out of the ordinary.

Coincidently, Bethanie's cousin, Maria Greene-Ware, was reported missing in June 1998. Two weeks later, police found her body in her own apartment. She had been dead for months. Her death was considered suspicious but due to the extreme state of decomposition, investigators could not determine a cause of death. No one has been named a person of interest or been charged with Maria's murder. It is not known whether or not Maria's homicide has anything to do with Bethanie's disappearance. Her loved ones believe she was taken against her will.

*(Bethanie at the time of her disappearance)*

At the time of her disappearance, Bethanie Dougherty had red hair, stood between 5'9" - 5'10", and weighed 160 pounds. She was last seen wearing a solid purple or purple and white pajama top and purple pajama bottoms with designs on them. She is Caucasian with blue eyes, a gap between her upper teeth on the left side of her jaw, and five piercings in each ear. She has the following tattoos: a vine with flowers on her left ankle, a purple butterfly over tribal markings on her lower back, and three Chinese scroll symbols on her upper back. She wears eyeglasses, but she left them behind. Her nicknames are Buffy or Beth, and her maiden name is Curtis. As of this writing, she is fifty years old.

If you have any information regarding this case, you are urged to call one of the following numbers:

*Broome County Sheriff's Office at 607-778-2053*

*Federal Bureau of Investigation (FBI) at 1-202-324-3000*

## Colin W. Gillis

Eighteen year old Colin W. Gillis was last seen in Tupper Lake, New York on March 11, 2012 after he got into an altercation and left a party at a private residence on Paskungameh Road. A passing motorist saw him at 1:45am walking southbound on State Route 3 near the Franklin/St. Lawrence County line, towards the town of Piercefield. He has never been heard from again. His mother reported him missing at 5:30pm. Searchers found his driver's license near the county line, but there was no sign of him.

He was studying pre-medicine at New York State University and was on Spring Break at the time. It is uncharacteristic for him to leave without warning, and his family believes he is in danger.

*(Colin at the time of his disappearance)*

At the time of his disappearance, Colin Gillis had blonde hair, stood 6', and weighed 170 pounds. He was last seen wearing a men's size medium white short-sleeve American Eagle v-neck shirt with black stripes, size 34/32 blue boot-cut Levis jeans, size 10 red high-top Nike Air sneakers, and an orange L.L. Bean backpack containing a reversible black and red L.L. Bean coat. He is Caucasian with blue eyes and a scar on his left shoulder blade. As of this writing, he is twenty-four years old.

If you have any information regarding this case, you are urged to call the New York State Police at 518-897-2000.

## Audrey May Herron

Thirty-one year old Audrey May Herron was last seen at 11pm on August 29, 2002 in Catskill, New York. She had just left her job at the Columbia-Greene Long Term Health Care Facility in the Jefferson Heights area. The drive from her place of employment to her home in Freehold, New York was about fifteen minutes. On the night she went missing, there was fog and rain in the area and she may have taken a shortcut to avoid it. She was supposed to arrive home at 11:30pm, but she did not and has never been heard from again. Her husband reported her missing at 6am the next morning.

She was driving her black 1994 Jeep Grand Cherokee with New York plates X233UV. The vehicle had some minor damage to the front passenger side bumper. It disappeared with her and has never been found.

She has not used her cell phone or her credit cards since she went missing. Her case is now being investigated as a homicide, even though there is no proof that she is in fact deceased. There have been no suspects or persons of interest named.

*(Audrey at the time of her disappearance)*

At the time of her disappearance, Audrey Herron had light brown hair, smoked cigarettes, stood 5', and weighed 105 pounds. She was last seen wearing a blue turtleneck, dark green scrubs, a yellow gold necklace with a pendant reading #1 Mom, and a watch with a white leather band and white metal face. She is Caucasian with hazel eyes, a scar on her right thumb that covers a portion of her hand, and a mole on the inside of her right knee. She may wear eyeglasses. As of this writing, she is forty-seven years old.

If you have any information regarding this case, you are urged to call the New York State Police at 518-622-8600.

## Robert J. Long

Sixty-two year old Robert J. Long was last seen in Long Island, New York on the afternoon of December 21, 2010. He left his home on Hillsdale Avenue to go to the nearby Miller Place Wine & Liquor Store on Route 25A. He made it to the store and bought a bottle of liquor, but he never returned home and has never been heard from again. He was carrying little to no cash. He had his cell phone but not the charger. His off-white 2007 Chrysler PT Cruiser with a yellow Support the Troops ribbon decal on the back and New York plates EEH4237 disappeared with him and has never been found. Foul play is suspected.

*(Robert at the time of his disappearance)*

At the time of his disappearance, Robert Long had brown hair and a graying beard, wore eyeglasses, stood between 6' - 6'2", and weighed between 270 - 280 pounds. He was last seen wearing a plaid flannel shirt, a black t-shirt, sweatpants, and moccasins. He is Caucasian with blue eyes. He has diabetes. His nickname is Bob. As of this writing, he is seventy years old.

If you have any information regarding this case, you are urged to call the Suffolk County Police Department at 631-852-6000.

## Bambi Lyn Madden

Thirty-one year old Bambi Lyn Madden was last seen walking away from her residence on Winding Way in Binghampton, New York at 11pm on January 11, 2006. She said she was going to a convenience store to buy beer, but she was not seen on the surveillance footage at any local stores the night she went missing. She was only carrying $5 in cash at the time. She has never been heard from again. Although there is no hard evidence of foul play, the possibility has not been ruled out.

*(Bambi at the time of her disappearance)*

At the time of her disappearance, Bambi Madden had blonde hair, smoked cigarettes and drank beer, wore eyeglasses for reading, stood between 5'4" - 5'8", and weighed 110 - 115 pounds. She was last seen wearing a size medium dark-colored puffy jacket, size 3 black jeans, size 6 black Timberland boots, gold earrings, and a gold ring with a red stone. She is Caucasian with blue/hazel eyes, pierced ears, and a scar on her right hand. She has the following tattoos: a unicorn with a crescent moon on her right thigh, a flower and a rainbow on her left shoulder, a rose on her right breast, a guitar with music notes on her right ankle, and a guitar with the name Tommy on her right shoulder, and the letters SWF, CMG, and TOM on her left shoulder. Her nickname is Bam Bam. As of this writing, she is forty-three years old.

If you have any information regarding this case, you are urged to call the Binghamton Police Bureau at 607-772-7080.

## Stacy A. Pennant

Twenty-one year old Stacy A. Pennant went to the movies with a friend during the evening of February 9, 1995 in Canarsie in the New York City borough of

Brooklyn. She was last seen dropping her companion off on east 85th Street between Avenue M and Avenue N in Canarsie at 11:30pm. She has never been heard from again. She was driving her blue 1990 Honda Civic Del Sol with New York plates E478RT that she had only recently purchased. The vehicle disappeared with her and has never been found.

The friend she was with that night said she had acted normally and appeared to be in good spirits. She was a business student at Queensborough Community College and worked nights as a cargo agent for Delta Airlines at Kennedy International Airport. She is described as a responsible individual who did not have a drug or alcohol problem or any other issues in her life which might have caused her to disappear.

*(Stacy at the time of her disappearance)*

At the time of her disappearance, Stacy Pennant had black hair, stood between 5' - 5'1", and weighed 117 pounds. She was last seen wearing a green ski jacket, gray sweatpants, and white shoes. She is African-American with brown eyes and a scar on her left eyebrow. As of this writing, she is forty-four years old.

If you have any information regarding this case, you are urged to call the New York Police Department at 646-610-6914.

## Roger Jermaine Chambers

Thirty-four year old Roger Jermaine Chambers was last seen at a gas station talking to a friend along Highway 211 outside of Red Springs, North Carolina on September 4, 2010. He had left his home on Army Road in Raeford at 6:15pm. He said he had an appointment in the Red Springs area, but he didn't say exactly where or with whom. Some believe he may have been going to see someone who owed him money. His wife spoke to him briefly on the phone after he left home. She tried to call him at 9:45pm, but the call went straight to voicemail. She eventually fell asleep and when she woke up at 2am, he still wasn't home. He has never been heard from again.

His green 1993 Toyota Camry with North Carolina plates YZF-4849 disappeared with him and has never been found. The car has chrome rims, lightly-tinted windows, paint peeling off the hood, and dents in the passenger side. Foul play is suspected.

*(Roger at the time of his disappearance)*

At the time of his disappearance, Roger Chambers had black hair and a mustache, stood 5'11", and weighed between 140 - 185 pounds. He was last seen wearing a black polo shirt with a red logo, black shorts, red sneakers, and a gold band. He was carrying a money clip. He is African-American with brown eyes, scars on his right leg and both shoulders, and a mole on the back of his right leg. His nickname is Jay. As of this writing, he is forty-two years old.

If you have any information regarding this case, you are urged to call the Hoke County Sheriff's Department at 910-875-5111.

## Troy Lee Jacobs

Twenty-one year old Troy Lee Jacobs was last seen at a BP service station along Highway 211 in Red Springs, North Carolina during the early morning hours of February 26, 1996. He was getting into a black Pontiac Grand Prix with multiple unidentified occupants. He has never been heard from again. He had told his father earlier that day that he was having some trouble with someone and was concerned for his safety. Investigators believe he was taken against him will.

*(Troy at the time of his disappearance)*

At the time of his disappearance, Troy Jacobs had dark brown hair with a mustache and a goatee, stood 5'6", and weighed 130 pounds. He was last seen wearing a long-sleeve blue and white zip-up shirt, black jeans, a

Tar Heels baseball cap, and size 9 white Nike sneakers. He is Native American with brown eyes. As of this writing, he is forty-four years old.

If you have any information regarding this case, you are urged to call one of the following numbers:

*Hoke County Sheriff's Department at 910-875-5111*

*North Carolina State Bureau of Investigation (NCSBI) at 919-662-4500*

## Stephen Victor Meeks

Thirty-two year old Stephen Victor Meeks was last seen in Reidsville, North Carolina on November 24, 1988. His wife stated they had had an argument and he left at 6pm. The couple's three children, however, said they had not seen their dad at all that evening. His sister reported him missing on December 4th. His black 1973 Ford truck with North Carolina plates CTS7429 disappeared with him and has never been found.

*(Stephen at the time of his disappearance)*

At the time of his disappearance, Stephen Meeks had dark brown hair, stood between 5'6" - 5'8", and weighed 175 pounds. He is Caucasian with blue eyes and a tattoo on his left arm of an orange Tasmanian devil with his initials S.V.M. underneath. His nickname is Steve. As of this writing, he is sixty-one years old.

If you have any information regarding this case, you are urged to call the Rockingham County Sheriff's Office at 336-634-3238.

## Kenneth Earl Mohler

Seventy year old Kenneth Earl Mohler was last seen in Newton, North Carolina on August 17, 2012. He worked third shift as a maintenance employee at Gregory Wood Products on Woodtech Drive. He texted his wife at 7:30pm and then his boss at 8:05pm, saying he had finished a waterline repair. He has never been heard from again. The next morning, his truck was found in the parking lot of the business. His keys and cell phone were lying in the dirt near the truck and his glasses were in the bed of the truck. There were signs of a struggle but no bloodstains present. Foul play is suspected. Both authorities and his family believe he was taken against his will.

*(Kenneth at the time of his disappearance)*

At the time of his disappearance, Kenneth Mohler was bald, wore eyeglasses, stood 5'5", and weighed 190 pounds. He was last seen wearing a white or gray t-shirt, blue jeans, and mid-calf work boots. He is Caucasian with hazel eyes. His nickname is Ken. As of this writing, he is seventy-five years old.

If you have any information regarding this case, you are urged to call the Catawba County Sheriff's Office at 828-465-8345.

## April Michelle Pickens

Twenty-nine year old April Michelle Pickens was last seen at the Pisgah View Apartments where she lived in Asheville, North Carolina on December 27, 2011. She told her sister that she was going to meet an unidentified male friend. She has never been heard from again. She did not have a vehicle at the time. It is uncharacteristic for her to leave without warning.

*(April at the time of her disappearance)*

At the time of her disappearance, April Pickens had black hair, stood 5'4", and weighed 155 pounds. She is African-American with brown eyes, a scar on her upper right arm, and pierced ears. She has the following tattoos: the name Eric on her upper back, Chinese characters on her left breast, and a Gemini sign on her right thigh. As of this writing, she is thirty-five years old.

If you have any information regarding this case, you are urged to call the Asheville Police Department at 828-259-5923.

## Tyarra Cacique Williams

Nineteen year old Tyarra Cacique Williams was last seen at the Stoneybrook Apartments off Webster Road in Greensboro, North Carolina at 8:30pm on January 7, 2016. She walked away from the apartment complex with friends. Her phone's GPS indicated she did arrive at a friend's apartment in the same complex and was on her way home when she disappeared. She never returned home and has not been heard from since.

She was within a week of starting classes at Guilford Technical College when she went missing. She and her mother had plans to go shopping for textbooks and a laptop the following day. Her family says it is uncharacteristic of her to leave without warning. Authorities believe she is missing under suspicious circumstances and may have been the victim of foul play.

*(Tyarra at the time of her disappearance)*

At the time of her disappearance, Tyarra Williams had brown hair, stood 5'5", and weighed 120 pounds.

She was last seen wearing a pink shirt, a black North Face jacket, dark blue Levis jeans, white Jordans sneakers with blue and green trim, and a royal blue knit cap. She is African-American with brown eyes, a piercing in her left nostril, and a nickel-size burn scar on her right wrist. As of this writing, she is twenty-one years old.

If you have any information regarding this case, you are urged to call the Greensboro Police Department at 336-373-2222.

## Shaniece Mona Briggs

Twenty-six year old Shaniece Mona Briggs was last seen at her apartment on east Long Street in eastern Columbus, Ohio on June 19, 2013. She walked out the back door at 1am, taking her wallet and cell phone. She did not take her purse or her keys, however. She left the door unlocked with her four young children still inside. A neighbor reported seeing her being pushed into a black car parked in front of the apartment complex. She has never been heard from again, and there has been no activity on any of her financial accounts. Foul play is suspected.

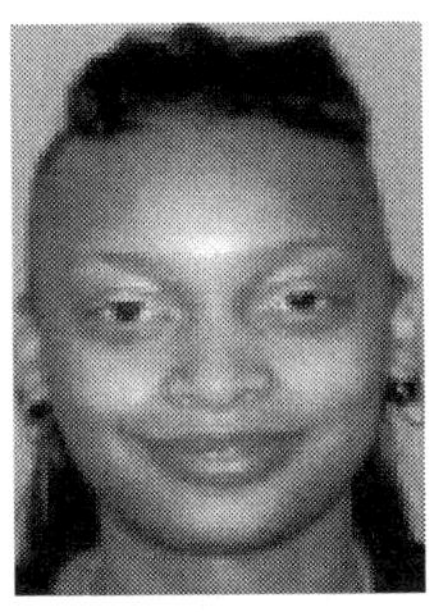

*(Shaniece at the time of her disappearance)*

At the time of her disappearance, Shaniece Briggs had black hair, stood between 5'3" - 5'5", and weighed between 130 - 140 pounds. She was last seen wearing a pink and gray shirt and black sweatpants. She is African-American with brown eyes, pierced ears, an upper lip piercing on the right side, and a tattoo of a crown with a name on the left side. As of this writing, she is thirty-one years old.

If you have any information regarding this case, you are urged to call the Columbus Police Department at 614-645-4545.

## Jonni Clemett

Forty year old Jonni Clemett had attended a baseball game between the Cleveland Indians and the Detroit Tigers in Cleveland, Ohio on May 27, 2001. She parked her vehicle in the parking lot of The Little Bar on Frankfort Avenue during the day. She returned to the location after the game ended. She was last seen leaning against her black four-door 2000 Dodge Neon with Ohio plates CQY-5786. A witness told authorities that it appeared as if Jonni was having trouble breathing at the time. She has never been heard from again. Her vehicle disappeared with her and has never been found. She left all her personal belongings behind, and there has been no activity on either her bank account or her credit cards since she went missing.

*(Jonni at the time of her disappearance)*

At the time of her disappearance, Jonni Clemett had blonde hair, wore eyeglasses, stood between 5'7" - 5'10", and weighed between 150 - 200 pounds. She was last seen wearing a leather Tribe jacket and jeans. She is Caucasian with blue eyes, a unicorn tattooed on her shoulder blade, and a tattoo of Chief Wahoo on one of her ankles. As of this writing, she is fifty-six years old.

If you have any information regarding this case, you are urged to call the Cleveland Police Department at 216-623-5200 or 216-623-5227.

## Shaylene Marie Farrell

Eighteen year old Shaylene Marie Farrell was last seen leaving her family's residence on Haverhill Drive in Piqua, Ohio at approximately 10am on August 8, 1994. She planned to run a quick errand to buy some tea at the nearby Pick - N - Save grocery store on Covington Avenue, where she worked part-time. She never returned home and has never been heard from again. She was reported missing after she did not show up for her 7pm shift at work. Her mother's car, which she had been driving, was found in the parking lot later in the day. There were no clues in or around the vehicle as to

Shaylene's whereabouts. She had no money, clothing, or identification with her when she went missing.

*(Shaylene at the time of her disappearance)*

At the time of her disappearance, Shaylene Farrell had dark brown hair, smoked cigarettes, stood 5'3", and weighed 135 pounds. She was last seen wearing a boy's white t-shirt with the words No Fear in blue lettering on the front, blue Piqua High School shorts, and black sandals. She was carrying a blue sapphire and diamond heart-shaped key ring with approximately five keys. She is Caucasian with hazel eyes, pierced ears, a mole under her lower lip, a birthmark on her left thigh above the knee, and a scar on her right leg above the knee. Four of her teeth are missing, and she has filings in eleven others. She may wear glasses. As of this writing, she is forty-one years old.

If you have any information regarding this case, you are urged to call the Piqua Police Department at 937-778-2027.

## Jesse Howard Flaugher

Eighty-five year old Jesse Howard Flaugher was last seen leaving his sister's house in Brookville, Ohio on October 2, 2006. He was driving his red 1989 Buick

LeSabre with Ohio plates DKL3867. The vehicle disappeared with him and has never been found. Prior to his disappearance, he had believed someone was out to get him. It is not known if his fears were rational or if he was suffering from paranoia.

*(Jesse at the time of his disappearance)*

At the time of his disappearance, Jesse Flaugher had graying red hair, stood 5'11", and weighed 195 pounds. He is Caucasian with blue eyes. He suffers from depression and a heart condition. As of this writing, he is ninety-seven years old.

If you have any information regarding this case, you are urged to call the Brookville Police Department at 937-833-2001.

## Christopher Lee Haas

Thirty-seven year old Christopher Lee Haas was last seen at the R & R Grocery on Greasy Ridge Road in Scottown, Ohio at 3pm on July 15, 2010. He was supposed to be on his way home, but he never arrived. The next day, his car was found abandoned on a rural road at Johns Creek. His girlfriend of fifteen years says that he was well-liked, had no enemies, and was not involved with drugs. It is uncharacteristic for him to drop out of sight for any extended period of time. His loved ones fear he came to harm.

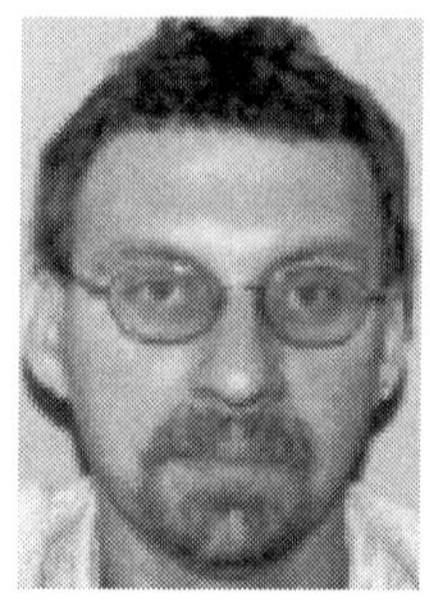

*(Christopher at the time of his disappearance)*

At the time of his disappearance, Christopher Haas had brown hair, wore eyeglasses, stood 5'11", and weighed 185 pounds. He was last seen wearing camouflage shorts, flip flops, and an earring. He had a blue t-shirt with him but he was not wearing it. He was carrying his wallet, a keychain with his name on it, and a silver cigarette lighter. He is Caucasian with brown/hazel eyes, a piercing in his left ear, skin discolorations on his buttocks and chest, and a tattoo on his left arm. He has scars on his right finger, his hand, his arm, and his head. He had previously fractured his ribs. He suffers from chronic back pain. His nickname is Chris. As of this writing, he is forty-five years old.

If you have any information regarding this case, you are urged to call the Lawrence County Sheriff's Office at 740-532-3525.

## Charles E. Koch

Nineteen year old Charles E. Koch was last seen at a trailer park in Ravenna, Ohio at 3:30pm on July 14,

1983. He had just completed his paper route. Two children saw him talking to a Caucasian man in a blue compact car. He has never been seen or heard from again.

*(Charles at the time of his disappearance)*

At the time of his disappearance, Charles Koch had blonde hair, stood 5'8", and weighed 120 pounds. He was last seen wearing a blue t-shirt with a bowling design, blue jeans, brown suede oxford shoes, and a gold watch. He is Caucasian with blue eyes. As of this writing, he is fifty-four years old.

If you have any information regarding this case, you are urged to call the Portage County Sheriff's Office at 330-296-5100.

## John J. Markley Jr. & Shelly Renee Markley

Thirty-six year old John J. Markley Jr. and his wife, thirty-one year old Shelly Renee Markley, were last seen at their home on Greenville Road in rural Bristolville, Ohio on December 15, 1995. Their five children went to school that morning, and when they returned home they found the house unlocked and their parents gone. Their red and silver Chevrolet pickup was also gone, and they had not left a note. A gun cabinet upstairs was found open, and a small safe in the master bedroom was also open. Birth certificates and other papers were scattered around the room. The beds were unmade and some of the couple's clothing was on top of the bed. A coffeepot in the kitchen was still on. In the garage, the tarps that normally covered John's prized 1978 Corvette were missing. Shelly's cigarettes and lighter were on the kitchen counter, and John's wristwatch was on a shelf above the stove. They normally had those items with them when they left the house.

The children initially believed their parents would return in a short time. They went to their aunt and uncle's house nearby and waited. The aunt and uncle reported John and Shelly missing at 12:30am. Their truck was later found locked and abandoned in the parking lot of a store in Bristolville, about ten miles from their home. The keys were missing, but their cell phone was inside the cab. A semi-truck tire and the Corvette's tarps were in the bed of the couple's truck.

The last transaction on their checking account was made at 10:36am on the day they went missing, approximately two hours after they were last seen by their children. A personal check for $1,000 made out for cash and signed by Shelly was cashed at Bank One in Bloomfield, Ohio. The bank teller at the drive-through window said she remembered seeing the couple pull up in their pickup. John was driving and Shelly was sitting between her husband and another man, whom the teller was neither able to describe nor identify. Authorities suspect the couple met with foul play.

*(John at the time of his disappearance)*

At the time of his disappearance, John Markley Jr. had brown hair, stood 5'10", and weighed between 150 - 170 pounds. He is Caucasian with green eyes, a mole and a scar on his back, and a scar on his right forearm. As of this writing, he is fifty-eight years old.

*(Shelly at the time of her disappearance)*

At the time of her disappearance, Shelly Markley had brown hair, stood 5'4", and weighed 125 pounds. She was last seen wearing stud earrings and a round gold ring with two diamonds. She is Caucasian with blue eyes, freckles, and pierced ears. As of this writing, she is fifty-four years old.

If you have any information regarding this case, you are urged to call the Trumbull County Sheriff's Department at 330-675-2540.

## Phillip Jason "PJ" Modlin

Twenty-six year old Phillip Jason "PJ" Modlin was last seen at approximately 8:30am on February 17, 2004 at his residence on Marsha Lane in Dayton, Ohio. He has never been heard from again. His family does not believe he left of his own accord.

*(PJ at the time of his disappearance)*

At the time of his disappearance, PJ Modlin had black hair, stood between 5'9" - 5'11", and weighed 230 pounds. He was last seen wearing a white t-shirt, a yellow jersey, blue jeans, sneakers or Timberland boots, a black and white baseball cap, and diamond stud earrings set in gold. He is African-American with brown eyes, a dark mark on his left thigh, pierced ears, a birthmark on his neck, and tattoos on both calves and both arms. As of this writing, he is forty years old.

If you have any information regarding this case, you are urged to call the Dayton Police Department at 937-333-2677.

## Robert Stephen Mohney

Twenty-nine year old Robert Stephen Mohney was last seen at his residence on Central College Road in Westerville, Ohio on July 18, 1996. He was in the process of eating dinner when he left his home, leaving his food on the table. He also left his wallet behind. His roommate said his behavior moments before he left was uncharacteristic. He was reported missing two days later. His red Pontiac Firebird was found parked above the Hoover Reservoir a few days after he was reported missing. Authorities believe he met with foul play, but no one has been charged in his case.

*(Robert at the time of his disappearance)*

At the time of his disappearance, Robert Mohney had brown hair, stood 5'11", and weighed 190 pounds. He is Caucasian with blue eyes, a scar on his right thigh, and a scar on his right finger. His nickname is Rob. As of this writing, he is fifty-one years old.

If you have any information regarding this case, you are urged to call the Westerville Police Department at 614-901-6481 or 614-882-7444.

## Catherine Parisi

Twenty-five year old Catherine Parisi was last seen on Clifton Boulevard in Cleveland, Ohio on April 18,

1997. She worked as a professional escort at the time. That night she went to an address in Parma, Ohio. At 6:30pm, she called the escort service she worked for and said that no one answered the door at the designated address. She has never been heard from again. The next day, her 1991 Chevrolet Lumina was found in the parking lot of a shopping center on Pearl Road with the keys inside and $350 cash in the console. The phone call from her prospective client was traced to a pay phone outside a Cleveland donut shop.

A few months before her disappearance, she had been violently attacked and robbed at gunpoint. The assailant tried to kill her by suffocating her with a plastic bag. She survived and the assailant was indicted for attempted murder, aggravated robbery, and felonious assault. Her assailant was a convicted drug trafficker. When Catherine went missing, he was out on bond, but it is unknown whether or not he had anything to do with her disappearance. Foul play is suspected.

*(Catherine at the time of her disappearance)*

At the time of her disappearance, Catherine Parisi had brown hair, stood 5’9”, and weighed 140 pounds. She was last seen wearing a black leather jacket, a gray button-down sweater, and blue jeans. She is Caucasian with brown eyes. Her nickname is Kathy. As of this writing, she is forty-six years old.

If you have any information regarding this case, you are urged to call the Cleveland Police Department at 216-623-5118.

## Janis D. Pringle

Thirty-two year old Janis D. Pringle was last seen in Dayton, Ohio at 3am on August 14, 2003. She has never been heard from again. A friend reported her missing on November 7th.

Janis' sister, Michelle Napier, disappeared from her own Dayton apartment in October 2003. Her body was later found wrapped in a tarp behind the Siebenthaler Company Nursery in Harrison Township, Ohio in May 2004. Her murder remains unsolved. It is not known whether or not Janis' disappearance is related to Michelle's murder.

*(Janis at the time of her disappearance)*

At the time of her disappearance, Janis Pringle had black hair, stood 4'11", and weighed 190 pounds. She is African-American with brown eyes. She has scars on her face, chin, and lower lip. Her nickname is Lil Bit.

She has a history of drug abuse. As of this writing, she is forty-seven years old.

If you have any information regarding this case, you are urged to call the Dayton Police Department at 937-333-1070.

## Brian Randall Shaffer

Twenty-seven year old Brian Randall Shaffer was last seen at the Ugly Tuna Saloona in Columbus, Ohio, near the Ohio State University Campus, between 1:30am and 2am on April 1, 2006. He had gone there with several male friends to celebrate the beginning of Spring Break. He was last seen speaking to two college-age women inside the bar. He has never been heard from again. Security cameras show him entering the establishment but not leaving it. A camera directed at the only other way in or out of the bar did not show him leaving the bar either. He seemingly vanished into thin air. When his friends could not find him, they assumed he had gone on home, so they left as well.

He was planning to propose to his girlfriend while on a Miami Beach vacation. The couple was scheduled to depart on their trip on April 3rd, but Brian never arrived at the airport. That was when his family reported him missing.

His car was parked at his apartment, which was near the bar. Nothing was amiss, nor were any of his personal belongings gone from inside the apartment. His cell phone, credit cards, and bank accounts have not been used since the day he disappeared. The Columbus Police Department put up missing person posters, combed through trash cans and alleys, and brought in dogs to track his scent, but their efforts turned up no clues as to his whereabouts. Neither witnesses nor cameras can place him outside of the bar after he went inside that night. If he had somehow managed to leave the bar without going through one of the doors, the surveillance footage from nearby bars would have picked him up, but none did. Everyone who entered and exited the bar that night was shown on at least one of the cameras, but authorities can find no evidence that Brian ever left.

In the years since Brian's disappearance, his father and brother have given media interviews, worked closely with law enforcement, hung up posters, and consulted with psychics in hopes of finding out what happened that night. Brian's mother had passed away with cancer nearly a month before he vanished. His father has since passed too, but his brother is still searching for clues as to his whereabouts. He hopes to one day have closure.

Authorities do not believe he left of his own accord. He was a second year medical student at Ohio State University, and he had already gotten his bachelor's degree in microbiology three years prior. He made good grades, and he had no reason to want to walk out on his life.

*(Brian at the time of his disappearance)*

At the time of his disappearance, Brian Shaffer had light brown hair, wore wire-framed eyeglasses, stood 6'2", and weighed 165 pounds. He was last seen wearing an olive green short-sleeve polo shirt over a white long-sleeve shirt, blue jeans, white Adidas sneakers, and a yellow rubber cancer awareness bracelet. He is Caucasian with hazel eyes, a tattoo of a Pearl Jam symbol on his upper right arm, and a black spot on his left iris. As of this writing, he is thirty-nine years old.

If you have any information regarding this case, you are urged to call one of the following numbers:

Columbus Police Department Unsolved Unit at 614-645-4041 or to remain anonymous, call 1-877-645-TIPS

## Lisa Alaria Szasz - Lazzaro

Thirty-seven year old Lisa Alaria Szasz - Lazzaro was last seen in the Andover, Ohio area on March 23, 2000. She has never been heard from again. Her white Chevrolet Blazer was found illegally parked at Youngstown - Warren Airport in Vienna Township, Ohio on March 24th. The keys were still in the ignition. Her parents reported her missing on March 27th. Prior to her disappearance, she had stated that she felt as though she was being stalked. It is unknown if police have any clues to confirm whether or not she was.

*(Lisa at the time of her disappearance)*

At the time of her disappearance, Lisa Szasz - Lazzaro had black hair, stood between 5'5" - 5'7", and weighed 135 pounds. She was last seen wearing a light blue jacket, jeans, multiple bracelets, a wedding ring, and a necklace with a cross pendant. She is Caucasian with hazel eyes and pierced ears. As of this writing, she is fifty-five years old.

If you have any information regarding this case, you are urged to call one of the following numbers:

*Ashtabula County Sheriff's Office at 440-576-0055*

*Federal Bureau of Investigation (FBI) at 1-202-324-3000*

## **Stephan Mitchell Adams**

Twenty-six year old Stephan Mitchell Adams called his girlfriend on his cell phone at 11am on December 13, 2004 and told her he was giving a man a ride to Keys, Oklahoma. Authorities later determined that at the time he spoke to his girlfriend, he was south of Tahlequah, Oklahoma. All calls made to his cell phone after 11:30am were sent straight to voicemail. Between 11:30am and 12pm, he was seen at a convenience store in Cookson, Oklahoma. He appeared to be upset and agitated at that time. He purchased a soda, and then he stood outside the store for about five minutes before he left in his pickup truck. It is believed he was alone at the time. He has never been seen or heard from again.

Authorities consider his disappearance suspicious and foul play is possible in his case. His vehicle, a white 1995 or 1998 GMC SCI one-ton truck with short bed, chrome bedrails, no taillight covers, and Oklahoma plates SEQ714 disappeared with him and has never been found.

Investigators would like to identify and interview a possible witness in Stephan's disappearance. The individual is a Caucasian male standing 5'11" and weighing between 180 to 200 pounds with brown and salt and pepper collar length hair and about four day's growth of salt and pepper facial hair. He was between forty and fifty years old in 2004. The man was seen at a Dollar General Store on east Downing Street in Tahlequah, close to Stephan's apartment, on the morning of December 13th. The man was wearing a tan Carhartt jacket, faded blue or black jeans, a flannel shirt, a dark green stocking cap, and eyeglasses. He drove a charcoal-colored or faded black 2000 Ford Ranger pickup truck with a chrome toolbox. Authorities stated that the individual arrived at the store at 7:50am and hung around the parking lot for hours. He claimed he was waiting for someone, but no one showed up to meet him. He mentioned to passerby that he worked at a construction site in Keys. The man left the parking lot just before 11am, around the time Stephan went missing. The man is not being called a suspect, but police feel he may have information that could assist the investigation. The man has yet to be identified.

Stephan was involved in a very heated custody battle with his ex-wife over their daughter at the time. He wanted to at least be able to see the child, but his ex-wife refused to comply with the court's visitation order. Twice he was charged with molesting the child, but neither time could enough evidence be found to take him to trial. The custody battle had been going on for over two years, and there was an important meeting about it scheduled in Muskogee County District Court for a few days after Stephan went missing. Authorities do not believe the timing was a coincidence.

A few weeks after Stephan went missing his family received a telephone threat from an individual who stated that they would be harmed if the investigation into his disappearance did not end. The caller has not been identified.

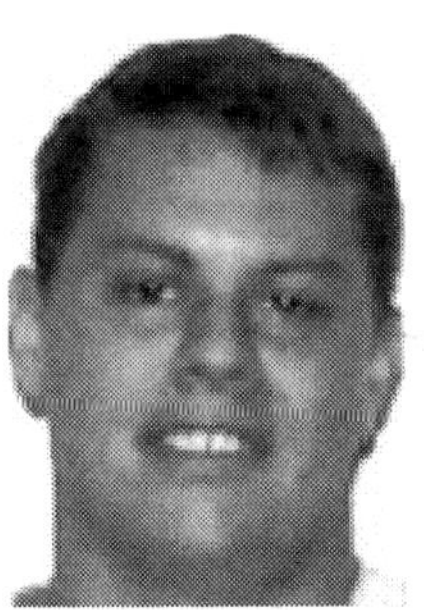

*(Stephan at the time of his disappearance)*

At the time of his disappearance, Stephan Adams had brown hair, stood 5'7", and weighed between 164 - 200 pounds. He was last seen wearing a black t-shirt, and jeans. He was carrying a dark-colored book bag. He is Native American with brown eyes. He has severe asthma and may need an inhaler. As of this writing, he would be thirty-nine years old.

If you have any information regarding this case, you are urged to call one of the following numbers:

*Tahlequah Police Department at 918-456-8801*

*Oklahoma State Bureau of Investigation (OSBI) at 1-800-522-8017*

## Karen Margaret Kincaid

Fifty-eight year old Karen Margaret Kincaid was last seen on the afternoon of October 3, 2002 at the Safeway store on northeast Stephens Street in the Metz Hill area of Oakland, Oregon. She has never been heard from again. Her dog, a neutered Pomeranian named Pippen, disappeared with her and has never been found. She left two other pets behind. It was initially believed that she left of her own accord, but foul play is now suspected. Investigators think that finding Pippen may be the key to solving Karen's case. They believe that whoever caused her disappearance, may have also taken the dog and either sold it or given it away. As of 2007, Pippen would have been seven or eight years old.

*(Karen at the time of her disappearance)*

At the time of her disappearance, Karen Kincaid had red hair, stood 5'5", and weighed 180 pounds. She is Caucasian with brown eyes. She has been diagnosed with bipolar disorder, but it is unknown whether or not she was taking medication for it at the time. As of this writing, she is seventy-four years old.

If you have any information regarding this case, you are urged to call the Douglas County Sheriff's Office at 514-440-4458.

## Gary Alan Larsen

Twenty-eight year old Gary Alan Larsen was last seen at Shari's Restaurant in Redmond, Oregon on September 16, 2001. He has never been seen or heard from again. His family reported him missing eleven days later. His white 1995 Dodge pickup with Oregon plates XTN945 disappeared with him and has never been found. Foul play is suspected.

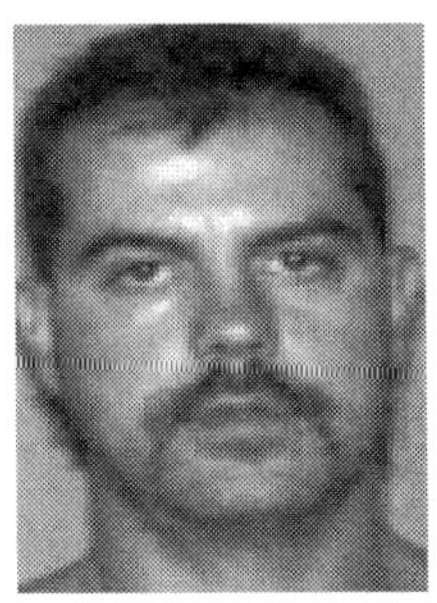

*(Gary at the time of his disappearance)*

At the time of his disappearance, Gary Larsen had brown hair, stood 6'3", and weighed 210 pounds. He is Caucasian with brown eyes. As of this writing, he is forty-five years old.

If you have any information regarding this case, you are urged to call the Deschutes County Sheriff's Department at 541-617-3393 or 541-693-6911.

## August Richard Schwabenland

Seventy-five year old August Richard Schwabenland was last seen at approximately 4pm on November 13, 2004 in Gold Beach, Oregon. He had been shopping and was returning home. He never arrived and has never been heard from again. He was driving his maroon 1996 Buick LeSabre with Oregon plats YWZ-945. The vehicle disappeared with him and has never been found. He was reported missing three days later.

*(August at the time of his disappearance)*

At the time of his disappearance, August Schwabenland had white/gray hair, wore eyeglasses with steel frames, stood between 5'10" - 6'1", and weighed 210 pounds. He was last seen wearing a dark-colored long-sleeve jacket or sweatshirt with a zipper up the front and a zipped left breast pocket, gray sweatpants, and a gray sweatshirt. He is Caucasian with blue eyes and a scar on his chest from heart surgery. He has diabetes and heart disease and requires medication. As of this writing, he is eighty-nine years old.

If you have any information regarding this case, you are urged to call the Curry County Sheriff's Department at 547-247-3242.

## Joseph Sireci

Sixty-three year old Joseph Sireci was last seen between 10pm and 4:30am on May 27, 1983 at his residence on Daly Street in Philadelphia, Pennsylvania. He was going to stop at the local laundromat near 3rd and South Street in Philadelphia on his way to work at Penns Landing Condominiums, but he never arrived. He has never been heard from again. His dark blue four-door 1972 Mercury Montego with Pennsylvania plates Y75089 disappeared with him and has never been found.

*(Joseph at the time of his disappearance)*

At the time of his disappearance, Joseph Sireci had balding brown hair, wore eyeglasses with brown plastic frames, was missing three teeth, stood 5'10", and weighed 190 pounds. He was last seen wearing a Timex watch and either blue jeans or checkered pants. He is Caucasian with brown eyes, a large mole under his left armpit, and a scar on his upper right arm. His blood type is AB. As of this writing, he is ninety-eight years old.

If you have any information regarding this case, you are urged to call the Philadelphia Police Department at 215-685-3258.

## John Thistlewood

Thirty-seven year old John Thistlewood dropped his two children off at a relative's house on South American Street in Philadelphia, Pennsylvania at approximately 7:30pm on September 11, 1992, and said he would return shortly to get them. He has never been heard from again. His white two-door 1992 Ford Expo with Pennsylvania plates XTX-633 disappeared with him and has never been found.

*(John at the time of his disappearance)*

At the time of his disappearance, John Thistlewood had brown hair and a mustache, stood 6'2", and weighed 210 pounds. He was last seen wearing a red silk shirt, black jeans, and black sneakers. He is Caucasian with brown eyes. As of this writing, he is sixty-two years old.

If you have any information regarding this case, you are urged to call the Philadelphia Police Department at 215-686-3013 or 215-686-3014.

## Dail Boxley Dinwiddie

Twenty-three year old Dail Boxley Dinwiddie attended a U2 concert with friends in Columbia, South Carolina on September 23, 1993. The concert ended at approximately 11:15pm. Dail and her friends then stopped at a nightclub called Jungle Jim's in the Five Points area of Columbia. Her friends lost track of her and assumed she had gone home. They left at approximately 1am. Dail was last seen talking to a bouncer about fifteen minutes before she left between 1:15am and 1:30am. She walked out of the nightclub and headed north on Harden Street. She has never been seen or heard from again. Her father reported her missing at 8:30am, after he had checked with her friends to see if any of them knew where she was.

The police treated her case as a kidnapping from the beginning. Everyone who knew her at the time said it would be very uncharacteristic of her to leave without warning. She is described as a cautious person who did not like to be out alone.

*(Dail at the time of her disappearance)*

At the time of her disappearance, Dail Dinwiddie had light brown hair with blonde highlights, stood 5', and weighed 96 pounds. She was last seen wearing a long-sleeve olive green pullover, a bright blue nylon L.L. Bean jacket tied around her waist, faded blue jeans, and either brown boots or new white Nike sneakers with a blue stripe. She is Caucasian with brown eyes, pierced ears, and severe asthma and allergies. One finger on each of her hands is slightly curved. As of this writing, she is forty-nine years old.

If you have any information regarding this case, you are urged to call the Columbia Police Department at 803-233-8474.

## Heather Rachelle Elvis

Twenty year old Heather Rachelle Elvis was last seen in Myrtle Beach, South Carolina at 2am on December 18, 2013. She went out with someone for their first date on December 17th, and he dropped her off at her house on White River Drive. Her roommate was visiting relatives out of state, but Heather called her at 3am to tell her how the date went. The conversation ended at 3:41am. Sometime after that, Heather disappeared never to be seen or heard from again.

On December 19th, her dark green 2011 Dodge Intrepid was found at the Peachtree Boat Landing along the Waccamaw River in Socastee, South Carolina. Her keys, purse, and cell phone were missing and have not been found. The location of her car was on the outskirts of Myrtle Beach, and only about an eight minute drive from her parent's home.

Prior to her disappearance, Heather had been romantically involved with a thirty-seven year old married man. Her roommate said the relationship had ended more than a month prior. But on the night of her disappearance, there were several calls back and forth between her and the man. The final call was at 6am. Her roommate said that Heather had told her that the man was planning to leave his wife to be with her. The man, however, denied saying that and stated he had not saw Heather since October. He admitted he had called her at 6am on December 18th, but said it was only to tell her to stop calling him.

In February 2014, the man and his wife of nearly twenty years were charged with Heather's kidnapping and murder, despite the fact that her remains have never been found. In March of the same year, the murder charges were dismissed. The kidnapping charges remained. The man was tried for those charges in June 2016, but it ended in a mistrial. It is unknown how either pled in their cases.

*(Heather at the time of her disappearance)*

At the time of her disappearance, Heather Elvis had brown hair, stood between 5' - 5'1", and weighed 110 pounds. She is Caucasian with brown eyes. She has the following tattoos: a compass rose on the inside of her left forearm, a stylized sea turtle on the left side of her torso, an infinity symbol on the right side of her torso, a small ocean wave on the outside of her wrist, and a sugar skull on her thigh. As of this writing, she is twenty-five years old.

If you have any information regarding this case, you are urged to call the Horry County Police Department at 843-915-5350.

## Brandon Rodrigues Graves

Twenty-four year old Brandon Rodrigues Graves was last seen in Sumter, South Carolina on January 30, 2010. He lived and worked in Myrtle Beach, but he had gone to Sumter on a spur-of-the-moment trip to attend Morris College's Homecoming. He went to Sebastian's Nightclub on Broad Street at 11pm. Shortly before midnight, a bouncer asked him to leave because he was drunk and unruly. He made two phone calls in the early hours of the next morning. He called a cousin and a friend, neither of whom answered their phone. He left voicemail messages for both, but his speech was incoherent. The last call was between 3:30am and 4am. He has never been heard from again. All calls made to his cell phone after 4am went straight to voicemail. Investigators were unable to determine where he was when he made those last two calls.

Brandon does not have a criminal record and did not associate with drug dealers. He was well-liked and had no known enemies. He had graduated from Coastal Carolina University with a degree in sports management.

(Brandon at the time of his disappearance)

At the time of his disappearance, Brandon Graves had black hair styled in long dreadlocks, stood 5'4", and weighed 150 pounds. He was last seen wearing a blue t-shirt over a black thermal shirt, black jeans, and a black baseball cap. He is African-American with brown eyes. He has asthma and requires medication. His nickname is Peanut. As of this writing, he is thirty-three years old.

If you have any information regarding this case, you are urged to call the Sumter County Sheriff's Office at 803-436-2700.

## Carlo Pfaff

Fifty-seven year old Carlo Pfaff was last seen at the Alpine Forest Mobile Home Park in Richland, South Carolina where he lived on March 6, 1998. He was a passenger in a dark blue 1987 Chevrolet Astro van with South Carolina plates CAR 564. He has never been heard from again. When police searched his home for clues as to his whereabouts, they discovered that his TV, radio, and VCR were missing. Foul play is suspected in his case.

(Carlo at the time of his disappearance)

At the time of his disappearance, Carlo Pfaff had balding black hair, stood 5'5", and weighed 160 pounds. He is Caucasian with brown eyes and a leopard tattoo on his left forearm. He is blind and has severe heart problems which require daily medication that he does not have with him. As of this writing, he is seventy-seven years old.

If you have any information regarding this case, you are urged to call the Richland County Sheriff's Department at 803-691-9000.

## Teresa Dianne Shannon

Forty-nine year old Teresa Dianne Shannon was last seen with a friend at the Western Sizzlin' Steakhouse in Lugoff, South Carolina at about 2:30pm on February 4, 1999. They had attended a battered women's support group meeting together earlier in the day. Later, Teresa dropped her friend off and was assumingly headed to her own home. She has never been heard from again. She was reported missing after she failed to attend her mother's wedding on February 11th.

All of her personal belongings were left behind at her home. There was no sign of a struggle. She was going through a contested divorce at the time, but it is not known whether or not authorities believe her husband had anything to do with her disappearance. A year before she went missing, her home in Kershaw County, South Carolina was destroyed by fire. It was worth $90,000, but she never collected any insurance on it. It is unknown what, if any, part the fire has to do with her later going missing.

Her burgundy two-door 1998 Oldsmobile Cutlass with South Carolina plates 605-CJY disappeared with her and has never been found.

*(Teresa at the time of her disappearance)*

At the time of her disappearance, Teresa Shannon had graying brown hair, stood between 5'4" - 5'9", and weighed between 215 - 275 pounds. She is Caucasian with green/blue eyes. She suffers from multiple sclerosis and requires medication. As of this writing, she is sixty-eight years old.

If you have any information regarding this case, you are urged to call the Sumter County Sheriff's Office at 803-436-2053.

## Shannon Elaine Riley Arif

Twenty year old Shannon Elaine Riley Arif was last seen by her husband at 9:40am at her home in Clarksville, Tennessee on March 17, 1998. She was scheduled to work at Wal-Mart from 4:30pm till 9:15pm, but she never clocked in. Her car and purse were found in the Wal-Mart parking lot, but there were no clues as to her whereabouts. She has never been heard from again. Foul play is suspected.

*(Shannon at the time of her disappearance)*

At the time of her disappearance, Shannon Arif had blonde hair, wore contact lenses, stood between 5'4" - 5'6", and weighed between 90 - 100 pounds. She was last seen wearing a red and blue Tommy Hilfiger shirt, jogging pants, and Nike sneakers. She is Caucasian with blue eyes, pierced ears, and a mole on the left side of her upper lip. As of this writing, she is forty-one years old.

If you have any information regarding this case, you are urged to call the Clarksville Police Department at 931-648-0656.

## Michael Edwin Hearon

Fifty-one year old Michael Edwin Hearon was last seen leaving his home riding his ATV on Bell Branch Road in Tallahassee, Tennessee at 11am on August 23, 2008. His Yamaha ATV was found a few days later on someone else's property and in a location where Michael would have had no reason to be. The ignition switch had been left on. He has never been seen nor heard from again.

He is described as being kind-hearted, generous, and easy going. He had no known enemies. His sons believe he met with foul play, because he would never have left his family without warning otherwise.

*(Michael at the time of his disappearance)*

At the time of his disappearance, Michael Hearon had dark brown hair, stood 5'10", and weighed 185 pounds. He was last seen wearing a faded red t-shirt, khaki cargo shorts, and Teva sandals. He is Caucasian with hazel eyes, a snake bite scar on one foot, caps on his teeth, a scar on his leg between the knee and the thigh, a surgical scar on his abdomen and the back of his knee, and a tattoo on his lower back. One of his feet is slightly smaller than the other one. His nickname is Mike. As of this writing, she is sixty years old.

If you have any information regarding this case, you are urged to call the Blount County Sheriff's Department at 865-273-5001 or 865-273-5200.

## Miriam Ruth Hemphill

Eighty-four year old Miriam Ruth Hemphill was last seen in Oak Ridge, Tennessee on July 22, 2005. She was driving a beige- or bronze-colored 1999 Buick LeSabre with Tennessee plates ABA-676. The vehicle disappeared with her and has never been found. She did not take any clothes and she had very little money with her. There has been no activity on her bank accounts or credit cards since she went missing. Her husband describes her as a social individual with an excellent memory. She was active in church at the time.

*(Miriam at the time of her disappearance)*

At the time of her disappearance, Miriam Hemphill had white hair. She is Caucasian. Her other distinguishing characteristics are unknown. As of this writing, she is ninety-seven years old.

If you have any information regarding this case, you are urged to call the Oak Ridge Police Department at 865-425-4399 or 865-425-3502.

## Elvin Cecil Hodge

Sixty year old Elvin Cecil Hodge was last seen walking out of his residence on Central Avenue in Chattanooga, Tennessee at 8am on May 24, 1990. He was walking towards Rossville Boulevard to pay bills. He has never been heard from again. He did not drive at the time and usually rode the bus to where he needed to go. He is missing under suspicious circumstances, and foul play is possible.

*(Elvin at the time of his disappearance)*

At the time of his disappearance, Elvin Hodge had graying black hair and a mustache, wore eyeglasses with heavy black frames, stood between 5'8" - 5'11", and weighed between 149 - 165 pounds. He was last seen wearing a burgundy jacket and beige pants. He is African-American with brown eyes. His left leg is severely weakened from arthritis and he needs a cane to walk. As of this writing, he is eighty-eight years old.

If you have any information regarding this case, you are urged to call the Chattanooga Police Department at 423-643-5055.

## Soon Chon Hwang

Forty-four year old Soon Chon Hwang left J & C Community Grocery, the store he owned, on Castalia Street in Memphis, Tennessee at approximately 12:30pm on September 5, 2006. He went to a wholesale grocery store he frequently visited called Tri-City Wholesale. Employees there said Soon was shopping in the store when he received an urgent phone call and left in a hurry. He left his groceries sitting in the cart. He has never been heard from again. His red 2002 Nissan truck was found that same night off of Interstate 55 in West Memphis, Arkansas. His own grocery store had been robbed several times prior to him going missing, but it is unclear whether or not authorities believe there is a connection. Foul play is suspected in his case.

*(Soon at the time of his disappearance)*

At the time of his disappearance, Soon Hwang had black hair, stood 5'7", and weighed 155 pounds. He was last seen wearing a yellow pullover shirt, dark-colored khaki pants, and a pink baseball cap. He is Asian with brown eyes. As of this writing, he is fifty-six years old.

If you have any information regarding this case, you are urged to call the Memphis Police Department at 901-373-3883.

## Marcus T. Rutledge

Twenty-three year old Marcus T. Rutledge was last seen at his residence on Park Dale Drive in Nashville, Tennessee on June 8, 1998. His red 1995 Plymouth Neon was found abandoned across town from his home in the parking lot of the Riverwood Apartments on Cabot Drive shortly after he disappeared. There were no clues as to his whereabouts inside or around the vehicle. He has never been heard from again. When his relatives checked his apartment, they found his dog shut in the bathroom with no food and only the toilet to drink from. His family says he would not have left his dog shut up in a room with no food. Authorities believe foul play is possible in his case.

*(Marcus at the time of his disappearance)*

At the time of his disappearance, Marcus Rutledge had black hair, stood 6', and weighed 190 pounds. He is African-American with brown eyes. As of this writing, he is forty-three years old.

If you have any information regarding this case you are urged to call one of the following numbers:

*Metro Nashville Police Department at 615-862-7557*

*Nashville Police Department's Crime Stoppers Division at 615-74-CRIME*

## Marsilene Smith

Sixty-nine year old Marsilene Smith was last seen in Murfreesboro, Tennessee on December 6, 2007. She went Christmas shopping at 1:30pm that day. She would normally return to her home on Village Green by dark, but on that day she did not. Her husband of fifty-one years reported her missing at 6pm. The next day, her champagne-colored Lincoln Navigator was found abandoned in the parking lot of the Wal-Mart on south

Rutherford Boulevard. The keys were in the ignition and the passenger side door was open. Surveillance camera footage showed a man get out of the driver's side of the vehicle at 2:30pm on December 6th. He removed a bright green bicycle from the back and rode away. The bicycle appeared to be a girl's or woman's bike, but it was not Marsilene's and her loved ones did not recognize it. According to the camera footage, she was neither in nor near the vehicle when it was left in the parking lot.

Her husband quickly stopped cooperating with police and hired a lawyer. He has not been charged in his wife's disappearance, but in March 2009 he was charged with two counts of evidence tampering and six counts of making false statements to police involving various aspects of her case. The couple's adult son testified against his father in an April 2010 trail, saying the man was physically and mentally abusive. Marsilene's husband maintained his innocence, even though he was convicted on all charges. He was sentenced to a year in jail and six years of probation.

Marsilene's loved ones believe she was abducted or possibly had some type of diabetic issue that contributed to her going missing. Authorities believe foul play may have occurred in her case. They have not ruled out the possibility that a family member or someone she knew was involved.

*(Marsilene at the time of her disappearance)*

At the time of her disappearance, Marsilene Smith had blonde hair, stood 5'4", and weighed 139 pounds. She was last seen wearing a beige long-sleeve t-shirt, a blue denim jacket, faded blue jeans, black zip-up ankle boots, a yellow gold band with diamonds on her left hand, and a yellow gold band with three diamonds on her right hand. She is Caucasian with blue eyes and a dime-size birthmark on her forehead. She is a diabetic and insulin-dependent. Her nickname is Marcie. As of this writing, she is seventy-nine years old.

If you have any information regarding this case, you are urged to call the Murfreesboro Police Department at 615-893-1311.

## Laresha Deana Walker

Twenty-three year old Laresha Deana Walker was last seen in Nashville, Tennessee on November 19, 1999. She dropped her two year old son off at her sister's home on Gayle Street for the night. She said that she planned to drive to Murfreesboro the following morning to get a mechanical repair estimate on her car. She called her father from her home on Edwards Avenue between 9:30pm and 10pm that night. Later, a neighbor heard her arguing with someone outside her home. She has never been heard from again.

One of her sisters checked her home after she failed to answer her phone the following day. The lights were on and the stereo was playing loudly, but there was no sign of Laresha. Her maroon 1995 Oldsmobile Achieva with Tennessee plates 419-ABG disappeared with her and has never been found. Her family reported her missing on November 21st. Foul play is suspected.

*(Laresha at the time of her disappearance)*

At the time of her disappearance, Laresha Walker had black hair, stood 5'7", and weighed between 190 - 200 pounds. She is African-American with brown eyes, pierced ears, and a surgical scar on the left side of chest. She has a heart condition and requires medication. As of this writing, she is forty-two years old.

If you have any information regarding this case, you are urged to call the Metro Nashville Police Department at 615-862-7557 or 615-862-7546.

## Maria Dolores Alcorn

Fifty-seven year old Maria Dolores Alcorn was last seen in Dallas, Texas on February 24, 2017. She has never been heard from again. Few details are available in her case, but authorities believe she may have been taken against her will.

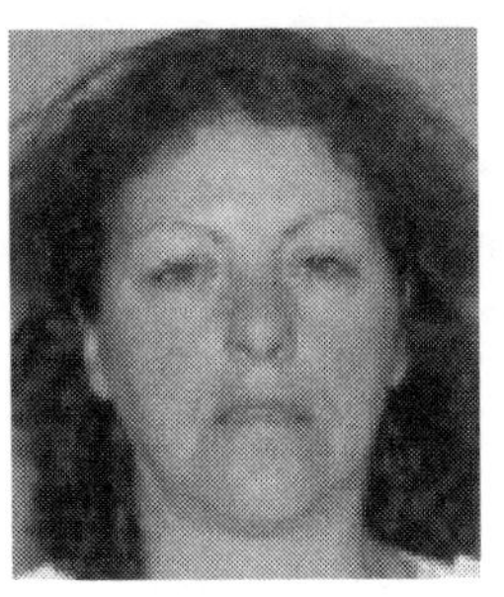

*(Maria at the time of her disappearance)*

At the time of her disappearance, Maria Alcorn had brown hair, stood 5'8", and weighed 120 pounds. She is Hispanic with green eyes. She may use the first name Lola. As of this writing, she is fifty-eight years old.

If you have any information regarding this case, you are urged to call the Texas Department of Public Safety at 1-800-346-3243.

## Jennifer Apreciado

Eighteen year old Jennifer Apreciado was last seen in the vicinity of 19th Street and Arizona Avenue in San Antonio, Texas at 3pm on October 26, 2006. She left her boyfriend's home on Arizona Avenue and was en route to the bus stop near Wall Street and General McMullen Drive. She called her boyfriend and said she noticed a car slowly circling the block, and she was frightened. She did not describe the vehicle or its driver. Her boyfriend tried calling her back an hour later and some other woman answered. The woman said she had found the phone. Jennifer has never been heard from again.

*(Jennifer at the time of her disappearance)*

At the time of her disappearance, Jennifer Apreciado had brown hair, stood between 4'7" - 4'10", and weighed between 95 - 105 pounds. She was last seen wearing a short-sleeve red blouse, blue denim shorts, and flip flops. She is Hispanic with brown eyes, the name Jacob tattooed on her right ankle, and Jennifer tattooed on her upper right arm. As of this writing, she is thirty years old.

If you have any information regarding this case, you are urged to call the San Antonio Police Department at 210-207-7660.

## Jennifer Joyce Barton

Twenty year old Jennifer Joyce Barton went to the movies with a friend in Austin, Texas on May 16, 1976. She was last seen getting into a brown or tan van with California plates outside a bar in the vicinity of east 11th Street and Waller Street in Austin. There were two African-American men inside the vehicle. She has never been heard from again.

Two other African-American women disappeared from Austin in the spring of 1976, and it is possible that the three cases are related. None of the three have ever been located.

*(Jennifer at the time of her disappearance)*

At the time of her disappearance, Jennifer Barton had brown hair and a light freckled complexion, stood 5'7", and weighed 135 pounds. She was last seen wearing a burgundy body suit, blue jeans, and sandals. She is African-American with brown eyes, a scar on the calf of her right leg, and pierced ears. She may go by J.J. As of this writing, she is sixty-two years old.

If you have any information regarding this case, you are urged to call the Austin Police Department at 512-974-5250.

## Andrea Lynn Unger Augsburger

Nineteen year old Andrea Lynn Augsburger was last seen in McAllen, Texas on November 29, 1999. Few details are available in her case, but authorities believe she may have been taken against her will.

*(Andrea at the time of her disappearance)*

At the time of her disappearance, Andrea Augsburger had blonde hair, stood between 5'6" - 5'7", and weighed between 120 - 130 pounds. She is Caucasian with blue eyes. As of this writing, she is thirty-seven years old.

If you have any information regarding this case, you are urged to call the Texas Department of Public Safety at 1-800-346-3243.

## William Nolan Bass

Eighty-seven year old William Nolan Bass was last seen driving his tan and brown two-door 1977 Chevrolet Caprice with Texas plates C82-MRB in Bellmead, Texas at 9am on October 21, 2000. He was on Highway 84 near Loop 340 at the time. He was headed to Waco, Texas to have his vehicle inspected and to purchase new tags. He never arrived, and he has never been heard from again. His vehicle disappeared with him and has never been found. Investigators are unsure what happened to him.

*(William at the time of his disappearance)*

At the time of his disappearance, William Bass had gray hair, wore eyeglasses, stood between 6'3" - 6'4", and weighed 160 pounds. He was last seen wearing a plaid button-down shirt, dark green khaki pants, and possibly a small-brimmed fedora. He is Caucasian with blue eyes. He suffers from high blood pressure. As of this writing, he is one-hundred-and-five years old.

If you have any information regarding this case, you are urged to call the Limestone County Sheriff's Office at 245-729-3278.

## Chester Lee Bell Jr.

Fifty-nine year old Chester Lee Bell Jr. rented a 1990 Ford U-Haul truck with Texas plates AA47808 in Dallas, Texas on May 4, 2001 for work-related purposes. He has never been seen or heard from again. Authorities believe he may have been taken against his will. It is unknown whether or not the U-Haul truck has been located.

*(Chester at the time of his disappearance)*

At the time of his disappearance, Chester Bell Jr. had black hair, stood 5'11", and weighed 200 pounds. He was last seen wearing overalls and black boots. He is African-American with brown eyes. As of this writing, he is seventy-six years old.

If you have any information regarding this case, you are urged to call the Texas Department of Public Safety at 1-800-346-3243.

## Scott Allen Brown

Twenty-five year old Scott Allen Brown was last seen sometime during the month of June 1996 in his apartment on Greens Parkway in Houston, Texas. He was driving a red 1986 Mazda RX7 with Texas plates MSJ05X at the time. He has never been seen nor heard from again. The vehicle disappeared with him and has never been found.

*(Scott at the time of his disappearance)*

At the time of his disappearance, Scott Brown had brown hair, stood 6', and weighed 180 pounds. He is Caucasian with brown eyes and his first name tattooed on his right arm. As of this writing, he is forty-seven years old.

If you have any information regarding this case, you are urged to call the Houston Police Department at 713-731-5223.

# EPILOGUE

The cases in this book are only but a few of the thousands of unsolved missing persons cases in the United States and its outlying areas to date. Many more have likely been opened since I started putting this book together in May of 2018. I tried to get the facts of each case as straight and as accurate as possible, however, if there are some inaccuracies I do apologize.

The desire to compile the cases for this book came from following along with a few of them since the beginning, in particular the Kyron Horman, Tabitha Tudors, Marsilene Smith, and Myra Lewis cases. I cannot begin to imagine what the families of those missing must go through every day. When you lose a loved one through death, it is a traumatic and trying experience, but to never know what happened to your loved one I am sure would be nearly unbearable.

I hope that at least one of these cases reaches out to someone who can help solve the case and give the family some closure. And if not, then maybe at least this book will help raise awareness of these cases to the public so that the missing's faces will remain out there in the world.

It has been proven time and time again that with programs like the Amber and Silver Alerts can and do get quicker results in locating the missing with the help of the public. In our day and age where just about everyone has a smartphone, Facebook, Twitter, Snapchat, or some way to view and share the details when a person goes missing, tons of people view and share the recent missing persons cases. But please when you are not hesitating to share those missing today, take a moment to share the cold cases too.

Several of the cases in this book have Facebook pages dedicated to them. Others have websites. A search of their name on Google or Bing will bring up those pages and sites. From there, you too can become active in helping these families find their missing loved one or at the very least to find closure.

# REFERENCES


*Gage & Chloie:*

- *http://wkrn.com/2016/09/23/brother-sister-still-missing-4-years-after-deadly-bedford-county-fire/*
- *http://abcnews.go.com/US/tennessee-children-missing-house-fire-kills-step-grandparents/story?id=17335838*
- *https://www.cnn.com/2012/09/29/us/tennessee-missing-children/index.html*
- *http://www.columbiadailyherald.com/sections/news/local-news/search-bedford-county-children-endures.html*
- *http://ldesherl.blogspot.com/2014/07/missing-chloie-levette-gage-daniel.html*
- *http://wkrn.com/2015/06/28/birthday-party-held-for-2-kids-missing-since-2012-bedford-county-house-fire/*
- *http://www.newschannel5.com/story/22757551/new-revelations-in-case-of-missing-bedford-county-children*

*Lauria & Ashley:*

- *https://www.usatoday.com/story/news/2016/01/26/case-girls-missing-since-1999-gets-new-look/79342834/*
- *http://www.insideedition.com/newly-found-investigation-notes-provide-leads-1999-cold-case-missing-girls-3950*
- *http://www.miamiok.com/news/20171229/long-lost-notes-breathe-new-life-into-freeman-bible-missing-girls-case*
- *https://www.facebook.com/OurMissingHearts/posts/1639651699429421*
- *https://www.smithsonianmag.com/history/the-children-who-went-up-in-smoke-172429802/*

*Sodder Children:*

- *https://historichorrors.wordpress.com/2014/05/13/what-was-the-fate-of-the-five-sodder-children/*
- *https://en.wikipedia.org/wiki/Sodder_children_disappearance*
- *https://www.npr.org/templates/story/story.php?storyId=5067563*

- https://theghostinmymachine.com/2016/04/18/unresolved-what-happened-to-the-sodder-children-after-the-fire/

*Rebecca Coriam:*

- http://www.greeningz.com/interesting/new-evidence-missing-disney-crew-member/45/
- http://www.rebecca-coriam.com/
- https://en.wikipedia.org/wiki/Disappearance_of_Rebecca_Coriam

*Annette Mizener:*

- http://abcnews.go.com/US/vanished-sea-baffling-cruise-ship-missing-persons-cases/story?id=15380865#1
- https://www.cruiseshipdeaths.com/2004/12/04/annette-mizener-passenger-cruise-ship-death-carnival-pride/
- https://www.theguardian.com/uk/2007/jan/18/ukcrime.cruises
- https://michellesaysso.blogspot.com/2005/11/wisconsin-woman-mysteriously.html?view=flipcard

*Glenn Sheridan:*

- http://www.foxnews.com/story/2004/11/27/search-off-for-missing-cruise-passenger.html
- https://www.cruiseshipdeaths.com/2004/11/02/glenn-sheridan-passenger-cruise-ship-death-carnival-celebration/
- http://www.cruiseshipmissing.com/2004/11/24/glenn-sheridan-passenger-carnival-celebration-november-24-2004/

*Rama Forman:*

- http://www.dailymail.co.uk/news/article-2036056/Scores-people-gone-missing-cruise-ships-Its-time-say-parents-girl-vanished-Disney-liner.html
- http://www.cruiseshipmissing.com/2004/10/09/rama-forman-passenger-silversea-cruises-silver-cloud-november-9-2004/

*John Halford:*

- *http://www.dailymail.co.uk/femail/article-2040248/Why-165-people-gone-missing-cruise-ships-recent-years.html*
- *https://www.miltonkeynes.co.uk/news/mystery-deepens-over-city-s-missing-cruise-passenger-1-2631055*
- *https://www.ranker.com/list/cruise-ship-disappearances/juliet-bennett-rylah?page=2*
- *http://www.missingpersonsdata.com/person-details/2011-56105*

*Sister Eileen Christie:*

- *http://www.ncregister.com/blog/astagnaro/prayers-requested-for-sr.-eileen-christie-missing-in-austria*
- *http://licatholic.org/new-yorkers-gather-to-pray-for-local-nun-missing-in-austria/*
- *https://www.ranker.com/list/people-who-disappeared-on-vacation/cheryl-adams-richkoff?ref=collections_btm&l=2520285&collectionId=1158*
- *http://licatholic.org/new-yorkers-gather-to-pray-for-local-nun-missing-in-austria/*

*Althea & Jeffrey Blankinship:*

- *https://www.findthemissing.org/en/cases/22894/45*
- *https://m.seattlepi.com/local/article/Photos-Washington-s-cold-case-missing-persons-3442104.php?cmpid=pinterest-mobile#photo-2749203*
- *https://www.findthemissing.org/en/photos/full/17352*
- *http://www.missingkids.com/poster/NCMC/1170648/*

*Matthew Garnes:*

- *https://www.findthemissing.org/en/cases/10196*
- *https://m.seattlepi.com/local/article/Photos-Washington-s-cold-case-missing-persons-3442104.php?cmpid=pinterest-mobile#photo-2749203*
- *http://www.doenetwork.org/cases/4363dmwa.html*
- *https://www.seattlepi.com/seattlenews/amp/Photos-Washington-s-cold-case-missing-persons-3442104.php*

*Sean Turner:*

- *http://www.wmcactionnews5.com/story/36890505/family-desperate-for-answers-after-ca-man-visiting-memphis-goes-missing*
- *http://www.missingpersonsofamerica.com/2017/11/23/sean-turner-goes-missing-while-visiting-tennessee/*

*Sherry Marler:*

- *http://www.dothanfirst.com/news/top-stories/enterprise-woman-seeks-daughter-missing-26-years/132100589*
- *http://www.pollyklaas.org/missing/kids/sherry-marler.html*

*Stella Evon:*

- *http://www.sitnews.us/0910news/092710/092710_cold_case.html*
- *http://www.pollyklaas.org/missing/kids/page-27044750.html#.Wpo1xWrwblU*

*Jacqueline Vasquez:*

- *http://www.phoenixnewtimes.com/news/avondale-infant-missing-since-2001-is-still-missing-cops-need-help-6651239*
- *http://www.pollyklaas.org/missing/kids/jacqueline-vasquez.html#.Wpo7TWrwblU*

*Mikelle Biggs:*

- *https://www.azcentral.com/story/news/local/mesa/2015/11/04/missing-arizona-biggs-sister-speaks-mikelle-cns/75166706/*
- *http://www.pollyklaas.org/missing/kids/mikelle-diane-biggs.html#.Wpo--WrwblU*

*Morgan Nick:*

- *http://www.thv11.com/article/news/local/missing-persons-reports/timeline-morgan-nick-disappearance/500638150*
- *http://www.pollyklaas.org/missing/kids/page-27044923.html#.WppDn2rwblU*

*Vanessa Smith:*

- http://kmph.com/news/local/girl-missing-for-19-years-mother-still-hopeful
- http://www.pollyklaas.org/missing/kids/vanessa-smith.html#.WppLvWrwblW

*Crystal Tymich:*

- https://www.fbi.gov/wanted/kidnap/crystal-ann-tymich
- http://www.pollyklaas.org/missing/kids/page-28571907.html#.WppPY2rwblU

*Melissa Espinoza:*

- http://www.pollyklaas.org/missing/kids/page-27044993.html#.WppSYGrwblU
- http://charleyproject.org/case/melissa-ann-espinoza

*Abby Jo Blagg:*

- http://charleyproject.org/case/abby-jo-blagg
- http://www.pollyklaas.org/missing/kids/abby-jo-blagg.html#.WppZOGrwblU
- http://www.missingkids.com/poster/NCMC/924029/1/screen

*Trenton Duckett:*

- http://charleyproject.org/case/trenton-john-duckett
- http://www.pollyklaas.org/missing/kids/trenton-duckett.html#.Wp4KTmrwblU

*Zachary Bernhardt:*

- http://charleyproject.org/case/zachary-michael-cole-bernhardt
- http://www.tampabay.com/news/zachary-bernhardt-case-in-clearwater-to-be-featured-on-missing-persons-show/2324534
- http://www.pollyklaas.org/missing/kids/zachary-bernhardt.html#.Wp4KaGrwblU

*Sabrina Aisenberg:*

- http://wfla.com/2017/05/24/what-happened-to-baby-sabrina-aisenberg-who-vanished-in-1997/
- http://www.tampabay.com/news/courts/Twenty-years-later-baby-Sabrina-Aisenberg-s-disappearance-still-a-mystery_162708412
- http://www.pollyklaas.org/missing/kids/sabrina-paige-aisenberg.html#.Wp4SdmrwbIU
- http://www.tampabay.com/news/courts/Twenty-years-later-baby-Sabrina-Aisenberg-s-disappearance-still-a-mystery_162708412
- http://wfla.com/2017/05/24/what-happened-to-baby-sabrina-aisenberg-who-vanished-in-1997/

*Paula & Brandon Wade:*

- http://charleyproject.org/case/brandon-lee-wade
- http://www.paulawade.com/
- http://www.pollyklaas.org/missing/kids/brandon-wade.html#.Wp4dQ2rwbIU

*Ruben Felix:*

- http://charleyproject.org/case/ruben-david-felix
- http://www.pollyklaas.org/missing/kids/ruben-felix.html#.Wp4nImrwbIU

*Trudy Appleby:*

- https://www.nbcnews.com/feature/cold-case-spotlight/sunday-marks-20-years-illinois-girl-trudy-appleby-vanished-n634526
- http://www.pollyklaas.org/missing/kids/trudy-leann-appleby.html#.Wp4r9mrwbIU

*Diamond Bynum & King Walker:*

- https://www.facebook.com/groups/diamondbynumandkingwalker/
- http://charleyproject.org/case/king-rajan-walker
- http://www.chicagotribune.com/suburbs/post-tribune/news/ct-ptb-diamond-bynum-king-walker-tips-0202-20180201-story.html
- http://www.pollyklaas.org/missing/kids/king-walker.html

*April Wiss:*

- *https://www.findthemissing.org/en/cases/5392/0/*
- *http://charleyproject.org/case/april-susanne-wiss*
- *http://www.pollyklaas.org/missing/kids/april-susanne-wiss.html#.Wp7jLGrwblU*

*Erica Fraysure:*

- *https://www.wcpo.com/news/insider/i-team-unsolved-20-years-later-classmates-say-erica-fraysures-disappearance-ruined-their-lives*
- *http://www.pollyklaas.org/missing/kids/erica-lee-fraysure.html#.Wp7pTmrwblU*

*Randy Sellers:*

- *http://deaniepeters-missingangels.blogspot.com/2012/05/randy-lee-sellers-missing-32-years.html*
- *http://www.doenetwork.org/cases/14dmky.html*
- *http://www.pollyklaas.org/missing/kids/randy-sellers.html#.Wp7uS2rwblU*

*Kristopher Lewis:*

- *http://www.fox25boston.com/news/mother-pushing-for-answers-2-years-after-13-year-old-went-missing/335646231*
- *https://missingadultskids.com/find-missing-kristopher-lewis/*
- *https://www.facebook.com/FINDKRISTOPHER/*
- *http://www.pollyklaas.org/missing/kids/kristopher-lewis.html*

*Andrew Amato:*

- *http://charleyproject.org/case/andrew-john-amato*
- *http://www.doenetwork.org/cases/790dmma.html*
- *http://www.pollyklaas.org/missing/kids/andrew-amato.html#.Wp780mrwblU*

*Angelo Puglisis:*

- *https://www.bostonglobe.com/metro/2016/09/01/lawrence/Q4GykXjV047cKG09IIAH1M/story.html*

- http://www.haveyouseenandy.com/characters.html
- http://charleyproject.org/case/angelo-gene-puglisi

*Leigh Savoie:*

- http://archive.boston.com/news/local/massachusetts/articles/2009/09/24/a_new_search_for_boy_who_never_came_home/
- http://charleyproject.org/case/leigh-frances-savoie
- http://www.pollyklaas.org/missing/kids/page-27640490.html#.Wp8NRGrwblU

*Steven Kraft:*

- http://wsbt.com/news/local/cold-case-files-the-disappearance-of-steven-kraft
- http://charleyproject.org/case/steven-earl-kraft-ii
- http://www.pollyklaas.org/missing/kids/page-27044165.html#.Wp9pn2rwblU

*LeeAnna Warner:*

- https://www.twincities.com/2013/06/13/chisholm-leeanna-warner-vanished-10-years-ago-but-case-still-open/
- http://charleyproject.org/case/leeanna-susan-marie-warner
- http://www.pollyklaas.org/missing/kids/page-27043909.html#.Wp9v92rwblU

*Myra Lewis:*

- http://www.wjtv.com/news/metro/vanished-4-years-since-the-disappearance-of-myra-lewis/1000908973
- https://www.facebook.com/MyraLewisHelpFindMe
- http://charleyproject.org/case/myra-lewis
- http://www.pollyklaas.org/missing/kids/myra-lewis.html

*Leigh Occhi:*

- http://www.cnn.com/2009/CRIME/11/13/grace.coldcase.occhi/index.html
- https://www.facebook.com/helpfindmissingleighmarineocchi/

- *http://www.pollyklaas.org/missing/kids/page-27045007.html#.Wp99V2rwblU*

*Shemika Cosey:*

- *http://fox2now.com/2013/12/29/family-still-looking-for-answers-five-years-after-teenager-disappears/*
- *http://charleyproject.org/case/shemika-keyanta-cosey*
- *http://www.pollyklaas.org/missing/kids/shemika-cosey.html#.Wp-Gh2rwblU*

*Karla Rodriquez:*

- *https://www.reviewjournal.com/crime/courts/las-vegas-girl-vanished-in-1999-leaving-grieving-family-frustrated-police/*
- *http://charleyproject.org/case/karla-carolina-rodriguez*
- *http://www.pollyklaas.org/missing/kids/page-27044261.html#.Wp-OcmrwblU*

*Tristen Myers:*

- *http://www.doenetwork.org/cases/4638dmnc.html*
- *http://charleyproject.org/case/tristen-alan-myers*
- *http://www.pollyklaas.org/missing/kids/tristen-alan-myers.html#.WqBFjGrwblU*

*Aaron Cody Stepp:*

- *http://www.columbusmonthly.com/article/20140922/LIFESTYLE/309229577*
- *http://charleyproject.org/case/aaron-cody-stepp*
- *http://www.pollyklaas.org/missing/kids/aaron-stepp.html#.WqBVmGrwblU*

*Amber Barker:*

- *http://charleyproject.org/case/amber-renee-barker*
- *http://www.pollyklaas.org/missing/kids/amber-rene-barker.html#.WqG1ZmrwblU*

*Jamie McChurin:*

- *http://charleyproject.org/case/jamie-michelle-mcchurin*
- *http://www.pollyklaas.org/missing/kids/page-27044709.html#.WqG10WrwbIU*

*Tabitha Tuders:*

- *http://charleyproject.org/case/tabitha-danielle-tuders*
- *https://www.nashvillescene.com/news/article/13016007/tabitha-tuders*
- *http://www.pollyklaas.org/missing/kids/tabitha-danielle-tuders.html#.WqHgIWrwbIU*

*Alexandria Lowitzer:*

- *http://www.alexandrialowitzer.com/Ali-Lowitzer.html*
- *http://charleyproject.org/case/alexandria-joy-lowitzer*
- *http://www.pollyklaas.org/missing/kids/alexandria-lowitzer.html#.WqHgVGrwbIU*

*Angela Jaramillo:*

- *https://www.dallasnews.com/news/news/2013/10/09/dallas-woman-hopes-new-leads-can-help-her-find-daughter-almost-four-years-later*
- *http://charleyproject.org/case/angela-rene-jaramillo*
- *http://www.pollyklaas.org/missing/kids/angela-jaramillo.html#.WqHh4GrwbIU*

*Dorien Thomas:*

- *http://www.newschannel10.com/story/28243019/the-case-of-dorien-thomas-still-haunts-the-amarillo-police-department*
- *http://charleyproject.org/case/dorien-deon-thomas*
- *http://www.pollyklaas.org/missing/kids/dorien-thomas.html#.WqNVaGrwbIU*

*Shelby Wright:*

- *http://www.heraldnet.com/news/detectives-renew-efforts-to-find-long-missing-boy/*
- *http://charleyproject.org/case/shelby-raistlin-wright*
- *http://www.pollyklaas.org/missing/kids/shelby-wright.html#.WqNfbGrwbIU*

*Teekah Lewis:*

- *http://charleyproject.org/case/teekah-latres-lewis*
- *http://www.angelfire.com/jazz/jazzyrose/Teekah.html*
- *http://www.pollyklaas.org/missing/kids/teekah-lewis.html#.WqNnT2rwbIU*

*Jeffrey Klungness:*

- *http://charleyproject.org/case/jeffrey-allen-klungness*
- *http://www.pollyklaas.org/missing/kids/jeffrey-klungness.html*

*Bryce Herda:*

- *https://www.strangeoutdoors.com/mysterious-stories-blog/2017/10/25/bryce-herda-strange-disappearances-from-us-national-parks*
- *http://charleyproject.org/case/bryce-florian-herda*
- *http://www.pollyklaas.org/missing/kids/bryce-herda.html#.WqN4WWrwbIU*

*DaShawn McCormick:*

- *http://www.missingkids.com/poster/NCMC/1228477/1/screen*
- *http://charleyproject.org/case/dashawn-leon-mccormick*

*Matthew Wade Crocker:*

- *http://www.missingkids.com/poster/NCMC/1244530/1/screen*
- *http://charleyproject.org/case/matthew-wade-crocker*

*Daniel Barter:*

- *http://charleyproject.org/case/daniel-barter*

*Tarasha Benjamin:*

- *http://charleyproject.org/case/tarasha-benjamin*

*Christina Lynn Carter:*

- *http://charleyproject.org/case/christina-lynn-carter*

*Fred Wright:*

- *http://ireport.cnn.com/docs/DOC-568799*
- *http://charleyproject.org/case/fred-wright*

*David Borer:*

- *http://charleyproject.org/case/david-michael-borer*

*Scott & Amy Fandel:*

- *https://www.nbcnews.com/feature/cold-case-spotlight/theories-fandel-children-s-disappearance-n385361*
- *http://charleyproject.org/case/scott-curtis-fandel*
- *http://charleyproject.org/case/amy-lee-fandel*

*Michael Palmer:*

- *http://charleyproject.org/case/michael-timothy-palmer*

*Victor Tolentino Cruz:*

- *https://blingee.com/blingee/view/122385800-Victor-Manuel-Tolentino-Cruz-ENDANGERED-MISSING-01-07-2010-*
- *http://charleyproject.org/case/victor-manuel-tolentino-cruz*

*Roland Himebrook & Richard Gorham:*

- *https://www.findthemissing.org/en/cases/show/14035*
- *http://charleyproject.org/case/richard-gorham*
- *http://charleyproject.org/case/roland-himebrook*

*Karen Grajeda:*

- *http://charleyproject.org/case/karen-rosalba-grajeda*

*James Hendrickson:*

- *http://charleyproject.org/case/james-a-hendrickson*

*Cynthia & Jackie Leslie:*

- *http://charleyproject.org/case/cynthia-ardina-leslie*
- *http://charleyproject.org/case/jackie-lynn-leslie*
- *http://www.forthelost.org/leslie.html*

*Robert Parks:*

- *http://charleyproject.org/case/robert-raymond-parks*

*Randy Parscale Jr.:*

- *http://charleyproject.org/case/randy-doyle-parscale-jr*

*Dorothy & Danielle Pitcher:*

- *http://www.willcoxrangenews.com/news/article_ea142e1f-cf88-5c6f-8115-4ce95bef3bf5.html*
- *http://charleyproject.org/case/danielle-therese-pitcher*
- *http://charleyproject.org/case/dorothy-jeanne-pitcher*

*Jennifer Douglas:*

- *http://charleyproject.org/case/jennifer-anne-douglas*

*Jonelle Matthews:*

- *http://charleyproject.org/case/jonelle-renee-matthews*
- *http://www.doenetwork.org/cases/198dfco.html*

*Lashaya Stine:*

- http://charleyproject.org/case/lashaya-nae-stine

*Christopher Vigil:*

- http://charleyproject.org/case/christopher-william-vigil

*Bianca Lebron:*

- http://charleyproject.org/case/bianca-elaine-lebron

*Marisela Pino:*

- http://charleyproject.org/case/marisela-pino

*Diana Alvarez:*

- http://charleyproject.org/case/diana-belinda-alvarez

*Bonnie & Jeremy Dages:*

- http://charleyproject.org/case/jeremy-lee-dages
- http://charleyproject.org/case/bonnie-lee-dages

*Adji Desir:*

- http://charleyproject.org/case/adji-desir

*Bryan Dos Santos-Gomes:*

- http://charleyproject.org/case/bryan-dos-santos-gomes

*Yakelin Llanes, Mario Mordoche, & Jonathan Mordoche:*

- https://www.bocalifemagazine.com/features/after-nephews-disappearance-broward-woman-founds-guardians-missing-solve-south-florida-cold
- http://charleyproject.org/case/jonathan-mordoche
- http://charleyproject.org/case/yakelin-llanes
- http://charleyproject.org/case/mario-antonio-mordoche

- *https://www.findthemissing.org/en/cases/8935/0/*

*Andrew Brown:*

- *http://charleyproject.org/case/andrew-lee-brown*

*Teresa Dean:*

- *http://charleyproject.org/case/teresa-melissa-dean*

*Desmond Dix:*

- *http://charleyproject.org/case/desmond-santonio-dix*

*Raymond Lamar Green:*

- *http://charleyproject.org/case/raymond-lamar-green*

*Alisha Smiley:*

- *http://charleyproject.org/case/alisha-smiley*

*Richard Bendele:*

- *http://charleyproject.org/case/richard-willis-bendele*

*Aram Dowell:*

- *http://www.bonnersferryherald.com/news/article_af9c26ae-b64b-11e5-80c5-eb3d70b5f718.html*
- *https://www.gofundme.com/2erwky4*
- *http://charleyproject.org/case/aram-wade-dowell*

*Daniel Glennon:*

- *http://charleyproject.org/case/daniel-glennon*

*Steven Asplund:*

- *http://wqad.com/2014/01/09/break-in-the-case-on-20th-anniversary-of-missing-moline-man/*

- https://missingadultskids.com/find-missing-steven-r-asplund/
- http://charleyproject.org/case/steven-r-asplund

*Michelle Bianco:*

- http://charleyproject.org/case/michelle-renee-bianco

*Anthony Klama:*

- http://www.missingin.org/reg3785/anthony_keith_klama.htm
- http://charleyproject.org/case/anthony-keith-klama

*Jerrica Laws:*

- http://charleyproject.org/case/jerrica-lizette-laws

*Hiep Luu:*

- http://charleyproject.org/case/hiep-t-luu

*Mark Miller:*

- http://charleyproject.org/case/mark-allen-miller

*Karen Schepers:*

- http://charleyproject.org/case/karen-l-schepers

*Janet Tillman:*

- http://charleyproject.org/case/janet-lollisa-tillman

*Marina Boelter:*

- http://charleyproject.org/case/marina-pearl-boelter
- https://www.facebook.com/Help-Find-Missing-Marina-Pearl-Boelter-1543737695887665/
- https://www.facebook.com/pg/FindMarinaBoelter/about/?ref=page_internal

- *https://www.facebook.com/1499983450293419/photos/a.1499985416959889.1073741828.1499983450293419/1499986713626426/?type=3&theater*

*Eva Mae Hale:*

- *http://webiographies.org/aub0000019/index.htm*
- *http://charleyproject.org/case/eva-mae-hale*

*Danyel Pauley*

- *http://missingpersonsdata.com/usa/Kansas/missing-recent/case-details/17147*
- *http://charleyproject.org/case/danyel-pauley*

*Daniel Reaves:*

- *http://finddanielreaves.blogspot.com/*
- *http://charleyproject.org/case/daniel-reaves/*

*Larissa Sam:*

- *http://charleyproject.org/case/larissa-marie-sam*

*Mark Tomich:*

- *http://charleyproject.org/case/mark-d-tomich*

*Dora Villarrea-Tolx:*

- *http://charleyproject.org/case/dora-maria-villarrea-tolx*

*Wanda Washington:*

- *http://charleyproject.org/case/wanda-elaine-washington*

*Jodi Huisentruit:*

- *http://www.fox9.com/news/new-leads-emerge-in-the-jodi-huisentruit-case*

- *http://charleyproject.org/case/jodi-sue-huisentruit*

*Ethan Kazmerzak:*

- *http://hamptonchronicle.com/content/remembering-ethan*
- *https://www.findthemissing.org/en/cases/22526/34*
- *http://charleyproject.org/case/ethan-bert-kazmerzak*

*Jane Bousley:*

- *http://charleyproject.org/case/jane-m-bousley*

*Albert Mitchell:*

- *https://canupplaw.com/have-you-seen-this-man-albert-gary-mitchell/*
- *http://charleyproject.org/case/albert-gary-mitchell*

*Melvia Roarx:*

- *http://charleyproject.org/case/melvia-kaye-roarx*

*Claude & Martha Shelton:*

- *http://www.wkyt.com/home/headlines/45840667.html*
- *http://www.unsolvedappalachia.org/2017/11/08/marth-sue-and-claude-shelton/*
- *http://charleyproject.org/case/claude-shelton*
- *http://charleyproject.org/case/martha-sue-shelton*

*Robbin Slaughter:*

- *http://www.doenetwork.org/cases/1171dmky.html*
- *http://charleyproject.org/case/robbin-lewis-slaughter*

*Sharon Sons:*

- *http://www.doenetwork.org/cases/1845dfky.html*
- *http://charleyproject.org/case/sharon-rose-sons*

*Barbara Blount:*

- http://charleyproject.org/case/barbara-ann-blount

*Jim Delaney:*

- http://identifyla.lsu.edu/profile.php?id=672
- http://charleyproject.org/case/jim-william-delaney

*Donna O'Banion:*

- http://charleyproject.org/case/donna-christine-obanion

*Adrian Planells:*

- http://charleyproject.org/case/adrian-juan-planells

*David Carter:*

- http://charleyproject.org/case/david-edward-carter

*Marilyne Chamberlain:*

- http://charleyproject.org/case/marilyne-chamberlain

*James Cole:*

- http://charleyproject.org/case/james-arthur-cole

*Mason Gomez:*

- http://charleyproject.org/case/mason-armani-gomez

*Mary Greene:*

- http://charleyproject.org/case/mary-kathryn-greene
- https://www.baltimorecountymd.gov/Agencies/police/homicide/unsolvedmissingpersons/greene1966

*John Morris Jr.:*

- http://charleyproject.org/case/john-james-morris-jr

*Tu Tran:*

- *http://articles.baltimoresun.com/1990-12-13/news/1990347221_1_umbc-tran-baltimore-county*
- *http://charleyproject.org/case/tu-thi-cam-tran*

*Lynn Burdick:*

- *http://charleyproject.org/case/lynn-burdick*

*Jennifer Mbugua:*

- *http://charleyproject.org/case/jennifer-kabura-mbugua*

*Charlita Harris:*

- *http://www.doenetwork.org/cases/3786dfmi.html*
- *http://charleyproject.org/case/charlita-sonya-harris*

*Margie Ranshaw:*

- *http://charleyproject.org/case/margie-ann-ranshaw*

*Robert Vance:*

- *http://charleyproject.org/case/robert-louis-vance*

*Lisa Walton:*

- *http://charleyproject.org/case/lisa-walton*

*Carla Anderson:*

- *http://charleyproject.org/case/carla-beth-anderson*

*Dawn Carlson:*

- *http://charleyproject.org/case/dawn-joy-carlson*

*Mark Folz:*

- *http://charleyproject.org/case/mark-duane-folz*

*Lucia Perez:*

- *http://charleyproject.org/case/lucia-chilel-perez*

*Kelly Allen:*

- *http://charleyproject.org/case/kelly-l-allen*

*Diana Braungardt:*

- *http://charleyproject.org/case/diana-jane-braungardt*

*Byron Davis:*

- *http://charleyproject.org/case/byron-lee-davis*

*Cheryl Kenney:*

- *http://charleyproject.org/case/cheryl-ann-kenney*
- *http://charleyproject.org/case/angela-marie-hammond*

*Cheryl Scherer:*

- *http://www.doenetwork.org/cases/338dfmo.html*
- *http://charleyproject.org/case/cheryl-ann-scherer*

*Jonathan Williams:*

- *http://www.missingveterans.com/1994/jonathan-williams/*
- *http://charleyproject.org/case/jonathan-williams*

*Dorothy Freeman:*

- *http://charleyproject.org/case/dorothy-geneva-freeman*

*Jose Concepcion:*

- *http://charleyproject.org/case/jose-concepcion*

*William Jamison:*

- *http://charleyproject.org/case/william-joseph-jamison*

*Patrick Francis Carnes:*

- *http://charleyproject.org/case/patrick-francis-carnes*
- *http://charleyproject.org/case/judith-ellen-casida*

*Opal Parsons:*

- *http://charleyproject.org/case/opal-marie-parsons*

*Shonna Wesley:*

- *http://charleyproject.org/case/shonna-dannette-wesley*

*Tanisha Watkins:*

- *http://charleyproject.org/case/tanisha-lorraine-watkins*

Lee Wackerhagen Jr. & Chance Wackerhagen:

- *http://charleyproject.org/case/chance-lee-wackerhagen*
- *http://charleyproject.org/case/lee-herman-wackerhagen-jr*

*Jamal Abdul'Faruq:*

- *http://charleyproject.org/case/jamal-abdulfaruq*

*Abraham Jimenez:*

- *http://charleyproject.org/case/abraham-romero-jimenez*

*Raquel Rodriguez:*

- *http://charleyproject.org/case/raquel-lucina-rodriguez*

*Pernell Tewangoitewa:*

- http://charleyproject.org/case/pernell-lloyd-tewangoitewa

*Corrie Anderson:*

- http://charleyproject.org/case/corrie-lynn-anderson

*William Anderson:*

- http://charleyproject.org/case/william-anderson

*Catherine Chiang:*

- http://charleyproject.org/case/catherine-chiang

*Bethanie Dougherty:*

- http://charleyproject.org/case/bethanie-lynne-dougherty

*Colin Gillis:*

- http://charleyproject.org/case/colin-w-gillis

*Audrey Herron:*

- http://charleyproject.org/case/audrey-may-herron

*Robert Long:*

- http://charleyproject.org/case/robert-j-long

*Bambi Madden:*

- http://www.binghamton-ny.gov/unsolved-cases
- http://charleyproject.org/case/bambi-lyn-madden

*Stacy Pennant:*

- http://charleyproject.org/case/stacy-a-pennant

*Roger Chambers:*

- http://charleyproject.org/case/roger-jermaine-chambers

*Troy Jacobs:*

- http://charleyproject.org/case/troy-lee-jacobs

*Stephen Meeks:*

- http://charleyproject.org/case/stephen-victor-meeks

*Kenneth Mohler:*

- http://charleyproject.org/case/kenneth-earl-mohler

*April Pickens:*

- http://charleyproject.org/case/april-michelle-pickens

*Tyarra Williams:*

- https://www.facebook.com/Help-Find-Tyarra-Cacique-Williams-1121733044533558/
- http://charleyproject.org/case/tyarra-cacique-williams

*Shaniece Briggs:*

- http://charleyproject.org/case/shaniece-mona-briggs

*Jonni Clemett:*

- http://charleyproject.org/case/jonni-clemett

*Shaylene Farrell:*

- http://charleyproject.org/case/shaylene-marie-farrell

*Jesse Flaugher:*

- *https://www.facebook.com/missingpersonfromohio/posts/missing-jesse-flaugher-was-85-years-old-when-he-was-last-seen-on-october-2-2006-/1805230919554125/*
- *https://www.namus.gov/MissingPersons/Case#/9639*
- *http://charleyproject.org/case/jesse-howard-flaugher*

*Christopher Haas:*

- *http://charleyproject.org/case/christopher-lee-haas*

*Charles Koch:*

- *http://charleyproject.org/case/charles-e-koch*

*John Markley Jr. & Shelly Markley:*

- *http://charleyproject.org/case/john-j-markley-jr*
- *http://charleyproject.org/case/shelly-renee-markley*
- *http://www.wfmj.com/story/30759163/new-leads-in-20-year-old-trumbull-county-unsolved-mystery*
- *http://www.tribtoday.com/news/local-news/2015/12/mystery-remains-two-decades-later/*

*Phillip Modlin:*

- *http://charleyproject.org/case/phillip-jason-modlin*

*Robert Mohney:*

- *http://charleyproject.org/case/robert-stephen-mohney*

*Catherine Parisi:*

- *http://charleyproject.org/case/catherine-parisi*

*Janis Pringle:*

- *http://charleyproject.org/case/janis-d-pringle*

*Brian Shaffer:*

- *https://melmagazine.com/a-guy-walks-into-a-bar-53c784e7369b*
- *http://www.newser.com/story/233690/man-missing-for-a-decade-mightve-never-left-this-bar.html*
- *http://www.findbrianshaffer.com/*
- *http://charleyproject.org/case/brian-randall-shaffer*

*Lisa Lazzaro:*

- *https://missingadultskids.com/find-missing-lisa-alaria-szasz-lazzaro/*
- *http://charleyproject.org/case/lisa-alaria-szasz-lazzaro*

*Stephen Adams:*

- *http://charleyproject.org/case/stephan-mitchell-adams*

*Karen Kincaid:*

- *http://charleyproject.org/case/karen-margaret-kincaid*

*Gary Larsen:*

- *http://charleyproject.org/case/gary-alan-larsen*

*August Schwabenland:*

- *http://usa.51xrw.com/MissingPersonNotice-Abductions-Oregon%20Lost-2891-August%20Richard%20Schwabenland_2891.html*
- *http://charleyproject.org/case/august-richard-schwabenland*

*Joseph Sireci:*

- *http://charleyproject.org/case/joseph-sireci*

*John Thistlewood:*

- *http://charleyproject.org/case/john-thistlewood*

*Dail Dinwiddie:*

- http://charleyproject.org/case/dail-boxley-dinwiddie

*Heather Elvis:*

- http://charleyproject.org/case/heather-rachelle-elvis

*Brandon Graves:*

- http://charleyproject.org/case/brandon-rodrigues-graves

*Carlo Pfaff:*

- http://charleyproject.org/case/carlo-pfaff

*Teresa Shannon:*

- http://charleyproject.org/case/teresa-dianne-shannon

*Shannon Arif:*

- http://charleyproject.org/case/shannon-elaine-riley-arif

*Michael Hearon:*

- http://www.findmikehearon.com/
- http://charleyproject.org/case/michael-edwin-hearon
- http://archive.knoxnews.com/news/local/happy-valleys-sad-mystery-sons-reflect-on-fathers-mysterious-disappearance-ep-360183632-356731721.html/

*Ruth Hemphill:*

- http://charleyproject.org/case/miriam-ruth-hemphill

*Elvin Hodge:*

- http://charleyproject.org/case/elvin-cecil-hodge

*Soon Hwang:*

- *http://charleyproject.org/case/soon-chon-hwang*

*Marcus Rutledge:*

- *http://charleyproject.org/case/marcus-t-rutledge*

*Marsilene Smith:*

- *https://www.facebook.com/TNMissingUnsolved/posts/marsilene-smith-aka-marcie-was-69-years-old-when-she-disappeared-from-rutherford/1322694957837257/*
- *http://www.wgnsradio.com/update-the-7-year-old-case-of-a-missing-69-year-old-murfreesboro-woman--cms-19912*
- *http://charleyproject.org/case/marsilene-smith*

*Laresha Walker:*

- *http://charleyproject.org/case/laresha-deana-walker*

*Maria Alcorn:*

- *http://charleyproject.org/case/maria-alcorn*

*Jennifer Apreciado:*

- *http://charleyproject.org/case/jennifer-apreciado*

*Andrea Augsburger:*

- *http://charleyproject.org/case/andrea-lynn-unger-augsburger*

*Jennifer Barton:*

- *http://charleyproject.org/case/jennifer-joyce-barton*

*William Bass:*

- http://charleyproject.org/case/william-nolan-bass

*Chester Bell Jr.:*

- http://charleyproject.org/case/chester-lee-bell-jr

*Scott Brown:*

- http://charleyproject.org/case/scott-allen-brown

*Thomas Brown:*

- http://charleyproject.org/case/thomas-kelly-brown

*Robert Casto:*

- http://charleyproject.org/case/robert-dale-casto

*Margaret Chauncy:*

- http://charleyproject.org/case/margaret-jane-chauncy

*Donna Cloud:*

- http://charleyproject.org/case/donna-kay-cloud

*Melissa Crabill:*

- http://charleyproject.org/case/melissa-gail-crabill

*Mauro Escobar, Jose Gonzalez, & Silvia Perez:*

- http://charleyproject.org/case/mauro-elias-escobar
- http://charleyproject.org/case/jose-guadalupe-gonzalez
- http://charleyproject.org/case/silvia-perez

*Thomas Flowers:*

- http://www.doenetwork.org/cases/4460dmtx.html
- http://charleyproject.org/case/thomas-flowers

*Frank Frazier:*

- *http://charleyproject.org/case/frank-d-frazier*

*Hipolito Garcia & Jose Molina:*

- *http://charleyproject.org/case/hipolito-sanchez-garcia*
- *http://charleyproject.org/case/jose-c-molina*

*John Giddens:*

- *http://charleyproject.org/case/john-allen-giddens*

*Elida Guzman:*

- *http://www.missingin.org/reg4498/elida_mendoza_guzman.htm*
- *http://charleyproject.org/case/elida-mendoza-guzman*

*Stephen Hamshire:*

- *http://charleyproject.org/case/stephen-douglas-hamshire*

*Tot Harriman:*

- *http://charleyproject.org/case/tot-tran-harriman*

*Mitchelle Hicks:*

- *http://charleyproject.org/case/mitchelle-deborah-hicks*

*Linda House:*

- *http://charleyproject.org/case/linda-ann-house*

*Dorothy Kelley:*

- *http://charleyproject.org/case/dorothy-smith-kelley*

*Randall Lee:*

- http://charleyproject.org/case/randall-dewayne-lee

*Maria Llamas:*

- http://charleyproject.org/case/maria-jesus-llamas

*German Machuca:*

- http://charleyproject.org/case/german-machuca

*Carmen Mares:*

- http://charleyproject.org/case/carmen-magdalena-mares
- http://foxsanantonio.com/news/local/help-us-find-carmen-mares-05-28-2016

*James "Jamie" Mayberry Jr.:*

- http://charleyproject.org/case/james-h-mayberry-jr
- http://www.doenetwork.org/cases/3732dmtx.html

*Salar Mohammed:*

- http://charleyproject.org/case/salar-jaafar-mohammed

*Trung Ngo:*

- http://charleyproject.org/case/trung-quang-ngo

*Carey Parker:*

- http://charleyproject.org/case/carey-mae-parker

*Modesto Robles Jr.:*

- http://charleyproject.org/case/modesto-robles-jr

*Dudley Scott*

- http://charleyproject.org/case/dudley-truett-scott

*Jessica Schreiber:*

- https://charleyproject.org/case/jessica-dawn-schreiber
- https://www.legacy.com/obituaries/statesman/obituary.aspx?n=sadie-lynn-blevins&pid=19225360

*Glenn Towery:*

- http://charleyproject.org/case/glenn-layne-towery

*Cassandra Hailey & Keith Call:*

- http://charleyproject.org/case/richard-keith-call
- http://charleyproject.org/case/cassandra-lee-hailey
- http://www.wavy.com/news/local-news/newport-news/30-years-later-the-colonial-parkway-murders/1109159329
- https://www.wavy.com/news/local-news/williamsburg/possible-developments-in-colonial-parkway-murders-family-says/1315929593

*Miller Harlow:*

- http://charleyproject.org/case/miller-smith-harlow

*Eric Smith:*

- http://charleyproject.org/case/eric-grady-smith

*Israel Smith:*

- https://www.findthemissing.org/en/cases/2828/230
- http://charleyproject.org/case/israel-ray-smith

*John Wingler Sr.:*

- http://charleyproject.org/case/john-william-wingler-sr

*John Akkerman:*

- http://charleyproject.org/case/john-allen-akkerman

*Beverly Cummings:*

- http://charleyproject.org/case/beverly-ann-cummings

*Nancy Glovick:*

- http://charleyproject.org/case/nancy-e-glovick

*Phyllis Lewellen:*

- http://charleyproject.org/case/phyllis-ellen-lewellen

*Ramon Moore:*

- http://charleyproject.org/case/ramon-castro-moore

*Nancy Moyer:*

- http://charleyproject.org/case/nancy-kareen-moyer

*William Summers Jr.:*

- http://charleyproject.org/case/william-kermig-summers-jr

*Eugene Wekesa:*

- http://charleyproject.org/case/eugene-bush-wekesa

*Karen Adams:*

- http://charleyproject.org/case/karen-sue-adams

*Carlene Brown:*

- http://charleyproject.org/case/carlene-brown
- http://charleyproject.org/case/deborah-rae-meyer
- http://charleyproject.org/case/sharon-baldeagle

- *http://charleyproject.org/case/cinda-leann-pallett*
- *http://charleyproject.org/case/charlotte-june-kinsey*
- *https://rapidcityjournal.com/news/man-s-hope-for-missing-daughter-renewed/article_014658e7-f2cc-50e5-90b8-2c7d0ad44cad.html*
- *https://billingsgazette.com/news/state-and-regional/wyoming/montana-woman-hopes-to-close-rawlins-cold-case/article_13602736-88a7-5689-916f-bce02010f3de.html*
- *https://whereaboutsstillunknown.wordpress.com/2013/04/10/carlene-brown/*

*Latoya Brown:*

- *http://charleyproject.org/case/latoya-t-brown*
- *http://www.cbs42.com/news/local/tuscaloosa-mother-searches-for-missing-daughter/957441937*
- *https://www.weather.gov/bmx/event_04272011tuscbirm*
- *http://tuscaloosacountyema.org/4-27-11-tornado-fatalities/*

*Oscar King:*

- *http://charleyproject.org/case/oscar-lewis-king*

*Stephen Pearson:*

- *http://charleyproject.org/case/stephen-horace-pearson*

*Shanna Peoples:*

- *http://charleyproject.org/case/shanna-genelle-peoples*

*Reginald Short:*

- *http://charleyproject.org/case/reginald-jermaine-short*

*Kierra Stubbs:*

- *http://charleyproject.org/case/kierra-stubbs*

*Erin Gilbert:*

- *http://charleyproject.org/case/erin-marie-gilbert*

*Frank Johnston:*

- *http://charleyproject.org/case/frank-h-johnston*

*Sheila McBroom:*

- *http://charleyproject.org/case/sheila-kathleen-mcbroom*

*Mary Thill:*

- *http://charleyproject.org/case/mary-kathleen-thill*

*Gilberto Gonzales & Jose Chavez:*

- *http://charleyproject.org/case/jose-d-jesus-chavez*
- *http://charleyproject.org/case/gilberto-gonzales*

*Miguel Cisneros:*

- *http://charleyproject.org/case/miguel-angel-cisneros*

*Bobby Davidson:*

- *http://charleyproject.org/case/bobby-davidson*

*Ruth Doss:*

- *http://charleyproject.org/case/ruth-t-doss*

*Bruce Evans:*

- *http://charleyproject.org/case/bruce-allen-evans*
- *http://www.missingpersonsofamerica.com/2013/09/10/bruce-evans-missing-from-tucson/*

*June Goodman:*

- *http://charleyproject.org/case/june-goodman*

*Adela Mendoza:*

- *http://charleyproject.org/case/adela-guzman-mendoza*

*Aleca Manning:*

- *http://charleyproject.org/case/aleca-renee-manning*

*Hurbert Turner:*

- *http://charleyproject.org/case/hurbert-turner*

*David Lamb:*

- *http://charleyproject.org/case/david-allen-lamb*

*Gloria McDonald:*

- *http://charleyproject.org/case/gloria-white-moore-mcdonald*

*Mary Shinn:*

- *http://charleyproject.org/case/mary-jimmie-shinn*

*Terkessa Wallace:*

- *http://charleyproject.org/case/terkessa-wallace*

*John Yates:*

- *http://charleyproject.org/case/john-r-yates*

*Hugues Bellevue:*

- *http://charleyproject.org/case/hugues-bellevue*

*Richard Davison, Robert Black, & Patricia Laxer:*

- *https://charleyross.wordpress.com/tag/goldie-swanger/*

- *http://charleyproject.org/case/robert-vincent-black*
- *http://charleyproject.org/case/richard-dean-davison*
- *http://www.doenetwork.org/cases/2084dfca.html*

*Heather Bloom:*

- *http://charleyproject.org/case/heather-bloom*

*Agnes Bross:*

- *http://charleyproject.org/case/agnes-bross*

*John Campbell:*

- *http://charleyproject.org/case/john-stewart-campbell*

*John Chesley:*

- *http://charleyproject.org/case/john-darwin-chesley*

*Le Tung Dinh:*

- *http://charleyproject.org/case/le-tung-dinh*

*Sheila Franks:*

- *http://charleyproject.org/case/sheila-sherrell-franks*

*John Goodman:*

- *https://oag.ca.gov/missing/person/john-carl-goodman*
- *http://charleyproject.org/case/john-carl-goodman*

*Kathleen Haney:*

- *http://charleyproject.org/case/kathleen-ann-haney*

*Roger Her:*

- *http://charleyproject.org/case/roger-her*

*Jorge Hernandez:*

- *http://charleyproject.org/case/jorge-cruz-hernandez*

*Johnnie Herrera:*

- *http://charleyproject.org/case/johnnie-joe-herrera*

*Jeannette Kamahele:*

- *http://charleyproject.org/case/jeannette-kamahele*

*Barbara Larkin:*

- *http://charleyproject.org/case/barbara-ann-larkin*

*Bryce Laspisa:*

- *http://charleyproject.org/case/bryce-david-laspisa*

*Donnie Lee & Aleksey Shelest:*

- *http://charleyproject.org/case/donnie-dale-lee*
- *http://charleyproject.org/case/aleksey-leonidvich-shelest*
- *https://www.namus.gov/MissingPersons/Case#/37986*

*Cindy Mellin:*

- *http://charleyproject.org/case/cindy-lee-mellin*

*Audrey Moran & Jonathan Reynoso:*

- *http://charleyproject.org/case/audrey-louise-moran*
- *http://charleyproject.org/case/jonathan-david-reynoso*
- *https://www.desertsun.com/story/news/crime_courts/2018/05/09/missing-couple-disappeared-exactly-one-year-ago/586719002/*

*Arnel Narvaiz:*

- http://charleyproject.org/case/arnel-nagal-narvaiz

*Myoung Noah:*

- http://charleyproject.org/case/myoung-keun-noah

*Vidal Orobio:*

- http://charleyproject.org/case/vidal-reyes-orobio

*Edrel Pierce:*

- http://charleyproject.org/case/edrel-mae-pierce

*Leslie Porter:*

- http://charleyproject.org/case/leslie-anne-porter

*Isabel Quair:*

- http://charleyproject.org/case/isabel-maria-quair

*Charles Radice*

- http://www.missingveterans.com/1995/charles-anthony-radice/
- http://charleyproject.org/case/charles-anthony-radice

*Wallace Richards III:*

- http://charleyproject.org/case/wallace-arthur-manasseh-richards-iii

*Hector Rivera:*

- http://charleyproject.org/case/hector-noel-rivera

*Anne Robinson:*

- http://charleyproject.org/case/anne-marie-robinson

*Kristine Rodrigo:*

- https://oag.ca.gov/missing/person/kristine-maravilla-rodrigo-0
- http://charleyproject.org/case/kristine-grace-rodrigo

*Diana Rojas:*

- http://charleyproject.org/case/diana-raquel-rojas

*Pushpinder Sangha:*

- https://www.sacbee.com/news/local/crime/article131165684.html
- http://charleyproject.org/case/pushpinder-kaur-sangha

*Doris Scandalis:*

- http://charleyproject.org/case/doris-catherine-scandalis

*Chandra Taylor:*

- http://charleyproject.org/case/chandra-marie-taylor

*Donald Tobin:*

- http://charleyproject.org/case/donald-william-tobin

*Arlene Tsuji:*

- http://charleyproject.org/case/arlene-kazuko-tsuji

*Kenneth Chacon:*

- http://charleyproject.org/case/kenneth-anthony-chacon

*Patricia Cordova:*

- http://www.doenetwork.org/cases/3842dfco.html

*Andy Lepley:*

- https://www.namus.gov/MissingPersons/Case#/22979

- http://charleyproject.org/case/andy-joe-lepley

*Richard Meyer:*

- http://charleyproject.org/case/richard-stanley-meyer

*Rebecca Morris:*

- http://charleyproject.org/case/rebecca-sue-morris

*Jose Ortiz:*

- http://charleyproject.org/case/jose-ortiz

*John Ashley Jr.:*

- http://charleyproject.org/case/john-jay-ashley-jr

*Nefertiri Trader:*

- http://charleyproject.org/case/nefertiri-trader

*Judith Osteen:*

- http://charleyproject.org/case/judith-dunton-osteen

*Annie Paul:*

- http://charleyproject.org/case/annie-ruth-paul

*Cynthia Wilkins:*

- https://qctimes.com/news/local/fire-destroys-fulton-apartment-building-woman-missing/article_25fa3073-b950-53e2-8c4a-a23f12d6ef81.html
- http://charleyproject.org/case/cynthia-s-wilkins

*Steven Hendricks:*

- http://www.missingpersonsofamerica.com/2014/02/01/steven-hendricks-missing-from-indiana-since-1988/
- https://www.namus.gov/MissingPersons/Case#/10653/details
- http://charleyproject.org/case/steven-w-hendricks

*Albert Baker:*

- http://charleyproject.org/case/albert-lee-baker

*Delia Baxter:*

- http://charleyproject.org/case/delia-b-baxter

*Robert Harrison:*

- http://charleyproject.org/case/robert-gene-harrison

*Robert Helphrey:*

- http://charleyproject.org/case/robert-david-helphrey

*Enrique Valles & Jorge Pintado:*

- http://charleyproject.org/case/jorge-luis-pintado
- http://charleyproject.org/case/enrique-oscar-valles

*Deborah Poe:*

- http://charleyproject.org/case/deborah-deann-poe

*Yekaterina Belaya:*

- https://www.wftv.com/news/local/search-continues-mysterious-disappearance-brevard-/106770735
- http://charleyproject.org/case/yekaterina-gennadyevna-belaya

*Mark Thompson, Bradley Williams, James Shumaker, Jason Galehouse, Mark Jackson, David Rhodes, & Barry Block:*

- *https://www.tampabay.com/news/courts/criminal/steven-lorenzo-appears-in-tampa-court-13-years-after-torture-murders/2338959*
- *https://www.namus.gov/MissingPersons/Case#/5675*
- *http://articles.orlandosentinel.com/2004-02-06/news/0402060352_1_disappearances-anti-gay-gay-men*
- *http://wafmp.tripod.com/bradleyleewilliams/*
- *http://charleyproject.org/case/barry-alan-block*
- *http://charleyproject.org/case/david-george-rhodes*
- *http://charleyproject.org/case/mark-douglas-jackson*
- *http://charleyproject.org/case/jason-rodney-galehouse*
- *http://charleyproject.org/case/james-mark-shumaker*
- *http://charleyproject.org/case/bradley-lee-williams*
- *http://charleyproject.org/case/mark-allen-thompson*

*Diane Hollins:*

- *http://charleyproject.org/case/diane-hollins*

*Charles Huff:*

- *http://charleyproject.org/case/charles-franklin-huff*

*Tammy Huston:*

- *http://www.doenetwork.org/cases/1934dffl.html*
- *http://charleyproject.org/case/tammy-lynn-huston*

*Dennis Brown:*

- *http://charleyproject.org/case/dennis-lee-brown*

*Kristine Bruce:*

- *http://charleyproject.org/case/kristine-may-bruce*

*Tommie Jackson:*

- *http://charleyproject.org/case/tommie-eugene-jackson*

*Doris Carter:*

- *https://abcnews.go.com/US/severed-leg-belongs-missing-florida-woman/story?id=16020874*
- *https://www.tbo.com/plant-city/more-than-3-years-later-families-of-two-women-still-wait-for-answers-20150729/*
- *http://charleyproject.org/case/doris-wade-carter*

*Philistin Saintcyr:*

- *http://charleyproject.org/case/philistin-saintcyr*

*Douglas Selby:*

- *http://charleyproject.org/case/douglas-harlan-selby*

*Sandra Lemire:*

- *http://charleyproject.org/case/sandra-lee-lemire*

*Steven MacKrell:*

- *http://charleyproject.org/case/steven-james-mackrell*

*William Staggs:*

- *http://charleyproject.org/case/william-ronnie-staggs*

*Stephanie Edwards:*

- *http://charleyproject.org/case/stephanie-l-edwards*

*Carol McHugh:*

- *http://charleyproject.org/case/carol-joan-mchugh*

*Richard Estrada:*

- *http://charleyproject.org/case/richard-james-estrada*

*Newton Whidden:*

- *http://charleyproject.org/case/newton-humphrey-whidden*

*Noemi Gonzalez:*

- *http://charleyproject.org/case/noemi-gonzalez*
- *https://www.facebook.com/Noemi-Gonzalez-Missing-Person-1443566579209644/*

*Lottie Wise:*

- *http://charleyproject.org/case/lottie-albertha-wise*

*Brookelyn Farthing:*

- *https://www.nbcnews.com/feature/missing-in-america/public-s-help-requested-three-year-anniversary-kentucky-teen-brookelyn-n598571*
- *http://www.richmondregister.com/news/five-years-since-brookelyn-disappeared/article_7f1bf458-7658-11e8-8100-4726e38f61b6.html*
- *https://www.wtvq.com/2018/06/22/mystery-continues-madison-co-teen-still-missing-5-years-later/*
- *http://www.findbrookefarthing.com/brookes-story/*

*Kay Wood:*

- *http://charleyproject.org/case/kaidena-lozelle-wood*
- *https://iowacoldcases.org/case-summaries/bill-and-kay-wood/*

*Beth Ricketts:*

- *http://www.doenetwork.org/cases/2739dfia.html*
- *https://iowacoldcases.org/case-summaries/beth-ricketts/*

*William Rogers:*

- *https://iowacoldcases.org/case-summaries/william-rogers/*
- *http://charleyproject.org/case/william-francis-rogers*

*Paul Shrout:*

- http://charleyproject.org/case/paul-ward-shrout

*Pavel Chernov:*

- http://www.missingin.org/reg11537/pavel_sergeievich_chernov.htm
- http://charleyproject.org/case/pavel-sergeievich-chernov

*Bernard Rusness Jr. & Peggy Parmenter:*

- http://charleyproject.org/case/peggy-joyce-parmenter
- http://charleyproject.org/case/bernard-wright-rusness-jr

*Richard Hess:*

- http://www.missingpersonsofamerica.com/2014/01/06/richard-hess-missing-from-barnett-since-2010/
- http://charleyproject.org/case/richard-dewain-hess

*Anwar Green:*

- https://www.facebook.com/bamfiorg/posts/12-yrs-ago-today-anwar-green-vanished-in-nj-pls-share-and-help-his-family-receiv/136216923204971/
- http://www.missingin.org/reg624/anwar_green.htm
- http://charleyproject.org/case/anwar-green

*Michael Nash:*

- http://charleyproject.org/case/michael-brendan-nash

*Pamela Callahan:*

- http://charleyproject.org/case/pamela-marie-callahan
- https://www.charlotteobserver.com/news/local/article96138702.html

*Daniel Moses:*

- https://missingadultskids.com/find-missing-daniel-mccoy-moses/
- http://charleyproject.org/case/daniel-mccoy-moses

*David Morse:*

- http://charleyproject.org/case/david-cook-morse

*Joey Offutt:*

- http://charleyproject.org/case/joey-lynn-offutt
- http://www.findjoey.org/

*Kenny Ebarb:*

- http://charleyproject.org/case/kenny-dwayne-ebarb

*Aleman Gustavo:*

- http://www.texasequusearch.org/missing-aleman-gustavo-41-yrs-pasadena-tx-080306/
- http://charleyproject.org/case/aleman-bautista-gustavo

*Jeannie Bryant:*

- https://www.nbc15.com/home/headlines/15927722.html
- https://missingadultskids.com/find-missing-ricky-jean-bryant/
- http://charleyproject.org/case/ricky-jean-bryant

*Wayne Moore:*

- http://charleyproject.org/case/wayne-moore

*Amelia Smith:*

- http://charleyproject.org/case/amelia-martinez-smith

*Charles Monroe Jr.:*

- http://charleyproject.org/case/charles-william-monroe-jr

*Gloria Plunkett:*

- http://charleyproject.org/case/gloria-marlene-plunkett

*Patricia Schneider:*

- http://charleyproject.org/case/patricia-jean-schneider

*Willie Tobias:*

- http://charleyproject.org/case/willie-manuel-tobias

*Mariah Mickelwait:*

- http://charleyproject.org/case/mariah-ann-mickelwait

*Randall Leach:*

- http://charleyproject.org/case/randall-dean-leach
- http://www.doenetwork.org/cases/1292dmor.html

*Garren Beller:*

- https://www.nwitimes.com/news/local/porter/man-missing-a-month-now/article_762af2dd-e1e7-537b-9ae1-54d229eca7e4.html
- http://charleyproject.org/case/garren-rudolf-beller

*Cecil Baker:*

- http://charleyproject.org/case/cecil-o-baker

*Andrew Memmelaar:*

- http://charleyproject.org/case/andrew-memmelaar

*Mohammed Alghannam:*

- https://www.theadvocate.com/new_orleans/news/article_22f786d3-c0cb-5d7b-a07f-ec9f24e22f19.html
- http://charleyproject.org/case/mohammed-abdulmohsen-alghannam

*Wilson Dumars Jr.:*

- *http://charleyproject.org/case/wilson-dumars-jr*

*Robin Vaudreuil:*

- *http://charleyproject.org/case/robin-anne-vaudreuil*

*John & Jean Block:*

- *http://donsdiverdown.blogspot.com/2013/03/aircraft-vanishes-nearly-36-years-ago.html*
- *http://www.michiganmysteries.com/cessna-1977/4561059624*
- *http://charleyproject.org/case/john-b-block*
- *http://charleyproject.org/case/jean-gertrude-block*

*Georgia Smith:*

- *http://charleyproject.org/case/georgia-ann-clock-smith*

*Shelia St. Clair:*

- *http://charleyproject.org/case/sheila-st-clair*

*Deborah Dean:*

- *http://www.missingin.org/reg1141/deborah_lois_dean.htm*

*Bengie Tyson:*

- *https://newsone.com/3580789/bengie-lynn-tyson-missing-from-montana-seven-years/*
- *https://www.facebook.com/theawarefoundation/posts/missing-bengie-lynn-tyson-age-39-was-last-seen-in-billings-mt-on-11262009-please/737741053044331/*
- *http://charleyproject.org/case/bengie-lynn-tyson*

*Emma Tresp:*

- *http://charleyproject.org/case/emma-frances-tresp*

*Michelle Smith:*

- *http://charleyproject.org/case/michelle-lyn-hundley-smith*

*Nicholas McCray:*

- *http://charleyproject.org/case/nicholas-alexander-lee-mccray*

*Courtland Mumford:*

- *http://charleyproject.org/case/courtland-lee-mumford*

*Byron Freeman:*

- *http://charleyproject.org/case/byron-augustus-freeman*

*Jose Hernandez:*

- *http://charleyproject.org/case/jose-benjamin-hernandez*

*Eulaila LaPorte:*

- *http://www.missingin.org/reg4640/eulaila_renee_laporte.htm*
- *http://charleyproject.org/case/eulaila-renee-laporte*

*Timothy McKye:*

- *http://charleyproject.org/case/timothy-james-mckye*

*Charles Koller Sr.:*

- *http://charleyproject.org/case/charles-ray-koller-sr*

*James Brady:*

- *http://charleyproject.org/case/james-elwood-brady*

*David Lovely:*

- *http://charleyproject.org/case/david-vernon-lovely*

*Randal Gary:*

- http://charleyproject.org/case/randal-paul-gary

*Robert Thompson:*

- http://charleyproject.org/case/robert-joseph-thompson

*DeAnna Brooks:*

- http://charleyproject.org/case/deanna-kay-brooks

*Jose Leon:*

- http://charleyproject.org/case/jose-abel-munoz-leon

*Roberta Pagan:*

- https://www.cruiseshipdeaths.com/2003/01/30/roberta-muzquiz-pagan-passenger-cruise-ship-death-carnival-elation/
- http://charleyproject.org/case/roberta-musquiz-pagan

*Manuelita Pierce:*

- http://charleyproject.org/case/manuelita-dejos-pierce

*Sandy Seligman:*

- http://charleyproject.org/case/sandy-seligman

*Francis McKenna:*

- https://www.ocala.com/news/20111215/no-clues-found-for-missing-north-carolina-man
- http://charleyproject.org/case/francis-xavier-mckenna

*Wallace Gerrald:*

- http://charleyproject.org/case/wallace-tolar-gerrald

*Lloyd Gilsdorf Jr.:*

- *http://charleyproject.org/case/lloyd-raymond-gilsdorf-jr*

*Madeline Ponds:*

- *https://missingadultskids.com/find-missing-madeline-teresa-ponds/*
- *http://charleyproject.org/case/madeline-teresa-ponds*

*Daffany Tullos:*

- *http://charleyproject.org/case/daffany-sherika-tullos*

*Carolyn & Mark Martin:*

- *https://missingadultskids.com/find-missing-carolyn-sue-n-mark-steven-martin/*
- *https://www.fbi.gov/wanted/vicap/missing-persons/carolyn-sue-martin*
- *https://www.facebook.com/missingkids/posts/missingmark-and-his-mother-carolyn-martin-were-last-seen-on-august-31-1981-in-ha/10156343204956988/*
- *http://charleyproject.org/case/mark-steven-martin*
- *http://charleyproject.org/case/carolyn-sue-martin*

*Nadine O'Dell:*

- *https://www.clickondetroit.com/missing-in-michigan/michigan-woman-remains-committed-to-finding-sister-missing-for-more-than-40-years*
- *http://charleyproject.org/case/nadine-jean-odell*

*Aaron Anderson:*

- *http://www.fox9.com/news/family-of-missing-22-month-old-still-hope-for-his-safe-return*
- *http://charleyproject.org/case/aaron-mitchell-anderson*

*Melissa McGuinn:*

- *http://charleyproject.org/case/melissa-diane-mcguinn*

*Curtis Fair:*

- *http://charleyproject.org/case/curtis-mackeever-fair*

*Jason Cannon:*

- *https://www.facebook.com/EastIdahoColdCases/posts/two-year-old-jason-keith-cannon-has-been-missing-since-today-in-1983-on-march-16/455772231295567/*
- *https://www.isp.idaho.gov/mp_viewer/showMissingPerson.action?id=M646822685*
- *http://www.doenetwork.org/cases/130dmid.html*
- *http://charleyproject.org/case/jason-keith-cannon*

*Sarah Avon:*

- *http://charleyproject.org/case/sarah-elizabeth-avon*
- *https://patch.com/illinois/joliet/sarah-avon-abducted-37-years-ago-week-ferak-column*

*Tricia Kellett:*

- *http://www.chicagotribune.com/news/ct-xpm-2001-07-29-0107290401-story.html*
- *http://charleyproject.org/case/tricia-j-kellett*

*Tionda & Diamond Bradley:*

- *https://chicago.cbslocal.com/2018/07/06/tionda-diamond-bradley-missing-17-years-later/*
- *http://www.chicagotribune.com/news/local/breaking/ct-bradley-sisters-anniversary-met-20160705-story.html*
- *https://abc7chicago.com/new-age-progression-photos-released-of-missing-bradley-sisters/2289176/*
- *https://www.crimeonline.com/2017/01/09/largest-search-in-chicago-diamond-3-and-tionda-10-still-missing/*
- *http://charleyproject.org/case/diamond-yvette-bradley*

- *http://charleyproject.org/case/tionda-z-bradley*

*Timothy Davison:*

- *http://charleyproject.org/case/timothy-jacob-davison*

*Kelly Staples:*

- *http://charleyproject.org/case/kelly-juanita-staples*

*Vinyette Teague:*

- *https://chicago.cbslocal.com/2011/09/28/two-missing-person-cases-baffling-police/*
- *http://api.missingkids.org/poster/NCMC/601917*
- *http://charleyproject.org/case/vinyette-trudy-teague*

*Andrew, Alexander, & Tanner Skelton:*

- *http://charleyproject.org/case/tanner-lucas-skelton*
- *http://charleyproject.org/case/alexander-william-skelton*
- *http://charleyproject.org/case/andrew-ryan-skelton*
- *http://www.cnn.com/2011/CRIME/02/01/michigan.missing.boys/index.html*
- *http://skeltonbrothers.org/*

*Kristian Justice & Kaylah Hunter:*

- *https://www.usatoday.com/story/news/nation/2014/06/10/missing-woman-body-found/10276829/*
- *https://www.detroitnews.com/story/news/local/detroit-city/2017/11/22/missing-kids-detroit-travae-fox/107921972/*
- *http://charleyproject.org/case/kaylah-neveah-hunter*
- *http://charleyproject.org/case/kristian-dejuan-justice*

*Tangena Hussain:*

- *http://www.cnn.com/2009/CRIME/01/13/grace.coldcase.hussain/index.html*
- *http://charleyproject.org/case/tangena-hussain*

*Shannon Sherrill:*

- *http://charleyproject.org/case/shannon-marie-sherrill*

*Beverly Ward:*

- *http://charleyproject.org/case/beverly-ward*

*Marc Allen II:*

- *http://charleyproject.org/case/marc-james-warren-allen-ii*

*Guy Heckle:*

- *https://iowacoldcases.org/case-summaries/guy-heckle/*

*Jackie Hay:*

- *http://www.kten.com/story/38995620/missing-in-kansas-jackie-hay*
- *http://charleyproject.org/case/jackie-dene-hay*

*Jennifer Lancaster, Monique Smith, & Sidney Smith:*

- *https://missingadultskids.com/find-missing-jennifer-lancaster-sydney-smith-n-monique-smith/*
- *https://twitter.com/kansasmissing/status/631669609414967296*
- *http://charleyproject.org/case/sidney-keara-smith*
- *http://charleyproject.org/case/monique-rae-smith*
- *http://charleyproject.org/case/jennifer-dawn-lancaster*

*Eugene Martin:*

- *http://charleyproject.org/case/eugene-wade-martin*

*Rachel Pratt:*

- *http://www.kake.com/story/39228669/missing-in-kansas-rachel-pratt*
- *http://charleyproject.org/case/rachel-geraldine-pratt*

*Jaquilla Scales:*

- *https://www.kansas.com/news/local/crime/article1073230.html*
- *https://www.kwch.com/content/news/Despite-time-hope-remains-in-case-of-Wichita-girl-missing-since-2001-481570851.html*
- *http://charleyproject.org/case/jaquilla-evonne-scales*

*Denise El-Mansura:*

- *http://charleyproject.org/case/denise-el-mansura*

*Corey Gilbert:*

- *http://charleyproject.org/case/corey-gilbert*

*George Barksdale:*

- *https://www.facebook.com/blackandmissing/posts/george-barksdalemissing-since-apr-21-1969missing-from-baltimore-mddob-feb-10-196/10153140863002413/*
- *http://charleyproject.org/case/george-barksdale*

*Bob Boyes:*

- *http://api.missingkids.org/poster/NCMC/1151854*
- *http://charleyproject.org/case/bob-louis-richard-boyes*

*Tiffany Goines:*

- *http://charleyproject.org/case/tiffany-michele-goines*

*Douglas Chapman:*

- *http://charleyproject.org/case/douglas-charles-chapman*

*Kurt Newton:*

- *http://charleyproject.org/case/kurt-ronald-newton*

*Sarah & Jacob Hoggle:*

- *http://www.fox5dc.com/entertainment/podcast/the-disappearance-of-sarah-jacob-hoggle*
- *https://www.nbcwashington.com/news/local/Father-Will-Never-Give-Up-Search-for-Missing-Hoggle-Children-492733131.html*
- *http://charleyproject.org/case/jacob-gabriel-hoggle*
- *http://charleyproject.org/case/sarah-grace-hoggle*
- *https://wtop.com/montgomery-county/2018/09/it-doesnt-get-any-easier-father-of-missing-md-kids-reflects-4-years-later/*
- *https://findsarahfindjacob.com/*

*Melody McKoy:*

- *http://articles.baltimoresun.com/1991-12-13/news/1991347178_1_melody-mckoy-gregory*
- *http://charleyproject.org/case/melody-mckoy*

*Solomon Rose III:*

- *http://charleyproject.org/case/solomon-gomile-rose-iii*

*Jesus De La Cruz:*

- *https://www.wcvb.com/article/20-years-later-lynn-boy-who-disappeared-still-missing/8248387*
- *http://charleyproject.org/case/jesus-de-la-cruz*

*Giovanni Gonzalez:*

- *http://charleyproject.org/case/giovanni-ernesto-gonzalez*

*Susan Labbe:*

- *http://charleyproject.org/case/susan-rhonda-labbe*

*Wildredo Torres:*

- *http://charleyproject.org/case/wilfredo-torres*

*Catherine Davidson:*

- http://charleyproject.org/case/catherine-barbara-davidson

*Brain Grocki:*

- https://counteverymystery.blogspot.com/2017/09/disappearance-of-brian-grocki.html
- https://www.facebook.com/112909515401791/photos/missing-and-last-seen-in-trenton-24-years-ago-many-friends-that-knew-him-never-r/1073717192654347/
- https://www.pinterest.com/pin/576320083535055869/?lp=true
- http://charleyproject.org/case/brian-grocki

*Adele Wells:*

- http://charleyproject.org/case/adele-marie-wells

*Kevin Ayotte:*

- http://charleyproject.org/case/kevin-jay-ayotte

*Jennifer & Ashley Conroy:*

- http://charleyproject.org/case/ashley-nicole-conroy
- http://www.missingin.org/reg3298/ashley_nicole_conroy.htm
- http://charleyproject.org/case/jennifer-lynn-conroy

*Jackie Theel:*

- https://www.kare11.com/article/news/investigations/kare-11-investigates-mystery-of-jackie-theel/32554765
- http://www.paynesvillearea.com/news/headlinesarticles/archives/092204/0922theel.html
- http://charleyproject.org/case/victor-john-theel

*Kreneice Jones & LaMoine Allen:*

- https://www.fox13memphis.com/news/missing-children/lamoine-allen-and-kreneice-jones/12039935

- *https://www.facebook.com/FindOurMissing/photos/lemoine-allen-and-kreneice-jones-were-loved-like-any-other-children-in-fact-they/356459071053772/*
- *http://charleyproject.org/case/lamoine-jordan-allen*
- *http://charleyproject.org/case/kreneice-marie-jones*

*Jerry Armstrong:*

- *http://charleyproject.org/case/jerry-lee-armstrong*

*Joel Hoag, William Hoag, & Edwin Dowell:*

- *https://khqa.com/news/local/a-hannibal-mystery-48-years-in-the-making*
- *http://charleyproject.org/case/william-hoag*
- *http://charleyproject.org/case/joel-hoag*
- *http://charleyproject.org/case/edwin-craig-dowell*

*Lisa Irwin:*

- *https://people.com/crime/baby-lisa-irwin-2016-missing-update-parents/*
- *http://charleyproject.org/case/lisa-renee-irwin*

*Scott Kleeschulte:*

- *http://charleyproject.org/case/scott-allen-kleeschulte*

*Robyn Pettinato:*

- *http://charleyproject.org/case/robyn-ann-pettinato*

*Bethany & Tina Sinclair:*

- *https://www.wmur.com/article/new-hampshire-unsolved-case-file-tina-bethany-sinclair/15872561*
- *https://www.doj.nh.gov/criminal/cold-case/victim-list/tina-sinclair.htm*
- *http://charleyproject.org/case/bethany-anne-sinclair*
- *http://charleyproject.org/case/tina-marie-sinclair*

*David Williams & Steven Anderson:*

- *https://www.courierpostonline.com/story/news/2017/10/25/fbi-missing-persons-steven-anderson-david-williams-new-lisbon/798314001/*
- *https://www.nj.com/expo/Dkky-2017/10/c7674dc9b6ee141e7d0e/index.html*
- *http://charleyproject.org/case/david-edward-williams*
- *http://charleyproject.org/case/steven-eugene-anderson*

*Laura Ramirez & Allen McPeak:*

- *http://charleyproject.org/case/allen-michael-mcpeak*
- *http://www.missingin.org/reg3515/allen_michael_mcpeak.htm*
- *https://www.kveo.com/news/local-news/missing-allen-mcpeak/707635624*
- *http://charleyproject.org/case/laura-leticia-ramirez*

*Kimberly Norwood:*

- *http://www.411gina.org/cases/norwoodkimberlyrachelle.htm*

*Kyron Horman:*

- *http://charleyproject.org/case/kyron-richard-horman*
- *http://www.thekhf.org/missing-children/kyronhorman*
- *https://www.facebook.com/missingkyronhorman/*
- *https://www.yourtango.com/2018314231/what-happened-kyron-horman-new-details-and-updates-about-unsolved-case-missing-portland-7*

*Margaret Fox:*

- *http://charleyproject.org/case/margaret-ellen-fox*

*Mark Himebaugh:*

- *http://www.crimeonline.com/2017/01/02/mark-joseph-himebaugh-11-vanishes-close-to-home/*
- *http://charleyproject.org/case/mark-joseph-himebaugh*

*William Jones III:*

- *http://charleyproject.org/case/william-ebenezer-jones-iii*

*Anthony Franko:*

- *http://charleyproject.org/case/anthony-bernard-franko*

*Jennifer Martin:*

- *http://charleyproject.org/case/jennifer-lee-martin*

*Sasha Davis, Selah Davis, & Jarib Bennett:*

- *https://www.facebook.com/bamfiorg/photos/findingfriday-sasha-and-selah-davis-and-jarib-bennett-were-last-seen-leaving-the/10152036366287912/*
- *http://charleyproject.org/case/selah-davis*
- *http://charleyproject.org/case/sasha-davis*
- *http://charleyproject.org/case/jarib-bennett*

*Andre Bryant:*

- *http://charleyproject.org/case/andre-terrence-bryant*

*Sharaun Cole:*

- *https://whereaboutsstillunknown.wordpress.com/2018/07/18/sharaun-cole/*
- *http://www.blackandmissinginc.com/cdad/index.cfm?MissingInfoID=564*
- *http://charleyproject.org/case/sharaun-taree-cole*

*Cynthia Constantine:*

- *http://charleyproject.org/case/cynthia-dawn-constantine*

*Christopher Dansby & Shane Walker:*

- http://www.cnn.com/2009/CRIME/11/30/grace.coldcase.walker/index.html
- https://missingchristopherdansby.wordpress.com/
- http://www.forthelost.org/cdansby.html
- http://charleyproject.org/case/christopher-milton-dansby
- http://charleyproject.org/case/shane-anthony-walker
- https://www.namus.gov/MissingPersons/Case#/7460
- https://www.facebook.com/missingkids/posts/shane-walker-went-missing-29-years-ago-in-new-york-new-yorkhe-was-last-seen-play/10157208963151988/

*Tiffany Dixon:*

- http://charleyproject.org/case/tiffany-madia-dixon

*Sean Evans:*

- http://charleyproject.org/case/sean-wayne-evans

*Leslie, Julie, & Timothy Guthrie Jr.:*

- https://www.lohud.com/story/news/crime/2014/11/11/katonah-mom-kids-disappeared/18860597/
- http://charleyproject.org/case/timothy-patrick-guthrie-jr
- http://charleyproject.org/case/julie-anne-guthrie
- http://charleyproject.org/case/leslie-anne-guthrie
- https://bedford.dailyvoice.com/news/still-a-mystery-no-sign-of-mom-kids-who-went-missing-in-katonah/700849/

*Equilla Hodrick:*

- http://charleyproject.org/case/equilla-lynn-hodrick

*Frederick Holmes:*

- https://www.recordonline.com/article/20091108/NEWS/911080326
- https://www.facebook.com/WeWontForgetThem/posts/frederick-holmesmissing-since-may-25-1955missing-from-grahamsville-nydob-jul-2-1/1972981286049232/
- http://www.missingkids.org/poster/ncmc/1129018/1

*Jeremiah Huger:*

- *http://charleyproject.org/case/jeremiah-george-huger*

*Russell Mort:*

- *http://charleyproject.org/case/russell-john-mort*

*Kirk Quintons:*

- *http://charleyproject.org/case/kirk-quintons*

*Marlene Santana:*

- *http://charleyproject.org/case/marlene-santana*

*Donna Barnhill:*

- *https://www.nbcnews.com/feature/cold-case-spotlight/cold-case-spotlight-donna-michele-barnhill-n332216*
- *http://charleyproject.org/case/donna-michele-barnhill*

*Sherri Truesdale:*

- *http://www.ncmissingpersons.org/sherri-lee-truesdale/*

*Kathleen Shea:*

- *http://charleyproject.org/case/kathleen-ann-shea*

*Louis Mackerley:*

- *https://www.oxygen.com/blogs/what-happened-to-louis-mackerley-who-disappeared-while-walking-to-a-neighbors-house*
- *http://charleyproject.org/case/louis-anthony-mackerley*

*Lauren Jackson:*

- *http://www.missingkids.com/poster/NCMC/601776/1*

- http://charleyproject.org/case/lauren-maria-pico-jackson

*Michelle Lakey:*

- http://charleyproject.org/case/michelle-jolene-lakey

*Kristi Vorak:*

- http://charleyproject.org/case/kristi-lynn-vorak

*Christina White:*

- https://klewtv.com/news/local/a-look-into-the-suspect-in-christina-white-disappearance
- http://altereddimensions.net/2014/lewis-clark-valley-serial-killer-lewiston-clarkson-asotin-washington-idaho-killer-remains-free
- http://charleyproject.org/case/christina-lee-white

*Hattie Jackson:*

- http://charleyproject.org/case/hattie-yvonne-jackson

*April Williams:*

- http://charleyproject.org/case/april-nicole-williams

*Victor Shoemaker Jr.:*

- http://charleyproject.org/case/victor-dewight-shoemaker-jr

*Dennis Johnson:*

- http://charleyproject.org/case/dennis-eugene-johnson

*Deborah Meyer:*

- http://www.doenetwork.org/cases/749dfwy.html
- http://charleyproject.org/case/deborah-rae-meyer

*Jessica Delgadillo:*

- *http://www.amarillo.com/article/20110422/NEWS/304229825*
- *http://www.411gina.org/cases/delgadillojessica.html*
- *http://charleyproject.org/case/jessica-delgadillo*

*Thomas Estevis:*

- *http://charleyproject.org/case/thomas-estevis*
- *https://www.facebook.com/missingkids/posts/missingesteviss-photo-is-shown-age-progressed-to-12-years-he-was-last-seen-on-ju/10157219290571988/*
- *http://www.missingin.org/reg7185/thomas_estevis.htm*
- *https://lightingtheirwayhome.wordpress.com/2013/03/06/thomas-estevis-endangered-missing-july-1-2008-updated-03-06-2013/*

*Karina Gaitan:*

- *http://charleyproject.org/case/karina-michelle-gaitan*

*Megan Garner:*

- *http://charleyproject.org/case/megan-elizabeth-garner*

*Nicholas Munoz, Carlos Ortega-Gonzales, Luis Hernandez, Richardo Gomez, & Jiovany Gomez:*

- *http://www.missingin.org/reg5813/jiovany_gomez.htm*
- *https://www.facebook.com/missingkids/posts/missing-have-you-seen-jiovany-gomezjiovany-s-photo-is-shown-age-progressed-to-17/10154320053156988/*
- *http://charleyproject.org/case/jiovany-gomez*
- *http://charleyproject.org/case/ricardo-gomez*
- *http://charleyproject.org/case/luis-manuel-hernandez*
- *http://charleyproject.org/case/carlos-ortega-gonzales*
- *http://charleyproject.org/case/nicholas-a-munoz*

*Melissa Highsmith:*

- *http://charleyproject.org/case/melissa-suzanne-highsmith*

*Theresa Jones:*

- *http://charleyproject.org/case/theresa-vernell-jones*

*Jenna Robbins:*

- *http://www.411gina.org/cases/robbinsjennaray.htm*
- *http://charleyproject.org/case/jenna-ray-robbins*

*Judith Elwell:*

- *https://newsok.com/article/3866922/private-detective-explores-1967-abduction-of-two-girls-in-oklahoma*
- *http://www.forthelost.org/blog/2018/07/06/judith-elwell-missing-fifty-one-years/*
- *http://charleyproject.org/case/judith-ann-elwell*

*Kathleen & Royce Henson:*

- *http://www.doenetwork.org/cases/3584dmok.html*
- *http://charleyproject.org/case/royce-henson*
- *http://charleyproject.org/case/kathleen-h-henson*
- *https://www.facebook.com/OklahomaLostnmissing/photos/a.1450784328468890/1450785375135452/?type=3&theater*

*Rita Jolly:*

- *http://charleyproject.org/case/rita-lorraine-jolly*

*Joan Hall:*

- *http://charleyproject.org/case/joan-leigh-hall*

*Shaina Kirkpatrick & Shausha Henson:*

- *http://articles.latimes.com/2001/may/09/news/mn-61279*
- *http://www.missingpersonsofamerica.com/2013/10/20/shausha-henson-and-shaina-kirkpatrick-missing-since-2001/*
- *http://charleyproject.org/case/shausha-latine-henson*
- *http://charleyproject.org/case/shaina-ashly-kirkpatrick*

- https://www.fbi.gov/wanted/kidnap/shausha-latine-henson

*Allen Briscoe Jr. & Christine Green:*

- http://www.cnn.com/2010/CRIME/02/22/grace.coldcase.briscoe/index.html
- https://whereaboutsstillunknown.wordpress.com/2017/09/28/christine-green/
- http://deaniepeters-missingangels.blogspot.com/2013/10/christine-green-missing-28-years.html
- http://charleyproject.org/case/allen-briscoe-jr
- http://charleyproject.org/case/christine-green

*Corey Edkin:*

- http://charleyproject.org/case/corey-james-edkin

*Mary Ann Verdecchia & Marcella Krulce:*

- http://pennsylvaniamissing.com/verdecchiamaryann.html
- http://missingpersonscommentary.blogspot.com/2018/02/namus-mp-32981-marcella-krulce-and.html
- http://charleyproject.org/case/mary-ann-verdecchia
- http://charleyproject.org/case/marcella-krulce

*Marjorie West:*

- http://charleyproject.org/case/marjorie-west

*Sarah Boyd, Kimberly Boyd, & Linda McCord:*

- https://www.postandcourier.com/news/greene-column-for-years-memories-of-daddy-s-girl/article_c18cd55e-d855-5233-ba83-fa967e235774.html
- http://peasintheirpods.blogspot.com/2012/02/kimberly-janis-boyd.html
- https://www.facebook.com/314563652068964/photos/a.518938524964808/618143591710967/?type=1&theater
- http://charleyproject.org/case/kimberly-janis-boyd
- http://charleyproject.org/case/sarah-w-boyd

- *http://charleyproject.org/case/linda-mccord*

*Charles Hall III:*

- *https://www.nashville.gov/Police-Department/Get-Involved/Missing-Persons/Charlie-Hall-III.aspx*
- *http://charleyproject.org/case/charles-hall-iii*
- *https://www.tn.gov/tbi/tennessees-missing-children/missing-children-18-older.html*

*Jeremy Grice:*

- *https://www.wrdw.com/home/headlines/25_Yrs_Later--What_happened_to_Jeremy_Grice_109994114.html*
- *http://charleyproject.org/case/jeremy-james-grice*

*Zaylee Fryar:*

- *https://www.wkrn.com/special-reports/millersville-babys-disappearance-remains-mystery-7-years-later/1388915606*
- *https://www.murfreesborovoice.com/article/1701/how-did-shauna-fryar-end-up-in-the-cumberland-river-and-where-is-her-daughter*
- *http://charleyproject.org/case/zaylee-grace-fryar*

*Trenny Gibson:*

- *http://charleyproject.org/case/teresa-lynn-gibson*

*Michael Woodward:*

- *https://www.army.mil/article/126914/mps_reopen_case_of_boy_who_disappeared_42_years_ago*
- *https://www.thestate.com/news/local/crime/article13859291.html*
- *http://charleyproject.org/case/michael-j-woodward*

*Jeremy Bechtel:*

- *http://charleyproject.org/case/jeremy-lee-bechtel*

*Erin Foster:*

- http://charleyproject.org/case/erin-leigh-foster

*Tonetta Carlisle:*

- https://www.timesfreepress.com/news/news/story/2009/mar/15/leads-are-few-20-year-old-missing-person-case/211583/
- http://www.chattanoogada.com/carlisle-tonetta.html
- http://charleyproject.org/case/tonetta-yvette-carlisle

*Dennis Martin:*

- https://defrostingcoldcases.com/missing-dennis-lloyd-martin/
- http://charleyproject.org/case/dennis-lloyd-martin

*David Warner:*

- http://charleyproject.org/case/david-clayton-warner

*Marjorie Knox, Melissa Alaniz, & Cheryl Vasquez:*

- https://www.elpasotimes.com/story/news/2017/08/10/murdered-missing-women-tied-serial-killer-david-leonard-wood/551097001/
- http://www.crimezzz.net/serialkillers/E/EL_PASO_MISSING_GIRLS.htm
- http://charleyproject.org/case/melissa-alaniz
- http://charleyproject.org/case/marjorie-alice-knox
- http://murderpedia.org/male.W/w/wood-david-leonard.htm

*Emmanuel Birts:*

- https://www.namus.gov/MissingPersons/Case#/24055
- http://charleyproject.org/case/emmanuel-kalief-birts

*Desiree Carroll:*

- https://missingadultskids.com/find-missing-desiree-chaunessy-carroll/
- http://charleyproject.org/case/desiree-chaunessy-carroll

*Scott Sims:*

- *http://charleyproject.org/case/scott-andreas-sims*
- *https://www.chron.com/news/houston-texas/article/Questions-linger-47-years-after-boy-vanished-in-1589165.php*

*Norman Prater:*

- *http://charleyproject.org/case/norman-lamar-prater*

*Kimberly Orellana:*

- *http://charleyproject.org/case/kimberly-abigail-orellana*

*Pamela & Michael Mayfield:*

- *http://www.forthelost.org/mayfield.html*
- *https://www.khou.com/article/news/local/bring-them-home-the-stories-behind-the-photos/215052746*
- *http://charleyproject.org/case/michael-mayfield*
- *http://charleyproject.org/case/pamela-mayfield*

*Jesus Martinez:*

- *http://charleyproject.org/case/jesus-alvarado-martinez*

*Diane Robbins:*

- *http://charleyproject.org/case/diane-nguyen-robbins*

*Laurie Partridge:*

- *http://charleyproject.org/case/laurie-lynn-partridge*

*David Blockett:*

- *http://charleyproject.org/case/david-ezell-blockett*

*Samatha Clonch:*

- *http://www.justicefornativewomen.com/2016/01/samantha-clonch-missing-from-texas.html*
- *http://charleyproject.org/case/samatha-lynn-clonch*

*Joshua Davis Jr.:*

- *http://charleyproject.org/case/joshua-jayvaughn-davis-jr*
- *https://www.kxan.com/news/crime/five-years-later-police-still-seeking-leads-in-disappearance-of-new-braunfels-toddler/1049722404*

*Tasha Wright:*

- *https://www.namus.gov/MissingPersons/Case#/9889*
- *http://charleyproject.org/case/tasha-shante-wright*

*Jennifer Klein:*

- *http://charleyproject.org/case/jennifer-lee-klein*

*Allyson Dalton:*

- *https://wnep.com/2017/10/11/search-continues-for-missing-child-19-years-after-mom-found-murdered/*
- *https://www.facebook.com/SylenaAllysonDalton/*
- *http://charleyproject.org/case/allyson-kathleen-dalton*

*Darren Hillis:*

- *http://charleyproject.org/case/darren-bruce-hillis*

*Keir & Chloe Johnson:*

- *https://wtkr.com/2018/04/30/full-coverage-the-disappearance-of-keir-and-chloe-johnson/*
- *http://charleyproject.org/case/chloe-johnson*
- *http://charleyproject.org/case/keir-shante-johnson*
- *http://www.dailypress.com/news/opinion/editorials/dp-edt-cold-cases-0402-story.html*

*Jaisle Thomas:*

- *http://charleyproject.org/case/jaisle-elizabeth-thomas*

*Sky Metalwala:*

- *https://www.kiro7.com/news/local/bellevue-boy-sky-metalwala-missing-for-five-years/463779816*
- *https://www.king5.com/article/news/local/police-release-new-image-of-sky-metalwala-missing-for-more-than-5-years/281-439483228*
- *http://mynorthwest.com/144981/mother-of-missing-child-has-new-baby-declared-unfit-mother/*
- *http://charleyproject.org/case/sky-elijah-metalwala*
- *http://www.kirklandreporter.com/news/bellevue-police-still-searching-for-answers-in-disappearance-of-sky-metalwala-6-years-later/*

*Sofia Juarez:*

- *http://www.nbcrightnow.com/story/9676350/mother-of-missing-sofia-juarez-dies-in-sacramento*
- *http://charleyproject.org/case/sofia-lucerno-juarez*

*David Adams:*

- *https://abcnews.go.com/US/cold-case-missing-boy-david-adams-reopened/story?id=9302719*
- *http://charleyproject.org/case/david-william-adams*
- *https://www.seattlepi.com/local/article/Missing-child-case-reopened-41-years-later-893317.php*

*Catherine Sjoberg:*

- *http://deaniepeters-missingangels.blogspot.com/2015/06/catherine-lynne-sjoberg-missing-41-years.html*
- *https://themusingsofmegan.com/2011/03/03/where-did-they-go-five-mysterious-missing-persons-cases/*
- *http://charleyproject.org/case/catherine-lynne-sjoberg*

*Jeffrey Bratcher:*

- *https://letsfindthem.wordpress.com/2013/06/08/almost-39-years-since-jeffrey-bratcher-vanished-from-ocean-city-park-in-ocean-shores-wa/*
- *http://charleyproject.org/case/jeffrey-michael-bratcher*
- *https://truecrimediva.com/jeffrey-michael-bratcher/*

*Ann Marie Burr:*

- *https://owlcation.com/humanities/1961-Disappearance-What-Happened-to-Little-Ann-Marie-Burr*
- *https://www.crimetraveller.org/2016/02/ann-marie-burr-ted-bundy/*
- *http://charleyproject.org/case/ann-marie-burr*

*James Duffy Jr.:*

- *http://charleyproject.org/case/james-william-duffy-jr*

*Sharon, Clara, & Michelle Giusti:*

- *http://charleyproject.org/case/michelle-renee-giusti*
- *http://charleyproject.org/case/sharon-louise-giusti*
- *http://www.forthelost.org/blog/2018/03/05/clara-michelle-and-sharon-giusti-missing-fifty-five-years/*

*Tyler Inman:*

- *http://charleyproject.org/case/tyler-jennings-inman*

*Dontray Hunter:*

- *http://charleyproject.org/case/dontray-miquel-hunter*
- *https://www.facebook.com/blackandmissing/posts/coldcase-dontray-hunter-missing-since-1975-from-milwaukee-wisconsinbambnf-blacka/10151457350892413/*

*Alexis Patterson:*

- *https://abcnews.go.com/US/story?id=91531&page=1*

- *https://fox6now.com/2017/05/03/wreath-laying-ceremony-to-be-held-for-alexis-patterson-missing-for-15-years/*
- *http://charleyproject.org/case/alexis-s-patterson*
- *http://archive.jsonline.com/news/milwaukee/disappearance-of-alexis-patterson-journal-sentinel-archives-385123251.html*

*Timmothy Pitzen:*

- *https://truecrimedaily.com/2017/04/25/timmothy-pitzen-6-missing-after-mother-found-dead-by-suicide/*
- *https://www.mystateline.com/news/father-of-timmothy-pitzen-desperate-to-find-his-son-after-6-years/713983459*
- *http://charleyproject.org/case/timmothy-james-pitzen*

# COMING SOON

Unsolved (True Disturbing Files #2)

Made in the USA
Columbia, SC
28 March 2021

35178534R20426